RAIDERS & REFUGEES

Smithsonian Series in Ethnographic Inquiry

William L. Merrill and Ivan Karp, Series Editors

Ethnography as fieldwork, analysis, and literary form is the distinguishing feature of modern anthropology. Guided by the assumption that anthropological theory and ethnography are inextricably linked, this series is devoted to exploring the ethnographic enterprise.

ADVISORY BOARD

Richard Bauman (*Indiana University*), Gerald Berreman (*University of California, Berkeley*), James Boon (*Princeton University*), Stephen Gudeman (*University of Minnesota*), Shirley Lindenbaum (*New School for Social Research*), George Marcus (*Rice University*), David Parkin (*University of London*), Roy Rappaport (*University of Michigan*), Renato Rosaldo (*Stanford University*), Annette Weiner (*New York University*), Norman Whitten (*University of Illinois*), and Eric Wolf (*City University of New York*).

RAIDERS &
REFUGEES

Trends in Chamba Political Development
1750 to 1950

RICHARD FARDON

Smithsonian Institution Press
Washington   London

Edited by Johnson & Vranas Associates, Limited

Library of Congress Cataloging-in-Publication Data
Fardon, Richard.
  Raiders and refugees.
  (Smithsonian series in ethnographic inquiry)
  Includes bibliographies and index.
  1. Chamba (African people)—History. I. Title.
II. Series.
DT474.6.C48F37   1988   966.9′004963   87-23251
ISBN 0-87474-428-8
British Library Cataloging-in-Publication Data available

Manufactured in the United States of America.

10 9 8 7 6 5 4 3 2 1

97 96 95 94 93 92 91 90 89 88

CONTENTS

PREFACE

Raiders and Refugees is a historical monograph about a contemporary people, written by an anthropologist from an ethnographic viewpoint. The coincidence of these features has decided the character of this study, which offers a historical and ethnographic account of an important West African people, as well as an argument for a particular type of anthropologically informed history writing. I cannot recall an intention to write such a book when I left to begin initial fieldwork in 1976. However, by the time I returned in 1978, I could not see how to write anything else about Chambas before making the attempt to place them historically and politically.

A number of factors may have led to this conviction. Anthropology was becoming increasingly politically self-conscious and historically informed throughout the 1970s so that the general academic atmosphere was conducive to a decision to write politically and historically. The heterogeneity of Chamba communities and the problematic status of the ethnic term "Chamba" both seemed to beg historical explanation. Equally important—although it is only lately that I realize how our interests converged—was the way in which the educated Chamba of towns like Ganye, the administrative center of much of core Chambaland, consistently glossed the intentions of my research in pan-Chamba terms. Like me, they puzzled how people who differed from one another as much as Chamba could maintain so strongly that they were a single people. Some sought to discover a common home from which all Chamba had migrated and viewed present difference as evidence of the branching of a once-united stream. A Muslim friend confided that it had been the failure to locate the place in the east from which all Chamba came that had curtailed his own Chamba history at the first sentence; others proposed more cautious local reconstructions; yet others tried to reconcile local tradition with grander designs. To many interested local commentators, I offer my thanks for their encouragement to pursue the problem of Chamba ethnicity and their suggestion that I look for a historical solution. At the same time, I must apologize that the answer I propose is partial and falls far short of addressing origins.

Much of the information on which my argument is based is also contained in the doctoral thesis I completed in 1980. The local research I carried out between August, 1976 and April, 1978 mostly, though not exclusively, concerned Chamba Daka speakers living within Nigeria. A second period of research, lasting nine months in 1984, was largely spent living with Chamba Leko speakers of northern Cameroon and Bali Chamba of the North-West Province of Cameroon. During the Christmas vacation of 1985—86, I was able to pursue the briefest of comparative researches among the Pere (Koutine), southern neighbors of the Chamba. A month-long trip to Ganye in Summer, 1987 has allowed me to benefit from the expertise of friend and linguist Raymond Boyd.

While differences of interpretation are to be anticipated between a doctoral thesis and a book completed seven years later, some differences of fact as I report them, especially concerning Chamba Leko, are attributable to subsequent local research and access to archives I had not seen before 1980. Both of my longer Chamba research trips were financially supported by the Social Science Research Council, and the first research trip received additional help from the Central Research Fund of the University of London. For supporting my brief researches among the Pere in 1985 and in Ganye during 1987, I am indebted to the Hayter Travel Fund of the University of St. Andrews and the Carnegie Trust for the Universities of Scotland. Archival resources have been consulted in Nigeria, Cameroon, England, and France, and I am grateful to the University of St. Andrews for defraying the expenses of trips to the latter two places.

My greatest debts are human ones, especially to those Chamba on whose hospitality and forbearance I was able to rely. Chamba friends never let me feel that, in accepting their help, I was accumulating an overdraft against the future, which is as well, as the debt is beyond my ability to discharge. The ritual listing that follows

is a record of my pleasure in recalling help received. I spent my longest period of research, over a year, in Mapeo. My most public friend
was Titlesime, then in his fifties, and a respected practitioner of
the Mapeo variant of Chamba religion. He and his wives, Kɛlu and
Jamani (who died between my first and second visits), spent endless
time, effort, and friendship (not to mention food and beer) upon me.
My adoptive mother's brother, Dɔngwe, instructed me in the ethics
of matriclanship by example. Nyangsiri, sociologically my child
but my elder in years, assiduously fulfilled the obligations due my
doubly fictive paternity. The priests, Jɛla Jida (Ba Laru), Wan Jam-
bumi, Wan Tapare, Gang Tagitɛra (Yɛla Gangi), and the Mapeo elders
Mallam Gudi Latbutɛre, Mɔde, Sanwe, Daudu Kpemɛmbu, Daudu
da Kusumi, Pegore, and others with whom I spent my time took
pains to assist my understanding of Mapeo life.

Outside Mapeo, my work met with great assistance from the local authorities at Ganye. The Chief of Ganye, Alhaji Adamu Sanda,
was my host for periods at the beginning and end of my original
research. He and his councillors furnished me with introductions to
travel throughout central Chambaland. The District Heads of Sugu,
Leko, Toungo, Mbulo, Yelwa, and Tola, as well as a host of village
heads, assisted my extensive inquiries and offered most generous
hospitality. None of them, I am sure, would object to my reserving
special thanks for my late friend Dominic Mapeo, then Waziri of
Ganye. Dominic always insisted that his prolonged absence from
Mapeo prevented his helping me with matters of "tradition," but his
practical advice and support, as well as the sympathetic ears he lent
to the misgivings of a young European meddling in Chamba affairs,
were my constant practical and moral props. My place in Mapeo
Chamba life was arranged on the fiction of junior siblingship to
Dominic, and this fiction stuck so well that I briefly resumed the
position on returns to Mapeo in 1984 and 1987. His absence would
have made a literally unimaginable difference to the experience of
living in Mapeo, and it is to his memory that this book is respectfully dedicated.

Of the longer periods I spent outside Mapeo, I must mention
three months in Gurum where I was generously assisted by Bakase
(Jimillar Gurumpawo), Amza, Gbansam, Gbansi, Gangta, Gbana,
Sudi (my host), and many other local and traditional officials. In

1984, I lived for six months in Yeli (Dayela) in the home of my friend Bouba Bernard and his wife Asabe. His father, the late Chief of Yeli, and Dura, the priest to the Yeli chief, allowed me great insight into the workings of this most significant and secretive of the central Chamba places. I passed a further period of two months in the Bali Chamba chiefdoms of North-West Province, Cameroon and enjoyed the hospitality of the Chief and people of Bali Gangsin.

Having recorded these thanks, I am aware of the longer list of Nigerian, Cameroonian, and European friends who accommodated, advised, commiserated and variously provided for me during my time in West Africa, and hope that they will accept this collective acknowledgment of their help.

In both Nigeria and Cameroon I have benefited from official affiliations: to the Nigerian Federal Department of Antiquities and its successor the National Commission for Museums and Monuments, and to the Institute of Human Sciences in Cameroon. I thank the staff of both these organizations, especially those at Jos, Garoua, and Bamenda.

For my anthropological education I am indebted to staff at University College London during the 1970s and particularly to Professors M. G. Smith and Mary Douglas. The virtual absence of references to their very different published works is not intentional. I can only interpret it as a backhanded compliment expressing the difficulty I should have in separating how I see things from how they taught me to see them. I am certain that the influences will be obvious enough to readers. My dissertation on the Chamba was supervised by Phil Burnham, who has not ceased to be a friendly critic in subsequent years. As external examiner, John Middleton went beyond the call of duty to separate the central from the peripheral in an overlengthy script, and his suggestions encouraged me to begin the rewriting that eventually became this version. Specific debts are due to the late Hamman Erasmus Diori, Aliyu Njidda Mbangan, Isolde Zucker, and Nigel Barley for help with textual translations; to Peter Crane, once stationed in Chamba country, for a lengthy conversation about colonial administration; to Elisabeth Copet-Rougier for a close reading of Part 3; to Bert Bremmer for heroic efforts to interpret my muddled ideas about maps; to Adrian Edwards for advice on many matters for more than a decade; and especially to Sally Chilver for unstinting generosity in her efforts to help me correlate central Chamba and Bali Chamba sources, and to Eldridge Moham- madou for the amicable exchange of views which has forced me to think more clearly. At the Smithsonian Institution Press, Daniel Goodwin, Ruth W. Spiegel, Peter R. Johnson, and George J. Vranas have clarified, or encouraged me to clarify, the text in numerous respects. In different ways, sometimes specific, as often general, I have benefited from the advice, criticism, and presence of Marilyn Strathern, Mike Gilsenan, Ladislav Holy, Ivan Karp, and Barrie Sharpe. The conventional public rites of absolution from what fol- lows are duly performed for them all.

Orthography and Other Conventions

There is no agreed orthography for either Chamba Daka (*Sa- ma.mumi*) or Chamba Leko (*Samba.nyənga* or *Samba.nwɔnga*). Chamba Daka, the majority Chamba language, spoken only in Ni- geria, was transcribed by following very broad conventions in mis- sionary literature that appeared during the 1930s and 1940s, before the wider circulation of Christian texts in Hausa and English. Lit- erature in Daka is now rare. Pastor Musa Bɔnɔtem was kind enough to assist my early learning efforts by giving me a 1933 *St. Mark's Gospel*, published by the British and Foreign Bible Society, and an undated selection of Old Testament stories, published by the United Society for Christian Literature. Both were transcribed from Gurum dialect where the Sudan United Mission had built a church (see Nis- sen 1968). A catechism in Chamba was published in 1951 after the founding of a Roman Catholic mission in Mapeo in 1941. My early attempts to transcribe Daka were based on these orthographies. Since the 1940s, to the best of my knowledge, Chamba Daka has not enjoyed popularity as a written language. Chamba Leko, the other Chamba language, has more speakers in Cameroon than in Nigeria. Whereas early transcriptions of Chamba Daka were ex- tremely broad, recent transcriptions of Chamba Leko have been based upon a narrow orthography refined from transcriptions by

P. Noss (1976). The Samba Literacy Centre at Balkossa has begun to publish literature in the Chamba Leko dialect of Balkossa producing, in 1984, a gospel and a short primer.

The conventions I use, with only slight difference for the two languages, represent a compromise between the two versions. I omit the contrast between long and short vowels that is important to both languages, and I do not show tones, although three tones and various glides have been identified in both languages. The possibility of confusion between the few terms I need to use is virtually nil, and I have found that Chamba readers of the Balkossa literature do not normally need recourse to tones to translate from the written to spoken forms.

The transcription of consonantal values does not pose any great problems for the limited purposes of this work. As far as possible, I have retained ordinary symbols from the Roman alphabet. As shown in Table 1, I use three special characters with their conven-

TABLE I

Leko and Daka phonemic transcriptions

Consonantal sounds

labials	dentals	velar/ labio-velar	palatals	liquids	glottal stop
m	n	ng	ny	r	'
p	t	k	y	l	
b	d	g			
f	s	kp			
v	z	gb			
nw	j				
w					

Vowels

tional values to represent vowel sounds, and an apostrophe for the glottal stop.

Most Chamba terms and matriclan names are italicized in the text; full-stops (periods) are used to mark morpheme boundaries. Personal names, place names, ethnic or linguistic labels, and patriclan names are capitalized and not italicized to distinguish them. I have reverted to the practice of using place names that occur on Nigerian and Cameroonian ordnance survey maps. Variants and more accurate transcriptions of the spoken forms appear in the appendices, or in parentheses in the text. The problems of relating text to maps are sufficiently taxing not to complicate them further. For example, I have retained the French spellings for places in Cameroon and the English spellings of places in Nigeria. The French form, Tchamba, is used for the Fulani chiefdom of that name, and the English rendering, Chamba, for the people. Otherwise, terms are given in the dialect of the place to which I refer in the text. Where no other indication is given, Chamba Daka terms are in Mapeo dialect, and Chamba Leko terms are in Yeli dialect. One exception to this rule has been made for a number of terms that, in the Mapeo dialect, use a glottal stop as a replacement for an initial consonantal sound. In such cases I have used the equivalent Nakɛnyare terms. Thus, I write *wurum* for ancestor or sprite, which would be pronounced *'urum* in Mapeo.

PART I

INTERPRETING TRANSFORMATIONS

CHAPTER 1

ETHNICITY, AGENCY, AND HISTORY

How do you begin to write about a people, for Chamba see themselves as such, who do not obviously share a mode of livelihood, culture, political organization or even language? The project seems to strain the very notion of the monograph as a generalizing and encompassing form—a description of a people, their way of life, their worldview, and those other aspects of their society we construe as their possessions. Traditional monographs circumscribed an ethnic subject to which possessions could be attributed, and they did so in terms of preconceived notions about the kinds of possessions ethnic subjects should have. The well-rounded description covered them all—economics, politics, kinship, religion, symbolism, and so on. But, at first sight, Chamba share little other than the assertion they sometimes make that they are all Chamba. How is the disparity between an ethnic subject, Chamba, and cultural subjects, distinct Chamba regions, political organizations, villages, or clans, to be accommodated within the conventional monograph form?

Part 1 broaches the problem of heterogeneity from three vantages which have guided the writing and researching of this study. Chapter 1 presents a theoretical overview of the ideas informing my account of Chamba political development and an ethnographic introduction to the people who would call themselves Chamba in the most extensive sense. Chapter 2 is a case study of political organization from the area in which I have worked the longest and know best. Subsequent chapters try to align these three perspectives usefully, for they issue from sources that are distinguishable: a theoretical stance from the diverse influences of my education, culture, and personality; an extensive account from short periods of residence, archival writings, and secondary accounts; and a qualitatively different, interpretative grasp from a more intensive period of research. In distinguishing three perspectives I am not suggesting they are independent, only that methodologically it is useful to consider them separately. Different strands of the argument predominate in different parts of the book.

Part 2 pieces together a historical narrative of Chamba as a whole; it draws upon regional perspectives, secondary sources, and wide-ranging interviews. Part 3 relies upon an interpretative grasp of patterns of Chamba sociability to carry out a formal analysis of evidence that organizational change has occurred. Part 4 is able, by virtue of the conclusions of the first three parts, to contrast two polar forms of Chamba political organization and suggest how transformations have occurred between them. The theoretical perspective, which remains largely implicit in the body of the book, again takes over in the concluding part, which also presents a tabular summary of the developmental trends that have been identified, interpreted, and explained.

Five general points of anthropological theory need to be introduced prior to an initial sketch of Chamba themselves:

First, despite attacks on its privileged status, the extended monograph remains the paradigmatic form of anthropological writing because it allows for an elaborated interrelation of the twin aims of anthropological research: ethnographic reporting and theoretical accounting. Seen as an experiment, each monograph is evidence for the state of play in the relationship between these aims.

A second, related, issue arises from the fact that the conventions of traditional monograph form have tended by default to introduce misleading assumptions about the stability of ethnic units. This tendency can be challenged by consistently presenting ethnicity within a political context and by actively attempting to counteract the effects of such conventions.

Third, a condition for avoiding misplaced ethnic concreteness is the broader recognition that time and space are not secondary features of social activities from which abstraction can be made. Ethnic subjects call for critical monographs that are comparative and historical.

Fourth, to treat ethnicity as a political phenomenon is to beg the question of the proper content of a political anthropology. In the very broadest terms, I believe that subdiscipline should be concerned with the interrelations between distributions of power and activities construed politically. Minimally, political anthropology studies a relationship. The subdiscipline is also, logically, subject to regression—since all of its conclusions may become objects of a further political analysis, as may the conclusions to that analysis, and so on *ad infinitum*. In practice, a bottom line has to be drawn in order to circumscribe a study, even if temporarily. For the present purposes I draw a line under the way in which we construe activities in different cultures as implicitly political, in short, the way in which we imagine a political domain susceptible to our analysis. These four points were broached in E. R. Leach's classic work *Political Systems of Highland Burma*, as part of an early attempt to present ethnicity as both problematic and political. I try to resume Leach's perspective, but with a significantly different approach to problems of political agency.

Fifth, I use paired notions of agency and sociability to describe some aspects of political activities. By sociability, I mean the behavior and attitudes anticipated in different social relationships. I shall argue that Chamba entertain two ideal models of sociability, and that some order can be introduced into the comparative and historical variations between organized Chamba communities if we look at them in terms of their predominant forms of sociability. I shall go on to suggest that, over time, we can witness a gradual encroachment of one form of sociability upon the other. In talking of agency, I intend to focus on the distribution of the responsibility for, and effects of, activities. Human agency may be viewed against a background of sociability, or sociability viewed against background assumptions of agency, depending where we, or our informants, fix our attention at any time.

These tersely expressed points of theory and methodology are results of the attempt to think through an ethnographic scenario that poses particular types of problems, in terms of a personal understanding of a changing body of anthropological theory. Problems and perspectives tend to shift together however. For the moment, I want to hold these five points in abeyance in order to describe the

ethnographic encounter from which they emerged. I shall then be in
a position to discuss anthropology and ethnography in terms of one
another, which is a more honest reflection of the development of the
argument.

Chamba are a recognized people within the modern republics
of Nigeria and Cameroon. By recognized I mean that they appear
under variants of this name in government publications of one sort
or another, and that you could, if you were to visit Chambaland,
meet people who would volunteer Chamba as their ethnic identity.
Chambaland itself is scrub country in which granite hills rise about
3000 feet above otherwise level plains (see Figure 1). It lies at the
eastern end of what is often called the middle-belt (see Figure 2), on
the border between Nigeria and Cameroon, in an area of transition
between the southern forests and the northern savanna. The annual
transformation of such a landscape is dramatic. In the dry season, a
pall of dust hangs over the plains and obscures more distant peaks.
The rivers are dry and the grass burned; movement is correspondingly easy. The wet season ushers in a landscape crisscrossed by rivers that rush from the hills across plains that are locally reduced to
marsh. Movement at this time is laborious and, although the air itself has cleared, villages and villagers' fields are hidden in regener-
ated scrub and grass. These contrasts of hill and plain, and wet and
dry seasons, have been tactical givens in the military histories of
Chamba communities.

Politically, the middle-belt has tended to be described as a residual area between the savanna states and the different world of the
forests. In relation to both of these areas, it has suffered a relative
ethnographic neglect until recent years. Middle-belt populations
tend to be fragmented and some of their peoples are relatively inac-
cessible. For the most part, despite their central position, these
populations have been represented as politically and economically
peripheral: marginal, when viewed from the northern state centers,
or as part of a hinterland, when seen from the coast. A notion of
generalized remote pagan-ness has served as a blanket image until
recently for what is, in truth, a swath of linguistically, socially, and
culturally diverse peoples.

In areal terms, the Chamba are both numerous and widely distributed. Today there may be as many as a quarter of a million

Chamba, but it is difficult to be precise since they are scattered and often mixed with non-Chamba from whom they are frequently not distinguished in population returns. In the precolonial period, with which we shall be concerned for most of this book, we are probably talking about a population of less than seventy five thousand. But there is a need to exercise caution even at this initial stage of presentation. The conventional markers of an ethnic label, a population figure and a shaded area on a map, have already begun to weave their substantiating spell.

Viewing history ironically, it could be suggested that the Chamba name and population are results of little more than a series of accidents. The contingency of the term is both contemporary and historical. For example, regardless of the subtlety with which they are able to point to differences among themselves, there are contexts in which Chamba speakers lay claim to a single extensive identity. Such contexts generally involve affairs "outside the tribe," framed by regional or national concerns. However, as a researcher with interests largely internal to the Chamba I was more frequently treated to minute accounts of differences. These accounts were both highly contextual and extremely specific; early in my research, their contents seemed to tally rarely if at all, but they did share a form. A typical account would start with a detailed, initial statement of the essential Chambaness of whatever category my informant identified himself with, whether region, polity, village, or clan. It would then move to a second statement that considered the essential non-Chambaness of all others excluded from this paragon and would finally conclude by expatiating on the superiority of Chamba (including my informant) over non-Chamba.

"So," I would ask to corroborate my understanding, "you are saying that the people of such and such a village are not Chamba at all?"

"Not at all," my informant would usually reply, "we are all Chamba, all the same."

A first reaction to such apparent inconsistency might be to treat it in terms of changing context. My question introduced a new context; in relation to my non-Chambaness, context-specific differences among Chamba collapsed. There is something to this argument, but it also misses a great deal. All statements are indexed; the more interesting question is how and to what contexts. In a sense, all of this book is the answer, but provisionally a more economical response is needed.

My initial questions had been posed in English immediately following my arrival. Learning to ask the same questions in the Chamba Daka language revealed that the term Chamba operated in English with a range different from its counterpart in Chamba. Whereas the term as used in English most frequently included connotations of boundedness and absolute difference, in Chamba its senses could be relativistic. The indexing of my informant's statement was not as I had thought. The initial statement responded to my interest in things Chamba with a translation of the relativistic sense of the ethnic term. The second statement attempted to head off my misreading of relative difference as absolute difference in the official language of the state, which is English. The same analysis certainly holds for French, and probably for Hausa as an official Nigerian language and Fulfulde as the northern Cameroonian lingua franca. The Chamba-language counterpart to Chamba as an ethnic term has to be understood as one of a series of discriminations which carries what we translate as ethnic intention in terms of our notion of ethnicity. The Chamba languages have no term that translates well as ethnicity; instead Chamba speak of degrees of difference.

The tendency to describe social relations in terms of sameness and difference also turned out to be an important feature of Chamba discursive logic, insofar as it can be inferred from speech. But this generalization was obvious enough to elude me virtually throughout fieldwork. More evident was the way in which Chamba informants drew upon different contexts to support suppositions of difference. This was no neatly nesting series of discriminations, such as one might anticipate hearing in a society where classification was based on some single principle like a segmentary lineage charter. The distinctions proposed by Chamba informants appealed to different and specific historical processes and cultural traits. As fieldwork progressed, it became evident that these differences could be mapped in the image of a complex Venn diagram, with intersections, subsets, and unions. Thus, the Chamba speak two quite different languages, each of which is marked by dialectal variation. Traditional Chamba political organizations consisted of different types of chiefdom, based upon military conquest or ritual paramountcy, or various forms of acephaly. Some Chamba had lived in the plains and others in the hills; some had been raiders, and others refugees. Put crudely, Chamba clanship is variously based upon matrilineal, patrilineal, or double descent. But these, and the many other dimensions of difference upon which accounts drew, did not coincide; instead they tended to converge and overlap in some respects and not in others. When I began to ask the reasons for the differences, I was often referred to historical processes. In short, the contextual basis for discriminating degrees of Chambaness seemed to have accumulated historically; to some extent the past was considered to have been inscribed in the present as difference.

Given the importance of historical process to Chamba, I suggest a brief and provisional overall scenario for Chamba history. As the reader with a detailed interest will be able to confirm by reading Part 2, this simple account is assembled from a rich array of local narratives. The same scenario can be represented diagrammatically as a number of population movements, and for simplicity we can look at these in terms of a series of snapshots.

The Proto-Chamba Period

In the eighteenth century or earlier, the speakers of different languages (Leko and Daka), lived in settlements distinct from one another (see Figure 3). The Daka speakers lived to the west, on and around an extensive range of hills, the Shebshi Mountains; the Leko speakers lived to the east with concentrations around the confluence of two major rivers, the Faro and Deo. The frontier between the two peoples roughly followed another range of hills, as high as the Shebshi Mountains but less extensive; these appear on maps as the Alantika Mountains.

The Period of Chamba Ethnogenesis

From perhaps the middle of the eighteenth century, and probably earlier, the Leko and Daka speakers began to coalesce. The first step in this process took place with the foundation of the chiefdom of

Yeli in the Alantika Mountains, the old frontier between the two peoples (see Figure 4). Tradition relates that the immigrant chiefly clan was of Daka origin, but over time the rulers adopted the Leko language while remaining mindful of their Daka origins, recalled through a few self-consciously Daka customs. After they had established themselves at Yeli, the ruling clan sent out emissaries to the west, who introduced chiefship among the Daka in the southern area of the Shebshi Mountains. The Chamba of this area are often called Nakɛnyare, and the existence of this third regional identity seems to have allowed a mediation of the senses of Daka and Leko, which in turn permitted the emergence of a comprehensive Chamba identity that subsumed the speakers of two languages.

The Period of Jihad

Early in the nineteenth century, the Fulani people of present-day Nigeria and Cameroon rallied to the call to wage holy war. The easternmost of their emirates was called Adamawa, after its founder Adama, or Fombina, recalling his charter to conquer the "south." The foundation of the Adamawa Emirate in the area that concerns us was initiated with the implantation of a cordon of Fulani chiefdoms along the Faro—Deo river system, that is, in the homelands of the Chamba Leko. We shall need to look at this interrelation in detail to judge its exact nature, but the main upshot of Fulani penetration was a wholesale abandonment of the riverine plains by the Chamba Leko. Emigrants reestablished themselves in four other areas, two of which were within the older Leko and Daka homelands (see Figure 5).

Some chiefdoms retreated from the plains into the Alantika Mountains, where they found refuge from the attacks of Fulani cavalry. Other Chamba migrated farther west, across the plain that separates the Alantika and Shebshi Mountains, to colonize the Daka speakers of the northern Shebshi Mountains who had not been incorporated into the earlier chiefdoms established from Yeli. These new chiefdoms were later assimilated to an expanded Nakɛnyare identity.

Other groups left the old Leko homelands to quit Chambaland definitively. Numerous oral reports tell us that one or another splinter group from this movement fell upon villages to the south and southwest of their old homelands and plundered for food, goods, and slaves. These are the notorious Chamba raiders, the best-known elements of the Chamba people. By about the middle of the nineteenth century, the raiders had settled in two areas that had previously not formed part of Chamba country.

Perhaps three separate alliances of Chamba and their allies pursued a southwesterly trajectory to enter the plains below the Benue River. These alliances were subject to rapid fissioning, which the Chamba both compensated for and accelerated by recruitment of the people they raided. Gradual abandonment of the life of mobile mounted raiders led to the foundation of more than a dozen chiefdoms under Chamba domination. In some of these, Chamba Leko soon ceased to be the normal medium of daily communication, and in many, the Chamba minority was unable to retain its dominant position. I call these chiefdoms the Benue Chamba.

Another large-scale movement of Chamba Leko and their allies settled farther to the south in the Ndop Plain and the Bamenda Grassfields of present-day North-West Province, Cameroon. Here they established five chiefdoms, four of which came to use Chamba Leko as an everyday language. Since the names of the chiefdoms are prefixed by Bali, I refer to them as the Bali Chamba.

The Chamba Leko diaspora, and the Fulani jihad that precipitated it, can be seen as two elements of a single areal process that affected the future Adamawa and its borders (see Burnham 1979). Initially, parties of mounted raiders, whether Fulani, Chamba, or allies of either, were able to make rapid inroads into settled populations of village-based cultivators. Their success seems to have depended less upon new means of destruction than upon willingness to deploy their methods ruthlessly, without regard to the future survival of the communities that were raided. In the short term, an impact policy of this wasting kind is capable of yielding considerable gains, but without the constant opening of new areas to exploitation, the policy is unstable. Raiding breeds ever larger numbers of raiders as the alliances recruit, split, raid, recruit again, and so on, in a widening arc of disruption. With increasing competition for diminishing resources, the necessity emerged for a reroutinization of territorial relations to allow renewable resources of tolls, tithes, debt enslavement, labor demands, and controlled seizures to be tapped. Throughout the area, an early stage of impact policy was replaced by later attempts at consolidation and reroutinization.

From Proto-Colonialism to Annexation

Reroutinization of political boundaries was well under way by the late nineteenth century when agents of three colonial powers began to appear on the scene. Early travelers' exploits were a prelude to the annexation of most of Chambaland by Germany under the Treaty of Berlin, and the subsequent partition of Chambaland between Britain and France after the First World War. Chambaland remained peripheral to the economic and political ambitions of all its colonizers. Development remained slight up to independence, and the introduction of indirect rule tended to favor the Fulani at the expense of the Chamba in a way that has been undone only gradually and lately.

In short, Chamba history has been a complex story of fusion and subsequent dispersion. The representation of contemporary distribution shown in Figure 2 needs to be interpreted historically with the aid of the flow chart of Figure 5 to understand how and when the widely scattered Chamba communities got where presently they are. This historical account in turn explains the contemporary distribution of differences among Chamba, which takes us back to the earlier point about the way in which Chamba informants are able to index statements about their perceived differences.

Such differences however, do not predominate to the exclusion of theme. Despite complexity, and despite the external agencies of the Fulani and European colonizers, major trends can be detected in the detail of Chamba political development. A number of related trends can be summed up that are suggestive of change in the dominant idiom of sociability. Such indicators of change include the displacement of matrilineal by patrilineal forms of organization, the replacement of chiefships vested in matriclans by chiefships vested in patriclans, and the tendency for notions of collective ritual responsibility to give way to political organization through stratification and dominance. Concurrently, the predominating representations of violence reveal a tendency for ritually organized aggression to be displaced by overt physical domination. Together, these indices of change suggest a more fundamental reappraisal of the forms of relationship expected to hold between members of a political community or, to put it another way, of the way in which differences between men become arguments for the attempt to direct them.

Some Points of Perspective

Having provided a historic outline of the subjects of this study, I can now return to the five points of theory and methodology itemized earlier and discuss each in relation to my present ethnographic problems.

The Monograph in Contemporary Anthropology

Little that anthropologists write today is received with the conviction commanded by an earlier generation of fieldworkers who enjoyed the support of a broad consensus concerning the aims and methods of the discipline and the ways deemed appropriate to express them. Our competing theories may mirror the absence of certainties in our contemporary world; certainly, the intellectual history of anthropology can no longer convincingly be written as a succession of improvements in our theoretical armory that leads us inevitably to the present.[1]

If theory itself cannot provide a continuous thread to anthropological development, perhaps we need to look to a more practical set of procedures. Such a practical linkage might be the nexus that leads from anthropological research, as both experience and technique, to the monograph, as the most ambitious and comprehensive statement of the prevailing relation between general theory and particular research. In clearly related ways fieldwork and the monograph are specifically anthropological inventions. Recognition of the practical distinction between anthropology and its cognate disciplines may account for the burgeoning literature concerned with the carrying out of qualitative research, and the writing up of such data, efforts that are beginning to outweigh our continuing preoccupation with ways to think about theories.

Recent writers have suggested that the traditional monograph, the rounded discussion of the society and culture of a single people, was established in the context of particular theories, themselves related to colonial dictates, and on the basis of certain literary and stylistic conventions.[2] Surprisingly, given the charges of conservatism leveled against it, this is the model that many third-world anthropologists have adopted from the pioneer generation of European ethnographers. One of many reasons for this adoption may be the way in which traditional monographs maintain their hold on the anthropological imagination thanks to our professional induction. The beginner's course in social anthropology remains, by and large, an invitation to meet familiar characters in an old pageant. Trobriand hustlers, self-reliant Nuer, Dinka metaphysicians, pious Talis, and Zande inquisitors with basketloads of their doomed chickens, all demonstrate the possibility of pursuing a human existence different from our own.

If there is a significant addition to the course outline of a quarter of a century ago, then it is most likely to be thorough-going criticism of the methods by which these portraits in the anthropologists' gallery were created. Sophistication achieved since the great generation of fieldworkers returned from the village to the cloisters has undermined the assumptions that allowed the classic monographs to be written at all. One by one, the pretensions of addressing the human condition or the life of a single people, and to do so scientifically as well, have been demolished. Along with the rejection of such pretensions has gone the ability to produce the memorable caricatures that had been a major feature of the popular appeal of mainstream anthropology.

Of the criticisms made by a second generation of fieldworkers of their senior colleagues' work, the most telling at the time appeared to concern the brute amount of ethnographic reporting that found its way into monographs. The new generation demanded extensive case studies, more quantification, adequate techniques of sampling, and so forth.[3] But more subversive of the old tradition was a querying of the adequacy of the fieldwork experience alone to furnish the basis for a monograph. Initially, this was tackled as a theoretical issue; ethnographic reports were shown to be constructed in a double sense, by anthropological theory and by the anthropologist's subjectivity, itself indebted to the folk theories to which he or she subscribed as a member of his or her own society. Fieldwork could not, of itself, guarantee the objectivity the metaphor of "participant observation" seemed to imply. The fieldwork experience, more closely scrutinized for legitimacy, remained one criterion of truth value, among several.

Of the series of criticisms of structural functionalism that have now become formulaic, one is crucially related to all the others and to emerging interests in anthropological genre and writing. This concerns the way in which tribal names were used to define units of study. Other criticisms, such as static bias, the neglect of the colonial situation, mistaken attributions of homogeneity to peoples studied, or the lack of reports of individual notions, for example, can all be related in one way or another to the definition of units of analysis. Moreover, the tendency to attribute characteristics to a tribal name, to produce a collective tribal actor, can easily be traced back into anthropology's pre-professional past through the writings of travelers and explorers. Anthropological genres, such as the use of indirect speech without personal attribution (Sperber 1985), and the anthropological drive toward cultural coherence, necessarily produced boundedness and consistency. The Azande sits outside time clutching his chicken; the Trobriander is forever frozen in the act of receiving a *kula* valuable. The simple addition of an opening chapter on history hardly touches the problem, for the images are masterpieces of a particular genre that would be discomposed by additions rather than overthrown.

Problems of writing Chamba ethnography stand out starkly against this background. Although I had written up my materials on Chamba a first time before the parallels became clear, it is easy to explain the ways in which the conception of this study is indebted to Edmund Leach's mold-breaking book *Political Systems of Highland Burma*. Like many key twentieth-century works, Leach's book uses a traditional format in which to criticize the very conventions that underpin it. Leach explains the construction of his book in terms of the exigencies of his fieldwork, a short period of intensive work interrupted by war service, during which he gained superficial knowledge of a wider area, and the loss of his fieldwork notes, which forced him into greater reliance upon secondary sources than had been the normal practice. Leach emphasized diversity, change, and the distance beyond simple observation that had to be traversed before generalizations could be made. But in its desire to generalize about temporal and spatial variety, *Highland Burma* remained a traditional monograph.

Not all of Leach's specific solutions appear in this work, but parallels between the two books may make the unfamiliarity of this one easier to assimilate. In a sense, this is the other side of Leach's thesis. Whereas Leach sought to identify regularities in political process among peoples areally adjacent but culturally distinct, I am interested in the claim to cultural similarity made by people who seem to differ widely from one another. Leach held that ethnic differences persisted because they fulfilled functions within the political process—a view that can be related to his espousal then of *homo politicus*, or machinating man, as a theoretical tool. I do not think that this view ever seemed very convincing, although the antinomy between what Sahlins might call cultural and practical reasons for the persistence of ethnic differences is also maintained by the later Leach (Leach 1982:44—49). His functionalist view was too general an answer to a particular question, too intentionalist a reading of a process that surely encompassed a host of latent effects, and too restricted an account of agency. But the ethnic process had been resituated from a peripheral position, where it inconveniently complicated the already difficult matter of generalizing about a "people," to centerstage where it became an important element in the processes of power and politics.

In terms of anthropological genres, Leach's study potentially demonstrated that a missing middle between fieldwork and the written document had been concealed in traditional monographs by stylistic devices that generalized from the ethnographic situation to the collective actor by means of mechanisms such as unattributed reports, observational certainties, or sheer coercion through reiteration.[4]

The reading of Chamba ethnicity that I propose is less tidy than Leach's account of ethnic difference in highland Burma, but it depends upon three issues that he recognized to be of fundamental importance to the study of circumstances in which the relation between ethnic- and culture-bearing subjects is problematic: the cultural construction of ethnicity, our notions of human agency, and the ways in which social systems are made and remade in time and space. All three bear directly upon issues of genre and presentation, and more generally on the handling of the problematic middle ground between fieldwork and writing.

Ethnicity

Most monographs begin by defining a "people" and proceed to offer generalizations about "their" way of life. This one works the other way around. My abiding question concerns the ways in which people who differ from one another as much as Chamba do are able to consider themselves a single people at all. Like most fieldworkers, I followed a name from home to the field and, while carrying out local research, used this name as a simple practical device to bound my most extensive interests. This procedure has a good deal to recommend it as a practical expedient in overcoming some of the problems of access to another language and the ideas of its speakers. Wim van Binsbergen has pointed out from his own experience how fieldwork tends to foster an adoptive ethnic loyalty in the alien researcher, and other writers have underlined the importance of regional trans-ethnic networks in African studies.[5] I accept these views but would want to go further.

In an essay, I developed at length the argument that our term "ethnicity" has potentially distorting effects when applied to precolonial African communities (Fardon 1987). My point is that ethnicity is something the ethnically self-conscious are aware of having, and that this self-consciousness only becomes apparent in a modern political context that includes the nation state as an international norm. We now lack a term to describe those idioms of difference that existed precolonially and into which we are retrospectively able to read ethnic intention. Tribe, the old term for such tendencies, has irretrievably atavistic associations; a follower of Derrida might suggest "ethnicity" or ~~ethnicity~~ to indicate a concept that is simultaneously exploited and denied. I continue to use the term ethnicity, occasionally modified by "precolonial," while trusting my reader to recognize a covert category. The term "Chamba," and the possibility of the idea of a "Chamba people," are themselves objects of this study. I shall repeatedly stress the accidental nature of the Chamba people when history is seen in developmental terms and likewise stress the inevitability of ethnic distinctions under present-day political conditions.

This approach to ethnicity is not easily accommodated within the debate over what have been called "subjective" and "objective" approaches to ethnicity. In the first place, the debate presupposes the existence of a universal ethnic phenomenon, which I doubt to be the case, whereas "subjective" and "objective" have normally designated little more than a distinction between informants' statements about difference (subjective) and anthropologists' assessments of the distribution of distinct culture traits (objective) (see Isajiw 1974; R. Cohen 1978 for the distinction; Barth 1969 for a subjective view; Naroll 1964 for an objective view).

Dissenting voices have argued for various synthetic readings of ethnicity as both subjective and objective (e.g., Van den Berghe 1981), but this argument requires us to accept both that ethnicity is universal and that the subjective/objective distinction can be applied to it. The latter distinction is difficult to maintain within an anthropology that seriously desires to give evenhanded treatment to the agency of both actors and analysts. In what way are anthropologists' accounts of statements they have heard less objective than their accounts of culture traits? If ethnicity may be defined as a form of classification of people into categories on the basis of shared cultural attributes that express historical community (however culture and history may translate locally), then this form of categorization is clearly notional. Our access to it depends upon precisely those conditions that have to be satisfied to gain access to other notional constructions.

These problems involve inference from statements and actions, and their difficulty cannot be underestimated, but to see them in terms of subjectivity or objectivity is to smuggle in an assumption of universal ethnicity—in fact, it is to accept part of the rhetoric of some of the ethnic spokesmen. But to say that ethnicity is notional is not to fall into idealism. Notions become relevant to a world of situated practices. Ethnicity may consist of a series of notions, and ethnic notions may shade off into other types of difference into which we read less ethnic intention, but ethnicity does not have to be accounted for in notional terms nor are its effects restricted to the notional. Idealism is avoided by seeing ethnicity as contextualized practice.

In the Chamba case, this practical situating of ethnicity takes a number of forms. Most simply I show how the status of the terms from which Chamba derives changed over time. At different times in the past, and in different present-day contexts, the ethnic terms have created different categories of inclusion and exclusion of people and practices. This is a particular example of a truism that has been dressed up in various ways; it was put in its most general form by Louis Dumont (1970:294):

> . . . a particular feature, if taken not in itself but in its concrete position within a system (what is sometimes called its 'function'), can have a totally different meaning according to the position it occupies. That is to say, from a sociological standpoint it is *actually different.* [original emphasis]

Chamba terms for differences between people and their practices have to be seen as members of sets and in relation to adjacent sets that may appear non-ethnic. The rather arbitrary distinction between, say, patriclanship and ethnicity, which emerges in many anthropological studies, would have no counterpart in distinctions recognized by the Chamba, as they would rather see a difference in degree of difference. But I want to go beyond this contextualization of a unitary conception of difference to suggest that deutero-difference (to borrow a term of Bateson's) can be inferred from Chamba statements and practices. Not all differences are of the same kind, and ethnic distinction is a manifestation of one style of construing difference that has consistently gained in importance for Chamba during the political developments of the last couple of centuries. I begin to develop this point under the heading of sociability, at the end of this chapter.

Time and Space

Chamba variation poses the perennial problem of typicality in an unusually acute form. Historically, Chamba communities have undergone relocation and organizational change. Contemporaneously, Chamba communities in different areas display organizational dissimilarities. In the previous section, I even suggested that the emergence of Chamba ethnicity, in its present sense, was a modern phenomenon. Clearly, no case can be made for generalizing from a single village study to the level of the ethnic subject, or for approaching the contemporary differences among Chamba from an ahistorical viewpoint. Yet local research, from which the vital interpretative element of analysis is supposed to be derived, is, by its nature, of brief duration and, in any *intensive* sense, must be also restricted in geographic range. Specific problems of research methodology, explanation, and applied theory have to be confronted in order to justify a way of proceeding further.

To the degree that present Chamba variation can be shown to be a historical product, there is some justification for using comparative and chronological frames interchangeably in formal analysis. The potential pitfall in such an approach would be a tendency to treat some contemporary Chamba communities as historical fossils. But I regard this as a practical problem and not one of principle. The feeling that anthropology and history are necessarily adversaries in the field of social explanation is waning. Nevertheless, the precise contribution that one kind of understanding is supposed to make to the other continues to pose theoretical and methodological problems. The general principle that social systems have no static properties has been conceded, as time and space are not extrinsic factors from which abstraction can legitimately be made. Even, or perhaps especially, the absence of change is a temporal phenomenon.[6]

It is not possible to research with equal thoroughness into every section of a dispersed population. I carried out local research in one Chamba village for over a year (Mapeo), in another for six months (Yeli) and in two others for two or three months (Gurum and Bali Gangsin). The villagers of the four places spoke different dialects of two languages, and lived under political organizations that were the product of differing histories. I made shorter visits, often repeatedly, and conducted interviews in numerous other communities, and I consulted the unpublished archives listed in the References. This method has yielded a good deal of information, but that information is undeniably uneven, often partial, and biased in many ways. At best, I have had to resort to standard methods of cross-checking sources, of comparing accounts, and of trying to outguess their partialities. I have done my best to be open about these questions in the text and to admit to uncertainties.

In more theoretical terms, I think that anthropology can aid historical understanding in two ways. From an interpretative understanding gained through participation in the life of the community about which an anthropologist writes, we are better placed to hypothesize about historical agency. Anthropologists can attempt to put the people back into history, but with the cautious recognition that the extension of interpretative understanding in time or space is always a risky strategy that requires justification. More optimistically, the extension of an interpretative understanding seems to stand a better chance of illuminating our accounts than the extension of a solely armchair view of agency, as the latter almost inevitably tends to be vulgarly transactionalist. A grasp, however tenuous, of contemporary concepts, language, and behavior as close to that of local people as we can manage, is the best basis from which to address potential problems of anachronism.

Secondly, anthropological techniques of regional comparison, through the formulation and transformational reworking of typologies (which are also indebted to interpretative understandings) offer an approach to the analysis of change and persistence in the features of organized communities. I do not subscribe to the view that interpretative understanding and transformational analysis are necessarily antipathetic approaches to the study of society, although this is true of some techniques of transformational analysis. The proper use of the method requires typological categories to be constructed from the basis of interpretative understanding and abandoned once the scale of change renders them inappropriate as translations. With this proviso, I shall argue below that history and anthropology potentially make different, but complementary, contributions to understanding.

In terms of the organization of this book, my method requires different ways of organizing data and of writing them up. The poles of the analysis are, at the formal end, the creation of typologies and the analysis of transformations between them and, at the interpretative end, more detailed explorations of the organization of particular communities, the sense of certain terms, or the meaning of precise kinship or clanship relationships. The ambition of the study is to move between typology and interpretation in order to illuminate the meaning of the general, on one hand, and to generalize the significance of the particular, on the other. Although I have attempted parsimony, the argument could not carry any weight in the absence of substantial ethnographic evidence. Much of this may be tedious for other than the area specialist, so I take the opportunity of offering different directions through the text in the hope of persuading readers with varied interests to stay the course.[7]

Power, Politics, and Knowledge: The Problem of Agency

Despite disagreement about the way in which the researcher's empathy arises, most anthropologists concur that fieldwork is supposed to underpin an interpretative understanding of the way people's lives are shaped by their culture. Anthropological method privileges the way that motivation and intention can be understood in the activities of others. Meaning, symbol, intention, and the rest of the vocabulary that mediate activities and culture are important to anthropology to the same degree that they are elusive, shifting, and recalcitrant to stable definition.

History, on the other hand, is often ironic in tone. Popular and academic commentators, of all political persuasions, have noted the powerlessness of human intentions caught up in the inexorable machinery of history. The sentiment recurs in Marx's often quoted observation that men do not control the conditions under which they make history, in Weber's insistence on the ironic outcomes of human intentions, and his "sociology of fate" (Turner 1981), or in Ferguson's noting the "successive improvements . . . which bring human affairs to a state of complication, which the greatest reach of capacity with which human nature was ever adorned, could not have projected" (1966:182).

The same observation may be imbued with optimistic overtones, as in Adam Smith's notion of an invisible hand turning private interest to public good, or pessimistic overtones, as in Rousseau's laments for the baneful effects of society upon human nature. The humanitarian posture of anthropological fieldwork methodology and the ironic elegies that history composes to human intention seem inimical. Political anthropology, once described in terms of a progressive refinement in theoretical sophistication, may also be seen in cyclical terms, where sometimes power, as the shaping condition and practical environment of agency (structural functionalism, Marxism, or Foucauldian analysis in each of their quite different ways), and at other times politics, as the willed intention behind personal relations (as in processualism, exchange theory, or transactionalism), may be in the ascendancy (Fardon 1985a).

We are not alone in producing power-like and intention-like judgments about the outcomes of human endeavor. We can recognize similar dialectics in the attribution of responsibility in the cultures anthropologists study. Some cultures are reported to attribute great, even subliminal, weight to human intention; others subscribe to an ant-like version of human powerlessness; yet others distribute power unequally through notions of *mana, baraka, tsav, mahano,* or concepts of power channeled through persons. Our metaphors of power influence whether we see ourselves as enmeshed in the strands of pervasive constraint (Foucault 1980:98; Abner Cohen 1981:10), or as the agents of our own destinies (Riches 1985). Unfortunately, as ever, theoretical elegance accrues to the proponents of the extreme views; the middle ground enjoys the worst rhetoric (Lévi-Strauss 1976:61).

In the context of this discussion, our analysis of Chamba history, utilizing both interpretative and transformational approaches, requires some reconciliation of Chamba agency with the outcomes of Chamba activities. More broadly, the political process, or the transformational effect of their activities or of their refusal to act that agents anticipate must be allowed to compete for explanatory attention with the dynamics of power, with the way in which agency is itself construed and created, and with the conditions of enactment that confront it. Our problem, therefore, demands mediation of a series of contrastive relations between history and anthropology, power and politics, determinacy and agency. Speaking advisedly of mediation, since resolution would be undesirable and probably impossible, I introduce the notion of sociability as an attempt to hold the dimensions of the analysis together.

Sociability

"Sociation," Georg Simmel wrote, "is the form (realized in innumerable different ways) in which individuals grow together into units that satisfy their interests" (1950:41). He studied sociability as the play-form of this relationship. In this study, I adopt his term, and follow his insights, but I give the term a slightly different sense. By sociability I want to understand a set of mediating concepts that informs the perception of personal relationships. Sociability is a framework of knowledge and organization of feeling about the way in which people impinge upon one another. It informs social action doubly: by making relationships visible in their culturally constituted form, and by informing them normatively and emotionally. Since sociability identifies and models personal relations, it is related both to the conceptual and moral ordering of societies, problems that Durkheim showed to be related logically.

Following from the analysis of relations between close sociates in Chamba communities (see especially Part 3), I propose a binary distinction within the category of sociates. In this, I follow an idea of Schutz's, who distinguished we-relationships, or consociates, from contemporaries (Schutz and Luckmann 1973:61—68) but, again, I slightly alter the sense of the original distinction. By consociating idioms of relationship, I understand forms of relationship marked by normative and emotional components that represent the differences between those related as only apparent, and suggest that the basis for relationship is to be found in an underlying similarity, which outweighs the perception of difference.

In contrast to this, an "adsociated" idiom of relationship, to use a term coined here, is a form of relationship that brings people "toward" one another without any challenge to their personal integrity.[8] Analogous binary distinctions, but with different referents and a more general, cross-cultural classifying intention, occur in the works of many anthropologists (notably Mary Douglas and Victor Turner) and may even be a more general feature of western dualism.[9] My formulation is designed only to translate some elements of the differences between forms of relationship among Chamba and, to the extent that agency is directed toward others to achieve practical effects, to explain some aspects of the human orientation of Chamba agency.

In terms of the categories that I am proposing, the secular trend of Chamba political development may be restated as a movement from the dominance of consociating idioms of organization toward adsociating idioms. I shall argue that there are elective affinities among the different examples of these two forms of sociation; change tends to occur in a cluster of the attributes at the same time. Matriclan chiefship, ritual aggression, collective responsibilities, and relative attention to matrilateral connection (to take only a few examples) tend to co-occur, as do patriclan chiefship, physical violence, stratification, and patrilateral connection. In order to understand the meaning of the change from matriclan to patriclan ownership of chiefship, we have to place this change in a cultural context in which matriclan chiefship is associated with collective responsibility for community welfare, with a division of the ritual work designed to ensure this welfare, with an assertion of the broad matrilateral relatedness that underwrites this collective obligation, with a mythological placement of the origins of this organization, and so forth. Conversely, patriclan chiefship tends to imply a historical situation of conquest, a notion of patrilateral division, and domination within the community.

This chapter has described my theoretical perspectives and presented an ethnographic introduction to Chamba. Chapter 2 takes us to the anthropological side of the interpretative process through a case study of the single Chamba village, Mapeo, from which my ethnographic focus has been directed. The chapters of Part 2 adopt an extensive perspective in order to address the broad issues of contemporary and historical Chamba variation. Subsequent chapters, in Parts 3 and 4 of this book, further analyze the binary scheme of sociation present among the Chamba. This analysis is summed up, in the final chapter, in a table that synthesizes the major points of the study, following which, I briefly take up further methodological implications.

CHAPTER 2

MAPEO: THE POLITICS OF

A RITUAL INVOLUTION

Mapeo is the Chamba village I know best. It is the place where I lived for more than a year, in which I eventually came to feel at ease, and from which my ethnographic focus has been directed. From this experience, I came to realize that even granted the diversity of Chamba forms of government, Mapeo is unusual. Whereas other Chamba communities can at least be fitted into types, Mapeo may be unique.[1]

My choice of Mapeo as a fieldwork site had not been accidental. After my arrival in the local government headquarters at Ganye, I made trips to some of the Chamba communities of Ganye Division, meeting the chiefs and local officials, and collecting fairly stereotyped local histories through interpreters. My intention was to gain some regional perspective before choosing a village in which to settle down to detailed investigations. I could not understand Chamba Daka at this time, but nonetheless my interviews with representative elders soon became routine. Most of the elders belonged to chiefdoms of the southern Shebshi Mountains, and would volunteer histories about their chiefdoms that related the movements of a chiefly clan, the eventual settlement of these clansmen among earlier inhabitants of an area, and their agreement to share the functions of government in some way or other.

Unless I made strenuous efforts to counter the tendency, by insisting upon the collection of narratives from all the local clans, the history of a chiefdom would consist of the history of the chiefly clan. These accounts were relatively formal because, I surmised, they had been systematized over many years, a supposition that was

27

confirmed when access to colonial records revealed a high degree of consistency in the versions of oral traditions collected from the same chiefdoms throughout this century. Having come to anticipate systematic accounts of my informants, I was perplexed during my first visit to Mapeo when I encountered a marked lack of consensus.

I had been led by my Nakɛnyare informants at Ganye to expect my Mapeo hosts to be energetic in their pursuit of "traditional" rituals, enthusiastic in their appetite for beer, and less "developed" than their Nakɛnyare counterparts. However, I had not been prepared for the pandemonium that would attend my efforts to collect what I had come to expect to be a routine history. Beer and rituals were indeed prominent, and the Mapeo Chamba took little care to conceal their disdain for their Nakɛnyare cousins to whom they occasionally referred as "Fulani slaves." Above all, the simplest question provoked endless and, at that period of my stay, totally incomprehensible dispute. When the meeting's spokesman, the man who held the chiefship in the local administrative system, produced a response to my inquiry, it was clear that many of the gathering were, insofar as language barriers and a semblance of minimal deference permitted, visibly dissociating themselves from his account of the past.

This first visit to Mapeo had been planned to coincide with the major harvest festival of *jub.kupsa*, the largest in a series of four cycles of dances which are started in Mapeo and "passed on" to the hamlets of the plain or "in the bush" as, with metropolitan aplomb, the Mapeo Chamba refer to the satellites of the village.[2] *Jub.kupsa* is awaited with anticipation in both village and bush hamlet. Although many Mapeo villagers live some miles away on their farms during the rainy season, no one is absent from this end-of-the-year festival with its abundance of beer, dancing, and carousing. Enormous volumes of beer are brewed and exhausted by the thirsts of visitors from the local hamlets and, nowadays, of friends and prodigal sons from the nearby towns and the more distant, large cities. *Jub.kupsa* has few serious aspects, most of the rituals necessary for the commencement of the harvest having been carried out a month earlier in the festival of *jub.nyɛm*. As a consequence, the prevailing atmosphere of *jub.kupsa* is that of carnival.

It was to the effects of darkness, drums, dance, and drink that I attributed the relaxed and informal way in which the Mapeo

Figure 1 A Hillside Settlement at Mapeo

Chamba were able to cope with my presence. The deference and courtesy of the chiefdoms elsewhere were replaced here by a friendly curiosity to test my willingness to join in, to see just how much beer I could be persuaded to drink, and just how long I would thrash out the monotonous thump of the stick-beaten drum that accompanies, with a metronomic crashing, the more fluid rhythms of the hand drums in the *jub.kupsa* dances. The rituals, the beer, the directness, the energy, and the lack of deference; these, rather than any formal structure, were the impressions I carried away from a first brief visit. In part, it was this failure to find any order or design in the experience that intellectually persuaded me back to Mapeo; in retrospect, I realize also that I found Mapeo informality simpler to cope with than unearned deference.

I subsequently found other reasons for my initial experiences. Mapeo simply lacked any traditionally centralized set of offices and institutions onto which informants could hang the kind of structural description I had been hearing in the Chamba chiefdoms. Cer-

tainly, there were cults, and chiefly and priestly sorts of offices; in
fact, these existed in superabundance and extravagant particularity.
But the institutions and offices appeared to be unrelated formally to
one another. Whereas the other Chamba chiefdoms seemed like
well-knit orchestras, Mapeo more closely resembled an assortment
of soloists, each following his private inspiration in splendid disre-
gard of his fellow players. The resulting cacophony may be reminiscent of the chorus of protest that Leach discovered in the village
of Hpalang, a chorus that informed his comparative account of
highland Burma politics. Mapeo has something of this position in
Chamba terms; but it illuminates through aberrance. Mapeo's singular character can shed light upon more orthodox Chamba organizations in the way that the extraordinary illumines those characteristics that remain hidden in the run-of-the-mill. In Mapeo, Chamba
culture and organization are, as it were, at full stretch, grappling
with a historically unique set of conditions.

Mapeo is an organizational work of genius. The elements of different forms of Chamba chiefdom are present, but they are so finely
counterpoised against one another that no undisputed traditional
chiefship ever emerged. Mapeo is not acephalous or uncentralized;
it is continuously and pervasively decentralized in the face of all the
known processes that have tended toward centralization in other
Chamba communities. This difference between Mapeo and the remainder of central Chambaland was succinctly expressed to me a
year after my first visit by my adoptive mother's brother. The statement is typically Chamba in the disparaging attitude it strikes toward all other Chamba; referring to the Nakɛnyare of the plains (nɛ
puk.ɛn.bu), Dəngwe told me with pride, "We Mapeo Chamba don't
follow a man [i.e., a chief], we follow jubi."

Jubi is the term for the cult activity that permeates life in
Mapeo.

It is not clear whether Chamba-speakers were living at Mapeo
before the period of the jihad. Some Mapeo Chamba claim that
the area initially belonged to the Koma while others claim it for
Chamba Leko. Certainly the majority of the patriclans now settled
in Mapeo were impelled to find refuge there by displacement after
the onset of the Fulani wars. Mapeo was the most easterly of the
Daka-speaking Chamba settlements, and looked out over the plains

from a vantage point perched halfway up the north-facing slopes of the Alantika Mountains. Beyond Mapeo, the Alantika Mountains were inhabited by Koma and Vomni. I refer to Mapeo as a village, but it existed in the nineteenth century as a collection of adjoining hamlets strung out along the mountainside. The name Mapeo is in Chamba Leko Ma.peu (Ma + locative); in Chamba Daka, the place is called Dim Ma. Ma is a contraction of Mama, the name of a small hillock set slightly apart from the Alantika range and visible across the plains for miles around. All the hillside to the east of Mama was called Dim Ma or "behind Mama."[3] Properly then, Mapeo is a territory rather than a village (*Ma.nɛp.bu sə* or "Mapeo people's land"). The hillock Mama has never been built upon since it is known to be a favored haunt of *wurumbu*[4] or ancestral sprites, but it symbolizes all the land upon which the hamlets of Mapeo stand.

Vestiges of only two of the dozen or more nineteenth-century hillside settlements remain, huddled under trees about halfway to the summit of the mountains (see Figure 1). In these hamlets, the compounds are built in upon themselves in a way that speaks eloquently of the confinement of the refuge period, much more than does the bald statistic that an estimated five thousand people may have occupied the Mapeo hamlets at that time.[5] Now, almost all the Chamba have left the hills, and live in a series of modern hamlets at the foot of the mountain. The hamlets hug the rough, dry-season laterite road that passes through Tisayeli and Mapeo and links Ganye, the divisional headquarters, to Yola, capital of the old Fulani Adamawa Emirate and of Nigeria's Gongola State, or does so when the rain is not heavy.[6] However, not all the descendants of the inhabitants of the hills have settled in modern Mapeo or in its sister settlement of Tisayeli, also called Tapare, about two miles along the road toward Ganye. The soil at the foot of the Alantika Mountains is poor, witness to the heavy burden of cultivation upon areas adjacent to the hill refuges. Consequently, some farmers, valuing easy access to fertile land above the enjoyments of village life, have moved out into the central plain to live in small hamlets and to farm the land watered by the Ini and Sanchi Rivers and their tributaries (see Figure 7).

Present-day Mapeo suffers from chronic water shortage during the dry season when the village women must sit for hours by the holes they have dug in the river beds to collect a single bucketful of gray and fusty water. Thanks to all-season hillside springs, water had been in more plentiful supply at the nineteenth-century settlement sites. Although Mapeo Chamba continue to consider spring water superior to river water, daily water carrying is considered women's responsibility, and the onerous work of headloading containers from the hill is only occasionally undertaken by the younger men when building or beer brewing make abnormal demands. Nonetheless, if the enticements of life outside Mapeo, in terms of proximity to land and water, are considerable, the attractions of village life are greater, as demonstrated by the inconvenience and labor that the majority of Mapeo Chamba, both men and women, are willing to undergo in order to remain there.

A mind's-eye attempt to fit even the Chamba compounds of modern Mapeo[7] back into their earlier hillside sites is sufficient to suggest the overcrowding that must have prevailed. Instead of sprawling, as at present, the compounds would have been pinched and cramped into intricate labyrinths, comparable to those that survive on the hillside. This labyrinthine juxtaposition, reflecting an inward and concentrated growth, also gives us an image of the organization and ideas that the older men inherited from their fathers, and through which they live and recognize their daily concerns, arguments, and worries.

Attempts by the older men to induct their sons into this view of life frequently meet with misunderstanding. A new generation of schooled sophisticates, most of them adherents of world religions, and many habitués of cities their fathers think to be as distant as Ingila (England), Faransa (France), and Mecca, can find little point in the older men's cults, clans, and histories. And, in truth, such ideas offer scant help to the problems these young men face in their lives. Even for the older men, Mapeo culture is perhaps becoming an encumbrance. Mapeo organization became luxuriant in the hothouse environment of the hill refuges and now, through failure to recruit a younger generation, burdens the older men with demands upon their time and their resources that they might have expected younger shoulders to bear, as their's did for their fathers.

Religious change and formal education came to Mapeo less than half a century ago, but made rapid inroads into a culture that had already been colonially encapsulated for a preceding half century. Ten years ago the efforts of the older men still sustained the weight of the organization that they had inherited, but nowadays Mapeo culture no longer contains the seeds of its own continuation. Despite this, my ethnographic present is not wholly a reconstruction. Even at this late stage in its career it is posssible to discern the distinctive features of Mapeo Chamba culture, and to meet, possibly for the last time, men for whom this distinctive outlook is relatively uncontested and the basis for a satisfying interpretation of life. With the death of these men, Mapeo culture may only be maintained by a self-consciously traditionalist revival. This sense of transition is shared by elders, youngsters, and ethnographer alike. I express it as encapsulation; Mapeo commentators are more poetic and say "Death is finishing the big men."

The Mapeo variant of Chamba culture arose in circumstances specific to the nineteenth century. As Mapeo became a more populous hill refuge, so the heterogeneity of the elements of the community increased. But this heterogeneity was not equally marked in the patriclan and matriclan domains of organization. Chamba idioms of clanship tend to accentuate differences in the patriclan domain but submerge them in the context of matriclanship (see Chapter 7). Concurrent with the emergence in Mapeo of the dozen or so matriclans typical of central Chamba communities, more than a score of patriclans preserved their internal organizations, offices, rituals, histories, and customs along with their jealous sense of exclusion and their attendance to matters of relative prestige (see Appendix 1 for a statistical demonstration of this argument). On the basis of these cultural resources, the patriclans formed alliances. They adopted one anothers' major cults; they sought out "one-father" (*da non.si; noni,* "one;" *non.si,* "oneness" or "togetherness") relations with other clans that had common elements in their histories; they recognized limited rights and obligations in and toward one another's officials; they entered into joking relations (*kpɔmi,* sing.; *kpɔmbu,* plur.) with clans that, by and large, were of different origin; and they defined mutual responsibilities (*langsi non.si*) in the life crises of birth, naming, circumcision, and death. But out of this organization there emerged no clan hierarchy or community-wide chiefship; instead the clash of interests produced an unresolvable dispute over precedence, a dispute that is evidenced by every clansman having some account of the importance of his own clan.

We need only examine a few of the better-known claims to gain the flavor of the argument. The Gbanbu, who trace their origin from Dayela (*Da' Yɛla*, the Daka term for Yeli), claim their *Yɛla gangi* to be the legitimate Mapeo representative of that most revered of Chamba places, and argue that they should be granted the chiefship on the basis of the connection. The other Mapeo clansmen readily concede the role of the *Yɛla gangi* but construe his representative function to be a duty carried out by the Gbanbu on behalf of the Mapeo community, not one that entitles the Gbanbu to claim pre-eminence except in dealings with Dayela. In the same manner, the Jangbu and Sanbu patriclans support the claims of their priestly of-ficials, the *wanbu* (sing. *wani*), the Yangurubu, a sizable patriclan with a somewhat violent reputation, argue the preeminence of their *'ut gang*, or skull chief, and the few Sankirtanbu support their *ye gang*, python chief. Conversely, the *dəngkuni* matriclan acted as representatives to the Fulani and now holds the village headship within the system of local government. But even this office is en-visaged as a specific function rather than a general charter for ascendancy.

In general, claims to authority in the Mapeo community are not denied. Authority is attributed to all those who have attained age, office, or position, although the claims are circumscribed. Within a broadly defined communal etiology that construes power as the ca-pacity to affect well-being, some place can be found for the aspira-tions of each clan, cult, and official. In some respects, and in relation to some circumstances, each cult and functionary is important, but none has overwhelming authority except in the eyes of its closest supporters. The upshot is a convolution of consensus and dissensus in which the same abilities are differently interpreted by different sections of the community. An officeholder can simultaneously be considered the leader of a community, the head of a clan, the custo-dian of a limited power, a usurper, and a charlatan.

There is nothing unique about this situation in the anthropo-logical literature, except its pervasiveness. In Mapeo, no office, cult, or function is untouched by disagreement; the legitimacy of no po-sition is consistently defined. In short, dissension is pervasive; a

situation that proceeds from what I refer to as a ritual involution—
a competitive intensification of all aspects of cult ownership and
cult attributes.

The Centrality of Jubi

The predominance of the cult as a form of organization is marked in
Mapeo to an extent that finds no parallel among the other Chamba
communities. There are cults, *jubi* in Daka or *voma* in Leko, in all
the Chamba chiefdoms, but they are not the major means through
which political organization is effected. Instead, the most important
cults are usually found as attributes of offices whose relation to one
another is, at least in indigenous political theory, fixed. In Mapeo,
where no such relationship exists, the cult system serves to interrelate an unusually large and diversified set of clans. This results in
decentralization based around a multitude of small nodes of power
generated by the cult beliefs. Within this scheme, each clan and, in
their role as cult practitioners, virtually every adult in Mapeo, potentially occupies some position of importance. But since these petty
importances are related only in particular contexts, it is impossible
for the allocation of authority to become generalized. Politics in Mapeo rests on the particular, the contextual, and the personal. Lacking
the broad brushwork of centralized institutions or hierarchical conceptions, Mapeo organization resembles a pointilliste confection of
dots and splashes whose design emerges from density and cluster
rather than from block and line.

Political organization of this type presupposes practical knowledge in a particular form. Mapeo elders need to know the complex
networks of clanship of all their contemporaries. They need to know
the details of the numerous and subtly varied cults of the village,
and the relations between them. Most of all, they need to be able
to relate their knowledge of kinship and clanship to their knowledge
of cults in order to trace the intricacies of access to, and ownership
and control of, cults. Since access to cults is normally tied neither
to office nor, necessarily, to seniority, this inventory of knowledge
is characterized by breadth and span rather than by hierarchy. Potentially useful knowledge is virtually inexhaustible. Like the field of

socially useful knowledge in the chiefdoms, it is knowledge about
the circumstances of others. But whereas some of the positions
in the chiefdoms are only slightly affected by context, in Mapeo
the kaleidoscopic effects of situation dominate the organization of
knowledge about society. The Mapeo elder is, because he needs to
be, insatiably curious about personalities and the involvement of
personalities in the small nodes of power thrown up by the dominance of the cult system.

The informal inquisitiveness with which my first visit to Mapeo was received provided me an initial clue to this manner of
thought. A year later, I heard the aphorism I have already quoted:
Mapeo Chamba do not follow a man but *jubi*. So far, I have tried
to explain the contrast the statement draws between the Mapeo
Chamba and their Chamba neighbors; unpacking the notion of *jubi*
in Mapeo thought is a more difficult task. Its connotations are so
broad as to be virtually uncontrollable. It expresses and sums up
almost everything of importance in Mapeo life. *Jubi* is particularly
associated with ailments and disease, but its attributes also encompass wisdom, power, danger, eating and drinking, the lifetime and
annual cycles, the importance of clanship and the distinctions between clan domains, the relations between men and women and
youths and elders, the significance of ancestors and ancestral sprites,
and much more besides. *Jubi* is such a key notion of Mapeo Chamba
thought that its associations can be followed into virtually any
dimension of Mapeo traditional culture. In what follows, I limit attention to the political significance of the relations between time,
disease, cult activity, kinship, and clanship. I shall examine their
symbolic aspects in another publication.

The centrality of *jubi* in Mapeo thought allows it to act as a
symbolic transmuter, generating references between otherwise unrelated domains. The practical significance of *jubi* as a key notion
in Mapeo culture, and especially as a symbol of power, has to be
understood in relation to this referential plenitude. Multivalence is
a characteristic of all symbols; but the attributes of *jubi* in Mapeo
are so varied, and its capacity to chain-in trains of association so
strong, that it appears to be slightly out of control. To some extent,
the idea of *jubi* carries Mapeo actors through a series of connotations independent of their wills. At the same time, Mapeo cult prac-

titioners recognize this capacity and enhance the "noise" around the idea of *jubi* by a deliberate emphasis on the heterogeneity of its properties.

Such variety and confusion is possible because *jubi* has no specific meaning, or most-basic referent, to which others of its aspects can be related, and its essential nature is necessarily elusive even to its practitioners. When I translate *jubi* I use the term cult, although the English word does not cover all the meanings of the Chamba Daka term. A plural form exists, *jubbu*, but is used only in some contexts; in a number of its senses, the singular form *jubi* is inherently plural. For example, the totality of Mapeo cults is always referred to as Mapeo *jubi*, never as Mapeo *jubbu*. This totality, I estimate, consists of about forty named cults that are associated with particular diseases and misfortunes.[8] The named cults are also called *jubi*. The names and the associated symptoms are particularly well known to the older men and older women; their unfamiliarity to many youngsters is, I suspect, a recent trend. Knowledge about cults is not secret at this level. Rather, the functioning of the cult system requires the wide dissemination of such superficial information in order for diagnoses to be made. From this perspective, the indivisibility of *jubi* dissolves into names and symptoms that are widely known. Furthermore, various family resemblances are noted among the *jubbu* by reference to the diseases associated with them or to the manner and timing of the performances of their attendant rituals.

The organization of *jubi* as groupings with personnel depends primarily upon an association of named cults with named clans that are said to "own" them. These owning clans may be of the same type—all patriclans or all matriclans—or, less frequently, of different types. Nevertheless, the matter of ownership is important because the manner in which ownership of a cult is distributed makes a considerable difference to the way in which that *jubi* becomes significant in Mapeo political affairs. Some cults are widely owned, others are the property of a single clan. Some are cults of the patriclan and define patriclan alliances that are referred to as *da non.si*, "one-father," relations. Other cults seem to be randomly distributed between matriclans and patriclans, and gain their importance intrinsically rather than because of their ownerships. Mapeo Chamba informants insist that the major cults of patriclan alliances were given freely by the clans that owned them, although there is often dispute about the identity of the original owners. By contrast, the remainder of the cults are said to have been purchased, or occasionally stolen, by their present owners from clans that introduced them to Mapeo.

An association of named cults and named clans is the most common form of public statement about the ownership of *jubi*. An elder who lists the cults owned by his matriclan or patriclan will refer to them as his *jubbu*. However, the practical organization of cult activity is far more complex than this public account suggests.[9] As with the names of specific *jubi*, so the gross distribution of cults among the clans of Mapeo constitutes knowledge that is more or less well shared by the older men of Mapeo, and by many of the older women. Knowledge of this type would likewise have been more effectively disseminated before the influences of schooling and the world religions began to be felt. Such knowledge is not strictly secret, although direct questions about cult ownership may be evaded, as often as not in order for the respondent to conceal the state of his or her knowledge. However, beyond this point, knowledge becomes, self-consciously, an attribute of the participation in power of the knowledgeable man, and comes to be invested with secrecy.

A detailed statement concerning what is actually owned by the named clans would yield distinctive lists of paraphernalia, unique sets of performances and techniques, and, ideally, varied individual rights to ownership and performance. All the members of the clan take public pride in their joint possession, and traditionalist men belong to cults owned by their clans. Nevertheless, not all men are eligible to join all the cults they would like to, and some men belong to cults not owned by their clans. A number of reasons exist for this practical situation, but the most basic parameter that governs cult eligibility is clan ownership. In this regard, matriclan cults have more open criteria of membership than do patriclan cults. As I explain in Chapter 7, matriclans are internally divided into nonpublicized sections that are often, although not invariably, named and men tend to belong to cults that are the property of their own matriclan section. Furthermore, the men of a matriclan are all eligible to join a cult nominally owned by the matriclan, subject to their being old enough. In most cases this means being circumcised, although a few cults require a member to be a compound holder or elder. Within the matriclan, men of the owning section are most likely to turn this eligibility into actual membership. Men whose fathers were members of the matriclan, "children of the matriclan," are also eligible to join, and are likely to have done so if their initiations were arranged by fathers who were active cult members. The admission of other than these two basic categories of members varies from cult to cult. "Grandchildren of the matriclan," that is, men whose father's father or mother's father belonged to the clan, might be allowed to join. In some cults, matriclan joking partners are eligible for membership; in others, members of closely related matriclans, who are considered to share one mother, may be allowed to join. Conversely, only full patriclan members are admitted to all patriclan cults; children of patriclan women and patriclan-joking partners may be allowed to join, but they are often prevented from "seeing all" of the cult.

Within the broad governing parameter of eligibility, individuals exercise a wide choice as to the potential memberships they will pursue. Not all men join all the cults to which they are entitled. The reasons for this are numerous, but one of the simpler is expense. Cult membership requires an initiation payment and additional contributions for further stages of initiation as well as payments for the beer and meat consumed at regular meetings. Another straightforward reason derives from initiation into what is nominally the same cult owned by another clan. It is not normally judicious to pay twice to join cognate cults. Beyond these relatively simple considerations lies an area in which individuals have to balance obligations to matrikin and patrikin, decide whose company they find conducive, assess the possibilities of rising swiftly to a respected position, and on this basis act wisely to develop their network of positions within the cults. Joining too many cults risks failure to support the economic obligations they involve; but joining too few may mean being judged worthless.

Although the cults differ in their specific regulations, certain common initiation features can be discerned. All cults that are dangerous (*girani*) may be entered safely, literally "seen" (*nyeni*), only on payment of a fee. The scale of fees is highly variable, but it is usually paid in livestock and pots of beer, although a few cults have

other out-of-the-ordinary requirements. The entirety of cult myster-
ies is witnessed only by those initiates who have completed their
payments; such men are said to have "finished" or "seen all" the
cult. However, cult membership begins as soon as an initial payment
has been made and some, often rather trivial, aspect of cult practice
has been revealed. As a first requirement of membership new initiates are taught to remain silent about cult practices outside the cult
place. Nothing that is said or done when "*jubi* is made" may be
revealed to nonmembers, especially women and boys, since such
knowledge is dangerous (*girani*) to them. Revelation may result in
the careless cult member, the people in whom he confides his secret
knowledge, or both, being "caught by the *jubi*," that is, succumbing
to the sickness or misfortune the cult is designed to control. This
eventuality demands the payment of reparation to the *jubi* if it is
not to result in serious illness or in death.

The internal organization of the cult group derives fairly directly from the relations of kinship and, especially, clanship upon
which recruitment is based. The members of the owning clan will
all be known as the "fathers" of the cult, and one of the elders
among them will be recognized as the cult owner.[10] However, the
cult owner is not responsibile for running the affairs of the cult
group. Arrangements for the periodic meetings, the preparation of
beer, care and maintenance of the cult apparatus and the meeting
place, the collection of initiation fees, and the conduct of much of
the ritual are the responsibilities of men who stand in the relationship of "children" to the owner of the cult. In the case of a patriclan
jubi, this category will consist of "children" within the clan, but in
the case of a matriclan cult the "children" comprise men whose fathers belonged to the clan and who are also cult members. These
children of the matriclan, in fact elders in years, are said to take "the
jubi in hand" (*guri wa*).[11] Taking the cult in hand is the most active
role within the cult group, so it is usually filled by one or more of
the elders in youthful middle-age. It is not a job for the oldest men,
although they may remain owners of cults indefinitely. Both ownership and custodianship of cults are prestigious, and most active
elders fill both roles in different cult groups. Owners and custodians
are always those who have finished "seeing" the *jubi*, who "know
it all."

When individuals refer to their *jubi,* using the plural form with a possessive (*jub.me.bu,* my cults), the exact referent of the statement can be determined only through a knowledge of context. It might refer to the cults owned by the individual's matriclan and patriclan, of which he is not necessarily a member, or it might refer to the cults of which the speaker has attained any stage of initiation, however slight. In the latter case, not all the cults need belong to the individual's clans. Most narrowly, the speaker might refer to those cults of which he is owner or holder. Given that there are approximately twenty-five patriclans and twelve matriclans in Mapeo, that there are about forty named *jubi,* that cult groupings are perhaps four times more numerous than the named cults, and that there are different levels of initiation in each cult group, then, without broaching numerous further complications, the range of specific information necessary to function effectively as a Mapeo elder will readily be apparent.

By virtue of their ownership of disease-causing cults, clans and individuals also occupy positions within the communal etiology of illness and misfortune. Although they may have recourse to diviners, Mapeo Chamba do not think highly of them, preferring to reason deductively toward the cause of a disease. If there is reason to believe that a cult is responsible for some illness, the first task is to discover the type of named cult that can cause such symptoms and the second is to find out who owns the version of the cult that is at work. The first deduction requires knowledge of the conventional relations between cults and the diseases or misfortunes they engender. The second deduction allows reparation to be paid and ritual to be performed so that the afflicted individual may return to health. In general, misfortune is construed to be caused by breaking a taboo (*girani*) of the cult. *Jubi* are not randomly contagious; they "catch" people, in some cases their matrikin, who transgress against cult rules. These transgressions include the revelation of cult secrets, the unintended witnessing of cult rites, or the theft of properties protected by cult symbols.

In this context, the meaning of the term *girani,* translated above as dangerous and tabooed, is of great importance. The concepts associated with this Chamba term resemble others familiar to anthropologists. *Girani* can be seen most simply as the expression of su-

pernatural danger in everyday life. Things that are dangerous and
may cause disease are *girani*—they should be avoided, the ideas of
avoidance and danger being connoted simultaneously. Immediate
parallels with the Polynesian concept of *tabu* or the Nyoro notion
of *mahano* spring to mind. But *girani* cannot be assimilated wholly
to these better-known qualities. *Mahano* appears to have an active
quality that erupts into normal life with the impact of an uninvited
guest (Beattie 1960) whereas *tabu* has a direct relation to power. For
the Mapeo Chamba, *girani* is a negative injunction, and the relationship of *girani* to power is made through the mediation of knowledge
derived from *jubi*. Cults are *girani*, but cults are also sources of
knowledge; the *girani* of cults can only be avoided, given that men
join *jubi*, by payment. Knowledge of *jubi* is secret knowledge, that
is, knowledge that cannot be spoken because to do so is *girani*.
Thus, *girani* connotes secrecy and payment in addition to danger
and avoidance. Not all these senses are to the fore in each usage of
the term, but they form a background of meanings that may become
relevant. This is most simply illustrated by some examples of the
verbal and adjectival senses of the term.

In most contexts, *girani* is related to *jubi*; however in certain
situations other relations apply. Menstruation is called *gira*. *Girani*
and *gira* both derive from the verb root *git*, a specialized sense of to
forbid or avoid.[12] Menstruating women are *girani* to men: they may
not cook, they should enter and leave the village by special paths,
and they should wait to be handed water from a river in case they
accidentally pollute the source. Some Chamba, though not those of
Mapeo, used to build menstruation huts outside the compound. The
danger, we might note, is not to women themselves but to men. The
same is sometimes true of *jubi*; by breaking a *girani* a person may
endanger another, especially a matrikinsman.

A few patriclans recognize dietary prohibitions. The Gbanbu of
Mapeo do not eat cats and believe that they would go blind if they
were to do so. The cat is said to be *girani* to the clan, or alternatively
it can be said that Gbanbu avoid (*git*) cat.

In Mapeo, various of the priestly officers, both male and female,
must observe taboos once they have been installed. Some of these
girani are highly specific, but a general avoidance of extramarital
sexual intercourse is necessary on pain of death. The prohibition

seems to extend to sexual contagion in any form. Thus, a male cult priest (*wani*) or female priest (*jem gang*) cannot sit on a mat other than in his or her own compound in case sexual intercourse has taken place upon it.[13] The counterparts of these types of *girani* are found with hierarchical implications in the ritualized chiefdoms (see Chapter 9); the chief's conduct is hedged by *girani* and he is believed to become *girani* in some respects to his subjects.

During secondary funerals (three-day wakes held sometime after the death of an adult), a rite may be held that is called *pɛn.girani*, dangerous thing. The rite is held secretly and has the purpose of absolving members of Mapeo matriclans of complicity in causing the death through witchcraft. A representative of each clan, usually a relative of the deceased, attends and drinks from a dedicated pot of beer. Each drinker leaves lees in the bottom of the calabash, and the assembled dregs are used in a rite of hand washing. Retribution against a witch follows automatically.

Apart from such unusual types of usage, all cults are *girani*.[14] They are dangerous. It is necessary to pay in order to be shown them. What is seen should never be imparted to a nonmember especially to a woman. The person who breaches such injunctions to silence will be "caught" by the disease that the cult controls. Here *girani* means forbidden. In its verbal form, *girani* may be used to express the entrance fee that must be paid to see a particular cult. A particular cult, for instance, may require *(git)* a payment of two chickens and some beer. Usually, these comestibles may not be eaten by a nonmember once they have been donated to the cult. If a chicken is not immediately to be consumed by cult members, the final joint of one of its toes is cut off to warn others not to buy the fowl at market. The chicken has become *girani* to nonmembers of the cult. Likewise, beer dedicated to the cult also becomes *girani*; in the few cults where this is not the case, the fact is remarked as a special convention, or *langsi*, as discussed below.

The *jubi* impose prohibitions that vary in scope, duration, and inconvenience upon initiates and nonmembers. Cults are usually associated with a crop or soup ingredient, the new harvest of which may not be eaten by initiates before proper cult observances have been carried out. The foremost of these *girani* applies to the staple, guinea corn. Before the performance of the harvest cult (*jub.nyɛmi*), the entire population of Mapeo is not only barred from eating the new crop but for a month prior to the rite is banned from dancing and drumming. No loud noise or argument may be raised, no one may be struck in anger, and sexual intercourse is said to be forbidden. All the prohibitions are removed during the first cycle of harvest dances. Less general temporary prohibitions have to be observed by cult members with respect to many other edible crops. However, apart from the commandment to secrecy, few permanent abstentions are imposed upon the lives of cult members. The few men who have penetrated the innermost rites of the cult that controls impotence, *jub.nɔ*, the exclusive preserve of mature elders, abstain from goat meat and should not break chicken bones.[15] But such a permanent *girani* is unusual enough to be remarked upon. There is also a pervasive prohibition upon sexual relations on the nights prior to, or during, a cult meeting. Men who have had intercourse can take no part in the dedicatory rites and must not handle the paraphernalia of the cult; they sit apart from the main body of officiants and are given undedicated beer. Their condition is referred to obliquely, out of deference to the *jubi*, as *wa liga*, or dirty hand. Some cults impose *girani* during initiation. Informants especially remark on the *girani* of the cult *ya.gum.ani*, the patriclan cult of the Yambu. The unusual nature of the prohibitions placed upon initiates to the cult serve to underline the cultural distinctiveness of the Yambu and to reinforce an ambiguously respectful distrust that non-Yambu have of their cult. For several months following initiation, the new member is separated from everyday commensality. He carries a sleeping mat, drinking calabash, and gourd spoon with him, and is forbidden to eat with others or to have sexual intercourse.

Some *girani* apply only to argument within the cult place. Argument is believed to anger the ancestral sprites present in the cult and thus to be dangerous. For example, informants make it quite clear that the danger for two men who have slept with the same woman and attend rites together is the propensity to argument, rather than any fear of sexual contagion. Each meeting, therefore, starts with a heated exchange of grievances before any ritual is performed. The argument is itself a type of standardized behavior of a predominantly symbolic nature although true dispute is not precluded. In general, the vigorous harangue at the commencement of the meeting concerns little more than a disputed cult payment, or minor disagreement over cult duties, but even in the absence of true dispute, some detail must be found to haggle over. Nevertheless, a surprisingly fierce argument usually ends abruptly in smiles and laughs once the cult owner announces the discussion to be over (*tit duki*).

Cult practitioners are also able to render crops or goods *girani* by protecting them with a symbol of their *jubi*. The practitioners can do this for themselves or for others, usually clanswomen, on payment of a small fee. Informants are fond of likening the process to the guard duties of police. The symbol of the cult is a supernatural security device that can only be removed by a member of the same cult. It serves to warn potential thieves of the automatic consequences that would follow from stealing the protected goods. Cult practitioners may also activate their cults to "catch" a thief after the event although, given the severity of the effects of some cults, such action can be interpreted as an overreaction, especially if the cult catches innocent matrikin of a thief.[16] Setting the *jubi* as a precaution absolves the cult practitioner from the intention of doing more than warning off potential thieves.

Girani and *jubi* are intimately related, since *girani* underlines the danger and therefore importance of cults, explains aspects of their operation, and sets them apart from daily life. It also shapes the way in which the cults will be experienced across the division between domains that such injunctions establish. In terms of *girani*, some people can be construed to have penetrated the area of danger and power while others are coerced to avoid any sign of the encroachment of *jubi* into daily life.

Jubi and *girani* are, furthermore, supportive of unequal age and gender relations in Mapeo. Mapeo Chamba assume that age and status normally increase in direct relation to one another until senility sets in. Asked why this is so, they would be likely to answer in terms of knowledge rather than in terms of intrinsic properties, such as development toward ancestorhood. A "big" man * nɛ wari*, is a person who knows something, *nyi pɛni*. The most important knowledge a Mapeo elder can acquire is knowledge about *jubi*. *Nɛ wari* and *jub.tu*, "big man" and "cult practitioner," are virtually synonymous terms. An elder who has no knowledge and does not attend many *jubi* may be referred to as *nɛ wari bɛn.je,* an elder for nothing, or *nɛ nyang.an.je,* a man who spoils things without reason.

The high value placed on cult knowledge is explicable in terms of the therapeutic importance of the cults. However, even though *jubi* are sometimes justified in terms of their curative powers, I do not believe that they are normally thought about primarily in these terms. Older Muslim Chamba critics of their traditional religion, for instance, turn the argument around and claim that *jubi* are the cause of disease. In reply, cult practitioners retort that Muslims cannot possibly believe that doing away with *jubi* would banish disease. In defence of *jubi,* I have also heard a young Christian friend explaining to a youthful Chamba audience that the Catholic church had been wrong to see *jubi* just as a force for evil, since it was in part the traditional Chamba medical practice.

Overall, *jubi* has an ambiguous status in relation to the world religions. It is both the cure and cause of disease; *jubi* assimilates disease to an effect of human agency. But beyond their narrow association with the etiology of disease, *jubi* are prestigious: for their owners, holders, and initiates; for the clans with which their names are associated; and for older men *vis-a-vis* women and youngsters. Traditionally, a man of material means used his resources to "see" and "finish" *jubi.* By doing so, he could become a man who "knows something." The danger of *jubi* and the necessity for concealment of knowledge are mutually referential in this context. When Mapeo Chamba speak respectfully of knowledge in traditional culture, they usually have in mind concealed knowledge, a type that may not be freely communicated. And yet, given that cult ownership is prestigious, too much concealment would be counterproductive.

To avoid this problem, each cult has what might be called public and private faces. The public face identifies the cult to an audience and is designed to impress upon noninitiates the importance of the *jubi* and, by association, its adepts. The public faces of the *jubi* tend to be anthropomorphized and endowed with personalities. This is a view particularly impressed upon children, in much the same way that Christians have personalized an image of God, in order to make ideas comprehensible by creating a mental image toward which an attitude may be cultivated. Pressed on the point, informants say that personalizing *jubi* is just a way of talking; *jubi* are techniques that the grandfathers *(kalumbu)* received from the sprites *(wurumbu)*; they are effective because of the will of God (*Su*), because of the will of the sprites, or because of the intrinsic efficacy of the techniques. However, no one is very precise on this point. Even so, during their rites, the practitioners address the *jubi* as if it were a creature, and to an extent there does appear to be an implicit assimilation of *jubi* to the creatures of the wild. The public face of the *jubi* is believed to bring an external force into the village that endangers noninitiates, but must come in order to celebrate harvest, mourn individual or collective dead, or carry out curative ritual. The public faces of the cults dramatize the existence of secret knowledge. They draw attention to themselves through dance, song, and weird sounds, suggesting the danger of what is hidden, the complexity and impenetrability of the *jubbu,* and the importance of those who control them, but they do not reveal what is secret.

The two aspects of the cult, the public and the private, serve different ends. The hidden aspect of the cult concerns initiation and the routine use of ritual techniques designed to retain the power of the cult within the control of the initiates. The public aspect of the cult encompasses cycles of propitiation and initiation that openly draw livestock and beer into the cult places *(jub.bumi)*, away from the women and children in the compounds, where they are consumed in a boisterous men-only atmosphere of self-indulgence. The *jubi* is expected to provide meat and beer for its members, the resulting convivial atmosphere being no less a part of the *jubi* than the straight-faced business of the ritual carried out during the cult meetings.

The lack of conflict between these two aspects of the cult is remarkable. Cult meetings are quite publicly compared in terms of the drink and food consumed, and the prestige of the cult owners and custodians rises or falls accordingly. Nevertheless, the hidden quality of the cult meetings is not compromised by the fact that the substance of cult meetings is not entirely a mystery to outsiders, and that it is not possible or desirable to conceal too carefully the identities of those present, or the quantities of beer and animals they have taken with them. Cult affairs are conducted in secluded places—commonly in Mapeo the hill behind the present village—and are "not seen" by noninitiates. What goes on is "not spoken" of by initiates and the cult techniques are "not known" by nonmembers. The cult meetings are further isolated by negative injunctions, or *girani*, which separate daily behavior from *jubi*. For different elements of the community, overlapping areas of cult activity are actually or definitionally secret.

Because of their central importance in the affairs of the traditionalists among the villagers, cult meetings engage the attention of villagers not attending them in a number of ways. But in this matter it is difficult to separate intention and accident. It appears that there is little real desire to lessen the impingement of cult activity on everyday life, for to do so would undermine the prestigious aspect of cult membership that secrecy, paradoxically, enhances. Men attend cult meetings and are absent from the village, beer has to be brewed, chickens caught, and so forth. The cult instruments—iron rattles, and horns of differing length and therefore pitch, made from calabash stems attached to gourd mouths—are often stored within the compound. Some men simply leave these instruments under large inverted pots. Others build small huts for the *jubi*, or secrete cult apparatus in a small granary. The significance of any of these storage places is obvious to the other occupants of the compound. The presence of the cult apparatus among those vulnerable to its contagion is a constant reminder of the prestige and power of the cult owner. The instruments are removed from the compound by their owner to the accompaniment of frenzied blowings and rattlings, at once a sign for women, children, and noninitiates to avert their gaze and for fellow cult members to hasten to the meeting place. This exuberance is typical of Mapeo, and provides a setting in which the twin goals of concealment and publicity are simultaneously satisfied through a noisy dramatization of the injunction to avoid *jubi*. Concealment and revelation are repeated in the cult rites themselves. The instrumental accompaniments to the meetings on the hillside echo through the village, and the return of the cult members to spend the night in the village is heralded by the horns and rattles of the cult.

In Mapeo, the public impact of cult activity is calculated and self-consciously sought; for the cults link not only individuals but also clans. *Jubi* is a vehicle of clan alliance, and cult appearances, for those who can read the connection between performance and participation, symbolize the involvement of the owning clans. Of particular significance are the predictable forays made onto a public stage by the cults at regular times during the year and as regular accompaniment to events such as death or sickness. These appearances reinforce the associations between the cults and the passage of time as marked by annual and lifetime cycles.

The Chamba year is divided into twelve lunar months, each named by association with three crucially related sets of annual events: the alternation of wet and dry seasons, the progression of agricultural tasks, and changes in ritual interests.

The busy month of "planting the farm" begins at the onset of the rains around May and June. At the same time, the tamarind fruit, highly valued as a bitter additive to porridge, ripens. The crop is *girani* to many of the commonest cults of the matriclans, and so members of these cults have to abstain from the new fruit crop until rituals have been performed for the cults. "Planting the farm" is followed by "weeding the farm," during which the sorrel crop, *girani* to other cults, ripens. At the end of this month, the Yambu patriclan members return to the village to carry out the collective annual commemorative service for those who have died in the past year. This *we simi*, "death beer," consists publicly of a performance of *ya.gum.ani*, the major patriclan cult of the Yambu.[17] The rites are marked, in public, by wrestling and a formalized demonstration of violence by the clansmen and, in private, by secret rites of aggregation of the dead. The following month is that of the "guinea-corn children," when the plants begin to produce seeds. The chore of weeding is especially onerous in this month; however, the okra crop ripens and a few cults meet to allow their members to consume it. In this and the succeeding *su kɛla* month (of unknown Chamba Daka etymology), the esoteric rites of the elders' impotency cult *jub.nɔ* (cult-female) are held. This cult has no public rites, no dance, and no chant. Thus it can be held during *su kɛla*, a month during which the injunctions prior to the harvest festival come into effect, a time that is otherwise virtually devoid of ritual activity. At this time, furthermore, the maize ripens and forms a hunger breaker before the new guinea-corn crop can be eaten. Since maize is not a traditional crop, no restrictions are placed upon eating it and heads can be plucked from the field and taken home to eat as they become ready.

The first of the harvest festivals takes place in the black month, *su viri,* so called because of the exhaustion of food supplies. The harvest rituals remain the focus of attention for four months, during each of which one cycle of the full harvest festival is held. Each cycle consists of a series of similar performances owned by different clans. The cycles comprise *jub.nyɛmi,* in late September, *jub.kupsa,* in late October, *jub.nyɛm gog.ani,* in late November, and *jub.kupsa gog.ani,* in late January. The festivals mark the transition from wet to dry season and include both the onset and completion of the harvest. As their names suggest, the last two of the four cycles are seen as repetitions of the first two. *Nyɛmi,* in *jub.nyɛmi,* is said by some Mapeo informants to refer to home, because the corn is to be harvested and brought home.[18] *Gog.ani,* suffixed to the last two cycles, refers to grinding and continues the theme of the processing of the crop. No informant was able to tell me what *kupsa* meant. I followed up the suggestion that *kupsa* might be a Leko word, but inquiries in Yeli were blankly received. The importance of the first two cycles of the harvest festival far outweighs that of the later cycles, which have been subject to an almost total erosion of their public character in recent years.

Jub.nyɛmi is held by many to be the most important event of the Mapeo ritual calendar. Older people especially emphasize that harvest cannot begin before *jub.nyɛmi* has been danced. For this reason, *jub.nyɛmi* is interpreted by some to be an expression of the ownership of the land. In the vexed issue of the right to represent Mapeo in the system of local administration, the members of the Gbanbu patriclan argue that their preeminence is demonstrated by the fact that they conventionally begin the first of the harvest dances in their clan hamlet. Their right to begin the festival is generally conceded but their consequent claims to ownership of the land or to chiefship of Mapeo are not always accepted.[19] *Jub.kupsa* is the liveliest and most large-scale festival of the year. Consequently, the drinking, dancing, socializing, and singing associated with the event are eagerly awaited. At this time, Chamba farmers are nearing the end of their agricultural labors for the year and, in many cases, are preparing to leave the "bush" and return to the village for the dry season. Each of the ritual cycles of the festival consists not only of a number of stages of the central rite, essentially a dance led by drums and calabash horns concealed inside a matting enclosure that accompanies dancers outside the enclosure, but also of numerous rites carried out by cult groupings. Since guinea corn is *girani* to virtually all the Mapeo cults of both men and women, the rhythms of propitiations of the numerous cults merge at harvest time in a complex rite of renewal.

The months following the harvest cycle of festivals are the driest of the year, during which the countryside becomes thoroughly dessicated. Since no agricultural work has to be carried out, time can be devoted to chores around the compound. New structures are built (at least for as long as water supplies last), matting fences and granary lids are repaired, mats are made, awnings are erected to keep out the sun, and general maintenance is carried out. The time of firing-the-grass is also the hunting season. Elders can recall times when larger game was hunted, but now only the various types of monkey and baboon, along with smaller animals, are commonly killed.

We sim su, "death-beer month," coinciding approximately with February and March, is the month in which all the secondary funeral rites deferred since the wet season are held. Each of these wakes is a large-scale three-day event of considerable complexity. Part of the event requires visits to the "death compound" of certain cults to which an individual belonged during his or her lifetime. Not all of the *jubi* "cry a death" (*kpa we*), but the members of those that do bring parts of their cult apparatus to the cleared space before the "death compound" and perform a dance or songs associated with the cult. Generally, each of the clans related to the deceased through an extended clanship network, by joking or by co-residence, will bring some performance as a token of participation in the event. Beer must be brewed by the deceased's patrikin sufficient to offer to each of the visiting cult groups, for the *jubi* cannot safely be disturbed without some payment, and women must hide their faces in their wrappers to avoid being caught by the contagion of the cult. But these precautions apart, when they appear at wakes the cults seem almost wholly detached from their etiological significance. Informants insist that the cults have no role in affecting the passage of the deceased, who has already metamorphosed upon death. The performance of the cults serves to demonstrate that the person undertook the obligations of cult membership, that he was a *jub.tu* and not some worthless person. In a sense also, wakes are a cooperative performance in which all the often nominal relationships of significance in Mapeo society are actualized in the discharge of some precise duty.

The two months that follow the month of wakes are both called dry months *(susumi)*, the first of them suffixed by *wura*, for which I could find no gloss, the second by *wari*, the "great dry month." In this second month, the patriclans allied by their common ownership of the cult *bən.təng* perform commemorative rites for their collective dead of the previous year. Like the Yambu before them, the clansmen use the opportunity to take over the public spaces of some of the hamlets for a day while they execute the slightly menacing dances associated with their cult. Although wrestling does not feature in the *gbəng.təng* rite, the high-kicking dance raises clouds of dust and noninitiates coming too close to the dancers without removing upper clothing and shoes will find themselves menaced by knives or spears. This event is the last in the annual cycle, which will recommence at the onset of the rains and a new season of planting.

The relationship between the cults and life-cycle time is further illustrated by another Chamba category of activity: *langsi*. Interestingly *langsi* is a term that Mapeo Chamba informants claim to misuse. It is loosely used to describe any strange, singular, or unusual rite or observance, in which sense all clans, cults, and rituals have their peculiarities or *langsi*. It is also insisted that *langsi* takes place between patriclans that are said to make "one *langsi*." The occasions for such cooperative rites occur at life-cycle rituals: birth, naming, circumcision, accession to office, death, and skull-taking. The particular or unusual element in these performances comprises the specific way in which a patriclan performs the life-cycle rites, thereby establishing, if only by the slightest variation, its difference from other patriclans. These cooperating patriclans are usually joking partners or hamlet co-residents. A specialized set of cooperative relations is invoked specifically for circumcision, but *langsi* relations are most prominent during secondary funerals or wakes. The funeral rites necessitate the display of a full range of Mapeo Chamba performances and, because Mapeo patriclans are differentiated in their patrimony, require cooperation. Clans that have a dancing mask, *nam.gbalang,* a calabash-horn band (like that of the harvest festivals), or a *lera*-flute band, bring such resources as markers of their assistance to their *langsi* partners. *Langsi* relations thus create a series of dependencies between patriclans that crosscut the alliances formed on the basis of co-ownership of major patriclan cults, and add to the density of ties between the constituent Mapeo clans.

The Evolution of Mapeo Politics

This Mapeo case study could have been extended to book length, but I have chosen instead to use it as an interpretative anchorage for a comparative and historical treatment of Chamba communities and their politics. I began this chapter by admitting that Mapeo is atypical even in Chamba terms, so I ought to finish it by explaining why this is so. I have emphasized the many attributes of the idea of *jubi* in Mapeo life. Disease, time, feasting, concealment, danger, dancing, singing, music, responsibility, and cooperation are only a few of the connotations I have been exploring. To me, as an outsider, it appears that Mapeo cults are attempting to reconcile the irreconcilable. Halfway between secret societies and competitive exchange, the notion of *jubi* seems to make contradictory demands for publicity and concealment. But as a participant, I know that the Mapeo *jubi* organization has a logic in action that goes beyond formal logic to become part of the "good life" as Mapeo elders understand it. Part of the atypicality of Mapeo has to be sought in the prominence of the cults. This focus can be extended into the past to ask how the situation came about, and into the broader social fabric to pose questions about the sort of Chamba agency construed in such a society.

All the central Chamba have cults, and their cults seem to have many of the same properties. Particular to Mapeo is the absence of a clearcut ranking of the cults. This is not to say that people do not propose relative evaluations of *jubi.* They do; in fact, they propose them all the time. But there is no agreed ranking. There are obvious reasons for this. There is no inherent basis on which *jubi* can be ranked. *Jubi* are specialized institutions that are formally supposed to take care of different ailments. In the absence of a hierarchy of sicknesses, there is no basis for a hierarchy of cults. An unusual instance illustrates this. Mapeo Chamba claim most to dread smallpox. However, smallpox is controlled from the chiefdom of Yeli or Dayela and not from within Mapeo. Consequently the Gbanbu patriclan of Mapeo acts as intermediary to the chief of Dayela, making a small tribute to the Dayela chief on behalf of the Mapeo villagers. Other feared diseases, such as leprosy and epilepsy, which lead to "bad deaths," are controlled by matriclan cults within Mapeo, but rather than being a basis for respect, these diseases lead to a distinctly ambiguous attitude toward the cult owners. To use such diseases to protect property seems a misuse of power. In contrast, a rough and ready ranking of cults in the chiefdoms away from Mapeo is achieved by reference to the cult owners. Great importance is attached to the cults of the chiefs and priests, and the right to ownership of the land is implied by ownership of the harvest cult.

In Mapeo, the absence of hierarchy among the clans, the unstructured relations between corporate offices, and the lack of ranking among the cults are factors sufficient to create a self-sustaining ritual involution, a competitive intensification in all aspects of cult activity. There are more cults, with higher entrance payments, than elsewhere, and there is less use of other channels of ritual regulation. In the central chiefdoms, shrines are as important as cults in the regulation of the supernatural environment, and they tend to come under the control of the chief and his priests. Mapeo Chamba have no real shrines in this sense and, in contrast to elsewhere, pay relatively slight attention to graves and skull shrines. The cult organization bears a great weight of ritual regulation and, since the *jubi* are nominally clan owned, regulates the relations between clans. The outcome is a rough and ready egalitarianism. But it is not one based on the tacit acceptance of equality. Instead, the absence of effective hierarchy in Mapeo derives from a vigorous, perpetual, and finally unresolvable dispute about precedence. The terms of the dispute may involve the clans, their officials, or their cults. Most clans put forward claims for their cults being "big" *jubi, jub.wari.* However, since someone can be found to make out a case for the "bigness" of almost any cult in Mapeo, no intransitive order can arise. Altogether too many particular criteria are proposed for evaluating the importance of the cults. The cults that ally patriclans (*ya.gum.ani, bən.təng, jarɔ, jub.jangi,* among others) are important on that account.[20] The cult of *karbangi,* owned by most Mapeo matriclans, is important because it is so expensive to join and because its cult apparatus is believed to contain elements from the paraphernalia of a dozen other cults. The cult *ka* is important because it belongs to the priests, *wanbu,* of the Jangbu patriclans of Leko origin, and they use the cult to cleanse the polluting effects of breech births that would otherwise spoil the village. The Gbanbu cult of *sankini* starts the first harvest cycle of *jub.nyɛmi;* without *jub.nyɛmi* no one could eat the new guinea corn, thereby proving that the Gbanbu are owners of the land. The impotence cult *jub.nɔ* is important because only elders can belong to it. In short, everything and its opposite can be interpreted as a sign of importance. Cults that admit many people are "big" because everyman belongs to them; cults that admit few people are "big" for precisely the opposite reason. Cults with dramatic public appearances are "big" on this account, but cults with no public face are too "big" to be seen at all. Mapeo Chamba informants tend to find importance in every detail of the organization of *jubi,* and find themselves drawn into interminable arguments that attempt to compare the incomparable. The character of *jubi* organization has rather to be sought in the intense concern for detail that conjures public issues from the complex ramifications of the ownerships of a plethora of distinct cults, from a host of different charters for membership, and from diverse rites practiced by numerous named patriclans and matriclans, between which accusations of suborned ownerships are rife and disputes over precedence and organization are pervasive. The human agents of such an organization tend to be competitive, truculent, independent, and practical particularists. Each Mapeo elder is a repository of the minute details of the organization and histories of cults, their costs, their memberships, and the grounds on which members became eligible.

How did *jubi* become so crucial? The short answer seems to be by stages. Unlike the chiefdoms, which are represented in oral tradition to have undergone a single foundation from which charters for government arose, Mapeo underwent a kind of continuous foundation throughout the nineteenth century as displaced patriclan sections arrived to seek refuge in the hills. Because of the position of

Mapeo on the borders between speakers of Leko, Daka, and Koma, the sections were highly differentiated and the distinctive aspects of Chamba patriclan cultures were emphasized, resulting in the persistence of such differences. At different times, and sometimes with the support of Fulani, European, or independent-Nigerian outside powers, some clan would attempt to assert chiefship on a model copied from one of the other central Chamba places. But invariably these attempts were unsuccessful, since it was in no other clan's interest to support such an attempt, and no clan commanded sufficient ritual or military resources to complete a centralizing mission by itself. Instead, Mapeo underwent a ritual involution, and as more clans arrived they were inducted into the process. They would enter cooperative relations on the basis of co-residence, find joking partners, join a patriclan alliance, and seek out other patriclans with similar histories as "one-father" relations. It seems that ownership of the stages of the harvest festival was one of the first foci of competition. Many stages of the harvest festival belong to patriclans of Leko origin who, by and large, are accepted to have been among the earliest clans that arrived in Mapeo. In contrast, it is commonly asserted that the matriclans usurped their ownership of the stages.

With the harvest rites oversubscribed, ritual competition seems to have turned next to the major patriclan cults that perform annual rites of commemoration for the patriclan dead. The association between patriclan cults and collective commemoration rites, and its use as a vehicle of patriclan alliance, seems unique to Mapeo. An alliance of clans, largely of northern origin, formed around the cult bən.təng, and organized its public rites to occur during a lull in ritual activity after the end of the harvest cycles. The different Yambu clans, conceptually united around their co-ownership of ya.gum.ani, chose the middle of the wet season in which to perform their public rites. Another alliance, predominantly of clans from the west, installed their rites of the madness cult, jarɔ, just prior to the harvest festivals. Seen in terms of its patriclan cult organization, Mapeo came to consist of a number of blocs of allies who shared common jubi. The alliances were frequently subject to strain, and clans with "one father" in this sense were not necessarily in amity. All the performances of major patriclan cults that I witnessed were divided according to different owning clans who carried out their rites with the assistance of joking partners or co-residents.

Competition in the sphere of matriclanship took a slightly different course. Matriclans did not enter into conceptually fixed alliances; instead, particular relations of cooperation were cemented with respect to different cults. Matriclan cults, unlike major patriclan cults, are said to have been bought and sold, and the new purchasers would normally cooperate with the previous owners of a cult and thereafter attend one another's rites. Thus it became possible to organize series of rites that assured the elders a succession of eating and drinking events. Since membership of major patriclan cults was virtually obligatory, the scale and degree of individual participation in matriclan cults became a more optative area of competition. Some matriclans own a dozen or more cults that an individual might want to join. In addition, by an extension of clanship, a man may join cults belonging to the matriclans of which he is a classificatory "child" or "grandchild."

Once the pattern of competition between patriclans and between individuals in the matriclan domain was entrenched, it became difficult for any centralizing move to do more than fuel the process of ritual involution. Any attempt by a matriclan to command overwhelming ritual prestige, or by a patriclan to command overwhelming force, led to retaliation by other sections of the community thereby raising the stakes in the competition and making centralization a more distant prospect. To the extent that Mapeo Chamba have had headships, these have been imposed by external powers—Fulani, colonial, or independent-Nigerian—to answer the need for the community to be represented. But consistently these chiefs have been classed by all but their closest followers as outsiders' representatives to Mapeo rather than vice versa. Younger Mapeo Chamba are being educated into the ideal of nationhood and may be coming to see the matter differently, but in the late 1970s, prior to which there had been some sort of Mapeo headman virtually throughout this century, my adoptive uncle was able to treat this office as an irrelevance to his generalization that, "We Mapeo Chamba do not follow a man, we follow *jubi*."

PART II

CHAMBA VARIATIONS

CHAPTER 3

CONTEMPORARY VARIATIONS:

AN OVERVIEW

In the chapters of Part 2, I switch my attention from an intensive concern with the organization of a single Chamba community to an extensive overview of Chamba variation in spatial, linguistic, temporal, and ethnic terms. Intensive and extensive interests reconverge in Part 3, where I suggest that contrasting types of sociation identifiable in Mapeo reappear in differing mixes as spatial and historical variants of Chamba organization. The present brief overview is designed to outline some of the range of contemporary variation that Chapters 4 and 5 address from a historical perspective. Chapter 6, which concludes this part of the book, places both historical and contemporary variation in a regional context.

The survey of variation in this chapter provides a working classification of Chamba communities that will allow me to compare their similarities and differences. To arrive at such a classification, it is necessary to add a small amount of detail to the grosser features of difference discussed in Chapter 1. We can start by correlating the current geographical extent of the Chamba with the differences of language and dialect among their components.

As previously mentioned, the historical Chamba homelands were eventually transected across their southeastern corner by the Anglo-French international border that now separates the modern republics of Nigeria and Cameroon. The bulk of the Chamba found themselves to the west of the border in an area extending from the watershed along the Alantika Mountain ridge across the Nassarawo Plain and the Shebshi Mountains. A small part of contemporary Chambaland was ceded to Cameroon in the area between the Alan-

tika Mountains and the Faro and Deo Rivers.[1] At one time Chamba
Leko had been settled across the Deo River throughout the area
south of the Faro—Deo confluence, but this area was abandoned in
the late eighteenth and early nineteenth centuries. These Chamba
must have been heavily represented among the ancestors of the
present-day Chamba in the five Bali chiefdoms of Bamenda and Ndop
in the North West Province of Cameroon, and in the numerous
Chamba-led chiefdoms that established themselves as intruders to
the south of the Benue River in Nigeria.

The major features of language difference correlate with the
overall territorial distribution of Chamba in a straightforward way.
The two Chamba languages have become known in the literature
as Chamba Leko and Chamba Daka; little purpose would be served
by trying to change these terms, although Chamba might dispute
them. The terms have relativistic senses when used in Chamba languages, and they refer not only to language but also to culture and
ethnicity. Since no Chamba terms separate language, dialect, culture, and ethnicity in an absolute and consistent way, this would
also be true of any other borrowed terms. We can continue to use
the terms as long as we realize that only one potential sense of all
those possible is denoted and, equally important, that the local usage of the terms can only be understood in terms of a richer set of
connotations.

Chamba Leko speakers refer to themselves as Samba (plur. Sam.
bira) and their language as Samba speech. This is a gloss for the term
Samba.nwɔnga in the Balkossa chiefdom, for the term Samba.nyɔnga,
in Yeli and, distinctively, for Daga.nyɔnga, among the Bali chiefdoms.[2] Chamba Daka speakers of the central area call themselves
Sama (plur. Sama.bu) and their language Sama speech (Sama.mumi).
At least, these are the terms they might be most likely to offer in a
context understood to involve a contrast between Chamba and non-
Chamba. With an eye to distinctions among Chamba, they might
offer one of the more particular terms I shall be examining presently.
The term "Chamba" is presumably of Hausa origin, since Fulani
speak of Samba. Whatever the case, the term, in various spellings,
was adopted by British, French, and Germans, and is accepted by
Chamba when they speak these languages or Hausa.[3] Until recently,
the two Chamba languages were accepted as part of the same lan-

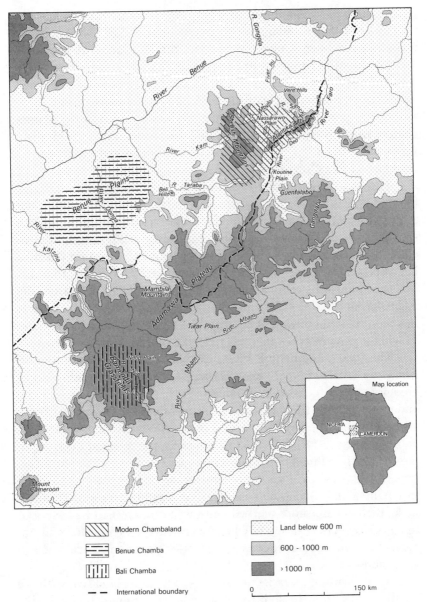

Figure 2 Contemporary Chamba in Nigeria and Cameroon

guage group, the Adamawa sub-branch of the Adamawa-Eastern (Greenberg 1963), or Adamawa-Ubangi (Samarin 1971; Boyd in press) branch of the Niger-Congo family. But the languages are mutually incomprehensible and, despite some grammatical similarities, share relatively few lexical items.[4] Lately, doubts have been expressed about the inclusion of Daka in the Adamawa language group (Bennett 1983; Boyd in press), and it may be better placed in the Benue-Congo group (Roger Blench personal communication 1986). The linguistic basis for Chamba ethnicity is more fragile than earlier commentators believed.

The gross distribution of Leko and Daka speakers is straightforward (see Figure 6). Where the emigrant Chamba of the Bali and Benue chiefdoms have retained their language, they are always Leko speakers.[5] In the historic Chamba homelands, Leko speech is associated with an easterly location. If we discount a few minor Chamba Leko-speaking groups (discussed in Appendix 2), it seems that, before the twentieth century, Chamba Leko was spoken only from the Alantika Mountains eastwards. During the twentieth century, there has been some migration of Leko speakers into the Nassarawo Plain, in what is now Nigeria, that has tended to complicate the picture.

The broad, and I think historically verifiable, interpretation of this gross distribution of Leko speakers is that the emigrant Chamba chiefdoms were founded by alliances that had drawn their leadership and some part of their personnel from an earlier concentration of Chamba Leko who lived to the east of the Alantika Mountains in an area more extensive than that occupied by the residual Leko population. The remainder of the contemporary Chamba of the old homelands are Daka speakers, who far outnumber Leko-speaking Chamba in Chambaland. Both languages have dialectal variation, although Daka dialects are more marked and more numerous. I have set out my working classification of Chamba dialects in tabular form in Appendix 2, and so introduce only the most pertinent historical features here.

Most contemporary Leko speakers in Chambaland live within a small arc running through the Alantika Mountains; they probably do not exceed ten thousand people in all. Many of their present settlements are at the foot of the Alantika Mountains, to which the communities descended during the colonial period. This was the

area that bore the brunt of the early stages of Fulani jihad in Adamawa, and most of the Chamba who did not emigrate took refuge in
the hills. To their north, these residual Leko populations neighbor
people whom they call Koma;[6] their neighbors to the south they call
by variants of the term Pere. In the literature the same people are
sometimes called Koutine or Potopo.[7] Chamba Leko informants derive the application of the term Leko to their language from their
habit of prefacing a statement with *mə.ba.le.kɔ,* "I say that . . . ."
They occasionally use the term to distinguish their language from
that of the Daka, who use the same term in a nonderogatory sense
for speakers of Chamba Leko (they also have various less flattering
terms).

There are several Chamba Leko dialects but not all are important for our present purposes. The most significant distinction in
historical terms appears to be that between northern and southern
dialects, which appears to correlate both with distinctive political
organizations and also with dialect differences among the Chamba
emigrants. The northern dialect is associated with an area of chiefdoms ruled by members of sections of the Sama patriclan, and may
be most closely related to the speech of the Bali Chamba. The southern dialect is found in an area where chiefdoms are ruled by the
gat.kuna matriclan, and this dialect may be related to that of the
Benue Chamba. Comparative linguistic research on Chamba dialects
is not advanced, so it would be rash to base too much upon linguistic
similarities, although the potential historical inferences are clear.
Another of several dialect variations recognized by informants within
southern Leko speech seems to correlate with the tradition, mentioned in Chapter 1, that the Yeli chiefly clan is intrusive. Some
informants suggest that Yeli derives from the same phrase as Leko,
which is rendered *mə.ba.yɛli.kɔ* in the speech of that chiefdom and
its surrounding hamlets.

Daka dialects cannot be dealt with quite so summarily. Many
speakers of what I call Daka dialects would be reluctant to accept
this term of themselves. Variants of the term are always used by
Chamba Leko to refer to the speakers of the other Chamba language
("Dara" in southern Leko; "Daga" in northern Leko), but centrally
placed Daka speakers consider the term to have western connotations. Only Daka to the west of the Shebshi Mountains would call

themselves Daka.bu and their language Daka.mumi.[8] Speakers living to the east of the Shebshi Mountains, as neighbors of the Leko,
claim that the mountain-dwelling Daka to the west are less civilized
than themselves; they prefer to call their own language Sama.mumi
or, failing that, Nakɛnyare. Like Leko, Nakɛnyare derives from a
common phrase in the language, n.nak.ɛn.nya.re, "how are you doing?"[9] It may first have been applied to Chamba Daka speakers by
outsiders, such as Fulani or Hausa, but the term has certainly been
current for well over a century, since we find Heinrich Barth record-
ing "Nyangeyarechi", as well as "Chambanchi," in his list of Adamawa languages (1857 II: 514—15). Language and dialect are, as I
have emphasized, intimately tied to Chamba notions of cultural and
ethnic difference; calling the second language Chamba Daka satis-
fies the requirements of indicating both that it is a Chamba language
and that it is distinct from Chamba Leko.

Just as with Chamba Leko, the distribution of Chamba Daka
dialects correlates with important historical data; again, I restrict
my discussion to those details directly relevant to establishing a
working classification of communities (for further information, see
Appendix 2).

The main Chamba Daka dialect Nakɛnyare, is associated with
the chiefdoms of the Nassarawo Plain and the Shebshi Mountains.
It is the speech form of the overwhelming majority of the central
Chamba and is expanding at the expense of minor dialects thanks to
its use in the growing towns of the Chamba area, such as Ganye and
Jada. Local variants of Nakɛnyare differ from one another in only the
slightest ways, although great local importance is sometimes attached to such features. Nakɛnyare speakers consider their dialect,
and therefore their culture, far more sophisticated than other Chamba
Daka forms. A separate dialect of Chamba Daka is spoken by the
people of the area around Mapeo and in the eastern part of the Nassarawo Plain. The speakers of this dialect insist that their speech
form is real Sama.mumi, "Chamba language," but also use the term
Ma.nɛ.mumi, "Mapeo people's speech," to distinguish their dialect
from that of people to the west.[10]

Other Daka dialects appear to be associated with politically less
well-organized peoples. There has been little research in these areas,
so it is wise not to attribute importance to detail, but the overall

pattern suggests a general distinction between the Daka dialects
of peripheral peoples, to the west and southwest of the major
Nakɛnyare-speaking chiefdoms, and the Daka dialects of ethnically
and, sometimes, residentially distinct groups within the major chiefdoms. This distribution appears to correspond to historical narratives, and suggests that a previously differentiated Daka population
was at least partly standardized in cultural and linguistic terms
through incorporation into the Nakɛnyare chiefdoms.

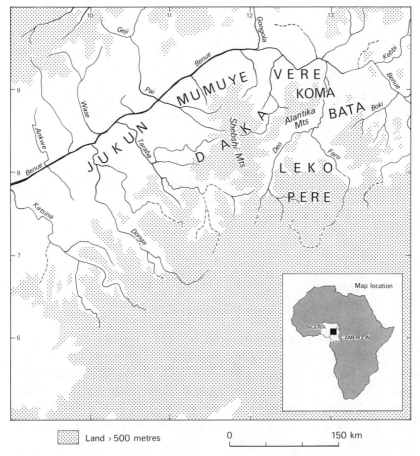

Figure 3 Stages of Chamba Implantation: The Proto-Chamba Period

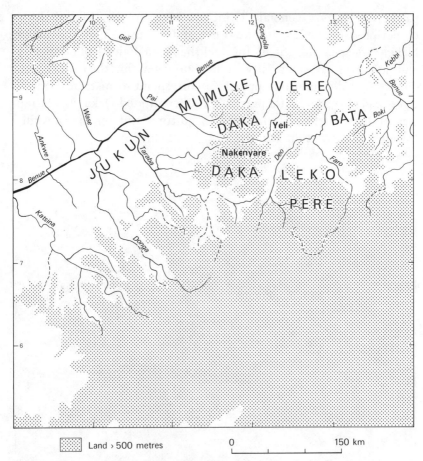

*Figure 4 Stages of Chamba Implantation: The Period of Chamba
Ethnogenesis*

Classification by language and dialect is a major step toward a
set of working categories. Therefore, only the addition of some further discriminations among the central Chamba chiefdoms is required to arrive at a preliminary organization of materials (see Figure
7). To do this, I am forced to preempt parts of the data on history and
clanship that form the subjects of later chapters. A first task is to
distinguish three areas among the Nakɛnyare-speaking chiefdoms:
the southern, central and northern.

The Southern Nakɛnyare, or Gang.kuni *Chiefdoms*

Aside from their common location around the eastern slopes of the
Shebshi Mountains, the members of the southern group share a
number of cultural features. Historically, all claim a close relationship to the Leko-speaking chiefdom of Yeli or Dayela, from where
their royal matriclans are supposed to have migrated. This clan,
gang.kuni, or the matriclan of the chief, is a literal equivalent of
gat.kuna, the chiefly clan of Yeli and the southern Leko chiefdoms

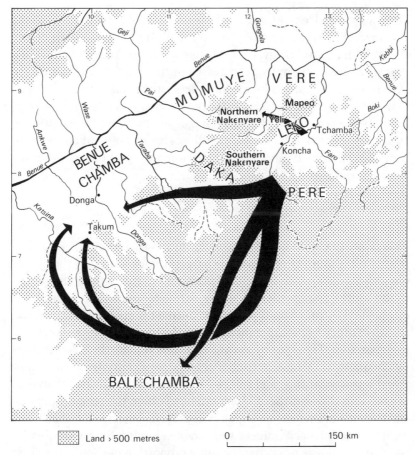

Figure 5 Stages of Chamba Implantation: Emigration Routes

more generally. Indeed, all the southern chiefdoms of Chambaland, whether Leko or Daka speaking, were once ruled by members of, what is nominally, a single matriclan. This shared feature is indicative of other features. In the most general terms, matriclan chiefship and a southern location correlate with a ritualized organization of the chiefdom and with a defensive, or refugee, response to the onset of the nineteenth-century jihadic wars. These correlations are not accidental.

The Central Nakɛnyare of Gurum and Yebbi

The two central chiefdoms of the eastern Shebshi Mountains are also medial in terms of their history and organization. Both chiefdoms claim that their royal clans originated from Yeli, and chiefship appears to have originally been vested in the matriclan of the chiefs of the east, *gang.tim.nɔ.kuni*. Like the southern chiefdoms they appear to have been organized initially in terms of a ritualized model and to have reacted to the early stages of the jihad by adopting a refuge policy. However, both chiefdoms were later taken over by competing patriclans and relations between the two places appear to have deteriorated.

The Northern Nakɛnyare Raider Chiefdoms

This group of chiefdoms is internally more varied than those farther south. Yet, a number of common characteristics shared by the northern chiefdoms provide additional contrasts to the refugee chiefdoms to the south. The northern Nakɛnyare chiefdoms seem to have been established by immigrant patriclans during the first half of the nineteenth century, contemporaneous with the impact of the Fulani jihad in Adamawa. Their internal organizations reflect their foundation by conquest; they have patriclan chiefships, a centralized control of ritual responsibilities, and a degree of stratification greater than that of the central or southern chiefdoms. It is here that the ethnic distinctiveness of incorporated Daka peoples has been maintained most clearly. The intrusive raiders were themselves of diverse origins, as we shall see in the next chapter, but a proportion of them trace their origins from the northern Leko area across the Alantika Mountains,

where we also find political organizations that are headed by patriclan chiefs.

It may be as well to restate the distinctions I have been drawing
in summary form. Within Chambaland I discriminate five groups of
Chamba communities as follows:

I. LEKO SPEAKERS

1.a. Northern Residual Leko Dialect Group

Predominantly patriclan refuge chiefdoms vested in Sama.

1.b. Southern Residual Leko Dialect Group

Predominantly matriclan refuge chiefdoms vested in *gat.kuna*.

2. DAKA SPEAKERS

2.a. Nakɛnyare Dialect Group

1. Southern Nakɛnyare: predominantly matriclan refuge chiefdoms vested in *gang.kuni* and claiming an origin from Yeli.

2. Central Nakɛnyare: originally matriclan refuge chiefdoms
vested in *gang.tim.nɔ.kuni*, claiming an origin from Yeli; later they
became patriclan chiefdoms.

3. Northern Nakɛnyare: intrusive patriclan chiefdoms vested in
different clans, often belonging to the patriclan cluster of Yambu.
Many of the chiefly patriclans claim to have originated from the
northern residual Leko area.

2.b. Mapeo Dialect Group

Locality populated by refugee clan sections.

2.c. Indigenous Daka Dialect Groups

A large number of apparently distinct speech forms occur, found
within and on the southern and western margins of the Nakɛnyare
chiefdoms. Distinct Daka dialects are more discernible in the northern rather than central or southern Nakɛnyare chiefdoms.

Outside Chambaland I have distinguished between two areas of chiefdom foundation associated with the Bali and Benue Chamba respectively. The complexity of the classification reflects a complicated distribution on the ground, the result of a sequence of historical processes. An initial distribution of Leko speakers to the east and Daka speakers to the west was mediated following the foundation of Yeli and the later foundation of the southern and central Nakɛnyare-speaking chiefdoms. Further rearrangements in distribution followed events during the early years of the conflicts between the Fulani and the peoples of Adamawa. Emigrant Chamba clans with their allies founded chiefdoms outside Chambaland and within the old Daka homelands of the northern Shebshi Mountains. Other Chamba communities took refuge in the defensive fastnesses of the Alantika or Shebshi Mountains. Some traditional chiefdoms were reestablished in new areas, and others seem altogether to have disappeared. At the same time, Mapeo became a populous and uncentralized hill refuge composed of the displaced.

The emergence of an extensive Chamba ethnic identity took place later, especially during the period when the colonial and postcolonial states began to demand Chamba acknowledgment, and coincided with a process of reconstruing the manifold interrelations and resemblances that had earlier existed. Political context and local response reacted upon one another. The following chapters develop these themes.

Chapter 4 retells the histories of the Chamba raiders, in part to see how far we are able to reconstruct the events associated with their alliances during the nineteenth century. Chapter 5 contrasts these narratives with those of the ritualized chiefdoms founded earlier and under different conditions. The two chapters are concerned with two aspects of ethnohistory. I want to see how far a judicious use of Chamba historical sources allows a reconstruction, in our historical terms, of the trajectories of Chamba raiding parties, and a dating of their exploits. I am also concerned with the way in which history is recalled in Chamba sources as this affects the way in which the accounts can be used for the purpose of historical reconstruction.

The chapters show how the accounts of the raider chiefdoms are stylized differently from those of the ritualized chiefdoms and how this dissimilarity forms part of a larger complex of differences between them. The histories of raider chiefdoms are retold in terms of patriclanship, the divisive idiom of Chamba organization. These narratives may tend toward the legendary, although they are devoid of mythological elements, and they are particularizing, precise and sequential.

Histories of ritualized chiefdoms tend to involve matriclanship, in Chamba terms an idiom of solidarity. Stories of matriclan origin are typically vague and mythological. They are closely related to a genre of folktales that Mapeo Chamba call *tit.jɔni* (laughing tales), which often involve animals and shape-changing. Like *tit.jɔni*, the origin stories are virtually devoid of temporally located narrative; a mythological origin directly precedes the clan's contemporary circumstances or normatively this should be the case. The intrusion of historical narrative into matriclan history is often indicative of some breakdown in the solidarity that should prevail between members of the clan.

Chapters 4 and 5 demonstrate not only the distinction between these Chamba conceptions of history, with their different definitions of context and their distinct effects, but also show how the choice of idiom, as much as the choice of content, carries information about the histories of Chamba communities. Chapter 6 sets the histories of Chamba raiders and refugees into a broader regional context that includes the different Chamba communities, their neighbors, and a regional system of interrelationships that stretched beyond the frontiers of Adamawa.

CHAPTER 4

HISTORICAL VARIATIONS:

THE CHAMBA RAIDERS

Rather than following Chamba history from a strictly sequential viewpoint, I deal in Chapters 4 and 5 with two different Chamba reactions to the pervasive disruption of normal life that affected Chambaland during the nineteenth century. In this chapter, I outline the sequences of Chamba migratory movements that occurred from and within Chambaland during the period. In particular, I am concerned with what we are able to reconstruct of the exploits of the notorious Chamba raiders. In Chapter 5 I take up the histories of Chamba communities that broadly adopted a refuge strategy during the nineteenth-century raids. Raiders and refugees together formed elements of a regional system of sociation to which I turn in Chapter 6.

There is general agreement in the literature that the Leko diaspora from their eighteenth-century homelands had dramatic consequences for the populations of the eastern end of the West African middle-belt. Consensus extends to the broad features of the diaspora, but the precise dates and the geographical extent of the Chamba raids are disputed. In broad terms we know that raiding bands under Chamba leadership, and recruited from the different peoples through whom they marauded, established war camps, made local alliances, raided for slaves, and pillaged villages in a widening arc of disruption to the south and west of their old homelands. The bands seem to have kept open lines of communication, and they split and reconverged as they pursued their trails of destruction. All writers agree that, in the process, Chamba raiders largely redefined the political map of the region. Their activities probably also assisted the Fulani state-builders by reducing potential opposition to the formation of the Fulani lamidates and by carrying many of the local forces ahead as members of Chamba alliances. Beyond this broad agreement lies pervasive dispute over matters of regional importance. Because of this, I summarize my own view before looking in more detail at the Chamba traditions.

A matter of some discussion concerns the scale of Chamba emigrations. Given that the groups involved were probably small but numerous, and that their numbers and strengths were continually modified by splitting, it is difficult to follow the careers of particular groups. Because they were intimately related to the type of history Chamba raiders were making, the sources available further compound the problem of following the activities of particular raiding groups. Since the raiding bands had unstable compositions, were deflected by potential opposition, and were attracted by the possibilities of successful raiding, it is difficult, with certainty, to tie their movements to the activities of particular named leaders or bands. We must rely on the internal consistency of the Chamba's own traditions, collected by different people at different times, on the recollections of the peoples who were the victims of Chamba raids, and on the present compositions of the Chamba conquest chiefdoms into which were incorporated large numbers of allies picked up during the wanderings of the raiding alliances. These narratives were often related by interested participants mindful of the contemporary pertinence of historical traditions to European travelers and colonial administrators of a number of different nationalities. However, the general historicity of Chamba patriclan narratives and instances of internal corroboration between sources can be set against the partiality of the sources.

Consistencies between the accounts make it clear that, in the short term, and before Fulani consolidation began to curtail the conditions favorable to small operators like Chamba, a transition to a parasitic, raiding, way of life could be made easily and successfully. This suggests a lack of precedent. Chamba appear to have used tactics against which the people they raided lacked adequate defense. It appears that this transition occurred rapidly, and that it dates back to the earliest period of the Fulani jihad, possibly slightly predating

the official declaration of religious war in 1809. The scale and sud-
denness of the changes are paralleled by a rapid transformation in
the organization of the participating groups. In my opinion these
changes are best understood from a perspective that emphasizes a
rupture in historical processes around the beginning of the nineteenth century. I do not deny continuity—continuity and change are
in fact derivative of a point of view—but suggest that it may be
most useful to look for signs of change.

In this context I propose that the critical rupture in historical
process was not the Fulani jihad, but a thoroughgoing change in
the extent to which many different people were either impelled or
persuaded to turn to a way of life that relied on, in Jack Goody's
terms, the means of destruction as much as the means of production
(Goody 1971). I believe that the Fulani jihad in Adamawa was as
much an expression, as a cause, of this change. The means of destruction do not appear to have changed qualitatively until later in
the nineteenth century. We do not know how long Chamba Leko
had bows and poisoned arrows or horses, especially ponies, but these
were the destructive resources with which their names are associated in Grassfield traditions, and Chamba recollections do not encompass a time when they were without them. The historian's problem concerns the intensity of the deployment of their resources. It
is difficult to escape the sense that the last years of the eighteenth
century witnessed the breakdown of an existing regional system of
social organization into which the Fulani emirates then expanded.
My own feeling is that, by the eighteenth century, the existing system was not, as proponents of the Jukun or Kororofa Empire argue,
an empire, but a regional network of ritual, clan, and economic relations that encompassed many communities, some with, and others without, chiefs. An increasing willingness to engage in mutual
raiding, that itself may have had demographic, ecological, and tactical preconditions, marked the effective demise of the existing
forms of sociability upon which such a network had to depend. The
Chamba diaspora was the last act of the drama.

If we take Chamba traditions of dispersal at approximate face
value and, as discussed below, there are valid reasons for such an
attitude, then the diaspora appears to have occurred in a relatively
short period of about twenty-five years. This has not been a gener-

ally accepted viewpoint among writers pursuing an areal perspective, but it does accord with E. M. Chilver's deductions on the basis
of Bali Chamba materials (most recently Chilver 1981). The view is
also that of Chamba themselves, who do not maintain traditions of
having been warriors prior to the break-up of the Chamba Leko
settlements. The year 1830 provides a benchmark, subsequent to
which dates can be assigned to events with a certain degree of confidence. By 1830 all the original hero leaders recalled in the narratives of the alliances were dead, and their passing was associated
with the fragmentation of the raiding bands themselves. By 1830
also, Chamba raiders had entered the area in which they were eventually to settle down, although the process of settling and redefining
political boundaries was going to take another thirty years. I suspect
that the earlier dislocations occasioned by Chamba movements occurred in the preceding twenty or thirty years. To support such a
view I have to examine the source materials in some detail.

One source deserving special mention, since I shall refer to it
frequently, is the history of the Chamba of the Benue regions composed by the late Chief of Donga, Bitemya Sambo Garbosa II. As a
young man, and after he had received some European education,
Garbosa became an assistant to the British government anthropologist C. K. Meek. Meek wrote on Chamba following a short period of
research in Donga during 1927. This experience seems to have gal-
vanized Garbosa's ambition to write a history of his own people, and
he set about interviewing elders in the late 1920s. The two works
that resulted were privately published as a single volume.[1] They deal
respectively with the histories of all Benue Chamba chiefdoms and
the lives of the Chiefs of Donga. However, although Garbosa is an
invaluable source of information, some caution has to be exercised
in interpreting his text. In contrast to sources on the Bali Chamba,
concerning which there has been an intensive research effort, there
are few accounts against which to check the authority of Garbosa's
narrative. Furthermore, two potential biases in his text have to be
kept in mind. It is evident that he exaggerates the nineteenth-
century significance of a Chamba factor in the plains south of the
Benue and, since his particular concern is to demonstrate the legitimacy of the descent of his own line of Donga chiefs from the chief
credited with leading the Chamba alliance from their homelands, we

may suspect a similar bias in his treatment of Donga in relation to the other Chamba-led chiefdoms founded in the Benue plains during the same period. Nevertheless, in his defense as a historian, it should be mentioned that Garbosa includes information that serves neither of the purposes that we can read into his book.

The Raider Groups

Taking our sources together we can identify four main raiding alliances that set out from Chambaland (see Figure 8). Each was subject to occasional splitting, and periodic reconvergence, sometimes in cooperation with, but just as often in conflict with, other alliances. The original alliances, each of which is usually associated with a hero leader, comprised the Den Bakwa led by Loya Garbosa, from which Garbosa claims descent of the present Donga dynasty, the Daka of Gyando, whose descendants occupied the Takum area, the Pere led by Mudi (Modi in Benue traditions and Muti in Bali traditions), whose descendants live within the Bali chiefdoms and are also credited with introducing Chamba-led elements into the Kashimbila area, and the Ba'ni of Gawolbe, whose descendants founded the five Bali-Chamba chiefdoms of northwest Cameroon.

The sources are most reliable concerning the Den Bakwa and Ba'ni groups. Information about the two other groups has to be largely gleaned from their occasional appearances in traditions of the Den Bakwa or Ba'ni. Although not usually discussed in the same context, I include the nineteenth-century Chamba chiefdoms of the northern Shebshi Mountains within the category of Chamba raiders and discuss their origins at the end of this chapter. Important among groups active in the northern Shebshi Mountains were those under the leadership of members of the Yambu patriclan. Of these, the most widely recalled is the group led by Damashi that appears to have ventured to the west of Chambaland. Figure 8 illustrates the scale and extent of the Chamba Leko diaspora and resultant raids. The figure is of course no more accurate than the traditions upon which it is based, and we shall see that considerable doubt can be voiced about particular details of the fortunes of the individual alliances but, overall, the pattern of dispersion is beyond dispute.

Den Bakwa

Garbosa II's chronicle begins with the departure of a group of Chamba under the leadership of Loya Garbosa, the Den Bakwa, from an area of Chambaland he calls Dindin.[2] These mounted raiders left with their dependents, signifying a definitive migration rather than the start of a raiding adventure, and regrouped in a temporary camp called Tipchen (presumably Tipsan, fifteen miles southwest of present day Koncha). The party appears to have subsequently followed the valley of the Taraba and established a second camp called Gildu, close to the Beli hills, from where they may have raided the Ndoro.[3] From Gildu, most members of the alliance crossed the Gazabu River to found a more permanent camp at Gankwe.[4] Events crucial to the reconstruction of Garbosa's narrative occur at this point. Loya Garbosa, the original leader and a member of the Sama patriclan, drowned in the river crossing; a new chief, called Pyemishena and a member of the Kola clan, was appointed his successor, taking the title of Garkola. Loya Garbosa's oldest son, Shimbura, is said to have refused the chiefship in order to remain an active warrior (Garbosa n.d.:14). The succession and implied usurpation of Garkola, and his subsequent abuse of authority (on no rational grounds, according to our author), resulted in the fissioning of the original alliance and introduced conflicts between Chamba that were only partly healed during a subsequent reconvergence of elements of the scattered Chamba, and the restoration of the Sama to a position of preeminence concurrent with the foundation of Donga. This movement from unity through dissent to the reestablishment of unity constitutes the dramatic intention of Garbosa's narrative, and in the absence of corroboration from other sources we need to view it with some suspicion.

Dissent between Garkola and his popular rival, Shimbura, led the latter to slip out of the Gankwe camp by night, scarcely managing to assure the escape of his infant son, Nubumga Donzomga (Garbosa n.d.:15—16). Shimbura and his followers headed southwest to establish a walled settlement at Jenuwa, where Shimbura was installed as chief with the title Garkiye. From this base, his raiders conquered peoples between Takum and the Katsina Ala River.[5] Here, also, the first of the reconvergences between different Chamba raiding parties occurred, as described by Garbosa II, consisting of the arrival of Chamba Daka under the leadership of Kumboshi, the son of Gyando (Garbosa n.d.:17). However, dispute broke out between the two bands and Garkiye moved again, this time heading north.

Passing toward Arufu, Garkiye's group gained support by incorporating local peoples and was able to send out splinter groups to Chanchanji and Rafin Kada.[6] Shortage of food is given as the cause of a further move to Ganako, on the south bank of the Benue near Ibi. We know that this settlement was in existence in 1854, for in that year members of the MacGregor-Laird expedition met Garkiye (Meek 1931b I:330—31; Crowther 1855:82—84; Baikie 1856:125—28). "Gankera," as these visitors called Ganako, was a moated and stockaded settlement; its inhabitants possessed Arab horses used in annual slave raids against the "Mitshi" (presumably "Munshi" or Tiv). They appeared to be under threat from neighboring Jibu.[7] Moving his, now aged, father north of the Benue, Nubumga Donzomga set out to secure an alliance with the Fulani governor Ibrahim of Bauchi, from whom he received a flag, a charter to take part in the holy war, thirty horses, and reinforcements in the form of a group of Fulani Jafun warriors (Garbosa n.d.:18—21; Meek 1931b I:331—32). Strengthened, the group took a southeasterly course and settled close to Donga. When their food supplies ran low, they took to plundering the fields of a Chamba group already settled in the area, whom they drove off, to complete the foundation of Donga.

The destiny of the putatively direct descendants of Loya Garbosa is Bitemya Garbosa's major interest in his history, but he also gives us indications of the fate of the other members of the Den Bakwa. Fissioning within the alliance had been chronic from the outset. Just as in the case of Shimbura's secession, the Chamba leaders of the seceding groups were installed as independent chiefs. Such splintering could not have been possible without the incorporation of large numbers of the peoples among whom the Chamba temporarily settled. Chamba appear to have followed a policy of selective support for local groups, provoking or playing on local antagonisms. The contemporary results of this include the ethnic heterogeneity of the Chamba chiefdoms (a number of which have passed out of Chamba control) and a pervasive bickering among Chamba chiefdoms about the legitimacy of their respective royal families. Such conflict is focused particularly on claims and counterclaims of descent from the acknowledged leaders of the Chamba alliances.

Before crossing the Suntai River, and prior to the establishment of the Gankwe camp, the future founder of Kungana had already left the united alliance of Den Bakwa. This group later came to assist Garkola at Gankwe, and is claimed by Garbosa to have been misused without reason by that chief. Nukpo and Tissa are supposed to have been founded by other Chamba sections that left Gankwe[8] and the camp finally disintegrated in complete disarray during the succession crisis on the death of Garkola.[9] A section led by Nyonzuma of the Poba clan, who took the chiefly title of Garbanyi, moved near to Donga and was the group found in occupation by Nubumga Donzomga. Garbanyi's Chamba are said to have called upon the Jukun, Ankwe, and Fulani as well as Nyakola of Jibu in the attempt to displace the newly arrived Chamba, but were themselves defeated and forced to flee to Jibu under cover of darkness. They remained three years at Jibu, and a further seven years, until the death of Garbanyi, in Wurio. Wobkasa, the brother of the late chief, succeeded to the chiefship with the title Garnyisa; he made his peace with Nubumga Donzomga and settled at Suntai, about ten kilometers from Donga, around the year 1870 (Garbosa n.d.:23—24; Temple 1922:79; Meek 1931b I:333; probably not independently). A history recorded at Suntai by Roger Blench (Interview 12.4.84) basically endorses this sequence of events but construes Donzomga's attack as unwarranted aggression against people who had hospitably received his father.

Three years after the foundation of Donga, Garkiye, father of Nubumga Donzomga, died in advanced old age. His son formally assumed the responsibilities of chiefship he had undertaken in the chief's old age, taking the title Garbasa Nonga. The later nineteenth-century history of Donga coincides with the intensification of Fulani activity in the Benue plains and with the establishment of Gassol by the Muri Fulani. The population of Donga was swollen by both Chamba and non-Chamba who were, Garbosa tells us, escaping witchcraft allegations, following trade, or simply seeking security. Garbosa writes of the need to rebuild the city walls to incorporate new arrivals, and it seems generally to have been the case that Chamba settlements in the Benue plains were walled. He estimates that Donga reached a peak population of eight to ten thousand in the nineteenth century. The town's military fortunes varied: Donga resisted an attack from Gassol in the later 1860s, but suffered a crushing defeat when attacked by Jibu in alliance with Wukari in 1871. However, the support of Bayero, campaigning on behalf of the Sultan of Sokoto, not only led to the defeat of the combined Jibu—Wukari forces, but was followed by slave raids that ravaged Jukun territory (Rubin 1969:169).

Daka of Gyando

A second Chamba group first appears in Donga traditions as rivals of Garkiye's raiders around Takum. Two versions of the encounter and dispute have been recorded: Garbosa's, representing the Donga viewpoint, and a second from the Takum perspective.

Following the death of Loya Garbosa, and after his son, Garkiye, and his followers had defected from the Den Bakwa group, Garkiye's Chamba met, and disputed with, another Chamba group in the vicinity of Takum. This second group is identified in Garbosa's narrative as Daka led by Kumboshi, son of Gyando. Garbosa attributes blame for the dispute to Gban Kuna, one of Garkiye's chiefmakers, whom he had titled Gardanpua. While Garkiye was planning his conquest of the remaining Kutep, Gban Kuna slipped away to join the newly arrived Daka under Kumboshi, and persuaded Kumboshi to attack Lissam, Garkiye's next target. When this attack turned out badly the Chamba Daka turned on Garkiye's Chamba. However, Garkiye, again abjuring conflict between Chamba, as at Gankwe, left and moved to the north. Returning to these events later in his narrative, Garbosa claims the alliance of Gban Kuna and Kumboshi to have been little more than a pretext to attack Garkiye. We may be dealing with the rationalization of a reversal.

The Gazetteer of Muri offers our only Takum perspective on the events. In this account, the Chamba of Takum are referred to as Tikari, whereas the Donga and Suntai Chamba are called Dingyi, a variant of a common term for Chamba Leko in the Benue region. The Tikari are said to have arrived in two sections. One was led by Garuba and settled at "Zenoa" (Jenuwa), and the other by the three sons of Garuba's brother Gando (the Gyando of Garbosa's account).

The three sons of Gyando, Kumboshi, Boshi and Yakuba, had initially settled west of Takum among the Tiv. They rejoined Garuba to assist in an attack on the Markam, a Kutep group, in the course of which Garuba was killed. (Garbosa records the death of a Daka named Zoboi in the attack on Lissam.) Kumboshi is said to have continued the attack on the "Zomper" and to have captured their settlements at Kunabai and Lissam. When these operations were complete, "Galboshi," the leader of the Dingyi (Chamba), refused to pay tribute to Kumboshi's successor, Boshi, and was killed. "Gurki" (Garkiye), son of "Galboshi," left the Takum area for Wukari and Ibi before founding Donga (Fremantle 1922:39—40). The characterization of the Takum Chamba as Tikari is also followed by Temple (1922:80); Garbosa, as we have seen, refers to them as Daka, a usage that persists in Donga.

Some of the differences between these two accounts are predictably self-interested and, as things stand, impossible to adjudicate. In the Donga account, the Chamba under Garkiye are represented as the first arrivals; in the Takum version the order is reversed. Takum sources claim that Garbosa was killed in the course of the dispute; Donga sources claim he died earlier in the crossing of the Gazabu River. But in the broadest terms, the reports clearly concern the same events. Garkiye's Chamba, who had defected from the Gankwe camp and moved southwest, met other raiders, associated with the name of Kumboshi, who had most recently arrived at Takum from the west, and who were called Daka or Tikari.

The origin of the Daka raiders is uncertain. Temple states that Kumboshi was the son of the chief of Tibati whose reign coincided with the start of Chamba migrations (1922:80). In Garbosa's account, Kumboshi's father, Gyando, is said to have left Adamawa in company with Mudi of the Pyeri. According to Garbosa, Gyando's followers included people known as Tikari, Jidu, Pati, Lufum, and Jibawa (n.d.:44). Presumably these identifications are based upon researches carried out by Meek in 1928. Wordlists collected by him from Takum inhabitants show that Pati were speaking a Grassfields language, and that the Jidu may have been speaking Buti. Meek records that Kumboshi reached Takum from the west and was the son of an Akwana chief's daughter. The Jidu are said to have come from Banyo (Meek 1928 Wukari District Office, summarized in Chilver ms.). Whatever we may infer from Kumboshi's supposed parentage, both the oral tradition and ethnic composition of the Takum group suggest that the Daka raiders had earlier formed part of the southward Chamba migration associated with the Ba'ni. The German explorer Zintgraff recorded a conversation with a later ruler of Takum, Yakuba, in which the latter claimed that his father, Gyando, and the leader of the Ba'ni migrations were "cousins" (Zintgraff 1895:269; quoted in Chilver ms.). The presence of Buti and Tikar in the Daka group suggests that the Daka had passed through Buti and Tikari country, had perhaps skirted Bamum, and had reached areas inhabited by Tiv before turning east toward the Benue plains to arrive in Takum. The details of this journey are not clear, but it may be that the Daka were responsible for the early raids in the northeastern Grassfields that are otherwise difficult to tie into what we know of the Ba'ni migrations.

The Pere

The immigration of the Pere (Pyeri in Benue, and Peli in Bali traditions) into the Benue plains is treated by Garbosa as the third of three distinct intrusions—Den Bakwa, Daka, and Pere. Information from Chambaland helps to identify this group, since Pere is used by the neighbors of the southern residual Chamba Leko to refer to themselves. And in different pronunciations, this is also the term by which the Chamba Leko know them.[10] The Pere improperly appear in older texts under the derogatory name by which the Fulani knew them, Koutine. Garbosa claims that they had fought their way to Bafut in the Bamenda Grassfields before arriving at the Katsina Ala River in two groups under their leaders Modi and Gadi. Dispute broke out between the groups and they separated. Modi's group established a settlement named after him, while Gadi's people are credited with the foundation of Kashimbila (claimed to be Garshimbila in Chamba) (Garbosa n.d.:48—50). Although Garbosa is not wholly clear on the point, Kashimbila may have been allied with Takum.

Convergent traditions, apparently concerned with the same groups, occur among the Ba'ni for the earlier part of the story, and the Tiv, for the later stages. The Ugenyi, as the Chamba are known to the Tiv, may have been a catalyst of Tiv expansion during the nineteenth century (Bohannan 1969:12). Two groups of Chamba settled in the Kashimbila area, the principal one of which (Modi's group?) arrived about 1830, having been driven from the Tibati area by the Fulani. They joined Chamba who had earlier settled around Kashimbila (Gadi's group, or Gyando's Daka?) (East 1939:49fn.). East, and the Tiv historian Akiga, attribute considerable influence to these immigrant Chamba.[11]

The Daka and Pere were responsible for most of the Chamba raiding in the southwestern Benue plains. They appear to have made their earliest movements concurrent with the southward-migrating Ba'ni before they converged with elements of the Den Bakwa, whose initial movements had been toward the west (this is the hypothesis of Figure 8). It seems possible that the Daka and Pere had constituted the vanguard of Chamba advance.

Ba'ni of Gawolbe

The Ba'ni constitute the most southerly of the Chamba raider groups, and their migrations, begun under the hero-leader Gawolbe, are the most fully documented of those discussed so far. A magisterial synthesis of Bali Nyonga historical sources has been carried out by E. M. Chilver, upon whose work I draw heavily.[12]

By the time that the Chamba groups migrating south appear in Pere traditions between Koncha and Tignere, they already contained elements of differing origins. In addition to Chamba, the groups included contingents from the Chamba's neighbors to the north, the Bata or Bachama clans, and possibly Koma from the Alantika Mountains, and they rapidly absorbed numbers of Pere, especially of Potopo elements of the population.[13] It is most probable that the different groups were subject to the splitting, the formation of local alliances, and the periodic confrontations that characterized the Chamba migrations elsewhere. This makes it difficult to determine the routes that specific groups followed, but two broad paths are discernible (Mohammadou 1978:38). One group, perhaps predominantly composed of Potopo and led by Ga Muti, and possibly in company with Gyando's Daka, moved from Koncha toward Tignere, where some Buti groups, already raiders themselves, may have been incorporated. According to tradition, there were attacks on Nyam Nyam in the vicinity of Galim, and Mbum elements around Tibati were drawn into the alliance. In the Banyo region, we find Chamba raiders involved in a political dispute, supporting one local protagonist against another, and moving with Buti allies just ahead of approaching Fulani war parties. A second group is said to have pursued a slightly more westerly route from the Koutine plain, moving through present-day Gashaka onto the Mambila plateau. The groups then passed through regions inhabited by Tikari, incorporating members of the chiefdoms in the area, and on to Bamum, raiding and absorbing local populations as they went.

Records of their subsequent raids across the Grassfields are particularly numerous, but do not appear to indicate a single movement.[14] The records may be reconcilable with traditions of successive sweeps across the area, the earliest of them carried out by the vanguard groups of Pere (Pɛli or Pɛ.nɛbba in Grassfields traditions) and Daka. Raiding on a devastating scale accompanied the passage of Gawolbe's main Ba'ni group across the Grassfields. This, the largest group of raiders, is often said to have been following in the wake of Ga Muti's Peli. A large Chamba settlement established among the Bamileke at Nkəm was soundly defeated by a large-scale attack, and Gawolbe, the Chamba leader, was killed.[15]

These events represent a turning point in local history. The Chamba alliance split under different leaders, whose relations with Gawolbe are now the subject of lively local interest.[16] The founders of Bali Kumbad raided the Ndop plain before establishing themselves on a range of hills from which they had driven the previous occupants. The Bali Nyonga group settled on the southern border of Bamum, from which they were driven along with an allied group of Bati (or pa Tie). The Bali Nyonga then displaced the Chamba Bali Konntan group, which may have been predominantly Peli, and occupied their settlement. The incorporation of the Bati is credited with the introduction to Bali Nyonga of Munngaka, a Grassfields language that displaced Chamba Leko. Other Bali groups under their independent chiefs were responsible for the foundation of Bali Gham, Bali Gashu, and Bali Gangsin. The histories of these groups following the reverse of Nkəm have formed the subject of E. M. Chilver's publications, so I shall not pursue them here. Suffice it to say that the larger Bali groups remained a considerable political force in Grassfields politics subsequent to the establishment of permanent Bali settlements. In the case of Bali Nyonga, alliance with German colonial ambitions led, for a time, to this group of immigrants becoming the paramount local power (see especially Chilver 1967).

A synthesis of the scattered traditions of Chamba migrations highlights several key issues. The extent of the area that the emigrants raided is immediately striking. Chamba-led raiders foraged up to five hundred kilometers from their homelands. Also striking is the way in which an older political order crumbled before the determined activities of rootless raiding bands composed of the displaced and their displacers, such that each assimilation of the raided became the condition for a subsequent and more pervasive raid of the next people along. The cumulative nature of the Chamba diaspora has not always been appreciated, but the traditions reveal that the so-called Chamba migrations were in fact of multi-ethnic composition and comprised groups of different Chamba, Bata, Bachama, and Pere. Furthermore, the emigrants incorporated elements of every people through whom they passed: Buti, Tikar, Kutep, and even Fulani after Nubumga Donzomga had visited Bauchi.

The Chamba migrations are movements on a regional, rather than local or tribal scale, and the changes they effected were permanent. The advent of the raiding parties in the Bamenda Grassfields, for example, is recalled in apocalyptic terms by those they attacked, and the depredations they caused seem to have changed residence patterns and descent organizations (see Nkwi and Warnier 1982). Jack Goody's concern with the distribution of the "means of destruction" in explaining relations between West African political groups, appears to have found a limiting case in this area of the middle-belt during the first half of the nineteenth century (Goody 1971). But the scale of disruption caused by the Chamba-led alliances militated against a permanent reliance upon the same tactics; reroutinization was inevitable once local populations had made adjustments to the increasingly perilous conditions of everyday life.

The narrative accounts of Chamba expansion tell us little about the lives of the people concerned, or the stages by which they adopted their current organizations; we learn, simply, that they raided, settled awhile, split, disputed, were often threatened by Fulani advances on their heels, and moved on. Their knowledge of clan names and chief lists permits local oral historians to associate migratory routes and places along the routes, to the reigns of particular chiefs. By utilizing a similar type of interpretation, the contemporary organization of emigrant Chamba chiefdoms, their ethnic make-up, the offices owned by different sections of the population, and their relationship to the chiefly clan, can be read as evidence of a founding journey. Another way of saying this is that spatial and temporal variety have become internal properties and reflect the way political organization is viewed in communities derived from the raiding groups. Titles in the present possession of recruited peoples are indicative of their past responsibilities toward Chamba chiefs. A scrupulous concern with their pedigrees and mutual prestige is typical of all the emigrant Chamba chiefs and may have been encouraged by the pseudo-historical rationalizations of colonial indirect rule (see Chapter 11). The legitimacy of current chiefship has become crucial to the integrity of all the other elements of present organization that are tied to it. Contemporary Chamba patriclan chiefdoms are self-consciously historical products. The epic journeys of their founders account for an internal distribution of duties between elements of different ethnic origin, and the concept of movement and recruitment underpinned rights that henceforth were not to be subject to temporal vicissitudes.

The Northern Shebshi Chiefdoms

In the remainder of Chapter 4 I turn to the development of another group of raider chiefdoms, those of the northern Shebshi Mountains. Until the start of the Fulani jihad it seems reasonable to suppose that the Shebshi Mountains were inhabited by clans that spoke indigenous Daka dialects. The independence of these clansmen ceased upon the arrival of raiders, most of whom were retreating from the east in the face of the Fulani threat. The chiefdoms that emerged from this convergence represent a possible intermediary stage in the foundation of Chamba raider chiefdoms. Unlike the Benue and Bali conquest chiefdoms, the foundations of new political organizations in the northern Shebshi Mountains occurred within Chambaland, and the degree of ethnic heterogeneity within the political community was correspondingly less. It is conceivable that the northern Shebshi chiefdoms provide data concerning the early stages in the organization of the Chamba raiding alliances. These political organizations suggest comparison with the chiefdoms of the southern and central Shebshi Mountains, founded in much the same milieu but, if we are to believe their traditions, without the use of force. The oral traditions of the northern Shebshi Mountains are less spare than their recorded counterparts from the Benue and Bali Chamba chiefdoms, and allow us to explore further ideas about the association between types of political organization and forms of oral narrative.

The nineteenth-century history of the northern Shebshi Mountains is complex, but apart from ambiguous matters of local detail the overall picture is fairly clear. The complexity derives in equal part from the numbers of population movements that occurred within the region, and from the instability of the political organizations that emerged. Two factors contributed to this instability. No single political organization was able to marshal sufficient military resources to allow it to dominate its neighbors for more than brief periods. Furthermore, all the Chamba communities of the northern Shebshi Mountains came progressively under threat from Fulani groups that by the middle of the nineteenth century owed allegiance to the emirate capital of Yola.

Early in the nineteenth century, disparate Chamba elements, along with Bata and Vere allies, converged in apparent independence upon a settlement immediately east of the Shebshi Mountains. The groups attempted to establish individual areas of influence among the resident, mainly Daka-speaking peoples who had not been organized into chiefdoms during the earlier period of migrations from Yeli. As the century wore on, the small immigrant chiefdoms retreated west, or sent out splinter groups into the mountains. These movements removed the chiefdom centers from close proximity to the Fulani villages that were concurrently becoming established in the Nassarawo Plain. The movements also allowed the immigrant chiefdoms to exercise enough control over the trading and grazing paths that traversed the mountains to be able to demand payment for passage over their lands.

During the period under consideration the principal groups of people present in the region included chiefdoms founded by members of the intrusive Yambu cluster of patriclans, chiefdoms founded by other intruders claiming Chamba Leko or Bata origins, and indigenous settlements of Daka-speaking ethnic groups, Mumuye, and other chiefdoms whose founders pressed claims to a western origin. However, a significant feature of political organization in the northern Shebshi Mountains was that, with few exceptions, the processes of arrival, dispersion, and retreat into the mountains occurred in such swift succession that the immigrant chiefdoms achieved little stability before their subsequent descent into the plains during the colonial period.

Oral traditions record that the first two categories of people, by and large, imposed themselves upon the third. In passing, the traditions also stress alliances between the immigrant groupings, in terms of the assistance they lent one another, and the superiority they considered themselves to share with respect to indigenous peoples. This assumption is just as clearly revealed in an opposite sense when, for instance, an immigrant patriclan threw in its lot with local interests and lost its right to compete for succession to chiefship.

The Yambu are one of the most widely distributed patriclan clusters of Chambaland. Among Leko speakers, the Jengnɛbba are considered to belong to the same grouping. "Patriclan cluster" is an unconventional term for a category that fits awkwardly into conventional anthropological terms of translation. All Chamba patriclans are culturally differentiated in ways that seem, in translation, to carry ethnic intention. The Yambu cluster is a particularly clear example of this general tendency. Although differing numbers of Yambu patriclans in different areas are distinguished by suffixes— three such clans exist for example in the northern Shebshi Mountains[17]—the patriclans also have a strong shared identity as Yambu and are, therefore, culturally distinguishable from other Chamba. Elements of this identity include a pervasive association with particular patriclan *jubi,* a martial reputation (largely on account of the exploits I am about to recount), and a general presupposition that they once lived in an ancestral Yambu homeland, although the location of this homeland is disputed. Another example of differentiation in the idiom of patriclanship is provided by indigenous Daka groupings such as the Mangla discussed below.

In general, the traditions of the three Yambu patriclan in the northern Shebshi Mountains are quite broadly consistent; interclan disputes principally concern traditions bearing on their relative pre-eminence. Informants of the chiefly clan in Polla Djalo ruled by Yam.də.nɛpbu, for instance, recall a migration north from an area around the confluence of the Faro and Deo into Bachama or Bata areas. Vere elements were incorporated into the alliance during this movement, and the resulting grouping, under the leadership of Ki'be, eventually reached the eastern approaches to the northern Shebshi Mountains and settled at Vanku. Subsequent events form the subject of a narrative known to all northern Shebshi informants to whom I have spoken.

> When the Yambu settled at Vanku the Mangla already lived on Mangla Hill. Yambu held a festival at Vanku and danced and beat their drums. The Mangla were angry at this because they were owners of the land and descended from their hill to chase the Yambu away. After this, the Yambu soaked the drumhead so that its sound would not carry to Mangla Hill. Three Bata then arrived and asked the Yambu why they were soaking the drumhead. Told about the Mangla and their attack on the Yambu, they advised the Yambu to put the drum in the sun to dry. In the evening, the Yambu resumed beating their drum, and when the Mangla heard it, they came down off their hill to beat the Yambu with whips. While they were beating them, one of the Bata men removed the point from his spear and threw the shaft into the side of a Mangla. When the Mangla removed the spear, he thought that the spearhead remained inside him, and all the Mangla ran away. They were chased up their hill, and one of them was killed. The Bata then told the Yambu to put grass coils on their heads [like those used for

headloading]. They circled Mangla Hill telling the Mangla that if they did not come down, they would carry off the hill on their heads. On account of this ruse, the Mangla came down to found villages at the foot of the hill.[18]

Among the purposes served by the story, one explains the alliance between the Yambu and Bata (Kam) by recounting their mutual interest in subjugating the Mangla. The importance of the ruses employed to this end recalls that Chamba, Bata, and especially Bachama, enact a relation of privileged, joking abuse (Stevens 1973; 1976). The alliance's effective dominance rests on the greater sophistication of the immigrants, who were able to dupe the Mangla, and an escalation, from whips to spears, of the means of violence. From the Mangla perspective, for they tell the same tale, the story explains how their ownership of the land was lost to the immigrants, and how they especially became subject to the Chamba-influenced Bata of Gang Bakɛni (now Mbulo). Apart from its purpose as a charter for current northern Shebshi relations, the tale also indicates some general characteristics of patriclan histories. Although the tale has legendary elements, the types of event narrated differ from the oral traditions of the ritualized chiefdoms (see Chapter 5). It does not deal, as do many of the stories of matriclan origin, with the shape-changing proclivities of animals; in fact, there is no element that is not conceivable in the mundane Chamba world. Even though it contains references to ritual, the story hinges upon military subjugation, in contrast to the accounts of the foundation of the ritualized chiefdoms that are examined in the next chapter.

Hardly different are the conventions of another equally well-known story that depicts the relation between the Farang and the Yambu in their subjugation of the Lamja. Farang and Lamja are two more examples of Chamba conceptual groupings of people that share attributes of both patriclanship and ethnicity. The Farang claim that they were displaced from a location in the western part of the Jukun region by Fulani raids, perhaps the raids by Buba Yero that preceded the official onset of jihad. The Farang ancestor, Bula or Samviri (dark Chamba), settled with the Lamja Chamba on their hill, Lam Kusum. The story relates that:

Bula was an only child, and for this reason extremely strong—
each bone of his arm was as thick as the arms of other men,
and in combat he could throw off ten assailants. The Lamja
began to fear this stranger and, when it was time to circum-
cise his oldest son, who took after his father in strength and
forcefulness of character, considered what trouble a father
with such sons would make among them. So they castrated
the boy, who died on the next day.

Bula then left Lam Kusum and sat alone in his grief on
a small hill called Na Kosi. From Na Kosi, Bula saw the
smoke of the kitchen fires of the Yambu living at Vanku,
and he left to find the people living there. In the bush he
met the daughter of Dumi [the chief who had succeeded
Ki'be as leader of the Yam.də.nɛpbu] carrying grass to feed
her father's horse. At first he was timid, but eventually he
agreed to help her with the carrying and met her father. The
chief gave his daughter to Bula to be his wife. Bula farmed
and had children at Vanku. Dumi then decided to give him
a chiefship and, when Bula was reluctant to accept, threatened to have the Kambu (Bata) beat him unless he accepted.
For this reason, he accepted the chiefship.

The story demonstrates for the Farang that they were deputed by the
Yambu to rule over the Lamja as compensation for the wrong that
had been done to their founder; to this day a section of Yambu clansmen constitutes the chiefmakers of the Farang chiefdoms. Some
Yambu interpret the story in terms of an attempt by Dumi to divert
the chiefship to his daughter's husband, and claim that it was complicity in this plot that now prevents the chiefmakers to the Farang
from making any claim to chiefship in Yambu chiefdoms. The story
also portrays the Lamja, who seem to be an indigenous Chamba
Daka group, and the Bata, for a second time, as representatives of
force.

An otherwise identical version of this story is retold by the
Jumabu of Mbangan, who press a rival claim to be the ones who
assisted the Farang attack the Lamja. Clearly, these varied traditions indicate that the area around the now-abandoned settlement
of Vanku, the scene of these events, was an important area of con-

vergence of groups entering the northern Shebshi Mountains. These groups included Yambu, Bata, Farang, and Jumabu. The Bata chiefdom was already established among the Mangla when Europeans arrived in the late-nineteenth century. The descendants of the chiefdom claim that the Bata arrived at Vanku from the north, as part of a Bata movement when their capital was established at Demsa. The Jumabu take their name from Juma, one of the hills in the Alantika Mountains, and claim to have reached Vanku after crossing the Nassarawo Plain, staying awhile among the Vere, and losing cattle that they had earlier raided from the Fulani.[19]

Vanku may have been typical of the many Chamba camps to which there is only passing reference in the traditions of the emigrant Chamba groups. For a short time, several parties grouped and regrouped there, but apparently without achieving political cohesion. The settlement probably broke up as Fulani activity in the Nassarawo Plain intensified, although the process was hastened by the competing ambitions of a number of Chamba leaders. By the time the earliest European travelers traversed the area, the members of the Vanku camps had dispersed into the hills to found a number of petty chiefdoms (see especially the maps of the Shebshi Mountains and Garoua by Moisel (1912 D2 and D3), which are based upon reports from the first decade of the twentieth century.)

In the early colonial period, the Bata-derived chiefdom of Gang Bakɛni, or Mbulo, then installed in the Mangla Hills, appears to have enjoyed the greatest local power (Passarge 1895; Strümpell 1907a). By this time all the northern Shebshi chiefdoms had ceased paying even nominal tribute to Yola, the Fulani emirate capital, although the suggestion that they had ever done so might have been of Fulani inspiration. According to Strümpell, and to modern informants, the chiefs recognized no relations of precedence among themselves, although the orbit of territorially defined chiefdoms included particular villages. In short, the large number of political units that occupied the area organized very small populations, and achieved only temporary territorial definition prior to the colonial period. Nevertheless, these chiefdoms demonstrate Chamba tactics for the organization of ethnically heterogenous populations and provide clues to the earlier stages in development of the major raiding chiefdoms (see Chapter 10).

The Damashi Traditions

Binyeri, northwest of Mbulo (see Figure 7), a convergence site similar to Vanku, but on a larger scale, demands closer attention. Binyeri was a chiefdom founded by Damashi of the Yam.tub.bu, the most celebrated of the central Chamba warrior leaders. Oral traditions concur that Damashi entered into an alliance with Adama, the founder of the Adamawa Emirate, for a period when, between 1809 and 1831, the first capital of the emirate was at Gurin. Delegated to fight on behalf of the jihadists, Damashi and his war bands conducted raids west of the Shebshi Mountains and in the plains south of the Benue. However, beyond this bare agreement, the details of his career are disputed and have been variously interpreted to support misleading chronologies of wider Chamba raiding outside Chambaland.

Although all accounts claim that Damashi met Adama at Gurin, they do not agree about the identity of the place he left to arrive at that meeting. This disagreement reflects a general uncertainty about the location of a supposed Yambu homeland. The most likely candidate is a settlement in the middle of the Nassarawo Plain that appears in traditions of different Yambu sections as a pre-dispersion homeland, although other interests point to sites west or east of the mid-plain.[20] Some interpreters claim that Yambu left the plain in the face of the Fulani menace, but there are also indications that Damashi's followers were already active as raiders, and that Damashi might himself have been the son of a warrior leader.

The commonly accepted account of the meeting between the Chamba warrior and the Fulani Emir is stylized in a conventional manner. Damashi is supposed to have given the Emir a bow and arrow and to have instructed the Fulani in its use. For his part he received a section of the Koran (ngitiru in Fulfulde, a "small book"; presently in the possession of the District Head of Tola), as an assurance of success in battle, and he nominally accepted Islam. The story of Chamba donation of archery to the Fulani is a common expression of alliance between Fulani and local peoples (E. Mohammadou has a similar story from Tchamba sources, 1978:35; H. Relly records a Fulani alliance with Bata in terms of the same convention, Relly 1954; I. S. H. Garoua). Furthermore, the material symbols of alliances, such as the flag that the founder of Donga procured at Bauchi and, perhaps, the flags adopted by the Bali Chamba, recall that Chamba and Fulani interests were not always opposed in the early-nineteenth century. The nominal nature of Damashi's acceptance of Islam, expressed in the story as his refusal to accept the conventional Muslim limitation on polygyny, has contemporary ramifications. Chamba, both Muslim and non-Muslim, deny that true conversion occurred during the period of the jihadic wars. This denial serves two ends: it demonstrates that the Fulani holy war was such in name only, and it shows that particular groups of Chamba were allies rather than subjects of the Fulani. Chamba Muslims stress that their conversion to Islam took place during the twentieth century, independently of the Fulani (I examine this supposition in Chapter 11).

After alliance with the Fulani, Damashi's raiders entered the northern area of the Shebshi Mountains where they allied with the Tola Chamba and the followers of Gang Pana, both apparently independent groupings of Chamba Daka. The reinforced alliance pressed west to fight what is recalled to be a major and successful engagement against the Mumuye. Tola elders claim that the raiders continued through Yakoko to Kona and beyond, and that Damashi returned to die at Tola, where his grave is tended today. But the latter stages of Damashi's raids have been subjected to other interpretations. Logan, a colonial officer, presumably drawing on earlier Tola informants, writes that beyond Kona, Damashi reached Kundi and the Donga River before he returned to Tola (1932, Rhodes House). The Nassarawo District History states that Damashi died west of the Shebshi Mountains, in the vicinity of present-day Jalingo, and attributes the establishment of the chiefdoms of Gambe and Gandole to elements from his following (G2.2). Corroboration of these traditions is found in Lilley's report on the Chamba settlements west of the Shebshi Mountains, in which he writes that Damashi and his allies (including "minor chiefs" called "Shabshi" and "Binywa") spent a year defeating the Mumuye, first, of Zinna, and then of Daban Ranti. "Binywa" then left the alliance to defeat the Daka of "Kwavani" (Kpavani?; perhaps "Binywa" is Binyeri, founder of the chiefdom of that name and usually supposed to be a son of Damashi). Damashi and Shabshi reached Tapari, where the latter remained to defeat further Mumuye groups, while Damashi returned to Tola (J8 Lilley 1921).

These traditions, broadly convergent with those of the Yambu settled to the east of the Shebshi Mountains, suggest the relatively restricted importance of Damashi's raids. They lead us to suppose that events to the immediate west of the Shebshi Mountains were taking much the same course as those to the east, and that similar actors were involved. These traditions would not demand examination in such detail were it not for the misconceptions about Damashi's raids that have been generally accepted, and the misleading effects of this acceptance on attempts to reconstruct a Chamba factor in middle-belt West African history.

Meek's account of Damashi's raids is particularly confused, and has served to confuse later commentators, all of whom have taken it as their source text. He claims that Damashi "reduced the whole of the southern bank of the Benue," conquered as far as Tivland, caused the disruption of the Jukun capital of Kororofa, and was responsible for bringing the Chamba into Bamenda (Meek 1931b I:449fn.; 1931b II:501). The dates he attributes to these events vary between the mid-eighteenth and early nineteenth centuries. A later study of the Adamawa area by Kirk-Greene popularized the earlier of Meek's dates (1958:17).

Between them, the researches of Meek and Kirk-Greene encouraged historical speculation about Chamba responsibility for the fall of the "Jukun Empire." But such speculation is clearly not consistent with evidence provided by other sources, and it would appear that their conclusions were guided by reports of actions ascribed to Damashi that should be attributed to others. Bali traditions make no reference to the activities of Damashi, and it is impossible to understand why Meek claimed that Damashi, leader of a band of Chamba Daka, could have been responsible for the arrival of Chamba Leko in Bamenda, particularly since he clearly distinguished the two Chamba languages. The idea that a Jukun Empire was toppled by barbarians in the eighteenth century is, to say the least, debatable. Furthermore, if the eighteenth-century dating for the end of the Jukun Empire is accepted, then the consistent recollections of an alliance between Damashi and the Yola Fulani imply that Damashi could not have been active at that period. Nevertheless, traditions that associate Damashi with the resettlement of the Jibu are plausible; if Damashi's raiders reached Kona and Jalingo, then they may well have penetrated as far south as Beli, into the area of Jibu settlement.

Garbosa, our informant on the Benue Chamba, gives two accounts of the activities of Damashi. Both are treated tentatively and do not seem to derive from Donga tradition; they may not be independent of Meek's writings. According to the first account, Damashi left Dindin (that is, eastern Chambaland) with a thousand horsemen and arrived at Jibawa Nybal (Beli) where he gathered the Jibu before crossing the Taraba River. The group failed to conquer the Wurbo, whom Garbosa claims lived in a dense forest (Meek's account has them taking refuge in Lake Kundi, 1931a:46), and continued to Katsina Ala (Meek claims Mirimwai as the precise site, 1931b II:501). The Jibu then separated from the Chamba and went north to found the town named after them between Ibi and Bantaje. In approximately 1850 they were forced to abandon this settlement because of attacks under the auspices of Muri (Garbosa n.d.:68; Meek 1931b II:501). Garbosa and Meek's versions of events are clearly not independent, although it is uncertain which was the source of the other, or whose traditions are being recounted. The report may be designed to account for the presence of settled raiders on the southern bank of the Benue in the mid-nineteenth century as recorded by members of the MacGregor-Laird expedition.

Garbosa's second account is more terse. It claims that the Jibu, broken into sections by Damashi's attacks, went directly to Jibu town and later moved from there to Gajere and Beli (n.d.:68). It is certainly conceivable that elements associated with Damashi's push west were also responsible for displacing the Jibu. But if our sources on the Damashi-Yola alliance are to be accepted, and it would be difficult to reject such consistent indications of a Chamba-Fulani understanding, then the movements cannot have occurred before the second decade of the nineteenth century. Such a dating would still imply that the raids associated with the name of Damashi affected the southern banks of the Benue before the arrival of Chamba Leko groups derived from the Loya Garbosa confederacy, but not that the raids took place in the mid- or early eighteenth century, or were responsible for an eclipse of the Jukun Empire at that time. To retain the historicity of the relation between Damashi and Adama, it seems necessary to admit that an overwillingness to subscribe to some version of the fall of a Jukun Empire has persuaded writers to place Chamba raids in an earlier period than is warranted by such evidence as we have.

Settlement in the Nassarawo Plain, the accessible area sur-rounded by the Vere Hills to the north, the Shebshi Mountains to the west, and the Alantika Mountains to the east and south, is most conveniently treated together with the northern Shebshi Moun-tains. By the late nineteenth century, travelers reports indicate that the plain was occupied by both Chamba and Fulani, sometimes in mixed settlements (see Chapter 11). Fulani control of Chambaland was at its greatest here, and the Chamba communities at Garamba, Bakari Guso, and Dalami must all have recognized some form of dependency upon Yola. In the case of Dalami, located on an impor-tant trade route, the relationship had been recognized since the reign of the fourth chief, subsequent to the move from Kollu on the south-ern flank of the Alantika Mountains that had brought the chiefship into existence. At least since the movement of the emirate capital to Yola (1841), the Dalami chiefs had been invested by the winding-on of a turban in the presence of the Emir. Passarge (1895) describes Dalami as a town of reasonable size for the area, comprising a Fulani enclave among a predominantly Chamba population. Most travelers stress that Fulani control was insufficient to provide complete free-dom from attack by Chamba to the traders and grazers who crossed the plains, but the volume of trade on the routes suggests that con-ditions were not so unsettled as to deter hardier spirits. Another common theme of the accounts is the distinction made between the Chamba of the Nassarawo Plain whose men, however nominal their allegiance to the Fulani, dressed in robes, and the Chamba of the hills, the "free pagans," some of whom might occasionally send gifts to the Fulani to ward off attack but whose villages would be sub-jected to raiding. Dalami's alliance with the Fulani was particularly close, and remains a source of contention among Chamba, since Dalami's representatives took responsibility for delivering tribute from plains' villages to the Fulani, and appear to have done so to their own profit. When we look at the subject in more detail in

Chapter 6, it will be apparent that the trails crossing the Nassarawo Plain had become important arteries in a regional system of trade that had Yola as one of its major entrepôts. This encouraged the Yola Fulani in the attempt to realize secure passage through the area nominally within their orbit. Conversely, reaching this goal was expedited through an accommodation with the Chamba settled in the plain. The Fulani had a vested interest in curtailing the virtual independence of Chamba and their retreat into the hills, which meant that they had to control slave raiding against the Chamba farming communities of the plain.

In summary, we conclude that the available data allow a regional pattern to be detected in the detail of the Chamba migrations. The traditions recall that Chamba alliances and migrations originated under a number of hero leaders, but by the late 1830s these leaders (Loya Garbosa of the Den Bakwa, Gawolbe of the Ba'ni, Gyando of the Daka, Damashi of the Yambu, and other minor figures) were dead, and the alliances had begun to disintegrate. The next thirty years witnessed further fragmentation before an eventual settlement of the raiding groups, which by then consisted predominantly of non-Chamba. Chamba narrative accounts of the histories of the raiders are typically prosaic and deal with migrations, raids, disputes, splitting, recruitment, and further migration to repeat the cycle. Insofar as we are able to check them, the narratives appear to be relatively accurate historical records in our terms. In the next chapter, we examine the difference between these records of the Chamba raiders and those typical of the ritualized chiefdoms associated with the more southern of the Chamba chiefdoms of the old homelands.

CHAPTER 5

HISTORICAL VARIATIONS: CHAMBA REFUGEES

The Chamba refuge chiefdoms, the subject of this chapter, encompass all the centralized organizations of Chambaland that remained in their previous locations, or nearby refuge sites, throughout the nineteenth century. The distinction between raiders and refugees is pertinent specifically to the nineteenth century, as it was then that these two reactions to changing power relations exhausted most, but the Mapeo case reminds us not all, of the options open to Chamba. As the term suggests, refuge chiefdoms weathered the vicissitudes of nineteenth- century life by virtue of a number of defensive tactics. These included reliance upon inaccessibility to hostile cavalry, the nuisance value they could cause grazers and traders from their mountainous retreats, and the losses they could inflict with poisoned arrows upon attackers who tried to catch the refuge inhabitants unawares when they farmed in the plains.

The necessity of farming in the plains was the single factor that placed the greatest restrictions upon the refuge strategy. Except in the interior of the Shebshi Mountains and a few other favored hilly areas, Chamba of the refuge chiefdoms had to descend to the plains in order to find sufficient farmland to support themselves. If caught in their fields, they could be subject to seizure into slavery by Fulani or other Chamba. The problem must have been made acute by the coincidence of the relatively late harvest of guinea corn, the local staple, and the onset of the dry season, the period during which horses could most effectively operate in the plains. In the contemporary recollection of this period, harvest stands out as a time of insecurity for people and their sustenance. The precise tactics avail-

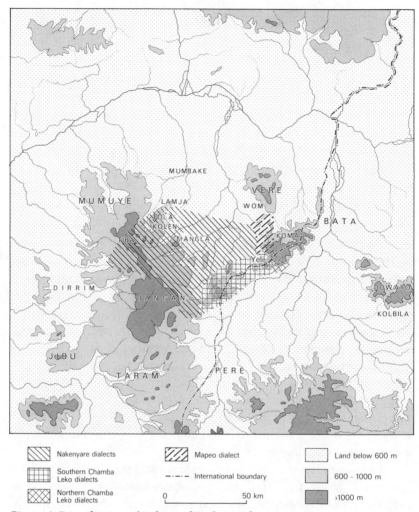

Figure 6 Distribution of Leko and Daka Dialects

able to the inhabitants of the refuge chiefdoms depended upon the
relationship between the local availability of fertile land that could
be farmed safely and the population density. Some refuge chiefdoms
were better placed than others, and Gurum, as we shall see, was
particularly favored in this respect.

   Another strategic factor concerned the proximity of Fulani centers and the ease of access Fulani had to the Chamba chiefdoms. In

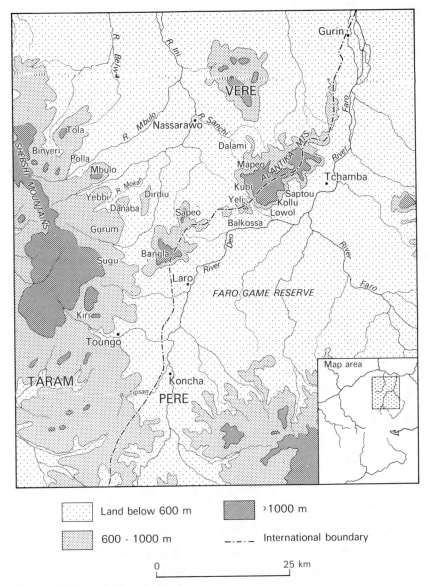

Land below 600 m   >1000 m

600 - 1000 m   _.._.._ International boundary

0   25 km

Figure 7 Central Chambaland

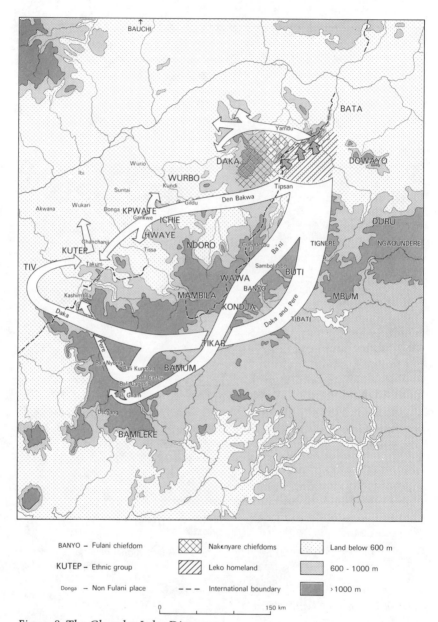

BANYO – Fulani chiefdom

KUTEP – Ethnic group

Donga – Non Fulani place

Nakɛnyare chiefdoms

Leko homeland

– – – International boundary

Land below 600 m

600 - 1000 m

> 1000 m

0 _____ 150 km

Figure 8 The Chamba Leko Diaspora

Figure 9 The Alantika Mountains Seen from the East

this respect, the residual Leko chiefdoms, the rump of Leko speakers left after the bulk of the population dispersed during the Leko diaspora, were poorly placed. The eastern slopes of the Alantika Mountains are precipitous and rocky (see Figure 9), quite unable to support hillside agriculture, at least in the area of northern Chamba Leko settlement. However, in the dry season, when the rivers subsided, the mountain slopes provided the only effective obstacles to Fulani attacks, and so it was there that refugee Chamba built their hamlets. The physical features of habitation, mode of livelihood, and location set general constraints to the capacity for maneuver of Chamba in the refuge chiefdoms, although these features varied locally within Chambaland. But there are more complex matters to be considered concerning the contrast between raider and refugee populations than can be deduced from these tactical givens.

We have seen that the narrative traditions of the descendants of Chamba raiders depict their histories as epic journeys marked by settlement, fission, the deaths of chiefs, and the prosecution of wars between different Chamba communities and between Chamba and other peoples. The order of events developed in these narratives corresponds relatively closely to what most westerners usually understand as relevant historical and chronological frameworks, and the idioms of Chamba raider organization and the conquest chiefdoms they established rest on presuppositions about the nature of time, history, and politics that converge with western presuppositions. However, in the case of the narrative traditions concerning Chamba refuge chiefdoms these historical frameworks and conceptual idioms are far less prominent.

The foundation narratives of the refuge chiefdoms in their nineteenth century or nearby locations appeal to events believed to predate Fulani advances into Chambaland associated with the establishment of the Adamawa Emirate. Like the settlement traditions of the raiders, these narratives are in part charters for the legitimacy of political organizations. However, they appeal to different kinds of events and make their appeal in terms of various narrative devices. The traditions emphasize ritual concerns rather than military conquest, matriclanship more than patriclanship, and relationship more than difference. The treatment of chieflists is an instance of the differences to which I refer that offers both an example of that difference and some clues to its quality.

Most chiefships in the refuge chiefdoms are customarily vested in matriclans, and the chiefs' roles historically tended toward the ritual end of a politico-ritual continuum of duties. Moreover, most of the matriclan chiefs belonged to what is nominally a single matriclan: the matriclan of the chief (*gat.kuna* in Leko, *gang.kuni* in Daka). In practice, chiefs may be drawn from a single section of the extensive matriclan or, if precedence has been subject to dispute, from one of the competing sections. Chiefship in raider chiefdoms is, in contrast, normally transmitted patrilineally or, more exceptionally, patrilaterally. Lists of the rulers of the raider chiefdoms collected from the early twentieth century onwards generally relate chiefs, in an agreed manner, to their paternal grandfathers or great grandfathers, men who are credited with the leadership of bands active fifty years or more earlier (see Appendix 1; Fardon 1980). In contrast, those of the refuge chiefdoms consist of longer, disorganized lists. Different informants provide lists that overlap rather than correspond, and tend to disagree about both the order and relationship between all but the most recent chiefs. All but these are identified as maternal brothers or sister's sons of their predecessors in an *ad hoc* manner. If pressed, the informants admit complete uncertainty about the identities of many of the earliest chiefs, the relationships between them, or the order in which they ruled. This uncertainty is consistent with the fact that the observance of rituals that are designed to solicit the collective assistance of past chiefs and assure the welfare of the present community demands the recollection and recitation of the names of only a limited number of previous chiefs. Some may stand for all.

The chieflists and the narratives I examine in this chapter are indications of collective and impartible characteristics that are attributed to facets of organization common to the refuge chiefdoms. Such characteristics relate to the connotations of feminine mediation and the form of sociation typical of matriclanship—what I have called consociating relationship. The presupposition of consociation, a relationship that subverts difference, pervades the organization of the refuge chiefdoms. It informs conceptions of their histories. Therefore, the narratives assume forms and carry practical relevances different from those found in the conquest chiefdoms founded by raiders, and different also from the dominant form of western historical consciousness. But these forms have similarities with less recognized products of historical efforts in the west to construct community through a denial of historical difference, particularly evident in some forms of nationalist rhetoric or in visions of the past created by advocates of class, or status, interest groups (e.g. Anderson 1983; Wright 1985). Translation of these idioms is facilitated by such convergences of perspective but, given the different political contexts in which the historical products have arisen, misrecognition of convenience in translation as identity would involve a drastic cost to our understanding. We need to see Chamba denials of difference in a context they have both created and had suggested to them by more general presuppositions of relationship in their thought.

My argument is that the relationships between predominant notions of hierarchy and of the past upon which narratives draw in the refuge chiefdoms differ from those that inform narratives in the con-

quest chiefdoms. This is the other side of my argument that the
nineteenth century saw a transformation in the political organization of Chamba emigrant groups. However, this is not to claim that
the refuge chiefdoms were historical fossils. The need to retreat into
the hills was itself a drastic form of change. Rather, the purveyors of
narrative about the past in the refuge chiefdoms had at their disposal
a set of idioms that predated the jihad and on which they continued
to draw in all the versions of their histories that have been collected
from the beginning of this century.

During the nineteenth and early twentieth centuries, refuge
chiefdoms came increasingly to resemble their counterparts established by Chamba raiders. Their chiefs reached varying types of
compromises with the Fulani, depending, among other factors, on
the tactical considerations that prevailed between particular Fulani
chiefdoms and particular Chamba groupings in the terms I described
earlier. The centralizing tendency was reinforced by the efforts of
different colonial administrations to govern Chambaland through
Chamba chiefs. In this changed political context, the matriclan
chiefs began to use their positions to extract the sorts of benefits for
themselves and their followers that routinely accrued to patriclan
chiefs. To some extent their ability to do this rested upon their privileged relation to outside powers (Fulani or European), and upon
changes in the internal organizations of their chiefdoms that had
occurred through efforts to resist or accommodate these powers. Significantly, one common change was for matriclan succession to
chiefship to be replaced by patrilineal succession. However, the
changes in matriclan chiefdoms that made them increasingly resemble their patriclan counterparts as time passed occurred later
than in the conquest chiefdoms. Because of the supposition that refuge chiefdoms represented the continuation of pre-jihadic organizations, the older idioms in which history and hierarchy had been
couched could still furnish an idiom to talk about contemporary circumstances. Thus, while refuge chiefdoms and conquest chiefdoms
tended to adopt common means of organization, they preserved different presuppositions in terms of which they explained and justified this organization to themselves, to generations of colonial officers who filed their reports, and eventually to an ethnographer.

Refuge Chiefdom Traditions

To illustrate these contentions, I turn to a detailed consideration of sources on the different refuge chiefdoms. The relevant parts of the typology of communities of Chambaland outlined in Chapter 3 can serve to organize the discussion. That typology rests upon language, dialect and chiefly family.

The Leko- and Daka-speaking areas approximately correspond to eastern and western locations within Chambaland (see Figure 6). The major Daka-speaking chiefdoms of the Shebshi Mountains belong to the dialect and culture grouping of Nakenyare. Within the Nakenyare grouping I distinguish a southern group of chiefdoms (Sugu, Kiri, Danaba, Nya Gangngwu, Da Dukdu) from a central Shebshi grouping (Gurum and Yebbi) on the basis of differences in their ruling families. The Leko speakers in the eastern Alantika Mountains are a residual part of the Chamba grouping that dispersed during the Leko diaspora. Among these residual Leko, a dialect difference between the northern and southern groupings correlates with a distinction in ruling clan. The southern group traditionally had chiefships vested in *gat.kuna* (the matriclan of the chief), whereas the chiefships of the northern grouping belonged to the patriclan of Sama.

Although divided linguistically, evidence suggests common organizational features among the refuge chiefdoms in the earlier nineteenth century (discussed in Chapter 9); as the century wore on, the distinctive differences between raider and refuge chiefdoms in the central Chamba area were reduced. The northern Shebshi chiefdoms (discussed in Chapter 4) retreated into the mountains as the Fulani expanded into the Nassarawo Plain, while some of the refuge chiefdoms began to adopt organizational devices from their northern neighbors. These changes produced a degree of convergence between the organizations of the two groupings.

Early in the nineteenth century characteristics of social organization crosscut divisions of language and dialect. Matriclan chiefship, for example, was characteristic of most of the southern and central chiefdoms. Regardless of their differing languages and dialects the southern residual Leko chiefdoms traditionally vested chief-

ship in *gat.kuna* (Yeli, Balkossa, Sapeo, Bangla), which is identical
to the chiefly *gang.kuni* matriclan of the southern Shebshi Nakɛnyare chiefdoms (Sugu, Kiri etc.). The chiefships of the central
Nakɛnyare (Gurum and Yebbi) were originally vested in the matriclan *gang.tim.nɔ.kuni* (the chief of the east). Later in the century,
chiefships at Sapeo, Gurum, Yebbi, and Dim Kusum, an offshoot of
Danaba, passed from a matriclan to a patriclan ownership.

Chamba traditions tell us that some time in the past almost all
the chiefdoms of southern Chambaland, whether Leko or Daka
speaking, were ruled by members of a single royal clan, the matriclan of the chief. In recent years, in many places, descendants of
these chiefly lines have continued to hold office in the newer systems of local administration. Whether informants emphasize that
all the chiefships belonged to a nominally single clan, or alternatively underscore the sectional divisions that exist within the clan,
depends on whether they wish to stress unity or diversity among
these chiefships.

The Sugu and Yeli Group of Chiefdoms

Sugu and Yeli belong to one of three groups of *gang.kuni* and *gat.kuna*
chiefdoms commonly distinguished by informants. Of the three,
only this group includes both Leko- and Daka-speaking places: Sugu,
Nya Gangngwu, and Da Dukdu are Nakɛnyare speaking; Yeli or
Dayela is Leko speaking. I suggested in the introductory historical
synopsis that the close relationship recognized between these places
formed the nexus that allowed Chamba ethnogenesis. Informants
typically explain the supposition of close relationship between these
chiefdoms by giving a version of the foundation stories of the chiefdoms, by emphasizing how each chiefdom may select a new chief
from members of the royal clan resident in any other chiefdom, or
by relating the continuing ritual relationship between Sugu and Yeli.

These considerations have important mutual implications. The
ritual and kinship relations are justified by, and offer contemporary
evidence for, the supposed historical relationship. Several versions
of the historical relationship between the chiefdoms have been recorded from different sources since early in this century. Although
they differ in detail, the broad features of the accounts concur: a

migration took place from the west, perhaps from an area with Jukun associations. The migrants first established themselves at Da
Dukdu and later at Sugu and Yeli. The order of settlement in the two
major chiefdoms, the names of the chiefs responsible, and the reasons for the moves vary between accounts. All detailed versions
record that the *gang.kuni* chiefs established their Sugu chiefship
among indigenous Chamba Jangani; one also claims this of the Yeli
chiefship. None of the versions make any reference to Fulani activities during the foundation period. The first account is the collective
work of Sugu elders whom I interviewed in 1977.[1]

> A movement from the west [Da Bɔnem, in the vicinity of
> present-day Jalingo] was led by Gang Lungen, a seer able to
> see the sprites and establish shrines to them. He settled at
> Da Dukdu and remained there for some years until his
> chiefmakers attempted to kill his sons and thereby prevent
> his diverting the chiefship to them. So leaving behind a sis-
> ter's son [Gang Duk], Gang Lungen and his sister [Nya jub
> kuna, mother-cult container] departed for Dayela. On the
> way he left *kamɛnbu* [priests] at places where he saw the
> sprites. At Dayela he appointed more priests, and spent each
> morning discovering more sprite places [*wurum.bum*]. He
> left a sister's son [Saboya] to be chief of Dayela and set out,
> with his sister, to expand the size of his chiefdom again.
> Strict instructions were given to his priests that if the chief
> died he was to be succeeded by a member of the royal ma-
> triclan, and that the property of the chief, his shield, spear
> and horn, should be forwarded to Gang Lungen at his new
> settlement of which he would tell them. Moving west,
> Gang Lungen arrived in Sugu, where he met Sansu Jimi
> who was leader, but not chief, of the Jangani. The Jangani
> were making *jubi*, and had brewed much beer. Gang Lungen
> dismounted from his horse and sat apart. Sansu Jimi sent a
> man to ask who Gang Lungen was. The seer gave his name
> and asked what the Jangani were doing; he was told that
> they were performing *jubi*. Gang Lungen said that he would
> help the performance by giving some salt (*gum.yɛlum*) to
> the *jubi*. The Jangani did not know how to manufacture

salt, and after one of Gang Lungɛn's men had licked the salt to show that it was not poisoned, the Jangani divided it among themselves and left none for the *jubi*. On the evening of Gang Lungɛn's arrival, the Jangani decided to ask him to stay and be chief. After the chiefmaking, Gang Lungɛn gave a whole sack of salt to Sansu Jimi to divide among the Jangani. The chief priest of the Jangani then suggested that Sansu Jimi be killed so that Gang Lungɛn could be put in charge of all the *jubi*. However, Sansu Jimi escaped, although no one knows what became of him. Gang Lungɛn left for Da Dukdu to rejoin the sister's son he had left as chief. He told the Da Dukdu people that his new settlement was to be Sugu and that if the chief of Da Dukdu died, his cap of chiefship should be brought to Sugu, where he would choose a successor. Returning to Sugu, Gang Lungɛn appointed his sister in charge of her own village. The expansion of Sugu began like this, and village heads who were members of the royal matriclan or "children" of the matriclan [sons of matriclan men] were sent to rule different areas.

Among other purposes, this version of the foundation history is designed to demonstrate the preeminence of Sugu among the southern chiefdoms. We can see this by comparing versions from the other *gang.kuni* chiefdoms that claim to have been established during the same founding journey. The version of the history proposed by the elders of the female chief of Nya Gangngwu (*nya.gang.ngwu*, "mother chief woman," the name of both her office and her village) differs in ways that demonstrate the seniority of the female arm of the chiefship. In the Nya Gangngwu version, the migration is claimed to have taken place from Kona (a more explicit Jukun reference than in the Sugu version), and it is a female chief who is supposed to have been leader. She led some of the migrants from Dayela to Sugu and later delegated her son to leave Sugu Hill and establish his village in the plain. The son's duty was to speak to outsiders for his mother, but power remained with her.

A Yeli version, collected in 1984, proposes that Sugu was founded prior to Yeli. Movement from Sugu to Yeli is attributed to rainmaking magic (*sugɛn.kina,* Sugu woman), which prevented Sugu women from drying their soup leaves in the sun. It was decided to remove the ritual objects, which were carried to the east in a cala-bash. At Yeli Hill, the migrants met members of the "chief red rock" and "baboon" matriclans (*gat.bəng.yɛl.kuna,zabongal.kuna*). These clans only knew of ash salt (*kəm.nwuma,* Koma salt) with which to "repair the land." The immigrants gave them mineral salt (*mum.yɛba*) and were able to be recognized as chiefs.

Although the three accounts show self-interested variation (in each case the differences between versions point to the preeminence of the community to which the narrator belongs), they draw upon similar presuppositions to support their cases. Each accepts that close matrilateral kinship existed between the three places, and ac-counts for the foundations in terms of a journey that was marked by meetings between previously separate peoples who are attributed unequal ritual potency. The preeminence of the *gang.kuni* family is explained by its ability to regulate the welfare of the community by ritual means, and this ability is tied, in turn, to the possession of salt and to an origin from the west. Disagreement does not affect the supposition of close relationship but concerns the reinterpretations necessitated by claims to seniority.

Within Chambaland generally, Yeli is recognized to be ritually senior to Sugu and, indeed, to all the Nakɛnyare chiefdoms, al-though Sugu is the larger and consequently more powerful chief-dom. The followers of the female chief of Sugu (*nya.gang.ngwu*) pro-pose that Sugu was previously twinned with Yeli as a dual chiefship. The male chief of Sugu is represented as a relative of the female chief. The followers of the female chief allege that the male chief functioned as a spokesman for her, since she was secluded. This role, they suggest, was misinterpreted by Fulani and Europeans who con-sidered him to be chief. In the Sugu version, the female chief is said to have been a sister to the male chief but, in the Nya Gangngwu version, she is said to have been his mother. Chamba Nakɛnyare outside Sugu tend to support the version of matters presented by the female chief of Nya Gangngwu. Although this does not necessarily vouch for the historical veracity of the version, it does demonstrate that Nakɛnyare Chamba tend to view their past in terms of a form of organization remote from their present.

Several oral accounts of the histories of these *gang.kuni* chiefdoms were recorded earlier this century, which allows us to identify
the stable elements of the stories. All versions contain the ideas of
migration from the west (with its Jukun associations), the notion
that chiefship was gained through ritual preeminence, and the exchange of salt for the recognition of chiefship (perhaps another reference to Jukun because of their control of the early salt trade). Furthermore, in some versions, references are made to attempts at
diverting the matriclan chiefship to the sons of a chief, a recurrent
problem confronting matriclan chiefs during the nineteenth
century.

Such oral traditions have led both Chamba and outside commentators to propose the existence of a far more encompassing political organization than any that had been known to exist during
the nineteenth century. This entity is believed to have included
most of the southern Nakɛnyare, and was only disrupted when the
Fulani occupation of the plains cut off the mountain chiefdom centers from one another. As discussed in the next chapter, this is a
proposition about which I have considerable doubt.

It is clear that recent accounts have telescoped events that were
separate in earlier versions, making it probable that earlier versions
are themselves telescoped accounts of even earlier accounts. For instance, Gang Lungɛn, the hero founder of Sugu in the version collected in 1977, appears as the son of the leader of the migration in a
version collected by a colonial officer, Glasson, in 1922 (J8), presumably from prior Sugu sources. On the basis of a rather literal reading
of the sequences implied in chieflists, and the necessity to place
some events before others, I infer that the earliest references in the
traditions refer in some way to the early to mid-eighteenth century.
This inference specifically accommodates the general Chamba recognition that the refuge chiefdoms were installed near their present
locations at the time of the Adamawa jihad. However, it is likely
that the events forming the basis for the stories, for I am assuming
that these stories may be interrogated both as legitimating devices
and as encoded historical records (see Willis 1981), bear some relation to a state of affairs that long predated the eighteenth century.

Unfortunately, the present state of our knowledge does not permit even an informed guess at the date when the chiefdoms of

southern Chambaland came into being. As narratives that refer to the early nineteenth century take the existence of the southern Chamba chiefdoms to be part of their context, any suggestion that the events described are more recent than the mid-eighteenth century would demand the rejection of all Chamba traditions. A final verdict on the founding dates of the chiefdoms will have to await the development of a fuller understanding of regional development than we yet possess.

The earliest British colonial account of the Sugu Chamba I have found is that compiled by B. Glasson in 1922, which contains another version of the *gang.kuni* foundation charter. From it we learn that a leader called Ganyekini left Kona with his wife and a few followers and settled at Mayo Aloru (the Fulfulde name for the place Chamba Daka call Da Dukdu) in the southern Shebshi Mountains. He left his followers at Mayo Aloru and continued with his wife until he reached Yellu (locative form of Yeli, or Dayela in Daka). Here, his wife bore him two sons, Sansogine and Ganlugeni, and a daughter, Ganwukumbe. Ganlugeni and his sister subsequently moved from Dayela to Sugu, where he obtained followers and became chief. Ganwukumbe was appointed Arnado Debbo (Fulfulde for the Chamba Daka *gang.ngwu*) by her brother and became "high priestess of the big juju, which remains the second biggest Chamba juju centre today," presumably after Yeli. In 1922, at the time Glasson collected his chieflist, Gang Kusum reigned as the ninth chief since the founder.

This skeletal account differs in interesting ways from other versions. We may assume that it was collected from sources close to the Sugu chief, since this was standard practice. On internal evidence, the account represents a Sugu perspective on events and seems to have gone through a Fulfulde speaker at some stage of its rendition into English. The order of settlement, from Kona, to Da Dukdu, to Yeli, and finally to Sugu, is that found in most accounts. The names of the actors in the narrative resemble those of the contemporary version I heard: Ganlugeni, founder of Sugu and son of the leader of the migration from Kona, is clearly Gang Lungen, credited in the contemporary Sugu version with leading the migration and founding all three *gang.kuni* chiefdoms. Sansogine is presumably Sansu Jimi, who appears as a brother to Gang Lungen in Glasson's account and has become a leader of indigenous Jangani at Sugu in the recent account. Significantly, Ganwukumbe, sister of the Sugu founder according to Glasson's informants, is named after her office, *gang-ngwu*, chief woman. In comparison with contemporary versions of these founding events, it appears that the relation between the male and female chiefs of Sugu is contested. In this regard, the present version, related by supporters of the female chief, has a woman leading the migration from Kona, and suggests that the female chief is always in the relationship of "mother" to the male chief, thus *nya.gang.ngwu*.

Overall, a comparison of the versions suggests that only certain aspects of the internal dynamic of the narrative are heavily dependent upon the interests of the narrator. Constant factors are the general direction of migration, the names used for participants in the story, the necessity to introduce male and female chiefship, and the association between immigration, ritual preeminence, and chiefship, all of which are referred back to a prestigious association with a Jukun area. The contemporary male actors, Gang Lungɛni and Sansu Jimi, may be held in contrastive relation by virtue of their names. Informants say that *lungɛni* in this context has the sense of "deserving" or "meritorious," *san.su* is said to be composed of the term for Chamba and that for a breech birth (*mi.su*, breech birth child). Breech births are extremely inauspicious for Chamba, and the infants were not traditionally allowed to live; perhaps the name connotes an extreme condition of unfitness for chiefship. The *jimi* of Sansu Jimi is explained by the verb to get up, referring to the flight of Sansu Jimi in the contemporary version.

The next reference to Sugu in extant colonial records occurs in the Ethnological Appendix to a report of 1924 on Toungo Division, which then included Sugu (B3.Z Glasson). The note is brief and suggests an unsupportable dating on no stated evidence, but it does reaffirm the western connections of the Sugu rulers. "Tsugu people" are said to be Chamba or Daka, who, at a date unknown, left Pe, west of Garbabi (in the territory of the Jibu grouping within the Jukun culture and language group) and during the 1860s established themselves in the Jangani Hills. The dating suggests that the Sugu chiefship was installed fifty years after the Fulani jihad, which is contrary to all traditions, but interestingly confirms another western origin with Jukun associations. It seems as though Sugu Chamba, if this account is indeed from that source, were less interested in precise connections than in the general idea of migration from a Jukun cultural area.

T. B. G. Welch, another colonial officer, reports as an aside to a proposal for administrative reorganization that Dirdiu, Bakari Guso, and Jaggu (which fell within an area to which Sugu claimed administrative entitlement) refuse to admit "close connection" with the known emigrants from Kona, although they have lived and moved with them (G3 Vol. I, 1933). Here we find the common acceptance of Sugu's claim to prestigious association with Kona being stood on its head as an argument for recognizing independence from the Sugu chief.

It appears that the tradition of a Sugu-Kona association was pervasive in British colonial writings, and coincided with a British interest in fostering the viability of the Jukun as indirect rulers. Another colonial officer, J. H. Shaw, in a further proposal for administrative reform, noted the "legend of origin" which claimed that Yeli was founded from Kona via Mayo Aloru (Da Dukdu) and that the founders of Sugu, Gurum, Yebbi and Binyeri all claimed an origin from Yeli. The historicity of the legend is argued in terms of the "godlike status of the chief of Kona," and a "playmate relation" between Sugu, Kona, and the Mumuye of Zin (G3 Vol. I, 1936).[2]

Another variant of the foundation traditions was recorded by R. Logan (1932 Rhodes House). "A very long time ago" the ancestors of the Sugu Chamba set out "peacefully" from Kona to look for a new country. Eventually, the main body settled at Da Dukdu, while other sections stopped at Ganlumeni and Kiri. Later, there was a dispute about chiefship, and the chief resorted to the expedient of killing all male children. A woman, Yasuno, bore a son and prevailed on her brother, Tumi, to flee with her to save the child's life. They fled north and settled at Yeli, or Dayela, in the Alantika Mountains. People following them swelled the population of Dayela. Later still, a chief of Da Dukdu, called Sansujumeri, went north to settle at Sugu. The Yeli people interpreted this movement as an attempt by Da Dukdu to regain control of Yeli and, under the command of their chief Ganbuneni, they "annihilated Sansujumeri's settlement at Tsugu, and established themselves there." Logan's chieflist claims that the Fulani jihad was declared during the reign of the fourth chief, after Ganbuneni had moved from Yeli to Sugu.

This version illustrates further historical vicissitudes in the career of the foundation traditions of the *gang.kuni* chiefdoms. In Logan's version, the name of Gang Lungen, hero founder in the current Sugu narrative, appears as a subsidiary settlement, Ganlumeni, in the early migrations. Sansu Jimi, whom we encountered previously as leader of the Chamba Jangani or as a brother to the Sugu founder, becomes chief of the Da Dukdu Chamba in the Logan version, and threatens the independence of Yeli. Apart from the broadest themes, the historical narratives recorded at different times from different informants are clearly incompatible. Logan's version seems to be guided by a Sugu interest in stressing connections with Yeli, by claiming that the Sugu dynasty is, in fact, the transplanted Yeli dynasty. Given the accepted ritual preeminence enjoyed by Yeli, the Sugu claims contain an implicit reference to those other southern Nakɛnyare chiefdoms that trace their origin to the Yeli chiefly family. It is possible that local administrative reform proposed during the 1930s had again brought the rivalry between the Nakɛnyare chiefdoms to a head (see Chapter 11).

It would be unwise to place reliance on any single version of these foundation stories. But their manner of telling does contain indications of the circumstances in which the stories were seen to be relevant. The circumstances include a prestigious center offstage, as it were, in the diffuse presence of the Jukun, and competition between several chiefdoms to relate themselves to this source of prestige more proximately than their competitors. The narratives both presuppose relationships between the active chiefly families, and make distinctions between the chiefly matriclan sections and the peoples, depicted as indigenous, who recognize their chiefship. The preeminence of Yeli is also presupposed, especially in the attempts to represent another place as either the source of the Yeli dynasty or the inheritor of Yeli's mantle. The narratives also share references to Da Dukdu as a center through which all the chiefly elements once passed, and the locale from which the matriclan chiefdoms among the southern Nakɛnyare were subsequently established.

Da Dukdu is situated on the Taraba River system where it enters the Koutine Plain from the Benue Plains, a likely route for prejihadic traders who had connections to Jukun. Only a remnant community survived into this century. D. A. Percival wrote in 1938 that Da Dukdu was recognized to be the source of many of the Nakεnyare chiefdoms, but it "has lost its importance and scarcely exists" (J8). In 1978, I visited the site, which then consisted of a small village of seven compounds. Elders there point out two previous sites, one in the plains and another in the hills. The plains settlement was devastated by a raid that seems to have come from Koncha around 1830 or slightly earlier. The village was destroyed and most of the survivors took refuge in Sugu. The hill settlement would seem to be the Da Dukdu of the foundation traditions. The names of the chiefs of the place are now forgotten; the list of chief's assistants, who generally hold their positions longer than chiefs, had eleven names but was considered incomplete.

Although the inhabitants of Da Dukdu recall the past importance of their village, more precise remembrance probably lost its pertinence in the catastrophe of the chiefdom's destruction. Perhaps Da Dukdu was already reduced in importance by the time Sugu and Yeli were founded. Whatever the case, little can be added to the record by sources in Da Dukdu today.

Some commentators have found evidence of a grand empire or large-scale migration in these traditions. Frobenius, the German ethnographer whose reports of Chamba custom are our earliest sound ethnographic sources, was inclined to believe that there had been a Daka empire that had been conquered by Chamba Leko, which caused the Daka capital to be moved from Yeli to Sugu (Frobenius 1913, 1925). But the notion seriously lacks evidence, even from Chamba's own recollections.

D. A. Percival, an assiduous and often perceptive synthesizer of colonial records, thought that the traditions recalled the introduction of chiefship by immigrants of Jukun origin. Here he echoes ideas current at the time, thanks to the writings of Palmer (1911), and his more cautious protégé, Meek (1931a; J.8 Percival 1938). However, both Percival's and Frobenius' notions require that we lend total credence to selected fragments of the traditions that have been recorded, which may themselves be presumed to be the smallest fragments of the conversations they represent. In my opinion, this is unacceptable. At best, the traditions indicate the terms in which precedence between chiefdoms of pre-jihadic origin continued to be talked about in post-jihadic times. It is not straining the evidence to suppose that they were talked about in similar ways before the nineteenth century. The context to which they refer appears to be one in which Jukun associations are prestigious and subject to claims phrased as origins. The chiefdoms engaged in dispute nonetheless recognize close relationships, despite other differences between them. Of greater significance, the chiefly family of the Yeli Chamba continues to maintain a claim to its Daka origin and selectively preserves what are considered to be Daka customs and names. To this end, it is still customary for the chief of Yeli to become a member of a section of the Jangani patriclan upon his accession to office, and he still carries the title *gang* rather than its Leko counterpart *gara*.

The Kiri and Danaba Group of Chiefdoms

In contrast to the Sugu chiefdoms, relatively little information has been recorded to document the histories of the Kiri and Danaba chiefdoms. Like Sugu and Yeli, these chiefdoms are presided over by chiefs of the *gang.kuni* matriclan, but their chiefs are said to belong to a different section of this clan. Nonetheless, they claim to have originated from Yeli and to have recognized the paramountcy of the Yeli chief in ritual terms. Most accounts claim that Danaba was established from Kiri (Logan 1932). Danaba was heavily raided and dispersed by the Yola Fulani late in the nineteenth century. When the Chamba returned, a second chiefdom was established at Dim Kusum and, significantly, this chiefship was vested in a patriclan associated with priests drawn from the Mangla and Yambu, in apparent imitation of the northern Shebshi model of chiefdom organization. Beyond these points of information the archival sources are mute, as Danaba and Kiri were not district headships during the colonial period. However, it is generally accepted that the chiefdoms form part of the Nakɛnyare grouping that characteristically recognizes the nominal ritual preeminence of Yeli.

The Gat.kuna *of the Southern Residual Leko*

Our sources on the *gat.kuna* are more helpful. They indicate that the "matriclan of the chief" also furnished chiefs for the southern residual Leko chiefdoms of Balkossa, the Bangla Hills, and Sapeo. It will be recalled that *gang.kuni* and *gat.kuna* are equivalents in the two Chamba languages. But there is an obvious and significant difference between the origin stories of the chiefly clan of the southerly Leko and those of Yeli and Sugu. Whereas the Yeli and Sugu origins seemed to point toward the west and the Jukun, the royal matriclans of the southerly Leko recall origins from the east, specifically from a concentration of Chamba Leko chiefdoms in existence prior to the Leko diaspora. Their relations with Yeli are ambiguous. Although the chiefdoms are related in the broad perspective of matriclanship, since both are ruled by the matriclan of the chief, they are distinguished by their ethnic origins, respectively Leko and Daka. Nonetheless, Yeli is for these southern Leko, as for the southern Nakenyare, the center from which smallpox and locust infestation were controlled, and the prestige of the southern Leko chiefly matriclan is enhanced by means of its relation to Yeli.

Among the elements common to many of the *gat.kuna* foundation traditions, the supposition of common clanship outweighs the claim to ethnic differences. However, one particular tradition collected from Balkossa in 1984 introduces additional ideas, including those of chiefly contagion and the theme of heat and coldness, to which we shall return in Chapter 9. This tradition recalls that:

> At Gatgu [*gat.gu*, the chief's place across the river] a bad marriage took place between a woman of *gat.kuna* [who was cold] and a man of the *vom.bira* [the custodians of *voma*, *jubi* in Daka; who was hot]. Following the birth of the woman's children, smallpox broke out; all the people of the village died or left during the night until a single daughter of the marriage remained in the village. She left Gatgu and crossed the Deo River to arrive at Denu where Gat Zanvala was chief. He saw that the girl wore a bracelet on her wrist and knew that she was of *gat.kuna*, the joking part-

ners of his own matriclan *sal.kuna*, so he decided to take responsibility for her upbringing. When the girl became grown he said to her, "You are nearly grown, so go to find the land of your grandfathers at Kolvanu." For the girl's mother had come from Kolvanu. At Kolvanu she stayed with Goykəkə, who was of *lam.kuna*, [the smith clan, but this need not imply he was a smith]. Goykəkə's son decided to marry the girl, at which one of his father's two wives said that she would leave the compound if the cold girl came to stay, because they were people of *voma*. The son became angry saying that he also would leave the compound if he could not marry whom he wanted. His father had become chief and advised his son to make the marriage, which he did, paying bridewealth to his own father for the girl. Na vala [mother of death] married Zig ding ya [put down spear] and they had three children: Val kosa [slave of death], Ding ke mu ga [spear hit me not], and Zera [year, i.e. leave me to live another year]. Later, Na vala left her husband and married a Koma by whom she had another son, Kom Gaji. Na vala had been the second wife of Zig ding ya. The children of the first wife were numerous, and this wife and her children accused the husband of favoritism towards the children of Na vala. So Zig ding ya said that he would show his children a proper *gat.kuna* place to live on the neighboring hill, called Wumkola, after the Chamba people there who were called Wuma. Here, Val kɔsa became chief.

The story goes on to recount how members of the Dənga patriclan left Dəngadiu (near Yelba), where they had been pressured by the Fulani, to help the Chamba of Balkossa. They divided the territory between them, and the Dənga became *vom.gara* (cult chiefs)[3] to the chiefs of Balkossa, named after Val kɔsa.

The Dənga and *gat.kuna* reappear as the actors in the foundation story of Sapeo, which I recorded in 1977, and which may be the source of Frobenius's idea that a powerful Leko imperial capital was once located at Dəngadiu. This story also starts with a migration from the confluence of the Faro and Deo Rivers.

Gat Tchimdekila and his sister [of the *gat.kuna*] led their people from Dəngadiu to Sapeo Hill, where the chief and his sister decided that it was time to die and arranged to be buried on the hilltop. Their grave became the most sacred place of the new chiefdom.

Subsequent to its foundation, the chiefship passed into the ownership of the Dənga patriclan, a development that the Balkossa elders attributed to be a consequence of the incumbent matriclan chief having contracted leprosy. Although Frobenius interpreted the breakup of Dəngadiu as indicative of a decline of an imperial capital, the name Dənga + locative supports the contemporary gloss that Dəngadiu was the home of people who are now called Dənga. Therefore, rather than being a capital, it was one of many sources of the contemporary Leko patriclans.

I have twice collected accounts of the foundation of the Bangla chiefdom. In both cases, the traditions recall attacks on the Chamba by Fulani, possibly with Bata assistance, that forced them to reestablish their chiefdom farther south on the Deo River. Eventually, they retreated into the Bangla Hills (Jubdiu) where, in one version, they drove out a matriclan settled there called *gat.wum.lɛrum.kuna* (chief ash-salt clan). The versions collected, from Chamba Muslim sources, do not embed these movements in more traditional narrative constructions.

Southern Leko traditions consistently associate *gat.kuna* with earlier Chamba settlements, probably those which predated the Leko diaspora, and which had to be abandoned in the face of the Fulani advance along the river system. The significance of the narrative themes these traditions employ are taken up in Chapter 9. Such themes, whose analogues appear in Sugu, include an association of chiefship with coldness and priestship with heat, an emphasis on diseases, especially smallpox and leprosy, and an importance given female actors. For now, it is sufficient to remark on the differences between the construction of these accounts and those of the raider chiefdoms.

Although both raider and refuge accounts incorporate founding journeys as a feature that precedes the foundation of chiefdoms, and both include traditions that acknowledge the threat posed by Fulani expansion, accounts of the founding journeys of the refuge chiefdoms consistently draw upon a vocabulary relevant to ritual interests, such as disease, rainmaking, ritual efficacy, and the establishment of shrines. These values are notably absent in the raider traditions. The southern traditions, as told by Leko and Daka speakers, share a tendency to construct foundation stories based on encounters between mobile matriclans and settled, named, and apparently indigenous, patriclans or patriclan clusters. Settled matriclans are only an occasional feature. Where the traditions of the raider chiefdoms explain the incorporation of differentiated elements into the political community in terms of the force of arms, the traditions of the refuge chiefdoms try to explain incorporation in terms of differential capacities for effective ritual action. These themes recur in central Shebshi traditions as well, although there they exist alongside others indicative of different understandings, possibly derived from the northern Shebshi raider chiefdoms.

The Central Shebshi Chiefdoms: Gurum and Yebbi

Gurum and Yebbi occupy a small, horseshoe-shaped plain surrounded on three sides by the Shebshi Mountains. To the north they are bounded by the northern Shebshi chiefdoms, and to the south and east by the *gang.kuni* chiefdoms. Their western border is called *nyɛm Daka*, the home of the Daka. The proximity of Gurum and Yebbi to contrasted types of political organization is reflected in the traditions of the two chiefdoms, which record a transition from matriclan to patriclan chiefship. Three clans (two patriclans and a matriclan) currently press claims upon the chiefships of the two places. Colonial records show that the contemporary arguments about precedence, which I heard in the late 1970s, have been recorded in much the same terms since the 1920s, and must have been current far earlier. Although variants are footnoted, I discuss here the most generally agreed versions of their foundation narratives. The traditions deal with four sets of events: the foundation of Yebbi from Dayela; the separation of the two chiefdoms; the loss of the chiefship by the original matriclan owners; and the temporary occupancy of the chiefship by a second patriclan claimant.

According to one version of the foundation:

Gang Wokni [chief of deep water] led the group to Yeli and Gang Kɔtsin [chief of the harmattan] brought them to Yebbi during the harmattan season. For five years there was a single chiefship at Yebbi until San.nyɛng.jimi [the Chamba who got up and left] went to Dim Nyɛnga.

There are several versions of Sannyɛngjimi's subsequent journey north, from Dim Nyɛnga along the Shebshi Mountains, since it is from this time that all the officials of Gurum prefer to trace the receipt of office by their forefathers. My version is an amalgam of the accounts offered by the different officials named in it. Accounts by other hands would include additional names, but the most important officials appear in most versions.

Leaving Dim Nyɛnga, Sannyɛngjimi moved to Lingbi, where he lived among the people of the hills and then to Da Silang, where he met Kɔm Po. It was Kɔm Po, of the Kpe.mɛmbu clan, who installed Sannyɛngjimi as chief and was appointed the first Gban Si, or head of the priests and chief-makers (*kamɛnbu*). To him were given the *jubi* of *ladin*, to make rain, and *gang gbi* (the chief's seed) which "eats the first guinea corn." From Da Silang, Sannyɛngjimi passed through Da Walum and San Gbɛm to reach Danubi, where he met the chief of Danubi who was put in charge of the sacred grove. From Danubi, he journeyed to Salam and met Gang Masi, the chief of the Lambabu patriclan, who became responsible for the burial of the members of the royal matriclan. Gang Masi showed a route by which the horses could descend to the plain, and Sannyɛngjimi then turned south to arrive at Gang Kusum [chief hill], where he founded a settlement called Nyɛmpa. There he met Nari Nyaksa, who became Gban Sam, the second ranking Gurum priest.

Because the story of Sannyɛngjimi's journey is so flexible it can be made to account for all the current positions within traditional

Gurum organization. Although many features of this organization
and corresponding features of the founding journey are disputed,
most traditions agree that three of the four great shrines were
founded during the initial journey (the fourth, the royal graveyard at
Dim Nyɛnga, was established on Sannyɛngjimi's death). The positions of the twelve chief's assistants (gang gbanbu), the twelve
priests (kamɛnbu), and the various chiefs (gangbu) and headmen
(misanbu) are customarily legitimized by appeal to meetings that
are supposed to have occurred during the founding journey. In practice, there is consensus about the senior membership of each category of officialdom, although precedence and the right of junior officials to membership of the chiefly set are frequently disputed. This
dispute occurs because the traditional Gurum political organization
has more named offices than can be accommodated within the dual
organization of twelve priestly offices balanced by twelve chief's assistants (see Appendix 3). The development is probably attributable
to the changes in chiefly family, as different chiefly families appear
to have favored different officials who had offered them support.

The separation of the chiefdoms of Gurum and Yebbi is retold
in the guise of a story about a dispute between brothers:

> Gang Kinkinmi, the Yebbi chief, was angry with his brother
> Gang Wemɔmɛn of Gurum, who had built a decorated clay
> dais, as though he were a chief. He plotted to kill his
> brother during the annual harvest rites. A shelter of guinea
> corn stalks was built to house Gang Wemɔmɛn and his fol-
> lowers, and beer was brought to welcome them. In the eve-
> ning, an elderly woman relative [grandmother] of Gang We-
> mɔmɛn came to his camp to warn him to drink only the red
> beer and not the white, which was drugged with a sleeping
> potion. When it was dark, Gang Wemɔmɛn and his people
> slipped out and crossed the Mokan River, from where they
> saw the shelter fired. Gang Wemɔmɛn ordered the royal
> drum to be beaten and shouted to his brother that he would
> have to come to "catch" him [gurumi, catch me]. After
> this the Mokan River became the boundary of the two
> territories.

Gang Wemɔmɛn was succeeded by Gang Miri, who was the last of the chiefs of the east matriclan (*gang.tim.nɔ.kuni*).[4] Gang Miri contracted leprosy and his sisters' sons (who should have taken responsibility for his bodily welfare) refused to "scratch" him down after he had washed. Because his sisters' sons had not "respected" him (*lari*, which also covers our sense, to fear), Gang Miri instructed his *kamɛn* Gban Sam not to allow them to succeed, but to give the chiefship to his son. *Gang.tim.nɔ.kuni* were not to be allowed to recover the chiefship until members of the clan had captured a bush-cow and a poisonous snake alive and delivered them to the *kamɛn*.[5] When Gang Miri died he was buried behind the royal graveyard, at a place called Dako, and his leopard skin was given to a close adviser (titled *gang.ta*, the chief's ear[6]) so that Gang Miri would recognize him when he came to make offerings on the grave.

The patriclan that assumed the chiefship traces descent from Gang Wokni, and is called Gang Woknibu. A further institutional change is explained by a narrative set during their chiefship:

> When the ancestral sprites [*wurumbu*] kept refusing to accept those nominated to chiefship, the chiefs died in quick succession, and all the candidates fled for fear they might be appointed. So the chiefmakers set a trap by placing a hunting net across the gap in the compound fencing of an elderly man. He tried to escape being made chief but was caught in the net [*sa*], and was made the first of the chiefs of the Taksabu patriclan. Perhaps four Taksabu chiefs reigned in Gurum, but they were never allowed to occupy the capital of the chiefdom, which was governed by a regent. The Taksabu and Gang Woknibu are sometimes collectively called Gurumbu, after the name of the chiefdom over which they ruled.

The Taksabu also occupied the Yebbi chiefship at various times, and some traditions suggest that they had claimed the Yebbi chiefship before that of Gurum. The two patriclan contenders have continued until the present to argue the merits of their respective claims to the chiefships of Gurum and Yebbi. These and the competing claim of the *gang.tim.nɔ.kuni* matriclan are alluded to in several reports of the colonial period. The reign of Gang Makɛn, at the beginning of this century, seems to have been marked by suppression of the *gang.tim.nɔ.kuni* claimants and an attempt to remodel the Gurum polity along lines reminiscent of the patriclan chiefdoms of the northern Shebshi Mountains. Raiding for slaves into the hinterland of the chiefdom is said by the Chamba of the hills to have intensified during the years immediately preceding the colonial period (see Chapter 11).

Gurum and Yebbi traditions draw upon devices noted among other groups, such as the migration of a matriclan from Yeli, the division of ritual responsibility with patriclans of indigenous peoples, the loss of chiefship because of the physical unsuitability of the chief, and rivalries between chiefs. An additional theme is an inference of danger associated with the assumption of chiefship by virtue of the proximate relationship between chiefs and ancestral sprites (*wurumbu*). This theme is elaborated in beliefs that express the mutual connotations of chiefmaking, circumcision, and death. Unlike all the chiefdoms to the south, with the exception of Sapeo, it is probable that chiefship in both Gurum and Yebbi passed from matriclan to patriclan ownership during the mid-nineteenth century.

The Northern Residual Leko Chiefships

Since the chiefships of Kollu, Nyemdelou, Saptou, and Vogba are not vested in the *gat.kuna* matriclan, it is not clear whether the northern residual Chamba are most usefully grouped with the refuge or raider chiefdoms. Like the northern Shebshi chiefships, those of the northern residual Leko are owned by patriclans, in this case by sections of the Sama patriclan. But like the southern Shebshi and southern Leko chiefdoms, the northern residual Leko spent much of the nineteenth century in hill refuges on the slopes of the Alantika Mountains.

I have carried out interviews in only two of the smaller chiefdoms, Kollu and Saptou. The foundation narratives obtained appear to refer back to events contemporary with the Leko diaspora. The members of the chiefly family of Kollu claim to have moved to their present location in the Alantika Mountains at the time that the Fulani of Turuwa made war on their old settlement of Lamurde, where they lived alongside the Bata. The Sama of Saptou say that they were once at Djubi, between the Faro and Deo rivers, where they lived with the Pɛla or Pɛlbira (terms for Koutine and Potopo). At first they lived peacefully with Fulani who came to settle at Dorba, near the Faro-Deo confluence but later, when Hamman Sambo founded Tchamba, war broke out and the Sama sought refuge in the hills. Their movement to the hills is said to have been contemporary with the emigration of other Chamba towards the south.

In their account of displacement from the east by Fulani, these reports recall those of the southern residual Leko of Sapeo, Balkossa, and Bangla. The references to connections with Bata and Pere can be related to the presence of clans of Bata and Pere origin in the Bali chiefdoms. The term Sama seems to function rather like Yambu, as a generic term for a cluster of patriclans that are only distinguished in some contexts. Sama sections appear to have migrated southwards during the nineteenth century. The chief priest of Yeli also belonged to a Sama section that arrived from the north or east. The clan sections are distinguished by the term for a female clan member (any man may be referred to as *sam.vana*); most of these terms are without known etymology, although a woman of the Kollu section of Sama may be called *kag.kina,* or Bata woman, which is said to recall the close association in which the Sama of Kollu and the Bata once lived around Lamurde. The opposition between chiefs (cool) and priests (hot), evident in the southern Leko traditions, is restated in the north in an extreme form that is consonant with the residence of the two types of officials in entirely separate communities. The northern Leko area is divided between communities headed by Sama chiefs and separate communities headed by priests (*wanbira*) who organize their ritual observances in relative independence.

It would clearly be unwise to approach the traditions of the refuge chiefdoms in literal terms. This already differentiates them from those of the raider chiefdoms which, once self-interest has been taken into account, can be interpreted in terms similar to our own historical understanding. But this is not to say that the refuge traditions are without historical interest; at a minimum, they indicate the type of society that produced them.

Where I have been able to trace the development of the oral record over a number of years, particularly in Sugu and Gurum, it has been apparent that, while the narratives vary greatly in detail, their overall form is relatively unchanging. They are clearly susceptible to analysis in terms additional to those that we may suppose preoccupied the teller at the time of telling. But this type of argument, which Peel dubs anthropological presentism, oversimplifies by assuming that effective legitimizing traditions can be contemporary works of fiction (Peel 1984).

Since they contain few references to events of concern to people other than local communities of Chamba, it is difficult to suggest the chronology of events that inspired the narratives. Some traditions do make reference to Fulani activities at the time of the reestablishment of the chiefdoms in the hills; this applies to some of the present residual Leko population (in the northern Alantika Mountains, and in the Bangla Mountains to the south). The establishment of the southern Nakɛnyare chiefdoms is recounted without reference to the Fulani, and allusions to the jihad, when they occur at all, are allotted to reigns subsequent to that of the chiefdom founder. Along with the evidence provided by chieflists, which are longer than those of the raider chiefdoms, it seems a reasonable inference that the southern central Chamba chiefdoms antedate the Fulani jihads. In turn, this suggests that these chiefdoms experienced a change in political environment at the turn of the nineteenth century. The foundation narratives owe their inception to this earlier period, as do the organizational forms of the matriclan chiefdoms. The changes that occurred during the nineteenth century had these earlier forms as context.

CHAPTER 6

REGIONAL VARIATIONS:

AN AREAL PERSPECTIVE

A train of events set in motion at the close of the eighteenth century redrew the political geography of the Chamba homelands during the subsequent fifty years. In the course of substantial relocations of population, a proportion of which quit Chambaland altogether, Chamba political communities were either redefined territorially or underwent changes that redefined their internal character. The world in which Chamba had lived was transformed by three concurrent events: the Leko diaspora, the Fulani effort to conquer Adamawa, and the search for refuge in central Chambaland. As a conclusion to this survey of Chamba variations, and as a means of reconstructing this eighteenth-century world, I want to see how far the differences among Chamba communities can be accommodated within a single historical narrative—to look for a story line to the diversity we have been examining, and to ask whether the story line is credible.

Pre-Nineteenth Century Chambaland

What was Chambaland like before the jihad? According to Chamba recollections, the few Fulani in Chambaland were grazers, dependent on local chiefs for their rights of pasturage. Their earliest settlements were established along the Faro River, and there are suggestions that these existed long enough for regular exchange relations to have developed.[1] Before the Leko diaspora, several chiefdoms populated by Leko-speaking Chamba occupied the plains around the

Faro and Deo Rivers. The names of a few of them, Dəngadiu, Gatgu, Sunbungba, and Papayo are still recalled by elderly informants. More generally, Chamba Leko claim that their old settlements occupied the area between the Faro and the Deo Rivers and between the Faro River and the Alantika Mountains (see Figure 7). The area between the rivers was in fact so depopulated during the nineteenth century that little movement of population was required to turn it into a game reserve during the twentieth century.[2]

In the southern foothills of the Alantika Mountains, which separate the speakers of Leko and Daka, a chiefly family that laid claim to prestigious association with the Jukun had established itself at Yeli and was accepted as ritual paramount by the peoples farther to the west. If we accept the chieflists of the refuge chiefdoms at face value, this situation of paramountcy may have prevailed during the first half of the eighteenth century. To the extent we think the chieflists are telescoped, then this has been the state of affairs for that much longer. Whether we wish to accept the dogma of immigration, or whether we want to see the claim to immigrant status made by members of the matriclan of the chief as a conventional expression of the claim to prestigious association, there is no doubt that such traditions are taken literally today. There is equally little doubt that the historical reconstruction of Yeli as a Leko-speaking place ruled by Daka, and of the Nakɛnyare chiefdoms as Daka-speaking places connected to the Leko through their ruling clans, was instrumental in making the emergence of an extensive Chamba identity a logical possibility.

On the more remote history of the relation between the two language groups, it is difficult even to speculate. It has only recently become clear that the two languages are not members of the same language family (see Appendix 2), which makes their shared semantic fields particularly interesting. Shared terms are particularly evident in the vocabulary of kinship and clanship, and in conceptions related to ritual interests and the natural environment. As a consequence, I infer that marriage, religion, and a common ecology may have been areas of mutual concern to Leko and Daka before the emergence of a common extensive ethnicity.

In addition to their juxtaposition to the Daka, the Leko chiefdoms in the plains were neighbors of the Bata to the north and of the

Pere to the south and southwest. On their borders, these peoples intermixed and intermarried, and they treated one another as joking partners, an indication of equality. Then, as now, the northern part of the Alantika Mountains was occupied by people whom Chamba referred to as Koma. Despite their provision of highland produce, they were not considered to share the level of civilization common to the Samba, Kaga, and Pere (Chamba Leko, Bata and Koutine). If we are to believe the oral traditions of the descendants of the Leko speakers, then the southernmost part of the area of Samba settlement was presided over by matriclan chiefs appointed from the *gat.kuna*. Here, the Samba were mixed with Pere. Again, according to contemporary traditions, the northern chiefdoms were interspersed among the Bata, who particularly settled along the rivers, and their rulers were drawn from the Sama patriclans. Perhaps it had long been thus, or maybe patriclan chiefship had been introduced by Bata. In the longer term, it is possible that the overall direction of settlement had been from north to south. It seems highly probable that distinctions in degree of centralization among Chamba Leko communities already existed in the eighteenth century. Some named Chamba patriclan clusters claim to have lived in the hills prior to the nineteenth century. They are also mentioned as the original occupants of hill territories in the foundation stories of southern Leko refuge chiefdoms, such as in the Balkossa narratives discussed in the preceding chapter.

To the west of the Alantika Mountains, settlement patterns probably changed quickly during the eighteenth century. Having reached Yeli from an earlier settlement in the south of the Shebshi Mountains, the immigrants who had Jukun pretensions expanded westward as their chiefship came to be accepted by Daka speakers living within the Shebshi Mountains. These Daka speakers claim to have lacked chiefs prior to the arrival of the immigrants. Perhaps the prestige of the immigrants was sufficient argument for devolving responsibility for some aspects of collective welfare upon them. Da Dukdu, Yeli, Sugu, Yebbi, Kiri, Gurum, and Danaba were established as chiefdoms that claimed foundation from Yeli. Furthermore, their traditions acknowledge that certain elements of their welfare were dependent upon Yeli, especially in matters concerned with the control of smallpox and locust plagues. Their chiefs were selected from the royal matriclans (*gang.kuni* and *gang.tim.nɔ.kuni*) by priests appointed from indigenous patriclans among whom they had settled.

Whereas the traditions of the Nakɛnyare and Yeli Chamba are concerned with the introduction of chiefship from outside, residual Leko traditions concern the transplantation of old chiefly families to new locations. A relatively recent centralization of Nakɛnyare communities can be argued, not only from their own traditions, but also by examining the distribution of other Daka-speaking communities that surrounded the new chiefdoms to the north, south, and west, but remained independent of them. The term Nakɛnyare itself was a means of separating the centralized from the uncentralized Daka speakers. The claim to matrilateral kinship with the Leko, which the Nakɛnyare press through their relation to the ruling clan of Yeli, seems to have served the aim of distinguishing them from the uncentralized Daka.

Given a general tendency to stress the prestigious relations of ruling families, we may be able to infer from the available traditions that Daka speakers of the earlier eighteenth century saw the organization of their Leko neighbors as more sophisticated than their own. It is difficult to argue that the relations recognized between Yeli and the places claiming foundation from it were ever more than a recognition of ritual interrelation. Although Frobenius wrote of a Daka empire based upon Yeli, his conception is based less on evidence than upon the rather restricted range of models of centralization available to writers of his period. Contemporary traditions recall only that Gang Yeli was the most important ritual functionary of the Chamba area, and that the outcome of rites held in Yeli were pertinent to the entire area. Yeli's position among central Chamba, therefore, depended upon notions of the way in which ritual could inflict, or threaten to inflict, violence upon others. I have repeatedly noted that the commonly recognized forms of these assaults that Yeli alone could control were smallpox and locust infestation, and such tribute as Yeli received was given on account of the fear with which these two visitations are, and were, held. Rather than an empire, we appear to be dealing with part of a regional system of interrelations, some of them predicated on the existence of differing capacities effected through ritual.

The notion that we may be dealing with a system of ritual interrelations is strengthened by the recurrent references in the traditions to Jukun origins for the chiefdom founder. The Jukun, or a congeries of people speaking Jukunoid languages, appear to have exerted a dominant influence over the plains south of the Benue prior to the nineteenth century. Earlier writers (discussed in Rubin 1969) saw in the Jukun the relic of a mighty empire, called Kororofa, that had, at its peak, menaced the northern states of the savanna. This empire was supposedly ravaged and brought low by the early Chamba raids. However, I have reservations concerning the concept that Chamba were eighteenth-century warriors. In part, this is because information on Jukun social organization is sparse; consequently it is not clear what the Chamba would have been attacking. The traditions, as discussed in Chapter 4, suggest that Chamba raids did not occur prior to the early nineteenth century, although the possibility that Chamba were launching raids before their diaspora cannot be discounted.

The conventional belief that the settled Leko chiefdoms became raiding bands suggests that they possessed military capacities before the migrations were set in motion, but no recollection of raids to the west remains. Additionally, proficiency in archery and horsemanship, at least sufficient to be able to menace agricultural communities, is likely to have developed in any community where men hunted and rode ponies. Even if Chamba Leko were raiders, it is not altogether clear why they would direct their attacks against the Jukun, rather than against less organized neighbors. Moreover, the transition from settled agriculture to the marauding life of the raiding confederacy is, perhaps, not as great as our terms make it seem. The techniques of warfare were not complex. Furthermore, the evacuation of their fields and homelands would have removed a major constraint, the possibility of reprisal, on the use of all available means of destruction. A more critical factor in the change to the raiding life was the probable willingness to deploy all means of destruction ruthlessly rather than the nature of the means themselves.

The concept of a Kororofa empire emerged in the dubious circumstances of a British search for rulers of the fragmented Benue populations who might discharge the sorts of administrative tasks undertaken by the northern savanna states. This need was abetted by the now discarded idea that Negro African states were necessarily founded by northern immigrants—the "Hamitic hypothesis" (Palmer 1911, 1930; Meek 1931a; dubbed "nonsensical" by Smith 1971:165; and demolished by Armstrong 1960). An impressive military record has been attributed to Kororofa on the basis of references in the chronicles of northern states such as Kano, Katsina, and Bornu (Meek 1931a:25–26; Rubin 1969:220–21, for fourteen references in primary sources). But the literary evidence does not convincingly clinch the relationship between the Jukun and people called Kona or Kororofa (Rubin 1969:134).

During the eighteenth century, the Jukun were active traders, particularly in salt (Rubin 1969:154; Meek 1931a:33; Adamu 1978: 38–43; Chukwudi Unomah 1982). Their chiefship was evidently much admired; not only do the Nakɛnyare gang.kuni and Farang chiefs like to claim a Jukun origin, but this origin was also favored by the chiefly Potopo immigrants among the Pere, the Kam to the west of the Shebshi Mountains (Meek 1931a:35; 1931b II:38) and the "Tigong" chiefs of Ashaku and Nama (Meek 1931a:38) among others.[3] The Hwaye and Kpwate, who were attacked by the immigrant Benue Chamba, classed themselves as Jukun and claimed chiefship over the peoples of the hills (Meek 1931a:38). Clearly, the Jukun enjoyed trade and prestige in the eighteenth century, and one may have followed the other.

Was this then Kororofa—nothing more than a web of resemblances relating numerous peoples living south of the savanna states between whom trade was pursued? A minimalist interpretation of the scant evidence might certainly suggest so. The break-up of Kororofa would have meant the fragmentation of the skein of relations among communites that together composed a regional system of clanship, trade, and ritual.

Early relations between the Chamba and the Bata/Bachama are equally intriguing. On the face of it we have two divergent accounts of the relationship: some sources emphasize a push by the Bata that displaced the Chamba southwards and expelled them from Lamurde and Tchamba before the jihad; other sources emphasize their joking relationship and the diffuse ritual and kinship relations between the two groups.[4] But we have seen how misleading it can be to approach problems of interpretation in terms of present ethnic identities. Traditions of displacement mostly refer to the Leko chiefdoms; ritual relationships are documented from the northern and central areas of the Shebshi Mountains. Clans of Bata origin are found in the northern Shebshi Mountains, the Mapeo hill refuge, and in the residual Leko chiefdoms. There is no reason to suppose that relations between the Chamba and Bata were identical in these different areas.

The founders of Mbulo, in the northern Shebshi Mountains, are supposed to be related to the Bata of Demsa. Their traditions of cooperation with the Chamba immigrants to the Vanku settlement were discussed in Chapter 4. Versions of a number of northern and central Shebshi Mountain chiefdom traditions refer to migrations through Bata settlement areas, or relations with Bata chiefs. The chiefly Gangwoknibu patriclan of Gurum and Yebbi recall that their ancestors passed through Demsa before reaching Dayela and that the daughter of the Chamba chief, Gang Kǝtsin, was given in marriage to the chief of Demsa.

For their part, the Bata/Bachama are said to recognize Gurum as the place from which the deity Nzeanzo leads their dead to the red land, and their descriptions of this place appear to be drawn from the grove at Danubi, which Gurum Chamba consider to be inhabited by the smallpox spirits (*kona*) (Stevens 1976). According to the custodians of the shrine, the forest sprang up from a stick brought from Dayela by the first chief of the nearby village, Dim Timi, and remains connected to Dayela by an underground tunnel through which the spirits may pass. Gurum was recognized by the northern Shebshi Chamba as the source of smallpox. So, the Gurum Chamba legitimized their shrine by association with Dayela, while the Yeli Chamba derived the efficacy of their smallpox shrine from its association with Kona and the Jukun. Ritual potencies are connected by a network of associations that appear to have had cross-ethnic significance. For instance, Meek recorded that the priestess who was the medium of the cult of Nzeanzo, "the most honoured cult of the Bachama, Bata and Mbula," was chosen as a virgin from Kona and had to live a life of "perpetual virginity, being regarded as married to the god" (Meek 1931b I:29). Yeli traditions maintain, furthermore, that the most important priestship of their community was delegated to a clan of Bata origin whose members showed themselves capable of spoiling rites from which they were excluded.[5]

E. Mohammadou has repeatedly challenged the tendency of earlier accounts of the Fulani jihad in Adamawa to ignore the associations that had existed between ethnic groups before the foundation of the Adamawa Emirate (1978; 1983), and has gone so far as to suggest a confederacy of Adamawa peoples prior to the nineteenth century. I would endorse his first point but feel the second is unlikely as the groups attained systems of political organization no larger than chiefdoms, each of which contained no more than a few thousand members. Interspersed among these chiefdoms were other communities, notably in the mountains, that lacked even this degree of centralization.

However, the different political organizations were crosscut by ties of common clanship, by the recognition of mutual ritual efficacy, and by their interest in trade. Ethnic identities formed the basis for joking relationships, but were themselves susceptible to change if clan members moved to a settlement that spoke a language different from their own. The most important units of organization were based on locality and clan, but the more diffuse relations between clans and localities might have furnished the basis for the mobilization of larger numbers of people.[6] Like most neighbors, it is probable that these chiefdoms periodically fell out with one another, that they were attentive to their mutual prestige, and that they cooperated when their political interests so dictated. The inception of the Chamba-led raiding alliances, characterized by the rapid recruitment and assimilation of followers to existing political and ritual organizations, may represent a hasty version of a more routine process, and suggests a basic compatibility between the cultures of the different peoples involved.

The Fulani Jihad

Although the Shehu, Uthuman dan Fodio, issued the call to holy war from Gobir in 1804, it was not until 1809 that Modibbo Adama received a flag at the Caliphate capital of Sokoto and returned to Gurin to become Lamido of the emirate of the south, Fombina or Adamawa (Njeuma 1978:28). Adama had set out on his journey in the previous year as the delegate of a number of Fulani leaders, *ardo'en*, who were already settled within the future emirate. Numerous accounts suggest that the assembled leaders were taken aback to find the young Adama, of relatively humble origins, installed as their leader, since they anticipated that he would return with mandates for them to pursue jihad independently (East 1935:19—21; Lacroix 1952:20–21; Abubakar 1977:56–57; Mohammadou 1978:162–63, 229–32; Njeuma 1978:25–32).

Problems of internal organization that were to characterize the affairs of the emirate for the remainder of the nineteenth century are evident even at this early stage. Fulani clans had entered the region with their herds long before the jihad and had reached arrangements with local peoples to permit grazing. These local interests were not always compatible with those of the emirate. But the impetus towards jihad was irresistable, and the *status quo* could not be maintained. North of the Benue, the military activities of Buba Yero and Bauchi Gordi were posing a threat to the autonomy of the Fombina Fulani, whereas south of the Benue some of the *ardo'en* may already have seized the initiative to consolidate territories around the Faro River. Moreover, Fulani refugees from the wars already joined in the north were reaching the south and probably exacerbating tensions between Fulani and non-Fulani (Abubakar 1977:43–45). Presumably, these northern disturbances would have disrupted the earlier regional trade routes running through Chambaland. To these local factors can be added the constructive religious vision that holy war held out to some, and the anticipations of economic gain entertained by others (Clarke 1982:Chapters 5–6; Last 1974). The relative independence from direct northern intervention that Chamba and other chiefdoms of the middle-belt had enjoyed was not long to be sustained.

By the 1830s, the Fulani had secured a cordon of chiefdoms along the Faro and Deo rivers from which they were able to mount a push towards the south. It was from these chiefdoms, Gurin (the early capital), Tchamba, Laro, Koncha, and Dodeo, east of the Alantika Mountains, that the Chamba were to face raids. The implantation and expansion of Fulani chiefdoms along the river system east of present day Chambaland and the emigration of the major Chamba raiding alliances formed a single movement. Fulani penetration west of the Alantika Mountains was not significant in the early years of jihad, and the Chamba of this area do not appear to have left their homelands in great numbers. West of the Shebshi Mountains, attacks on the Chamba Daka by the Muri Fulani seem to have occurred after the foundation of Donga. However, such attacks never reached east of the mountains. So, it is to the Faro-Deo cordon of chiefdoms that we must look for early activities precipitating the Chamba Leko diaspora.

The Kiri'en, who settled around Tchamba, were among the earliest Fulani immigrants to Chambaland. Their attacks on Bata and Chamba, which preceded the foundation of Tchamba, may have occurred just prior to the recognition of Adama as Lamido of Fombina (Mohammadou 1964:25–26; 1978:33–34, 40). Another group, the Wolarbe Fulani, established themselves under Ardo Usumatu at Wassamdu, near Laro, also before the formal onset of jihad, and claim to have exercised influence over local Chamba groups (Mohammadou 1978:160). When Hamman Dandi became leader of this group, Wolarbe war parties forced the Chamba into the hills and carried out attacks on the Pere in the course of founding Koncha and Laro (Strümpell [1912] 1982:76; Mohammadou 1978:162–66). Koncha and Laro appear to have recognized a border with Tchamba just to the north of Balkossa. Koncha became the largest of the Faro-Deo Fulani cordon of chiefdoms during the nineteenth century. It was responsible for raiding as far as Gurum and the Taraba River, and later became an important link in the north—south trading networks (Strümpell 1912). With the establishment of the Faro–Deo chiefdoms, the Wolarbe and Kiri Fulani turned their attention to the push towards the Adamawa plateau, closely following routes that the Chamba raiding bands had pioneered. The routes were, in all probability, those also used by traders plying their wares between the states of the north, the Benue Plains, and the Bamenda Grassfields.

The impetus to Chamba movement may have been an indirect result of conflicts farther north. S. Abubakar tells us that the earliest attacks launched from Gurin at the onset of jihad were against the Bata, the dominant ethnic group of the Benue valley (1977:59). At this time, or perhaps in anticipation of military action, we find traditions about a southward displacement of Bata clans and their Chamba Leko neighbors. The clans involved in these migrations appear to have been sections of a patriclan cluster called Sama. Some elements of these people sought refuge in the Alantika Mountains, while others moved south or west from the eastern part of Chambaland. The Sama clans of Saptou, Kollu, and Yeli probably arrived at their hill refuges about this time, for they recall Bata origins or strong Bata associations. The period may also have seen the emigration of the Ba'ni raiding band that was supposed to have been set in motion by an initial alliance between Kaga (i.e. Bata) and Djaba (ancestors of the present Leko inhabitants of Djap.kolu or Lowol, neighboring communities of the northern residual Leko). The Djaba of the Bali chiefdoms are especially associated with the cult rites of *voma*, and the Sama are responsible for the rites of *lela* (*lera* in southern residual Leko and Donga dialects), the royal flutes. Identical associations, though in a different political context, exist among the Djaba and Sama presently settled in northern residual Leko communities.

The resettlement of the founders of Dalami into the Nassarawo Plain from an area around Kollu may be part of the general movement associated with the onset of jihad, because their ruling clan is said to have been called Sama before it adopted the name of the river that flowed alongside the new village (Da Lami, Lami River; Lam.nepbu, the royal patriclan of Dalami). Loya Garbosa, the early leader of the Den Bakwa alliance, was also a member of the Sama patriclan that later became the chiefly clan of Donga. A general consensus emerges from quite separate bodies of tradition that Chamba clansmen known as Sama were displaced from a location some distance to the north and were active in many of the earliest Chamba relocations. The Sama most often appear as a royal clan. Bali traditions suggest that the alliance of Kaga, Djaba, and Sama later recruited clans called Nyema and Dinga.[7] The recruitment of Nyema tallies precisely with the recollection at Yeli that large numbers of Nyemnebba abandoned a hill settlement neighboring Yeli to join a migration with Bata elements already recruited to it. The tradition also claims that these Bata spoke Chamba.

Farther south, the same alliance recruited large numbers of Pere, who were perhaps already endangered by Fulani activities around Laro and Koncha; they are the Peli of present-day Bali. The Ba'ni headed south, led by their war flags, which they call *tutuwan*. This is quite clearly the Fulfulde term *tutuwal*, and we may recall that groups empowered to prosecute jihad were issued with flags by the Emir of Adamawa.

It is difficult to know whether the Chamba adopted the use of standards in emulation of the Fulani, or whether they had been directed to use them by one of the early Fulani chiefs of the area prior to setting out on their raids. However, as their own traditions frequently depict their departure from Adamawa as an escape from the Fulani, emulation is a more likely reason for the Chamba use of flags than a Fulani mandate.

On linguistic grounds, I have already argued that the Den Bakwa migrants might have had a higher composition of southern Leko than their northern counterparts in the Ba'ni bands. Chamba patriclans among the Benue Chamba named in the lists recorded by Garbosa and Meek are less easy to identify than the patriclans of Bali tradition. As is the case with Sama, there are certainly Pere or Koutine (Pyeri), Za (possibly Djabnebba), Nupabi (perhaps equivalent to the Nupabu from whom is appointed the chief of the Danubi shrine in Gurum) and others whose identification is problematic.[8] The migrations of this group may be associated with the activities of the Tchamba Fulani on the right bank of the Deo River. These migrations also appear to have moved clans to the southern refuges of the Bangla Hills, Sapeo, and Balkossa. Some names of these old settlements are recalled in present traditions, especially in the recollections of the histories of the gat.kuna royal matriclans that once ruled villages such as Gatgu and Dɔngadiu, which have long ceased to exist.

In the absence of traditions, the exact origins of the Kashimbila-Gadi and Takum Chamba are difficult to determine; it has already been suggested that their migrations might have slightly predated those of the better documented migrations of other groups. Given their names, it seems that Kashimbila migrants were largely of Pere origin, whereas the Daka must have incorporated elements which would warrant the use of the term Daka by Leko speakers—perhaps they were peoples associated with the earlier movement of western Chambas into the area around Yeli.

Various other migrations and settlements occurred elsewhere in the region around this time. There is some evidence (discussed in Chapter 4) of settlement, in the 1820s, by the Yambu under Damashi in approximately the middle of the Nassarawo Plain. Damashi's visit to Gurin led to his recognition as an agent of the Fulani and, together with his Vere allies, he set off on raids that emplaced Chamba chiefdoms west of the Shebshi Mountains. Other Yambu, Bata, and displaced Leko converged upon Vanku and began colonization of the northern Shebshi Mountains, establishing themselves among the Mangla.

It is difficult to determine how the southern and central chiefdoms specifically reacted to the onset of the religious wars. Gurum appears to have been the most intransigent in its refusal to come to terms with the Fulani, and there are no records of any form of alliance between Gurum Chamba and the various Fulani chiefdoms. Strategic location in the mountains appears to have been the key to Gurum's ability to withstand the Fulani threat; but it could also have been that the route through the Shebshi Mountains via Gurum could be avoided thanks to the existence of alternate southern and northern routes.

The chiefdom of Da Dukdu, which had been the source of the southern *gang.kuni* chiefly families at Sugu and Yeli, appears to have suffered a particularly devastating slave raid from Koncha. The raid caused the majority of its population to flee to Sugu; the remainder was forced to pay tribute to Koncha. Sugu itself appears to have come to some kind of arrangement with Koncha in which the payment of nominal tribute was accepted by Koncha in return for immunity from slave raiding.[9]

Throughout the earlier part of the nineteenth century, refugee patriclans of very diverse origins had been responsible for the emergence of a large series of settlements along the northern slopes of the Alantika Mountains at Mapeo. By the mid-nineteenth century, both Gurum and Yebbi chiefships had probably been transferred from matriclan to patriclan ownership. Traditions suggest that both Gurum and Sugu chiefs resorted to raiding their own hinterlands in order to secure slaves for sale. These sporadic raids, which may have been on the increase by the latter part of the nineteenth century, probably supplemented the more usual sales of undesirables who were traditionally removed from Chamba communities, such as witches, miscreants, and children who cut their upper teeth before their lower ones.

Mid- and Late Nineteenth Century Developments

Significant Fulani penetration of the Nassarawo Plain did not take place until about thirty years after the consolidation of the Faro-Deo cordon of chiefdoms. The Wolarbe and Kiri Fulani had founded Tchamba, Laro, Koncha, and their related settlements as entities virtually independent of the emirate capital, and had then pressed south into the Adamawa plateau in the hope of achieving total independence from their nominal overlord. The colonization of the Nassarawo Plain was a more centrally controlled affair, and relied upon two strategies. Chamba agents, such as Damashi and the plains chiefdom of Dalami, were recognized to be clients of the Fulani, and Fulani settlements were installed in the plains. By the 1830s two Fulani chiefs are said to have received flags from Adama and to have founded their villages at Pakorgel and Jauro Nuhu in the more northern portions of the plain. They do not appear to have engaged in military enterprises and presumably relied upon general recognition of their protection by Yola for such influence as they achieved.

In mid-century, the Yola Fulani attempted to secure their hold on the plain by establishing more settlements, and by sending Hamidu, a son of Adama, to found the village of Nyibango (G2.2 Nassarawo District History; Vicars-Boyle 1910). Although fighting between the Nyibango Fulani and the Chamba is not remembered, the establishment of Fulani settlements in the plains was instrumental in pushing the Chamba of the northern Shebshi area deeper into the mountains, where they were able to control the important trade and grazing trails that passed toward the Benue Plains. The role of Dalami as a way-station for traders and as a tithe-collecting agent for the Fulani seems to have been maintained throughout the period. Yola never exercised much direct influence over the southern area of the plain, where Koncha and Laro were the predominant forces. Under the protection of its alliance with Koncha, Sugu, or more precisely its male chief, now settled in the plain, appears successfully to have asserted authority over settlements to the west and south. In the latter part of the century, especially during the reign of Lamido Sanda, the fragile *status quo* that had assured relative tranquillity between the Chamba and Fulani in the plains appears to have broken down. It is recalled that slave raids were launched against Danaba, against chiefdoms in the northern Shebshi Mountains, and even against former clients such as Binyeri.

European accounts of interrelations in Chambaland in the last decade of the nineteenth century and the first decade of the twentieth present a confusing situation. Although Fulani were present in significant numbers in the plains, their administrative ambitions seem to have been satisfied by securing relative safety for traders and extracting generally nominal tokens of their authority from the Chamba. Chambaland was traversed by several significant trade routes that were principally utilized by long-distance Hausa traders. Traders from the south could follow a route from Laro, through the Alantika Mountains near Kollu, to Yola by way of Dalami, or else could follow the Deo River to its confluence with the Faro and then proceed from Tchamba to Yola. The first route was probably the more popular. A third route, to the west, involved crossing the Shebshi Mountains by way of a number of well-placed Chamba chiefdoms, such as Tading and Gang Bakeni (Mbulo).

All the early travelers noted differences between the inhabitants of the plains and the mountains. The Chamba of the plains appear to have been quite numerous and generally recognized Fulani authority. They dressed like the Fulani, in gowns bought from the Hausa. However, there is evidence as well that they were not averse to robbing and killing passing traders when they thought they were able to get away with it. In return for the payment of tithe to the Fulani, the Chamba were able to farm in the plains. The Chamba benefited from this arrangement because the loss of produce as tithe payment must have been outweighed by the high yield that could be obtained by farming near the river system of the plains.[10] Chamba villages on major trade routes across the plains often included small resident Fulani populations.

In contrast, the Chamba of the hills were either independent of the Fulani, or else made minor payments to them when it seemed to be advisable. Most of them lived in the hills but farmed in the plains, which put them in a strategically ambiguous position. Although their homes were relatively immune from attack, their fields were subject to firing and they themselves could be captured while on their farms. Typically, the hill Chamba carried bows and poisoned arrows. When the Germans first attempted administration through Fulani chiefs they quickly realized that Fulani authority was not always recognized by hill-dwelling Chamba groups. In 1907, Strümpell recorded the reluctance of the Gurum Chamba to deal with the Fulani. Before the end of the German colonial period they were brought under the jurisdiction of Fulani chiefs only by military means.

In Mapeo, the Fulani appear to have tried varied expedients to impose a semblance of external authority. Fulani were appointed as *jekada* (administrators) of Mapeo, particular clan chiefs were culti-vated as Fulani agents, and an attempt was even made to implant a more compliant Chamba clan to act as chiefs. None of these strategies appear to have met with much success, since the Mapeo Chamba continued to constitute a menace to traders passing by their hillside settlements.[11]

The remnants of the Chamba Leko living on the eastern slopes of the Alantika Mountains were less numerous than their Daka-speaking neighbors and less favorably placed to deal with the power-ful Faro-Deo Fulani chiefdoms. Although their villages were protected by the mountains, their fields were easily accessible. However, the Fulani chiefdoms of the Faro-Deo area were themselves diminished in size and importance after the implantation of their southern ex-tensions at Tibati and Banyo. The Alantika Mountain Chamba seem both to have paid tribute and to have been raided by their Fulani neighbors. Perhaps the most significant of the chiefdoms was Bal-kossa, which maintains that it was able to inflict defeat upon attack-ers from Yola during the late nineteenth century, while acting in support of a Fulani chiefly candidate at Laro.[12] Rivalries among vari-ous Fulani factions may have prevented the emergence of a clear dichotomy of interest between Fulani and Chamba.

Early European travelers understood this fluid set of circum-stances in overly stark terms. They envisaged that a Muslim and Fulani dominance of the plains was opposed to a pagan Chamba or Daka independence, which survived by virtue of refuge in the hills (e.g. Detzner 1923). Although geographical features were among the most important strategic factors in late-nineteenth century politics affecting Chamba, and were the most readily apparent to the eye of a passing European, matters were not so simple. As Chamba were later to argue to British administrators, there had never been a conquest of Chambaland as the Europeans understood this concept. The Fulani had never solved their internal problems of organization for long, and the Chamba had been both too elusive and too adept at turning Fulani competition to their own advantage. The fact that Chamba communities might be subjected to attack, or that Chamba might periodically pay the Fulani in order for this not to happen, did not imply conquest.

Conquest, as Chamba of the twentieth century envisaged it, using the Fulani's own rhetoric of jihad, would have involved genuine acceptance of Islam during the nineteenth century and a subordination of their chiefs to dictates emanating from Yola. Cooperation with some particular local Fulani chief or Fulani community was not, they were to claim, any indication of a general conquest of Chamba by Fulani.

As will be discussed in Chapter 11, early European rule represented the plains Chamba as conquered people. Resistance on their part to Fulani overlordship looked like an attempt to take advantage of the supposedly greater leniency that Fulani observed thanks to the colonial guiding hand. The Chamba of the hills were simply an anachronism, lawless and prone to destabilizing an area that was legitimately open to traders and grazers. In contrast to the Chamba of both hill and plain, the Fulani appeared to Europeans to be a noble race, similar in many respects to themselves—especially since the Fulani, like Europeans in Africa, were particularly receptive to the notion of having other people do their work for them. Because of these misleading simplifications, European rule through Fulani chiefs exacerbated the ethnic tensions that already existed. These stereotypes contributed to the creation of a dichotomy of interest between Fulani and Chamba as distinct peoples, which became the dominant vision of local politics in the British colonial and early post-independence times.

PART III

CHAMBA THEMES

CHAPTER 7

KIN AS SOCIATES, AND SOCIATES AS KIN

Many African peoples seem to have dogmatic and explicit views on the nature of the person, but in this, as in much else, Chamba informants are undogmatic and largely unconcerned.[1] I was never offered one systematic view of Chamba personhood, but by means of questioning and overhearing my informants over the course of my year's residence in Mapeo, I was able to gather, piecemeal, the account that I present as current Chamba conventional wisdom.

The body or substance of a child derives from the mother, from the blood that she retains and from the milk with which she suckles her child. One image suggests that body is like clay, and God is the potter who forms this clay in a continual activity of creating people. God-centered accounts are not the prerogative of adherents of world religions among Chamba and here, as elsewhere, Chamba are able to draw upon more or less God-centered or man-centered accounts according to their predilection in these matters. Similarly, spirit is seen both as something that God adds to the clay-like substance of the child, or as somehow associated with the father's seed (gbi). In either case, spirit is reincarnated in the patriclan. Alternative views are rarely encountered, and then only outside of Mapeo. God takes the spirit of a patriclan ancestor from his subterranean phase of existence and puts it into the substance of the child. Or, in a way that defies explanation, this spiritual connection is somehow the automatic consequence of the implantation of the father's seed. Not only is a child born, but an ancestor is reincarnated. An ancestor who was happy with the behavior of his descendants, who died without leaving outstanding disputes, and whose descendants buried and remembered him with respect, by arranging to remove his skull and by taking beer and food to his grave, will "return" as an immediate descendant of his last "becoming human."[2] His displeasure would be shown by his return to a more distant branch of the clan or (but never for Mapeo informants) a return within his matriclan.

The precise way in which reincarnation occurs is unclear. As a collectivity, the inhabitants of the underworld are termed *wurumbu*, a word that shares connotations with our notion of "sprite." However, in the context of reincarnation, Chamba normally, but not invariably, speak of specific kin (grandfathers or paternal aunts). In this context I write of spirits. There is a further equivocation as to whether the reincarnation implies metamorphosis of the *wurum* or transplantation of the breath, *gɔngsi*.

Similarly, Mapeo Chamba accounts of meanings associated with birth do not seem to recognize incompatibilities in attributing volition to God, to the ancestor, and to the seed itself. The newborn child is not fully human but retains elements of his sprite character (*wurum*). This character tends to reassert itself towards the end of life. I was quite frequently told that senile elders and young children both spoke the language of the *wurumbu*. My friend and tutor in Mapeo ways, Titlɛsime, ever the empiricist, was pleased to find this demonstrated to me on a day when we were keeping his extremely aged and senile maternal uncle company. While the old man was lying on his deathbed, slowly renouncing the human world for that of the sprites, his ramblings, which had lost all elements of lucidity a few days previously, seemed to be answered by gurglings coming from the newest member of the compound—here was evidence of a dialogue in *wurum.mumi*.

Upon becoming human again, a spirit should be recognized and given the name that it had had in its previous incarnation, otherwise it may be reluctant to resume human form and may "return" (not die, since death is for mature humans and animals). The use of the verb "return" (*peni*) for the movement by which a spirit becomes incarnate, or a child refuses to remain in the human world, underlines the facility of transformation at this stage of life. Often a baby has some distinguishing feature by which the spirit may be recognized; failing this the child is given a name and is thereafter observed to see if it will find the name acceptable. Should the child cry incessantly, an aged man or woman of the patriclan will be brought to recite the names of those who have died; the child's cries will cease as it recognizes the name it should bear.

The characteristics of humanity are slowly added to the child's natural endowments, and gradually displace its sprite like features. This slow process of transition to humanity, which begins with naming, continues with the acquisition of human language and passes, at adult initiation, into full human responsibility before tending again toward identification with the underworld.

The images evoked in these accounts of birth (and death) are consistent with other images pervasive in the notions that Chamba express concerning relations between people. Between the mother and child there is a relation of substance: formless, clay-like, and red (like clay and blood). Since this substance is maternally derived, it is shared by all maternal relatives. Matrikin are responsible for one another's bodily welfare, and the discovery of witchcraft substance in one member of a matriclan implicates all those who are close matrikin. Patrikin are associated in different idioms. They represent the names and incarnations of the patriclan.

Unlike substance, spirit has no aggregate state, even while in the underworld awaiting reincarnation. The *wurum* is a unique individual with a determinate character that can be good or evil, intelligent or stupid, rash or cautious, or brave or cowardly. Spirit is especially associated with the head, the seat of thought, and the skull, which is hard and preservable. The degradable seats of emotion, the stomach and heart (in Chamba, the insides), are elements of substance and may introduce maternal influences upon the basic paternal disposition of the individual. Life itself is associated with breath (*gɔngsi*), neither maternal nor paternal, but represents the (perhaps God-given) span that is allotted all living things and is either used up and "finished" or else prematurely "destroyed."

Patrikin and matrikin are the two most important categories of a person's sociates, but the form of the association is different in the two cases. Using the terminology of my introductory chapter, matrikin are consociates; the differences between them are only apparent and transient, for at bottom they all derive from undifferentiated substance. Patrikin are adsociates; they are radically distinct, have always been, and will always remain, such. Association can never compromise their immutable differences of spirit. Cooperation brings them together, but does not merge them as a body. The differences between these two views of human association constitute what Bateson might have called a deutero-difference, or difference between differences, and the ramifications of these views pervade Chamba politics, ritual and kinship.[3] The changing relationship between consociation and adsociation as idioms of Chamba association is a cultural theme that will allow us (in Parts 4 and 5) to examine the historical narrative reconstructed in Part 1 in a different light. First, I must demonstrate the pertinence of the distinction to an analysis of kinship.

By utilizing conventional anthropological kinship terms, which are useful as approximating and orienting devices, Chamba societies can be said presently to have three types of kinship systems. In central Chambaland, there is a double-descent system and, traditionally, a Yakö-type partible inheritance; the Benue and Bali Chamba have kinship systems that exhibit a more pronounced patrilineal bias, whereas the Daka in the south and west of Chambaland trace descent matrilineally. As a mnemonic guide (Chambaland—double descent; Benue and Bali—patrilineal; Daka—matrilineal), the typology has something to recommend it, but in cultural terms, the different Chamba systems probably share more features among themselves than they would with other members of a comparative sample slotted into the same categories.

In this chapter, I provide a detailed analysis of the idioms of kinship, clanship and local organization among central Chamba. The account is largely drawn from my intensive fieldwork in Mapeo, which was my interpretative starting point in Chapter 2. With slight modifications, it is generally applicable to Chamba living in the Shebshi Mountains and to the Leko refuge communities.

Idioms of Descent and Parentation

Mapeo Chamba draw on a limited range of concepts to describe a wide range of relations, from the closest personal kinship connections to the most distant ties of clanship. This tendency to work a few terms hard lends a particular character to their reckoning of kinship and clanship. These reckonings are clear about close kinship and named clan groupings but are rather vague about the area between the two. Analysis of the terminology shows a preoccupation with three types of discrimination: parentation, gender, and birth order. From the perspective of named clan groupings, an appeal to shared clanship can be made by simply stating that two people are members of the same clan; the same implication could be derived by saying that they had "one father" (the same patriclan) or "one mother" (the same matriclan), or that one father or mother "bore" them (translating *wani*, to bear, either of women or men).

The verb "to bear" warrants closer examination; its relationship to kinship terminology is tautological. Any person addressed by a lineal kinship term of the ascending generation (father or mother) may be said to have borne the individual, and common membership of any clan category implies an ancestor or ancestress who was the common parent of the members. Matrilineal and patrilineal descent among Chamba can be understood to refer to "genealogical continua." Chamba can look at descent genealogically, but the normal referent of descent is to the characteristics individuals share by virtue of their relation of common parentation. Relations are expressed as the direct consequences of sharing a mother or father, which is what I mean by parentation, and not primarily by reference to a larger time, which descent connotes. Since they have one mother, members of a matriclan share matrilateral and matrilineal characteristics involving substance and the responsibilities derived from it; they are consociates. Members of patriclans share attributes located in patriclan culture: name, spirit, incarnation, and the specific historical qualities of their patriclan origins and customs; they are adsociates. Appealing to common parentation or shared clanship refers directly to these qualities of association without recourse to the intervening idea of genealogical continuum.

To express the Chamba idiom "to bear" more precisely, we might envisage a notional space bounded at its poles by the ideas of genealogical descent and the closest parentation. Two such spaces are constituted for patrilateral and matrilateral connection, and the use of a single term, bear, can evoke some or all of the connotations appropriate to them. To control the range of evocations, Chamba use emphasizing particles tacked on to the relation of parentation (*da noni,* one father, *da non təng təng,* an emphatic form; identically for mother: *nya noni, nya non təng təng*). The number of emphasizing particles can be expanded virtually without limitation. But the same idiom may, depending upon context, emphasize the closeness of a relation or the importance the speaker attributes to it. Short of knowing from the outset what is being communicated, it is hardly possible to understand the import of a particular statement about kinship. This is no more than a kinship variant of the familiar problem of deciding the context to which a statement is indexed, since context and statement carry mutual implications. The statement may presuppose an agreed context (a known relation), or may alternatively have the effect of redefining its context (emphasizing the closeness of a relation not previously considered close).

Used in its widest sense, the verb "to bear" refers the hearer to Chamba clans and the relations between them. Both patriclans and matriclans are distinguished and named, and clan members share putative descent from a founder or founders, if they are known, who bore them all. Although maternal parentation is the dominant idiom of matriclanship and paternal parentation of patriclanship, nondominant idioms play important roles in the extension of clanship. The corporate clan categories are populated in the first instance by the direct descendants of the founders. The members of a matriclan (*kuni,* Daka; *kuna,* Leko) are consociated by the assumption of their common descent. Since Chamba genealogies are very short, only the genealogically arcane can progress far beyond the names of their grandparents. Clan membership effectively means the inheritance of membership of a named category from a parent, and a recognition of close common clanship with those who share that name.

Kuni/kuna, in a restricted sense, refers to the members of a named matriclan, but in a broader sense the same term includes this category and those whose fathers belonged to the clan. These are children of the matriclan; they are properly referred to as children borne by the clan. Collectively, they are brothers and sisters among themselves, and children in relation to the full members of the clan, who are addressed by terms for a senior generation relative (regardless of age). Thus all children of the matriclan call all male members of the matriclan "father," and may include an age marker in the designation. This relationship is one of the most important in traditional Chamba organization. As a further extension of the matriclan category, individuals whose father's father belonged to the matriclan stand in the collective relation of grandchildren to the full members of the clan, who are termed grandparents. Less commonly, individuals may be grandchildren of a matriclan by virtue of the membership of their maternal grandfather. Like the verb to bear, *kuni* has contextually shifting referents; it may refer to a group of matriclan members, or it may refer to the extended matriclan of full members, children and grandchildren. The referents used by Chamba informants would not distinguish the two notions in the way that I have.

Patriclanship is not quite a mirror image of the matriclan. The Chamba terms for patriclan that mean father's child or children (*da.mi*, sing., *da.membu*, plural, Daka; *ba.wa*, sing., Leko) refer primarily to the full members of the clan. Extension does not take place categorically, as with the matriclan, but by tracing the linkages of individuals through their mothers. Whereas the matriclan consists of three broad categories of members, patriclan membership is extended only to individual daughters' children, and their participation in patriclan affairs is crucial only in relation to a few ritual tasks, most particularly following their mother's death. The relative openness of matriclan organization, in its ability to co-opt the largest possible number of people into its activities (at least nominally, if not in fact), contrasts with the relative restriction of access to matters concerning the patriclan. This is a further feature of the more general contrast I have suggested between two forms of sociation.

Looked at from the vantage point of the individual, each Chamba may trace kinship connection to five or more clans (matriclan, patriclan, father's matriclan, mother's patriclan, father's father's matriclan, mother's father's matriclan, etc.), and may claim that some of the members of these clans bore him/her. Through these associations, the individual locates additional kin who are in different sociate relations, such as other individuals who are siblings because they were borne by the same matriclan. Alternatively, the local community may be envisaged in terms of its constituent clans: as a collection of patriclans or as a collection of matriclans. Who belongs in which category depends on the representation chosen. Patriclan and matriclan categorization are equally legitimate ways of looking at the community, although the terms differ in their appropriateness as circumstances change.

Taken together, these representations foster a distinctive style of thinking about association. Attention tends to be focused either on the personal network of ties, or on the clan framework of the community. Chamba have not elaborated the idea of lineages. Slightly more attention is paid to descent in the patriclan, but only as far back as a common grandfather or great grandfather, from whom their descendants might trace a close tie of parentation. Patriclans and matriclans may have internal sections, but these are not inter-related or internally organized in a strict genealogical idiom. In-stead, these sectional differences are represented as lesser versions of the differences between publicly transacted clanship categories.

Chamba representations move directly between the individual's unique network of kin ties and the community's shared framework of clan categories. But Chamba lack of interest in descent is more than compensated for by the extraordinary breadth of knowledge that active elders have of different individuals' places within the clan groupings—for it is the coordination between the individual and the corporate categories of the community that makes possible the calculation of responsibility and obligation. The tendency to rep-resent sociates as kin also undercuts the importance of specifically affinal relations; these relations are either terminologically assimi-lated to kin, or else neutralized by joking or avoidance. Virtually all sociates are treated as kin or quasi-kin, with the effect that Chamba communities are experienced as complex networks of different types of kin relations.

Kinship Terminology

Ego's Own Clanship

To penetrate the complex networks of different types of kin rela-tions, it is simplest to begin by looking at the terminology a speaker utilizes for members of his own unextended patriclan and matriclan (Table 2). The few differences in terminology that depend on the sex of the speaker, with one exception, occur in the first-ascending and first-descending generations away from ego. Alternate generational terms (grandparents and grandchildren) are forms of a single root, *ka*. Grandfather is composed of the root plus the male suffix *-lum*; grandchild is the same root plus a suffix which means small *ka.we*. The reciprocal of grandmother is *kag.we*. The relationship between grandparents and grandchildren is unmarked in Chamba culture; it is neither particularly indulgent nor particularly authoritarian, and is on the whole easygoing.

Sibling kinship terms are also simple. Elder and younger siblings are distinguished, and elder siblings, especially patrisiblings, should be shown respect. The eldest of a set of male siblings may simply be called big/old man, *nɛ.wari*, the general term of respect for adult men. Mapeo Chamba use the term *jigani*, "to follow" to express seniority of birth order. Those who follow in order of birth call their elder siblings, regardless of gender, *nena*, "older sibling," or *bɛ.we*, "younger sibling" (in which the diminutive suffix recurs). Siblings of different gender, who choose to suppress the reference to seniority, may use the terms *bɛ.lum.we* (sibling + masculine + diminutive) and *bɛ.ng.we* (sibling + feminine + diminutive). Seniority markers are never dropped between Mapeo men, and it seems significant that the cross-sex sibling terms suppress seniority by the use of reciprocal diminutives. Siblings tend to be very conscious of relative seniority.

The terminology for adjacent generations demands more attention to detail. There are four terms, two for lineal relations (mother, *nya*, and father, *da*), and two for collateral relations (mother's brother, *pɔbi*, and father's sister, *mala*). The terms are clearly paired. The reciprocal form for mother or father is child, *mi*; mothers and fathers "bear" *(wan)* children. The reciprocal terms for mother's brother and father's sister are their own diminutive forms: *pɔb.we*, sister's child, and *mala.we*, brother's child. These are collateral relations, since strictly the verb "to bear" should not be used directly to describe the link between the generations. Senior collaterals should express their relationship to their brothers' and sisters' children in mediated terms as "my sibling bore him/her." It is also significant that suffixes denoting seniority are used toward lineals, not collaterals of the first-ascending generation. Therefore, father and

TABLE 2

Mapeo Kinship Terminology

Terms for patriclan members

Generation	Male Alter	Female Alter
+2	ka.lum	ka
+1	da.wari (snr.), da.tiri (jnr.)	mala
0 (ego)	nena (snr.) bɛ.we (jnr.)	nena(snr.) bɛ.we(jnr.)
	bɛ.lum.we (B;fem. ego)	bɛ.ng.we (Z;male ego)
−1	mi (male ego)	mi (male ego)
	mala. we (fem. ego)	mala.we (fem. ego)
−2	ka.we (male ego)	ka.we (male ego)
	kag.we (fem. ego)	kag.we[4] (fem. ego)

Terms for matriclan members

(+2, −2, 0 generations as for patriclan)

	Male Alter	Female Alter
+1	pɔbi	nya.wari (snr.)
		nya.tiri (jnr.)
−1	pɔb.we (male ego)	pɔb.we (male ego)
	mi (fem. ego)	mi (fem. ego)

mother are marked for age relative to a person's own parents (*wari*, big; *tiri*, small), but collaterals are not marked in this way. Attention to seniority in Chamba terminology and in Chamba life especially concerns relationships between siblings, and between children and lineal relatives of the adjacent senior generation, namely, fathers and mothers.

At least in normative terms, if not always in practice, the roles of the four types of senior member of ego's own clans are clearly distinguished. A child should respect/fear (*lat*) his or her father. He should obey him, act with decorum in his presence, and never occupy a single mat with him. Sons may succeed to their father's compound, and take possession of a few objects with which he farmed

TABLE 2—*Continued*

Mapeo Kinship Terminology

Terms for members of ego's mother's patriclan

	Male Alter	Female Alter
+2	ka.lum	ka
+1	pɔb-təm-be	mi.nɔ
0	mi	mi
−1	ka.we (male ego)	ka.we (male ego)
	kag.we (fem. ego)	kag.we (fem. ego)
−2	no term, or assimilated to ka.we/kag.we	

Terms for members of ego's father's matriclan (all generations)

Male Alter	Female Alter
da.wari/da.tiri	mala/nya.tiri

Terms for members of ego's FF and MF matriclans (all generations)

Male Alter	Female Alter
ka.lum	mi.nɔ təng təng

[Abbreviations: B = brother; Z = sister]

and hunted; they will also be responsible for organizing the complicated observances following his death. Children should love their mothers (wɔ), and expect this affection to be returned. Like a son in the case of his father, a girl may inherit a few significant items associated with her mother, such as her farming implements, or perhaps the leg rattles she used for dancing, or her finery, her beads and suchlike.

Relations with collaterals are more strongly marked. *Mala*, the father's sister, is the most respected of relatives. Behavior in her presence, especially on a formal occasion, verges on avoidance. She may require the strictest etiquette of posture and address. *Pɔbi*, the mother's brother, occupies a slightly ambiguous position, at least in our terms. His relationship to his sister's son is built of elements that share the sense of closeness: the two have joint interests in property, in the condition and treatment of the body, and they are brought even closer through humor. The sister's son is the potential inheritor of his mother's brother's moveable goods, wealth objects, money, harvested crops, and fine gowns—everything, in fact, except the few objects that are commonly taken by a man's sons. A man may appropriate small items of property, beer, and fowl from his pɔbi's compound during the latter's lifetime.

During their lives, sister's children and mother's brother are bound together by their substantial relationship. Only the maternal uncle should inflict physical punishment on a child; only he can take the initiative to remove his sister's son or daughter from the community, by disposing of a breech birth, by giving away a child who cut upper teeth before lower, or by selling the child to settle a debt or gain goods or money. Should the child fall ill, it is the responsibility of the maternal uncle to raise the means from the members of the matriclan to pay for treatment to cleanse the violation of the cult rule responsible for the illness. Should any person or his or her pɔbi be implicated in witchcraft, guilt automatically descends upon both. Joking is permitted not only with the maternal uncle but also with his wife, the only senior-generation affine toward whom such behavior is enjoined.

Within the terms of my analysis of sociation, each individual is joined in consociated relations with the mother who bore him/her and her brother, who shares substance with her, and in adsociated relations with the father who bore him/her, and the sister who shares the qualities of patriclanship with him.

Ego's Extended Clanship

In addition to membership in their own clans, Mapeo Chamba occupy positions within a system of extended clanship. The English term "father's matriclan" is a direct translation of the Chamba terms, da.kuni (in Daka), and ba.kuna (in Leko); all those whose fathers were members of a clan are addressed as children by all clan members. In turn, they respond with terms for members of the senior generation: father, da, either older or younger than ego's own father, *mala*, for father's sisters, *nyatiri*, small mother, for women who call ego's own father *pɔbi*. This is the majority view. According to some informants, father's elder maternal sister may be called *nya.wari* and his younger half-sister *nya.tiri*. The clan members claim all these junior attached members as *mɛm wan.an.bu*, children borne by them. Since the ritual duties of extended clanship are not the concern of the youngest men, by the time these responsibilities are shouldered the father's matriclan is composed of two types of lineal relation: "small fathers" and "small mothers." Respect for their positions normally precludes the use of the modifier "small" (*tiri*), so in practice extended matriclanship between individuals and their father's matriclan revolves around three terms: children, fathers, and mothers. Members of each category are in classificatory relations of parenthood, siblingship, or childhood to the others.

One result of extended matriclanship is the elevation, by a generation, of a class of relatives which includes the patrilateral cross cousin (father's sister's son or daughter) (see Figure 10). Chamba offer two explanations for this. Some patrilateral cross cousins are children of the father's patriclan sisters (*mala*). As *mala* must be respected, likewise such respect should be extended to her children, who are therefore addressed by senior-generation terms.

However, this explanation cannot account for the extension of the term to the children of all women belonging to ego's father's matriclan, some of whom may be younger than ego. In these cases, informants explain the terminology in terms of the categorical relation of clanship between a father's matriclan and all the children it has borne. The pertinence of this distinction between two types of rationale becomes evident in Chamba communities where matriclanship has died out, since the close patrilateral cross cousins retain their privileged position so long as *mala* is respected, but the broader categorical relationship necessarily disappears along with the conception of matriclanship.

The terminological problem of extending clanship between individuals and their mother's patriclan requires a more complex solution (see Figure 11). The mother's patriclan is literally *nya.da.mi*, but more often the term for a woman of the ascending generation, *mi.nɔ*, discussed below, is used of the clan as a whole. Terminology is generational. Members of the alternate ascending generation are termed grandparents, and respond with the term grandchild. In the adjacent ascending generation we encounter two unfamiliar terms: for women *mi.nɔ*, and for men *pɔb.təm.be* Both terms have folk etymologies. *Mi.nɔ* is derived from the term for a woman who has given birth, especially a first birth (*mi*, child, *nɔ*, female) and *pɔb.təm.be* from mother's brother with, or of, the bow (*təmi*, bow). *Pɔbi* is said to be appropriate because the mother's paternal brother was "born with the mother," like her full or maternal brothers.

While logical in itself, this argument ignores the analogous case of the father's junior maternal classificatory sister, whom some claim should be called *nya.tiri*. The argument that she was "born with the father" would dictate that she be called *mala*. The suffix "with the bow" is subjected to different glosses: that he gives his sister's child his first arrow, that he is always prepared to defend his sister's child, and that he receives the back of any animal killed by his sister's child. None of these glosses is very convincing, nor do the rationales appear to be practiced.

Chamba kinship terminology seems to become ambiguous when

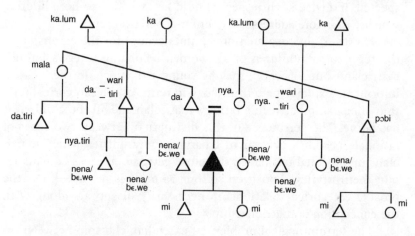

Parallel cousins = siblings
MB ch = children
FZ ch = parents
F = FB ≠ MB
M = MZ ≠ FZ

Figure 10 Mapeo Kinship Terminology Showing Skewing in Ego's Generation

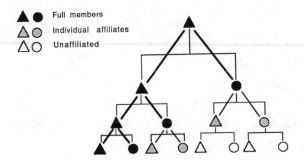

Figure 11 The Chamba Extended Patriclan

coping with relations between an individual and his or her mother's patriclan. If we compare the way in which the father's matriclan is handled, the problem becomes clearer. Extended matriclanship is based on the recognition of a relationship of parentation between two broad categories: parents and children. In contrast, Chamba patriclanship, a more closed idiom of organization, is incompatible with such broad-based recruitment. So, in the adjacent senior generation, always crucial to Chamba reckoning of relatedness, we find a modified collateral term, *pɔb.tɘm.be* and a new collateral term *mi.nɔ*. We can confirm that this is not a lineal term because its reciprocal is not child, *mi*. In fact, both of the terms have diminutive reciprocals, a feature that, as discussed earlier, characterizes collateral relations between adjacent generations. In short, the terminology has stopped short of recognizing parentation between a woman's paternal sisters and her children, although the choice of the term *mi.nɔ*, with its reference to childbearing, connotes parentation.

This seems an uncertain solution to the problem, and it may be significant that the term is so often used to refer to the mother's patriclan as a whole. Yet the alternatives, *mala* and *nya*, would clearly be inappropriate. In the absence of the maternally derived relationship of substance, the mother's paternal sister could not be called *nya*, mother. Similarly, the term father's sister would be inappropriate since there is no relationship of spirit to the father involved. To preserve the patrilaterality of the *mala* relation, and to avert the possibility of introducing considerations of shared substance to the patriclan, where they do not belong, there could be no alternative to introducing a new term. The example is instructive

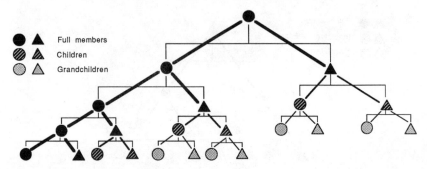

Figure 12 The Chamba Extended Matriclan

since the problem is intrinsic to the way central Chamba kinship is constructed, and the terminological resolution is found only in the kinship-term schedules of Daka-speaking Chamba communities that have double clanship.

To return to extended matriclanship (see Figure 12) is also to go back to the types of relationship Chamba kinship seems to cope with best, namely broad categories of parentation. Chamba are members of their paternal and maternal grandfathers' matriclans. All male matriclan members are addressed as grandfather, at least in ritual contexts in which the relationship is actualized. Female members of the matriclan are supposed to be called *mi.nɔ tɔng tɔng*. I must admit that I never heard this form of address used, but it derives from the ambiguous term that is applied to the mother's patrilateral sister, suffixed by two emphasizing particles that serve here to denote the distance between the people related.

In the course of constructing the clanship of a fictive Chamba individual, we have seen various points at which new kin may be discovered. Individuals may discover siblingship in their common relationship to a matriclan or patriclan, and they may develop their relationship in these terms if they find them conducive. Further room for maneuver in the definition of personal relations is created by the networks of ties between clan categories which we have yet to examine. As a result, Chamba frequently find themselves related in several ways. Where one relationship is clearly closer, and especially if it occurs within the limits of one's own clan, there is little reason to assert the more distant relationship. But in other cases, particularly where roughly equidistant multiple relationships are available, it is not unusual to find the same individuals occupying quite different relationships depending on the context of the moment.

Affinity

Mapeo Chamba terms of reference and address for affines, those who have married one's clanspeople, are susceptible to analysis in three classes: as proxy kin, respected affines, and familiar affines. The spouses of people called mother, father or grandparent are addressed by the appropriate kin term of the other gender—mother's husband is father, father's wife is mother, and so on. If seniority suffixes are used they are cued by reference to the status of the spouse belonging to ego's own clan; so *da.wari*'s wife (FeBW) is *nya.wari* regardless of her age. A person's own father's wives are ranked in relation to his or her own mother; "new wives," *nya pasi*, may be referred to literally as such. The affinal status of the spouses of senior generation kin is effectively ignored.

Two specifically affinal terms are used, though they are not subject to wide extension. *Mam.nwɔsi* is used reciprocally between mother's brother's wife and her husband's sister's children, and between the spouse of any older sibling and his or her spouse's younger siblings (eBW/HyB or HyZ; eZH/WyB or WyZ). The *mam.nwɔsi* relation is one of privileged abuse. The extension of this relation to *pɔbi*'s wife (MBW) seems especially significant, since no other spouse of senior generation kin is treated familiarly. The affix *mam-* indicates that this relationship belongs to a cluster of very close and familiar personal ties. Thus, *man.kasi* are a person's close age mates, with whom one shares lifelong obligations and an unwearying joking relationship. *Mana* means friend, and a Chamba saying avers that friends are greater than *kuni*, matrikin. On its own, *man* may be used in preference to *nɛ* to refer to someone close, like a coresident. Although not kin, members of this class are associated with relaxed, joking well-being. As such, they are integral to Mapeo Chambas' experience of a facet of their selves.

The husband of *mala* (FZ), the other main collateral, has no par-

ticular term applied to him and can only be referred to by the cir-
cumlocution "my paternal aunt's husband" (*mala.me suni*). The
spouses of the two senior generation collaterals are treated in diamet-
rically opposite fashions, both terminologically and behaviorally.

Apart from terms for husband (*suni*) and wife (*ngwu*), a single
root form, *gu*, is modified to express all other affinal relations within
which respect is required. *Gu.lum* (with masculine suffix) and *gu.nɔ*
(with feminine suffix) refer to men and women addressed by the
spouse as father and mother, or as younger sibling (yBW/HeB or
HeZ; yZH/WeB or WeZ). The reciprocal forms of these terms are
their diminutives, *gu.lum.we*, junior male affine, *gu.nɔ.we*, junior
female affine. The respect relation most actively informs the behavior of the younger affine toward the older, but the latter for his or her
part must respond with restrained conduct.

Clanship

Thus far, I have looked at multiple clanship from the perspective of
ego, the anthropologist's conventional individual. But the network
can also be envisaged from the perspective of the clan categories
themselves. All central Chamba are organized into named patriclans
and matriclans, but these two types of category are differentiated in
several ways.

The majority of common Daka names for matriclans are derived
from natural phenomena:

busum.kuni	ant clan
jam.kuni	mist clan
kongla.kuni	elephant clan
mi.san.ku.kuni	hare clan
mum.kuni	oil clan
wɔ.yit.kuni	loves guinea-corn clan
sa.mɛm.kuni	bird-children clan
su.kuni	sun clan
təmsi.kuni	sheep clan
wana.kuni	dog clan
wurum.kuni	spirit clan
yɛt.kuni	bushcow clan

Not all matriclans have origin stories, but those I have been able to record share a genre:

> The ancestress of the bushcow clan was a bushcow, one of a herd seen by a hunter removing their skins to wash. He stole the girl's skin and hid it [or covered it in stinging ants so that she could not bear to put it on]. She became his wife and bore him a son and a daughter. Later, the husband revealed the cow origin of his wife when he was drunk, and the mother and son resumed bushcow form and impaled him on their horns. They returned to the wild and left the daughter, from whom the clan is descended.[5]

> The ancestress of the dog clan gave birth while everyone was away farming. Her labor was assisted by a dog and so her descendants were known as the dog clan . . .

> Members of the loves guinea-corn clan are descended from an ancestress of enormous appetite, a trait which they are supposed to have inherited . . .

In a similar vein, the members of the elephant clan are descendants of an elephant and recount the same tale as the bushcow clan, but omit the later events involving the hunter's death. People of the sun clan are descended from a child born in the bush and left to dry in the sun after birth . . . and so forth. These origin tales are pleasing just-so stories. They are recounted with great gusto; clan members take the part of the animals involved and enact the events of origin in a spirit of fun. Sometimes the original characteristics of the clan names are supposed to descend upon the clan members: elephant clan members are large and clumsy; loves guinea-corn clanspeople are gluttons; members of the sheep clan behave like a flock and so on. Such associations are ammunition for a matriclan's joking partners, who taunt the clan members on all possible occasions, to the undiminished merriment of onlookers. Taunts of this type reflect the fact that much of the ethos of matriclanship, at this level at least, is lighthearted and jovial. History in any specific sense does not appear in these narratives, its place being taken by mythology.

Interrelations between matriclans, whether joking or cooperative, are based upon wordplay and associations between ideas evoked
by the clan names. So, in Mapeo, ritual cooperation is practiced between the dog, bushcow, elephant, and sun clans because they are
all people of the bush, a reference to associations in their origin
tales. In these terms, they have "one mother" and, during their rituals, they may choose to emphasize this relation by using sibling
terms for one another. For example, the joking relation between the
mist and sun clans began when they once tested the fortitude of an
old woman from each clan by leaving them outside to be respectively lashed by rain or scorched by sun. Again sociates are translated into a relevant kin category.

Both the stories of the origins of the matriclans, with their
shape-changing animals and their natural analogues, and the stories
of the inception of matriclan alliance in terms of "one mother" or
joking relations that draw on the same conventions, are marginal
members of a class of accounts that Mapeo Chamba call *tit jɔni*. *Tit*
literally means problem or account of events and *jɔni* is the verb to
laugh; a more idiomatic translation would be amusing tale. There
are scores of such tales that are told by adults to one another, for
instance to pass the time during collective farming, or by adults to
children, especially at evening around the hearth. These folktales
share genre characteristics with pan-African examples. The actors
are often animals or insects, although capable of metamorphosing
into humans and vice versa. The stories frequently offer explanations in "just-so" fashion and often deal with archetypal human foi-
bles: gluttony, avarice, lust, envy, cunning, greed, or general mischief-
making, by embodying these characteristics in animal exemplars.
Chamba do not say that the stories are untrue, but simply that they
have no way of knowing whether the events depicted took place
or not.

Matriclan tales are not strictly *tit jɔni*, which are defined as a
class by virtue of a prefacing statement in which the narrator announces the tale to be *tit jɔni* and the audience replies in the affir-
mative, but are said to resemble such tales. For a Chamba audience,
the factual basis of matriclan tales is much the same as that of the
amusing tales. The genre relies upon the credibility of events that,

considered possible, are nevertheless outside the range of everyday experience of most hearers.

I use the term mythological, in a restricted sense, to refer to these stylized features, which, at a conventional and public level, are credible and explanatory of certain aspects of matriclan and other organization. Mythological accounts are a form of social reckoning that is considered sufficient, providing pressing and divisive issues are not at stake. The absence of such accounts in most patriclan histories is indicative of a different form of social accounting that contexts of patriclanship almost always evoke.

Although matriclan accounts are characterized by mythology rather than history, in the restrictive senses in which I use the terms, matriclanship banishes history only apparently; historical accounts resurface in two contexts that share the characteristic of exerting duress on the conceptual impartibilities of matriclanship in general as well as of particular matriclans. The first context involves circumstances in which matriclans pursue claims to chiefly office or territorial prerogatives to the exclusion of the other matriclans of the community. Examples of this occurred in Part 1. The stories of the chiefly matriclans of *gang.kuni* (in Sugu, Da Dukdu, Nya Gangngwu, Kiri, and Danaba), its Leko equivalent *gat.kuna* (in Yeli, Balkossa, and Bangla), and the one-time chiefly clan of Gurum and Yebbi, *gang.tim.nɔ.kuni,* are all recounted in terms that share conventions with patriclan histories. The narratives of the chief of the red rock clan (*gang.van.ji.kuni* in Mapeo; *gat.bəng.yɛl.kuna* in Yeli) are similar since both clans press claims to have occupied the chiefships of these places at a time before the advent of the matriclan of the chief. The small "people of the hill clan" in Mapeo (*nɛ.kusum.be.kuni*), claims to have been settled on the hill with *gang.van.ji.kuni* before the expansion of Yeli influence and the arrival of their representatives, and presses a nominal claim to ownership of the land on this basis. The large *kɔm.kuni* clan, also of Mapeo, is believed to be descended from women taken as wives or slaves from the Koma, northern neighbors of the Mapeo Chamba, which again introduces historical elements. Finally, the *dəng.kuni* clan of Mapeo, which holds the present village headship under disputed circumstances, is remarkable because no convincing etymology of the name, which occurs only in Mapeo, can be agreed upon.[6]

A similar effect occurs in the event of duress within a matriclan. All but the smallest matriclans have internal sections. These sections may or may not be named, and knowledge of them is very unevenly distributed even among clan members. In intra-clan matters, the existence of sections is either passed over, since it is a breach of etiquette to mention them, or hotly denied. Most informants are reluctant to discuss the circumstances under which the sections arose; this reluctance is directly related to the historical circumstances of their formation. Regardless of the number of patriclans, every central Chamba community is divided into approximately the same number of matriclans. Given the substantial resettlement that has occurred, this implies regular processes of assimilation of new arrivals into preexisting matriclan categories. Despite their avowals in most contexts that all matriclan members have "one mother," in other contexts and in confidence, Chamba will say that in fact the different sections have "different mothers".

Sections were created by the arrival of immigrants and, most contentiously, by the purchase of slaves or the transference of members between matriclans in compensation for blood debts. It would be invidious to give examples I had been told in confidence but, apart from this, examples would be spurious. Nowadays, it is impossible to gain an accurate account of the sections with slave status since the matter is so contested. Accounts that have been offered to me rarely tally.

In a more public context, the identity of matriclan sections becomes public knowledge when accusations of witchcraft, a trait shared by close matrikin, are rife. Whether witchcraft is shared by the descendants of a common maternal grandmother, great grandmother, or clan section is not agreed as dogma. Other evidence is necessary to make a judgment in a specific case; in general, waves of suspicion emanate from the identified witch to closer and then more distant matrikin. Before external authorities took a hand, witches would either be beaten to death with staves and unceremoniously thrown into the bush or else sold into slavery. Now that such practices are illegal, matriclan members distance themselves from accusations by publicizing the internal divisions within the clan; in other words, they subvert the conventional assumption of a "one mother" relationship. In earlier times, such a strategy would probably have been the preamble to a resolution of the problem through expulsion of the witches and normal solidarity would be reinstated among the matrikin who remained. Now that expulsion is almost impossible, matriclan divisions may remain in the public domain.

It was only the persistence of this circumstance in the affairs of one Mapeo matriclan for several years that allowed me the initial discovery of the existence of matriclan sections. Without this circumstance, I am not sure whether I would have detected the presence of a level of matriclan sections between the named clan categories and the known relations of descent from a maternal grandmother or great grandmother. This may indicate the strength with which sections are conventionally denied.

Historical accounts of matriclan circumstances emerge under conditions of duress, as I have described them. There is therefore only an elective affinity, or a conventional appropriateness, between matriclanship and what I am calling consociation, and patriclanship and adsociation. If these two qualities of relationship were definitively tied to clan domains it would not be necessary to appeal to other terms. However, matters are more fluid and more complex.

The mixture of familiarity and authority that protects the matriclan slaves parallels the mother's brother/sister's son relation in which privileged humor is similarly juxtaposed to corporal authority. But privileged humor is not the prerogative of matriclanship. It occurs between patriclans in joking relations, between larger ethnic categories (like Chamba and Bachama), and between age mates. In each of these cases, humor is considered appropriate because there exists a context in which those involved may deny the apparent differences separating them and state "we are one." The play of similarity and difference in culture is contextual and nuanced. Only in simplified terms can we note the strong correlation between permanent states of "oneness" or "togetherness" (*noni*) and "difference" or "separateness" (*ti ti* or *gong gong*).

In these terms, the ethos of patriclanship contrasts strongly with that of matriclanship. Patriclan names derive from non-Chamba ethnic origins (such as Bata, Pere, or Yangur), from indigenous Chamba Daka groupings (such as Mangla, Jangani, or Tola), from patriclan clusters (Yambu, Sama), or from offices and places associated with the clan. Like their names, the narratives of the development of the patriclan are considered to be historical accounts of actual occurrences.

Patriclan historians are attracted to the legendary, especially when their founders are concerned, but hardly ever to the mythological. Legendary and mythological, as I use them here, imply different levels of plausibility. Legendary events are enacted by extraordinary individuals in a mundane world. The contrast between event and context highlights the extraordinary character of the actor. Mythological events involve actors and a context more remote from the mundane world. I have never heard a humorous account of a patriclan history. Patriclans are explicitly politicized in a way that matriclans become only under duress.

Further indication of the differences between the two types of clanship can be derived from their sizes and their mutual relationships. Although there is a large number of matriclan names in Chambaland, a local community is composed of about a dozen clans. Nominal and purely conventional equivalences are used to reduce the number of clans by assimilating incomers. So, wherever Chamba travel within Chambaland (and even among some neighbors like Koma, Vere and Pere, if we are to believe their accounts) they are able to find their own matriclan. Matriclanship is assumed to be pervasive, and a single grid covers Chambaland and beyond. When traveling, or moving to another village, an individual simply has to find the place that he assumes must exist for him in the new community.[7]

The obverse assumption is made of patriclanship. Since patriclans possess unique cultures and are historically differentiated, patriclanship is immutable. Patriclans are never, to my knowledge, merged, even when they appear to be on the point of extinction. Except where relationship is demonstrable, an incomer who is not a slave cannot be incorporated into a Chamba patriclan. Patriclanship stands aside from interfering with demographic processes with the predictable result that Chamba communities contain widely different numbers of patriclans depending on their histories, and that these patriclans range in scale much more widely than matriclans (see Appendix 1 for a numerical demonstration of this for Mapeo).

Both patriclans and matriclans are interrelated with clans of their own type in a number of ways. Joking relations (*kpɔmbu*) are recognized between matriclans and between patriclans in much the same way; in both cases, the relationship involves specific forms of cooperation in ritual, although cooperation between matriclans allows the joking partners greater participation in the more esoteric rites than does patriclan partnership. Relations of shared parentation are traced differently. One-mother relations between matriclans, as we saw from the example of the "people of the bush," rest on associations between mythological origins and relate large categories of people. One-father relations between patriclans are traced primarily on the basis of historical similarities involving ethnic or geographical origins. Not all patriclans have such origins in common with other members of the local community, and in this case they recognize no relations of shared parentation with them. In Mapeo, slightly exceptionally I think, patriclans may recognize parentation by virtue of sharing a single major cult (*jubi*) (see Appendix 1).

Since patriclans are co-resident groups or, more precisely, parts of them are co-resident at present, and because patriclan histories claim that all patrikin were co-resident in the past, they recognize a broader array of relations not available to the residentially dispersed matriclan categories. Co-resident patriclans, literally those of the compound entrance, *ya isa tu bu*, recognize ritual responsibilities of cooperation. Again, with regard to Mapeo, my impression is that the significance of this relation has been especially developed under circumstances peculiar to Mapeo history.

Patriclanship and matriclanship are further contrasted in terms of the activities they are encharged with. The patriclan, consistent with its idiom of relationship through spirit, is responsible for the passage of its members through life—a passage punctuated by naming, initiation, perhaps installation to patriclan office and, eventually, death and its complex of funerary observances. As a residential grouping, conscious of its prestige, the patriclan should respond to any call for group assistance by a member including, if need be, physical violence following the murder of a clansman, or the theft of his property or wife. In cases of murder, we find an interesting relation between the two clan domains. Although patriclansmen should seek to avenge the death of a kinsman, *quid pro quo*, a settlement may be arranged by the transference of a member of the slayer's matriclan, usually a child, to the victim's matriclan. Unlike the matriclan, the patriclan cannot accept a body equivalent for its slain member, whose unique spirit can be restored only by becoming human once more. The efforts of the patriclan only benefit the victim's matriclan. A similar contrast is made with respect to slavery. An individual may only have slave status (kǝsani, in Daka; kɔsa, in Leko) in the matriclan; Mapeo informants are dogmatic that nobody can be a slave in his or her patriclan.[8]

Matriclanship is consistently linked to body values and, as noted before, this linkage emerges frequently when matrikin find themselves collectively obliged to provide compensation that must be paid when a member is "caught" by a cult belonging to one of the other clans of the community. Some of the cults are considered to act indiscriminately against matrikin. A cult may "catch" a matriclan member other than the transgressor of the cult regulation and, if the cult is not "repaired," it will "follow" the matriclan, causing affliction, and maybe even death, to more of its members. The collective obligations of matriclanship are matched by their collective vulnerability to cult contagion and to witchcraft accusation.[9] Matriclanship reaps the consequences of extreme proximity between its members, whether these be desirable or not.

This chapter began with an account of the two debts Chamba children owe their parents: a spiritual debt to the father, and a fleshly debt to the mother. The ramifications of this distinction have carried us far. Two clan domains are distinguished by central Chamba and subjected to systematic contrast. Matriclanship, associated with the mother, lineally, and her brother, collaterally, is the domain of empathetic relations between people united through shared substance. Its organization is open, since the matriclan categories are large, pervasive within Chambaland, linked by relations of parentation to other matriclans, and categorically extended to "children" and "grandchildren."

The historical content of matriclanship is concealed in the interests of solidarity, and its past is treated as mythological play. It is the most permissive form of organization, and licenses privileged abuse between some members of adjacent generations. On the other hand, the bodily image of matriclanship also involves it with sickness, witchcraft, physical punishment, and slavery. The substantial theme of matriclanship recurs in the inheritance of property between mother's brother and sister's son, and the access the boy enjoys to his uncle's property during the latter's lifetime.

The patriclan is an assembly of unique individuals joined by history and distinct culture. Under the sterner guidance of the father and his sister, it is responsible for the individual's spiritual passage through life. Boys inherit a name, a place to live, fields to farm, a few implements especially associated with their father, and membership of a group that will assert their rights with physical violence should it be necessary. Patriclans are radically distinct, and membership rights are extended outside the patrikin only to daughters' children as individuals. Categorical extension of the patriclan is truncated in the ambiguous position of the mother's paternal sister, part lineal and part collateral. Girls leave their patrikin at marriage, but may return at divorce, and will certainly return to be buried in their patriclan graveyard. The memory of the deceased is the particular obligation of the patriclan and its skull shrine.[10]

The joint extent of the clan domains, and the tendency of Mapeo Chamba to convert other sociates into kin, places every Mapeo Chamba individual at the center of a ramifying and complex set of kinship relations. Different individuals devise different strategic uses for their kin networks; not everyone devotes the same degree of attention to matriclan and patriclan affairs. But the differences between the proper affairs of matrikin and patrikin, and between the two types of kin sociation, are relatively constant throughout Chambaland. Historically, this relation has been subject to change, and the next chapter demonstrates both the similarities between the central Chamba forms and the types of changes they may accommodate.

CHAPTER 8

TRANSFORMATIONS IN SOCIATION

The detailed investigation of Mapeo Chamba patterns of sociation presented in Chapter 7 makes it possible to pick out a few critical features to subject to comparative examination. Once the significant differences in patterns of sociation among a number of Chamba communities have been located, it is but a further a short step to begin to relate them to the historical narrative of Part 1, and thereby examine the degree to which transformational analysis can be made to yield data on historical change within a known chronology.

As in the more detailed analysis of kinship provided in the previous chapter, I approach patterns of sociation from the viewpoints of the individual (ego), and the larger categories of communal organization respectively. Taking Mapeo kinship and clanship as a baseline, I compare these data with those from other central Chambaland communities, from Gurum and Mbangan, to represent the Nakɛnyare Chamba, and from Yeli, to represent the residual Leko. Since Yeli is historically related to Nakɛnyare, I note any divergences between Yeli and Sapeo, which is a Leko-speaking community not sharing this relationship. Three other sets of data represent Chamba outside central Chambaland. The Daka data, the most deficient, are entirely based upon Meek's early researches, since I have not worked in a Daka area (Meek 1931b I:78 et seq.). The southwestern Daka need to be included in the survey, despite deficiencies in information about them, because they represent indigenous groupings that have not been subjected to Nakɛnyare influences. The Chamba of the conquest chiefdoms are represented by Donga from the Benue group, and Bali Gangsin from the Bamenda Grassfields group. The information on Donga Chamba kinship and clanship given by Garbosa and Meek, our major historical sources in Part 1, is slight, so I am reliant for most of it on incomplete notes taken during a very brief visit of my own. Bali Chamba kinship and clanship data are from my own researches, unless another source is specifically acknowledged.[1] Together, these communities are representative of most of the types of Chamba political organizations that came into existence in the two centuries before the present. The conquest chiefdoms, the most recent, were founded in the latter part of the nineteenth century; Mapeo had emerged as a hill refuge earlier in the century, whereas the central and southern Nakɛnyare chiefdoms and Yeli are of earlier foundation, certainly eighteenth century or earlier. We have no means of assessing the antiquity of the present Daka settlements. Local variations from these types can be suggested on the basis of less extensive data from other communities.

Comparative Kinship Terminology

Conventionally, conclusions follow the presentation of data, but matters will be clearer if the provisional results of our survey are given first. Formally, Mapeo kinship terminology is very similar to that of other central Chamba, regardless of language and dialect. This similarity throws doubt on some theories of Chamba development that propose a fusion of matrilineal and patrilineal peoples in relatively recent times. On the other hand, there is little reason to suppose that central Chamba kinship at the time of the diaspora was different from now. Differences show up in the three schedules of kinship terminology from outside Chambaland. Daka terminology is consistent with the reported absence of patriclanship, whereas the terminologies from Donga and Bali seem to represent different reactions to the disappearance of matriclanship. Convergent evidence that suggests an attenuation of matriclanship in the conquest chiefdoms can be derived from an examination of data from chiefdoms in the northern Shebshi Mountains where matriclan attenuation is less marked than in the emigrant Chamba communities.

The most significant terms in Mapeo kinship terminology are generally those extended to members of ego's own generation and the generations adjacent to it (see Table 3). Within ego's generation,

TABLE 3

Comparative Kinship Terminology: Ego's Generation

Parallel cousins and siblings

	Seniority denoting		Gender denoting	
Mapeo	nena	(eB/eZ)	bɛ.ng.we	(Z)
	bɛ.we	(yB/yZ)	bɛ.lum.we	(B)
Nakɛnyare	bɛ.wari	(eB/eZ)	bɛ.ng.we	(Z)
	bɛ.mi	(yB/yZ)	bɛ.lum.we	(B)
Yeli	nena	(eB)	kun.kena	(yZ/Z)
	moma	(eZ)	kud.vɛla	(yB/B)
	kuna	(B/Z)		
Daka	?		biangwu	(Z)
			biari	(B)
Donga	nia	(eB)		
	ma	(eZ)		
	kuna	(B/Z)		
Bali	ni	(eB)		
	ma	(eZ)		
	kun.je	(yB/Z)		
	kuna	(B/Z)		

Cross-cousin terms

	Patrilateral (FZD/FZS)	Matrilateral (MBD/MBS)
Mapeo	nya.tiri (FZD); da.tiri (FZS)	mi
Nakɛnyare	nya.sɔka (FZD); da.sɔka (FZS)	mi
Yeli	na.gira (FZD); ba.gira (FZS)	wa
Daka	nya.tirere (FZD); da.tirere (FZS)	mie/sangko
Donga	mala (FZD); bati (FZS)	(?wa)
Bali	as siblings	as siblings

Abbreviations: e = elder; y = younger; F = father; M = mother; B = brother; Z = sister; S = son; D = daughter; not shown: H = husband; W = wife. *Hence:* eB = elder brother; FZD = father's sister's daughter; MeZ = mother's elder sister, etc. (Note: Daka terms in this and subsequent tables in this chapter follow Meek's transcription)

Mapeo terminology assimilates parallel cousins to siblings, shifts patrilateral cross cousins up one generation, and matrilateral cousins down one generation. This terminology reflects the organization of Mapeo clanship. Parallel cousins are members of ego's own clans, thus terminologically siblings, sharing either male or female parentation. Patrilateral cross cousins are elevated by virtue of their membership in ego's father's matriclan, in the case of the father's full or matrilateral sisters, or by virtue of the respected position of the father's sister, ego's *mala*, in the case of the father's full or patrilateral sisters. The elevation by one generation of the children of the father's full sister is overdetermined, in the sense that informants may attribute it to two rationales. The demotion of matrilateral cross cousins by a generation is explicable in terms of the logic of extended matriclanship. Ego is a member of alter's father's matriclan and, therefore, in a relation of parentation to alter. Given the close relation between clanship and kinship terminology, changes in one would most probably be reflected in changes in the other.

Formally, the three central Chamba schedules make similar discriminations, although they do so in different languages and dialects. Many of the differences concern suffixes. Mapeo and Nakɛnyare share root forms for sibling (*bɛ*), mother (*nya*), and father (*da*), but use different modifiers for seniority and juniority. The only difference in terminology concerns older brother, for which Mapeo shares a form with the Leko speakers of Yeli. Since Sapeo Chamba have a similar term (*nia*), which occurs also in the Bali and Donga schedules, the Mapeo usage is presumably a Leko loan word. Yeli terminology develops most sibling forms from the root *kuna*, the sense of which is not restricted to matriclan, like the Daka *kuni*. Yeli Chamba use gender-marked terms for older siblings. As far as we can judge from Meek's incomplete data, Daka terms are minor dialectal variants of those used among Nakɛnyare and Mapeo Chamba. We know, from the previous chapter, that this arrangement of terms for zero-generation kin is compatible with the presence of extended matriclanship.

As shown in Table 3, major differences occur in the two Leko-language schedules of the conquest chiefdoms of Bali and Donga, outside Chambaland; the differences center on the treatment of cross cousins. The Donga schedule follows the central Chamba practice of raising patrilateral cross cousins one generation, but it does so differently. Central Chamba matriclanship creates the relation of parentation between an ego and his or her patrilateral cross cousins on account of the more inclusive relationship between the categories of "children" and the father's matriclan which bore them. Both patrilateral cross cousins (FZD and FZS) are merged with lineally related members of the adjacent senior generation. Donga kinship manages the same generational adjustment by merging patrilateral cross cousins and senior patriclan members. This does not alter the term used for FZS, but it does mean that FZD is addressed as paternal aunt and not as junior mother. Meek states that the terms for patrilateral cross cousins are "honorific," which I would interpret to mean that the reason offered for their promotion derives from the respected position of the paternal aunt, or *mala* (Meek 1931b I:381). Meek does not tell us whether matrilateral cross cousins are demoted a generation. Presumably, the reciprocal of *ba.ti*, small father, must be child; and the reciprocal of *mala* may either be the same, or a diminutive form of *mala* itself. But without matriclanship, this usage can be extended only to the children of the mother's full and patrilateral brothers. Among the central Chamba, the most important extension of the term occurs in the relationship between ego and the children of the mother's matrilateral brothers, who belong to the category of "children borne by the mother's matriclan." The Bali schedule differs more radically. Parallel and cross cousins are all addressed by sibling terms. In other words, the terminology simply distinguishes generation. This implies the absence of matriclanship and the ending of the practice which extends the honorific status of the father's sister to her children.

Concerning the parental generation (Table 4), Mapeo terminology draws distinctions between lineals and collaterals in the first-ascending generation, which is crucial to the construction of the twin domains of clanship.

In common with the terminological system for ego's generation, the three central Chamba schedules for the first-ascending generation are formally similar. All distinguish mother's and father's siblings, and recognize two lineal terms, mother and father, which are modified relative to ego's age, and two collateral terms, mother's brother and father's sister.

TABLE 4

Comparative Kinship Terminology: the Parental Generation

Father's full siblings

	FeB	FeZ	F	FyB	FyZ
Mapeo	da.wari	mala	da	da.tiri	mala
Nakɛnyare	da.wari	mala	da	da.sɔka	mala
		nya.mala.ngwu			nya.mala.ngwu
Yeli	ba.gba'a	mala	ba	ba.gira	mala
Daka	dabori	nyabori	ba	datirere	nyatirere
Donga	ba.we	mala	ba	ba.ti	mala
Bali	ba.gbo'o	mali.gbo'o	ba	ba.je	mali.je

Mother's full siblings

	MeB	MeZ	M	MyB	MyZ
Mapeo	pɔbi	nya.wari	nya	pɔbi	nya.tiri
Nakɛnyare	pɔbi	nya.wari	nya	pɔbi	nya.sɔka
Yeli	muna	na.gba'a	na	muna	na.gira
Daka	kawo	nyabori	nya	kawo	nyatirere
Donga	muna	na.we	na	muna	na.ti
Bali	muni.gbo'o	na.gbo'o	na	muni.je	na.je

The terms for father's sister differ among northern and southern Nakɛnyare. The northern Nakɛnyare, emigrants from the east, share with other eastern Chamba (Mapeo, Yeli, and Sapeo), as well as other emigrants from the east (Donga), the simple term *mala* for paternal aunt. Southern Nakɛnyare prefer the compound "mother–paternal aunt–woman" (*nya.mala.ngwu*), which is shortened to "mother," with the reciprocal "child," as a form of address. In this respect, the southern Nakɛnyare term is similar to the Daka schedule, in which mother is used of the father's sister. This strengthens the supposition that the development of patriclanship among southern Nakɛnyare may have been related to Leko influences. *Mala* would appear to be a Leko term, and the evidence suggests there is no equivalent term that derives historically from the Daka language.

However, both languages possess terms for the matrilateral col-lateral relative (MB). Meek, unfortunately, appears to have recorded a variant of the Fulfulde term *kawu* as a Daka term for maternal uncle. It seems probable that the Chamba Daka language term is found also among the southwestern Daka people. This distribution of terms is consistent with the argument that both Leko and Daka speakers of Chamba have recognized matriclans throughout the pe-riod for which a historical reconstruction can be proposed.

Many of the differences among the terms collected from the same language group involve the suffixes denoting seniority, which vary between dialects. With the exception of the Bali schedule, sen-

TABLE 5

Comparative Kinship Terminology: Parental Generation
(Parents' Half Siblings)

Father's matrilateral siblings

	FeB	FeZ	FyB	FyZ
Mapeo	da.wari	mala nya.wari	da.tiri	mala nya.tiri
Nakɛnyare	da.wari	mala nya.mala.ngwu	da.sɔkɑ	mala nya.mala.ngwu
Yeli	ba.gba'a	mala	ba.gira	mala
Daka	dabori	nabori	datirere	nyatirere
Donga	ba.we	mala	ba.ti	mala
Bali	bagbo'o	mali.gbo'o	ba.je	mali.je

Mother's patrilateral siblings

	MB	MZ
Mapeo	pɔb.tɜm.be	mi.nɔ
Nakɛnyare	pɔb.tɜm.be	mi.nɔ
Yeli	mun.tab.bea	na
Daka	kawo	nya
Donga	(ʔmuna)	(ʔna)
Bali	muni	na

iority modifiers are suffixed to lineal but not collateral terms. Senior, but never junior, suffixes may occasionally be employed by central Chamba as a sign of special respect.[2]

More far-reaching differences show up in the terms for parents' half siblings (see Table 5).

Since we are particularly interested in the extension of these terms to broad categories of kin, there are limitations to what may be inferred from secondary sources that provide terms with the conventional single genealogical referents. To compensate for these omissions, I utilize evidence from clanship. In the cases of the three central Chamba schedules, to examine these first, terms for parents' half siblings are also used in classificatory senses for all the members of the relevant clans of the same generation. Thus, terms for father's matrisiblings apply to members of the father's matriclan, and terms for mother's patrisiblings to the members of her patriclan.

The terms applied to male half siblings of either parent are straightforward. They are identical in the two central Chamba Daka language schedules, apart from dialectal variation in the junior suffix. Terms in the Yeli schedule are literal equivalents of the Daka language set. In all three cases, the father's half brothers who belong to his matriclan are termed "father," and the mother's half brothers who belong to her patriclan are "maternal uncles of the bow."

The terms for female half siblings are somewhat more complex. In the case of the father's maternal half sisters, central Chamba notions appear equivocal, and opinions on correct terminology vary. There is, however, no equivocation that father's maternal half-sister's children (FZS/FZD) are termed "small father" and "small mother." This follows from the fact that, despite their belonging to ego's generation, these relatives are members of the matriclan that bore ego. In practical terms, these ego-generation kin are the people whom an adult ego will most often encounter as representatives of that clan. To put it another way, the class of father's half-sister's children, rather than that of father's half sisters, is marked to indicate extended matriclanship. In the case of the father's maternal sister, reasonings derived from the contrasting logics of kinship and clanship conflict. Yeli informants consistently hold to the kinship logic: "women who address your father as brother are your paternal aunts, *mala*; those who address him as maternal uncle, *muna*, you call mother." Some Mapeo informants reason identically. But, following the logic of clanship, I have also heard father's maternal sisters in Mapeo addressed as mother, *nya*. In this case, informants reason that, as the woman in question belongs to the clan that bore ego, she must be called "mother." To reconcile these contradictory modes of thought, Mapeo informants propose two different compromises. One viewpoint holds that the closeness of the relation between father and father's classificatory maternal sister is crucial. If the relationship was demonstrable, the woman was "paternal aunt," if not, she was "mother." A second school of thought asserts that the distinction depends on seniority. Father's senior classificatory maternal sisters were classed with paternal aunts and his junior classificatory maternal sisters were classed with mothers.

More important than the specific solutions proposed, for my present purpose, is the way in which areas of uncertainty in the kinship terminology reveal the principles upon which informants consider the logic of the extension of terms to rest. The southern Nakɛnyare term for father's maternal half sister appears, from this perspective, to have the best of both kinship-and clanship-based logics. Like the father's full sister, his maternal sister is termed *nya.mala.ngwu*, (mother—paternal aunt—woman). In address, this term of reference is shortened to mother. Taking the Yeli, Mapeo, and southern Nakɛnyare solutions to this terminological quandary as a series, we can note that: the Yeli solution derives from the logic of patrikinship; the Mapeo solution draws ambiguously on the logics of kinship and clanship; and the southern Nakɛnyare solution favors the logic of extended matriclanship. This generalization is consistent with my supposition that patriclanship has developed more recently in the west than in the east.

Mother's paternal half sisters are called by the ambiguous term *mi.nɔ* (child—female), both in Mapeo and among southern Nakɛnyare. I noted in the previous chapter that this term appears to have connotations of both lineality and collaterality. I found no Leko equivalent to this term in Yeli, where mother's paternal half sisters are called by the same term as mother.[3]

Daka terminology, as previously remarked, apparently lacks a special term for father's sister. Meek records no term equivalent to the Mapeo term for mother's paternal half sister, and no modification of the maternal uncle term to refer to the mother's paternal half brother (although he could not discover this, even if it existed, having taken a Fulfulde term for maternal uncle). The data are admittedly poor but, accepting the presence of matriclans, I would expect that all father's maternal half sisters would be addressed as mother and all maternal half brothers as father, by virtue of their co-membership in ego's father's matriclan. Without patriclan groupings, the term for mother's paternal half siblings cannot be generalized beyond the polygynous household. In fact, the status may be anomalous, since Meek reports virtual monogamy among the Daka.

Donga and Bali schedules are formally not very different from their central Chamba Leko counterparts. In neither case could I find the modified term for maternal uncle applied by central Chamba to mother's male patrisibling. We have already noted one difference in the Bali tendency to add suffixes to collateral terms to denote seniority relative to ego's parents. But the apparent similarities conceal difference. Since there are no matriclans among Bali Chamba, father's matrisiblings cannot be traced far. Terms for such relatives are extended, according to informants, only to people addressed as siblings by their father, specifically, children of his mother's previous or subsequent marriages, and possibly the children of her full sisters. As matriclans are absent in Donga as well, the situation is likely to be similar. In both cases, the persistence of groupings in a patrilineal idiom permits wider extension of terms to the mother's patrisiblings, who are members of a named category. If this reasoning is correct, the Bali and Donga cases should be mirror images of the Daka case, at least to the extent that Daka matriclan groupings allow extension of kinship to the father's matrisiblings as a category, whereas kinship to mother's patrisiblings is restricted. In contrast, Bali and Donga patriclan groupings do the opposite. Most significantly, this implies different patterns of sociation from those found in central Chambaland, where kinship is generalized both patrilaterally and matrilaterally.

The Mapeo, Yeli and Nakɛnyare schedules all make a distinction between lineals and collaterals in the first-descending generation (see Table 6) that correponds to that made in the first-ascending (parental) generation. Accordingly, ego addresses as child anyone who calls him or her, father or mother; and ego responds with a

TABLE 6

Comparative Kinship Terminology: the First-Descending Generation

	Male or female speaker			Male Speaker	Female Speaker
	BS	BD	S/D	ZS/ZD	BS/BD
Mapeo	mi	mi	mi	pɔb.we	mala.we
Nakɛnyare	mi	mi	mi	pɔb.mi	mala.mi/mi
Yeli	wa	wa	wa	mun.vɛla	mala.vɛla
Daka	mie	mie	mie	pwa vi (ZS)	mie
				pwa me (ZD)	
Bali	wa	wa	wa	wa	wa

Note: known Donga terms are identical to Bali; unfortunately no information is available concerning cross-cousin terminology

diminutive term when addressed as paternal aunt or maternal uncle. The Daka terms differ because there is no specialized term for paternal aunt. Father's sister is merged with mother, which always has the reciprocal form of child. This characteristic is shared by southern Nakɛnyare, among whom paternal aunt (*nya.mala.ngwu*) is shortened to mother (*nya*) in address, with a reciprocal form child, *mi*. Among Bali Chamba, the distinction between lineals and collaterals, although made in the first-ascending generation, is completely ignored in the first-descending generation, all members of which are addressed as child. The symmetrical arrangement of lineal and collateral relatives in adjacent generations thus seems unique to Chamba double clanship systems, although it is ambiguous in the southern Nakɛnyare case.

I earlier noted the marginality of grandparental relations to Chamba reckoning of clanship, a feature that is consistent with the relative absence of interest in step-by-step descent, rather than parentation and shared descent. None of the schedules (see Table 7) makes distinctions based on patrilineality or matrilineality between grandparents or grandchildren. In the absence of extended matriclanship, grandparental terms cannot be used in Bali or Donga to mark

TABLE 7

Comparative Kinship Terminology: Grandparents' and Grandchildren's Generations

	Grandfather	Grandmother	Grandchild
	FF = MF	FM = MM	SS = DS = SD = DD
Mapeo	ka.lum	ka	ka.we/kag.we
Nakɛnyare	ka.lum	kaki	kang.mi/kak.mi
Yeli	do.ra	ka	wa.kasa
Daka	karim	kari	kangme
Bali	do	ka	wa.ka

the relationship between an ego and his or her father's father's or mother's father's matriclans, as happens among all central Chamba. We do not know if Daka matriclanship is extended to the same extent as among central Chamba. Meek had not understood Chamba extended clanship and therefore did not pursue inquiries that could help us.

All Chamba use the appropriate other-gender kinship terms to refer to the spouses of people they call grandparent, mother, or father. Mapeo Chamba and Nakɛnyare employ specifically affinal terminology to address spouses of the maternal uncle or an older sibling (joking affines) and spouses of younger siblings, children, or the parents of their own spouses (respected affines) (see Table 8). Yeli Chamba use similar terms, but claim that the separation of two types of relation to siblings' spouses is a Fulani custom; they include all siblings' spouses in the joking category. Throughout Chambaland, specifically affinal terminology is not applied more extensively than to spouses of actual siblings and parents. Daka usage seems to correspond to that of the central Chamba Daka speakers. Meek records distinct terms for older brother's wife and mother's brother's wife, but the first will probably transpire to be a contraction of the second. The Donga schedule is distinctive from that of Bali because Donga Chamba retain a joking affinal relation with the spouses of their maternal uncles and older siblings. This usage has disappeared in Bali, where the mother's brother's and older siblings' spouses are simply referred to by the kinship status of ego's relative, plus the relevant morpheme for husband or wife.

In summary, the detailed terminological data discussed here indicate that the Chamba within Chambaland share a broadly similar kinship system despite their linguistic and dialectal differences. It is a system of double-extended clanship, marked by shallow genealogies, and it utilizes as diagnostic terms those employed in ego's and ego's adjacent generations. In the first-ascending generation, the most important distinction is that between lineal and collateral relatives. In ego's generation, the significant feature is the distinction between parallel and cross cousins. In the first-descending generation, reciprocal forms of the adjacent senior-generation collateral terms are used, and the distinction between lineal and collateral relatives is maintained.

The lack of patriclan organization among the southwestern Daka groups correlates with the absence of the collateral term for father's sister in the ascending generation, and correspondingly, the absence of a reciprocal collateral term for a female speaker towards her brother's child in the descending generation. Instead, the relation is lineal, mother to child. Other features of Daka terminology suggest a central Chamba form of extended matriclanship.

Benue and Bali Chamba both retain the central Chamba distinctions between lineal and collateral relations in the adjacent senior

TABLE 8

Comparative Affinal Terminology

	Joking affine Reciprocal terms	Respected affine Senior terms (male/female)	Junior suffix
Mapeo	mam.nwɔsi	gu.lum/gu.nɔ	-we
Nakɛnyare	mam.nwɔsi	gu.lum/gu.nɔ	-mi
Yeli	mang.nara	gun.vana/gun.kena	-letera
Daka	mashi/mangwashi	gwom	?
Donga	mana	gun.vana/gun.kena	?
Bali	(none)	gun.vana/gun.kina	(none)

generation. Of these two emigrant groups, it seems that the Bali Chamba have fewer central Chamba features. There are no generational shifts of cross cousins in ego's own generation, although these are retained in Donga; and the reciprocal terms for collateral relatives of the senior generation are entirely absent from the junior generation, who are all addressed as children. Even the class of joking affines, which persists in Donga, is unknown to Bali Chamba.

Kinship Variation and Time: Historical Hypotheses

Based on the history of Chambaland, discussed in Chapters 4 and 5, a number of hypotheses may be suggested to account for the variations in kinship patterns evident among Chamba. Since Daka lack patriclanship, we may suppose that, at least in the southern area of Chambaland, organization into patriclans was somehow associated with the introduction of chiefship by peoples claiming Yeli associations. The presence or absence of patriclans appears to be the only significant kinship-related difference between the Daka speakers within the Nakɛnyare chiefdoms and those outside them. Early patriclan organization was probably based upon locality once the Daka rule of matrilocality was replaced by one of patrilocality.[4] Hypothetically, this might have occurred concurrent with an expansion of polygyny, reported by Meek to be unworkable under the Daka system of matrilocality. Even more tentatively, it could be suggested that the rate of polygyny would tend to rise with the establishment of a chiefship and chiefly officials, especially if this occurred at the same time that the chiefdom became tied into the Jukun trade network, possibly as an exporter of slaves. Local emigrations, as our Mapeo case history suggests, were probably instrumental in multiplying the number of patriclans within Chamba communities.

We have no reason to suppose that, when they departed Chambaland, the nineteenth-century emigrants had kinship systems different from those of their contemporaries who stayed behind; and there is no reason either, to suppose that the clanship system of their contemporaries differed radically from that of present-day central Chamba. In the emigrant cases, the attenuation of matriclanship among them must have occurred during their diaspora and subsequent settlement. A number of reasons for this development may be advanced. Intermarriage with non-Chamba women might automatically lead to matriclans dying out within a couple of generations, unless the women either had matriclans for which Chamba could find equivalents, or were given matriclan memberships, as central Chamba claim to have done with slaves.

However, as Chamba were to become a minority in their own alliances, a second argument suggests itself. Because matriclanship is the open idiom of Chamba organization, members of a politically privileged Chamba minority anxious to protect their status might want to retain for themselves and their older allies access to office and to officialdom. In this circumstance, the consociating idiom of matriclanship would become threatening to their position. A better strategy would be to emphasize patriclanship, already the appropriate form for the organization of violence among central Chamba, and retain matrilateral ties for individuals of Chamba descent.[5] In such a social climate the criteria of Chambaness might be relaxed to encompass the Chamba's homeland neighbors and oldest allies. Extension of Chambaness with a concomitant reinforcement of patriclanship would simultaneously create a shared identity for the raiders while maintaining the privileged position of particular patriclans. This would yield the kind of organization we now find among Benue and Bali Chamba—patriclanship modified by an emphasis on the importance of ego-centered kinship networks. An intermediary stage of development is suggested from data on the central Chamba immigrant chiefdoms of the northern Shebshi Mountains, where the formal organization of double clanship remains, but virtually all political and ritual offices are vested in patriclan ownership.

The historical hypothesis of longer term development would be that double clanship developed among the Chamba Leko with the emergence of patriclanship to supplement matriclanship. In the course of the developments associated with Yeli and the foundation of the Nakenyare chiefdoms, patriclanship became a significant organizing principle among the previously matrilineal Daka speakers. The dispersion of predominantly matriclan-ritualized chiefships during the late eighteenth and early nineteenth centuries took place under conditions that consistently favored devaluation of the importance of consociating idioms of organization. The political significance of matriclanship was carefully controlled in the northern Shebshi chiefdoms, and disappeared among Benue and Bali Chamba immigrants.

Clansmen as Sociates

To explore this reconstruction, we can look at Chamba kinship from the second perspective, that of clan categories. Throughout Chambaland, formal categories of clan organization are virtually identical to the type of double clanship we analyzed from Mapeo. However, political organizations are far from identical.

The ritualized chiefdoms of the southern and central Shebshi Mountain Nakɛnyare and Alantika Mountain Leko, the small intrusive conquest chiefdoms of the northern Shebshi Mountains, and the uncentralized refuge community of Mapeo have adapted a formally similar conception of clanship to dissimilar political circumstances. We shall see in Part 3 that the flexibility of the Chamba clanship and kinship idioms allows these same idioms to organize and express a range of political relations. Here, my interest concerns their formal similarities.

Outside Chambaland, within the conquest chiefdoms of the Benue and Bali Chamba, the idioms of clanship have been subjected to change. Although this change, as the kinship terminology implies, is toward an increasing emphasis on patriclanship in both instances, the Bali and Benue variants of the transformation differ in particular ways. Daka clanship, for which I am again reliant upon Meek's researches, repesents the obverse case of matriclanship stressed to the apparent exclusion of patriclanship.

Central Chamba Clanship

The two Chamba languages express the gross clanship categories in terms that are almost direct equivalents. *Da.mɛmbu*, father's children, the Daka-language term for patriclan, has a literal equivalent, *ba.wa* or father's child, among Leko speakers. *Kuni*, Chamba Daka for matriclan as a category, and also a suffix of individual matriclan names, is cognate with *kuna* among Leko speakers where it is used in the same ways. The categories of extended matriclanship, father's matriclan or *da.kuni*, grandfather's matriclan or *kalum.kuni*, have the direct equivalents of *ba.kuna* and *do.kuna*. There is a single difference in the use of the term *kuna*, which comes to greater prominence in the kinship organizations of the emigrant Leko speakers, since the Leko term shares a root form with the general term for sibling. Thus, *kun.ma.bira*, my brothers, has a bilateral reference to all classificatory siblings that is not shared by the Daka *kuni*.

Like matriclan names, patriclan names are formed in the same way in both Chamba language groups. Daka speakers append either a simple plural, *-bu*, or the term "people," *-nɛpbu*, to a patriclan name; the corresponding Leko suffixes are *-bira* or *-bɔra*, and *-nɛbba*. The mother's patriclan, literally *nya.dami* for Daka speakers, is mother's people, *na.nɛbba*, for Leko, who may refer to the children of patriclan women as *nyi.kin.wa*, literally "trunk–woman–child" (*i.e.*, offshoots of the trunk of a tree). Looking overall at clanship terminology, the evidence of historical convergence between Daka and Leko conceptions is strong, especially when we recall that their two languages may be unrelated.

Differences between the scale and distribution of matriclans and patriclans occur in both language groups. Most local communities in Chambaland have approximately the same number of matriclans. Mapeo has eleven named matriclans; in Sapeo (Leko speaking) I elicited twelve names (Frobenius 1913:278 recorded eleven including *lam.kuna*, the blacksmith clan, equivalent to *kpe.kuni* in Daka, which he mistakenly supposed to be composed solely of smiths). At Kiri, in the southern Shebshi Mountains, I was given ten names, and in Gurum thirteen names. Although the terms outside Mapeo were elicited formally, rather than picked up through participation, the numbers are sufficiently similar to suggest the relative invariance of the matriclan mode of organization. Nominal equivalences are established exactly or recognized conventionally. Thus, the elephant clan is found throughout both Chamba language groups in the central area, whereas the dog clan of the Daka speakers, *wana.kuni*, is recognized to be the same as the Leko *sal.kuna*, which takes its name from a type of grass that has to be weeded out of the fields and cleared areas around the compound, so, more generally, rubbish.

Leko patriclans, like their Daka counterparts, are more particu-

laristic. They have distinctive histories and customs, and are identified by names that are often supposed to refer to previous settlements. Interrelations between clans are handled by Leko in exactly
the same way as by Daka speakers. Matriclans and patriclans recognize common parentation, diffuse in the matriclan case and specific
in the patriclan case, and joking relations (*kpɔmi*, Daka, *man.zala*,
Leko).[6] In both languages, the same term is used to denote a relation
of privileged abuse between different clans and between different
peoples, especially Bachama.

The evidence of formal kinship and clanship analysis suggests
that there are no important differences between central Chamba regardless of differences of language and dialect. However, we need to
look farther afield than the Chamba to discern how widespread the
distribution of similar organizations may be. To do this, I have to
rely upon descriptions of uneven quality. It is nonetheless important, since features shared by neighbors nowadays identified by different ethnic labels suggest the previous existence of a more labile
regional network of resemblances.

Clanship among the Central Chambas' Neighbors

J-L. Siran has noted that matriclanship was an important organizational device among most of the Chambas' neighbors and among
some of the earliest adherents of the Chamba raiding parties (1981a:
266–267). His own researches concerned Buti, who lived to the
south of the Chamba, elements of whom were incorporated into the
alliances that eventually established the Bali Chamba chiefdoms.
The precise extent of the band of peoples who utilized matriclan
organization and who lived at the eastern end of the West African
middle-belt has yet to be determined (although I have offered a provisional survey in Fardon forthcoming). Despite such limitations in
the data, it is important to look briefly at the position of the Chamba
from a regional perspective in order not to attribute to them by default a cultural uniqueness they do not possess.

A survey can most usefully begin with the central Chamba's
closest neighbors. Geographically, culturally, and linguistically, the
Dirrim and Taram groups of Daka, living to the west and south of
the Nakɛnyare, are the closest relatives of the central Daka-speaking

Chamba. Here, as earlier, I am reliant upon Meek's data, which are suggestive rather than exhaustive. He reports the presence of matriclans among them, called *kona*, *kwon* or *kon* (presumably cognate with the central Chamba *kuni* and *kuna*) (Meek 1931bI:398). In contrast to the central Chamba communities, these peripheral Daka practiced matri-uxorilocal residence and lived in matriclan sections. The kinship terminologies I examined suggested that Taram and Dirrim matriclans might be extended on the Chamba pattern. This would imply the recognition of at least traceable relations of male parentation. Daka sons apparently did also inherit the small patrimony of axe, hoe, bow and spears that Chamba sons received on their father's death (Meek 1931bI:401). Sons were responsible for the organization of their father's funeral and graveside rites and, at least among the Dirrim, might inherit their father's cults. The major reservation that has to be registered against this series of convergences is that we have no way of assessing the degree of influence that might have been exercised over these groups by the emigrants from the central area who founded chiefdoms west of the Shebshi Mountains.

Further evidence for the existence of matriclans can be drawn from the Jangani of the southern Shebshi Mountains, an apparently indigenous group who speak a dialect of Daka and were assimilated into the southern chiefdoms, particularly after the foundation of Sugu. The Jangani seem to have a typical Chamba double clanship organization with matriclans identical to those recognized by Nakɛnyare-speaking Chamba. Their patriclan names are compounds that consist of the term Jangani with a suffix referring to the hilltop village from which the clansmen originally claim to have migrated. Versions of history that I elicited from Jangani informants were consistently retold in matriclan terms. This information, such as it is, is consistent with a relatively recent adoption of patriclan organization by people who previously favored matriclan organization, and is similar to the Dirrim and Taram to their south and west. Together with evidences from the southern area of Chambaland, we have indications of a broad belt of Daka- and Leko-speaking peoples with commensurate matriclan organization.

The Daka-speaking subgroups of Chamba, such as the Mangla and Tola, who were incorporated into the chiefdoms of the northern

Shebshi Mountains, appear to have clear conceptions of patriclanship. In the course of interviews with Tola elders, I was unable
to find evidence of matriclan names except where intermarriage
with Chamba had occurred. These indications may suggest that the
northern border of the matriclan belt traversed what is now northern
Chambaland. Some of the Vere groups, northern neighbors of the
Chamba, also seem to be without matriclans (see below).

Turning from materials on Chamba speakers to materials on
their neighbors, we seem to find corroborating evidence for this pattern. The Pere, direct southern neighbors of the Chamba Leko, are
reported to be a matrilineal people (Boutrais 1978). Brief researches
I have been able to carry out among Pere lead me to conclude that,
formally speaking, Pere matriclanship is virtually identical to its
Chamba counterpart and that, like the Taram and Dirrim, Pere lack
patriclans (Fardon 1986). Pere terminology makes the same critical
distinctions in kinship terminology as the central Chamba schedules: in the senior adjacent generation, lineals (M and MZ; F and FB)
are distinguished from collaterals (FZ and MB). A categorical relation of parentation is recognized between a matriclan and the children of its male members and, just as among Chamba, this shows up
in kinship terminology as a promotion of patrilateral cross cousins
to father and paternal aunt and a demotion of matrilateral cross
cousins to children. The two senior-generation collateral relations
are contrastively handled. Just as among Chamba, the maternal
uncle's wife is the only familiar affine of the senior generation, and
mother's brother and sister's son are closely related by bodily associations. As among Chamba, the maternal uncle was formally permitted to pawn his sister's child, and a partible inheritance transferred all but a man's weapons and tools matrilaterally.

Pere and Chamba conceptions of matriclanship are close counterparts. Pere distinguish three levels of matriclans, all of which may
be called *nim;* the most encompassing level can also be called *sabo,*
a word that also covers our sense of ethnic group. The levels correspond to levels in Chamba matriclans that I called matriclans, matriclan sections, and the descendants of a named common maternal
grandmother. As among central Chamba, matriclan sections developed as a result of migrations and enslavement, and to effect the
payment of death compensation by the transference of girls as pawns.

Pere seem less secretive than Chamba about the identities of matriclan sections, and this may be attributable to the absence of patriclans which, among Chamba, are held in strong contrastive relation
to matriclans. Pere and southern Chamba Leko have intermarried
over many years, and Pere clans are now represented in many of the
emigrant Chamba chicfdoms founded by raiders. At least in Bali,
Pere clans are now considered to be of Chamba origin. The two
peoples both recognize a close joking relationship between all Pere
and all Chamba Leko speakers.

Immediately to the north of the Mapeo Chamba and Chamba
Leko are peoples whom Chamba call Koma. This term is not used
by Koma to refer to themselves, and the validity of the term as an
ethnic category is not clear. I collected kinship schedules from informants who belonged to two groups (Gɔnu and Ritɔbe). In both
cases cross-cousin terms were skewed (patrilateral cross cousins
were promoted, and matrilateral cross cousins demoted), and both
informants described extended matriclan categories reminiscent of
their Chamba counterparts. No evidence was found for the existence
of patriclans.

The Buti, living to the south of the Pere, are reported to have
lost their matriclans. In their case skewing of cross-cousin terms
does not now occur (siblings, parallel and cross cousins are addressed
by the same terms, Siran 1981b:44–45). However, Siran's kinship
schedules are drawn solely from Buti who migrated south and lost
their matriclans. It is likely that these Buti groups, like the Bali
Chamba who shed this feature as a result of organizational adapta-
tions to the life of raiders, may concurrently have altered their kinship terminology. It seems probable that prior to their migration
Buti would have shared the matriclan organization and skewed cross-
cousin kinship terminology typical of members of the matrilineal
belt (J-L. Siran personal communication). Like Chamba, Buti recognize paternal parentation, with the effect that taboos are transmitted
patrilineally, although these nominal lines apparently have no organizational significance.

The Vere, whom Chamba call Momi (Daka) or Moma (Leko),
mostly live to the north of the Nassarawo Plain. Meek's Vere researches (1931bI, Chapter 7) were exclusively concerned with the
northern Vere among whom he found no indication of matriclan or-

ganization. Like Koma, Vere is not an indigenous ethnic term and seems to cover a congeries of people who differ substantially. Chamba informants in Mapeo are adamant that matriclan categories like their own are found not only among the Koma and Pere but also among the eastern Momi who are their neighbors. One Mapeo matriclan is in fact believed to be descended largely from women of Momi origins.

The tentative conclusion to be drawn from this brief survey is that Chamba matriclanship was simply one local variant of a more widely distributed regional feature. It seems likely that the feature did not extend to the immediate north of the Chamba, but in all probability it was shared by people farther west than Taram and Dirrim (Fardon forthcoming) and extended south as far as Pere, Buti, and perhaps beyond. This finding provides further support to the proposition that Chamba patriclanship was an innovative form of organization.

Chamba Marriage Regulations

Contemporary marriage regulations in Chambaland vary widely and consequently, different informants' accounts are not altogether consistent. Two factors appear to be involved in this situation. Exogamic restrictions are currently being eroded or changed with the adoption of new religious faiths and increased social mobility within Chambaland. This factor is explicitly noted by informants who contrast a present-day range of choices in marriage partners with those they believe applied in the past. The second factor is more hypothetical but accords with the understanding of earlier changes that I am proposing. This is that the restrictions recalled as "traditional" by contemporary informants had themselves emerged in the context of changing patterns of clan sociation. To illustrate this contention, I return initially to consider the information I collected from Mapeo.

Central Chamba, of Mapeo and elsewhere, apply specifically affinal terminology to a very narrow range of relationships: to the spouses of maternal uncles, siblings, and children, and to the close relations of a spouse. The spouses of lineal ascendants are terminologically assimilated to the appropriate category of kin. The obligations specific to affinity are extremely slight and mostly apply to relations of respect or privileged abuse between individuals but not groups. The significance of marriage, for Chamba informants, is its capacity to produce legitimate clanship rather than alliance or affinity. The ramifications of double extended clanship not only tend to supercede descent in importance, but also relations that, in many other societies, stem from marriages.

In Mapeo, patriclans are strictly exogamous but matriclans, and even matriclan sections, are not. Marriage to a mother's sister's daughter is disapproved by some, although I have found an example of it; matrilateral cross-cousin marriage is not disapproved. Other restrictions accumulate as a result of a person's own marriages and the marriages of close kin. Thus, affines in a respect relationship should not marry. Joking affines may marry provided no other regulation is violated, such as a prohibition against men and women taking partners from the same patriclan more than once. Extant marriages were tested for intra-matriclan unions. Roughly twelve percent of marriages were entered into with members of ego's own matriclan, and another twelve per cent involved members of a male ego's father's matriclan. This suggests a random distribution of marriages.

The rate of polygyny at any particular moment is low; only a few men have three wives and most have one or two (see Fardon 1980II, Appendix 4). However, life histories collected from older men suggest a very high rate of serial polygyny. Some individuals appear to have entered stable marriages relatively immediately, but many more have been married to between ten and twenty different women. Such a divorce rate evidently militates against marriage forming the basis for stable alliance between clans.

Chamba distinguish two means of taking a wife (*ten ngwu*). First marriages used to entail brideservice to the potential affines in the form of farming and building as well as transferences of goods in kind. The dissolution of such marriages without issue was supposed to be followed by payment of compensation to the husband. Nowadays, brideprice has replaced brideservice. Marriages subsequent to first marriage are termed wife stealing. In principle, only a small payment to the wife herself was necessary to regularize such a union, although some payment might also be accepted by the girl's close kin. Children of the marriage belonged to the new husband.

Despite the fragility of marriage bonds, I have never encountered any uncertainty about individual clan affiliations; children belong to the man to whom a woman is considered married when she becomes pregnant. Nonetheless, because wife theft could be followed by violent retaliation, it is easier to argue that marriage relations were a source of contention between patriclans, rather than a means of alliance.

Mapeo shares its rules of patriclan exogamy with the chiefdoms established by the raiders who settled in the northern Shebshi Mountains. However, informants from the southern Shebshi chiefdoms recall that matriclans were once exogamous and that the prohibition on remarriages was defined in terms of matriclanship and not patriclanship. These regulations appear to be shared also by the Pere, southern neighbors of the Chamba Leko, and by the Koma, to the north of the Chamba Leko. In contemporary Yeli, patriclans and the chiefly matriclan are exogamous. But there as well, remarriage into a matriclan from which a spouse has previously been taken is not permitted.

Throughout Chambaland, matriclan exogamy has been dying out over a considerable period. A colonial officer (Welch 1935) remarked that matriclan exogamy had disappeared in Gurum before the 1930s and that wife stealing was becoming a pressing problem to colonial officers as it often was a cause of violence. Significantly, he notes that Chamba did not steal wives from members of their "group," which corresponds to the Mapeo injunction against stealing from patrikin. This rule may indicate Chamba recognition that marriage was potentially disruptive of important clan solidarities.

One regulation, which I heard in Mapeo and among the northern residual Leko, suggests a further restriction on the choice of partners. In these communities, marriage with women of the royal matriclan was strongly disapproved because it introduced dangers associated with royal bodies, which had to be returned to their chiefly homes on death. The blood of girl's tooth evulsion and boy's circumcision also endangered the host community. In the boys' case, their foreskins had to be returned to their mothers' royal place of origin, to be buried in the royal graveyard. These regulations clearly refer us to the impartible associations of royal substance, and they are held to explain the absence of the royal clan *(gang.kuni* or *gat.kuna)* from places that were not under the rule of the matriclan of the chief.

In the context of a general tendency for patriclanship to increase in importance, it is likely that the erosion of matriclan marriage regulations was instrumental in contributing to the fragility of the marriage bond, at least for a period. In places where patriclanship became preeminent and was associated with chiefship, the scale of royal and officials' polygyny appears to have increased. According to Welch, royal polygyny and wife stealing appear to have increased concurrently in Gurum with the accession of patriclan chiefs during the nineteenth century (3058 Welch 1936).

The immigrant Chamba who founded their chiefdoms in the northern Shebshi Mountains recall that they preferentially married their daughters to fellow immigrants but they also took the daughters of the indigenous peoples of the area in marriage. This strategy would have permitted an increased rate of polygyny to the dominant stratum, which is what we might expect of people who represent themselves as conquerors.

The Bali ideal was for marriage not be entered into with traceable relatives over three to four generations; however patrilateral parallel-cousin marriages were found among the royalty (E. M. Chilver personal communication). The scale of polygyny in the Bali chiefdoms was very substantial. In an assessment report of 1925, figures from Bali Nyonga showed that twenty-three men in a population of 1,813 had ten or more wives (Hunt 1925). The chief declared himself to have ninety-nine wives, although the reporting officer noted an earlier estimate of two hundred wives belonging to a previous Bali chief. Of the adult males, 460 were reported to have no wife at all. A comparison between Bali Chamba and central Chamba is compromised to the extent that the Bali Chamba have adopted so many features of the Grassfields culture into which they entered, and where extravagant chiefly polygyny is a norm. Nonetheless, there does appear to be an association between the predominance of patriclanship and increasing polygyny.

Given the absence of matriclans, matriclan exogamy is necessarily absent in the emigrant Chamba conquest chiefdoms. In Donga, marriage restrictions are reported to apply to the patriclans, which were exogamous, as well as to known descendants of a common grandmother (Meek 1931bI:342). At the other end of the scale, Meek reports the Taram and Dirrim, without patriclans, to be virtually monogamous (Meek 1931bI:398-402). The indications from Mapeo are that the predominance of patriclan organization of marital affairs in the absence of centralization may be associated with pronounced marital instability. At present, through much of Chambaland, marriages are far more stable than those contracted by the older generation of Chamba informants and, especially among the more educated young people, marriages are now contracted between communities which once did not intermarry, such as between Gurum and Sugu.

Benue and Bali Chamba Clanship

Although matriclan categories are recognized in neither Donga nor the Bali Chamba chiefdoms, the term *kuna* persists, to denote brothers or kin bilaterally (a sense which has precedents in the usage of the Leko-speaking central Chamba). Patriclans persist in the Chamba chiefdoms of both the Benue Plains and the Bamenda Grassfields. Meek refers to "patrilineal kindreds" in Donga, in which component sections were not consistently related genealogically but between which it was "clear" that there existed a "real consanguinity" (Meek 1931bI:338). It is uncertain how Meek could be clear about this; we may assume that Chamba asserted it to be the case. Meek and Garbosa each gives a list of Donga patriclans. Some of the names appear on both lists, and some can be matched with counterparts in Chambaland (Garbosa:10; Meek 1931bI:338).[7]

Between the clans, Donga Chamba recognized two types of relationship: joking relations (called *man.zala*, as among Chamba Leko) and relations of "brotherhood" (presumably a literal translation, if Meek's *kumboa* is a contraction of *kun.ma.bira*, "my brothers"). Brotherhood is no more than another way of expressing a relationship central Chamba would be likely to express in terms of shared parentation. Among Donga patriclans, Sama, Janga, and Nyera, and Kola, Poba, and Kwasa are two groupings of patriclans that have a relationship of brotherhood. Ngwuma, Gbana, Zaa, Nupabi, and Lama (the smiths) are given as names of other clans. All of this is very clearly reminiscent of central Chamba patriclan organi-

zation. Meek also recorded evidence for the relation of shared substance that we have seen central Chamba posit between a mother's
brother and his sister's son. However, he felt forced to interpret this
relationship, erroneously in my opinion, as a relic of a previous stage
of "mother-right" rather than as the persistence of previous idioms
of double clanship. Thus, a man could pawn his sister's son, could
inflict physical punishment on him to the point of death, and was
implicated in any accusation of witchcraft made against him. For
his part, the sister's son was able to appropriate small objects from
his mother's brother, although his right to inherit material wealth
became relevant only in the absence of inheriting sons (Meek 1931bI:
344–345).

Together with the persistence of the respected role of the father's sister, as well as most features of Chamba kinship terminology
(including generational adjustment of cross cousins), these features of
Donga clanship suggest that the clanship system in existence at the
time of Meek's researches was a Chamba system without the matriclans, but one in which a matrilateral connection was still emphasized, particularly with respect to the relationship between a boy and
his mother's own brother. The Chamba elements of the Bali Chamba
confederacies traveled farther and recruited more non-Chamba
before settling in their present locations; their clanship system diverges from the central Chamba type in more complex ways.

In Chapter 6, I remarked on the persistence of patriclan names
among Bali Chamba that correspond to names of Chamba clans
(Nyɛmnɛbba, Djabnɛbba, Dinga), or of ethnic groups bordering Chambaland (Pɛli, Kaga; for Pere and Bata), and of allies recruited in
the southward push (Buti, Mbum, Tikari). These names identify a
minority of extant Bali clans, most of which trace descent from later
adherents of the alliance, recruited subsequent to its arrival around
Bamum and the Grassfields (Chilver unpublished 1970:Part Two). A
kinship terminology collected from Bali Gangsin (identical to that
from Bali Kumbad) had lost many of its Chamba features. Apart
from preserving the distinction between lineals and collaterals in
the ascending generation, the terminology marked only generation,
gender, and relative age. This suggested that changes in Bali sociation had been more radical than in Donga and were effectively influenced by Grassfields models of organization.

To explore this contention, I shall first look at clanship organization in Bali Gangsin, one of the four Bali locations in which Leko
remains the everyday language, and then, more briefly, at clanship
in Bali Nyonga, where Leko has been supplanted by a Grassfields
language.

The word Bali, which I use to identify the southwestern emigrant Chamba, derives from the term *ba'ni* in the Munggaka language of Bali Nyonga. In Mubako (i.e., Chamba Leko), the Bali
Chamba call themselves Ndagana. This term has contextual referents: it can also refer to speakers of Ndagan.nyonga (another term
for Chamba Leko), excluding the Munggaka speakers of Bali Nyonga,
or it can refer to the members of the Chamba alliance who had
joined Gawolbe's alliance prior to its arrival in the Grassfields. More
specialized usages contrast Ndagana with Sama; the former are custodians of the *voma* cults and non-royals, the latter custodians of
the *lela* flutes and royals. Earlier, I speculated that the contrast between Sama and Ndagana might be a variation on the opposition
between Sama and Daka known from the central Chamba area.

The term Sama also has shifting referents. As a personal name,
Sama, usually found with a suffix, is given to twins (*Sam.gba'a*, big
Sama, *Sam.jɛla*, small Sama) who, following Grassfields custom,
were sent for palace service. The name is also given to any child born
at the time of the annual *lela* celebrations, themselves associated
with royalty (see Chapter 10). Sama also means prince and can be
synonymous with chief's son; chief's sons are prominent members
of Sambila (plur.), the officials responsible for the performance of
lela. Finally, Sama retains the sense of a royal patriclan, since descendants of Sama may themselves be Sama, although there appear
to be mechanisms that limit the spread of Sama status that would
eventuate from very high rates of royal polygyny. A clear design relates these two terms: Sama has royal connotations and is associated
with the *lela* flutes; Ndagana, on the other hand, is a more general
term, since in some of its usages Sama are members of Ndagana,
although, when contrasted with Sama it connotes non-royal custody
of *voma*, the community cults. The division is found in the central
Chamba area, but seldom formulated with this clarity. The focal position of the chief, *gala*, or *Sam.gba'a*, big Sama, is particularly
emphasized. Women of the royal clan are addressed as *na'a*, the

chief's wives are all called by the term for mother, *na*, and any women addressed by the chief as mother should be addressed by others as grandmother, *ka*. This modification of kinship status to mark a relation to the chief, positional succession, or occupancy of office, is typical of the area in which Bali Chamba live, but not of Chambaland.

Although patriclan names persist in the Bali chiefdoms, patriclans have little significance as units of organization. Instead, we find a system of repeatedly segmenting patrilineal groupings that maintain testamentary, positional succession to a stool, a drinking horn, to kinship position, and for some, a title. Material wealth may be equally divided between sons. Non-succeeding sons become focal points for the proliferation of new succession lines. The shallow descent lines are termed seed, *luma*, or root, *lila*, and an individual may trace relation to the lines of his lineal ascendants (thus, *do.luma*, grandfather's seed, *ka.luma*, grandmother's seed, *ba.luma*, *na.luma*, father's and mother's seed). The primary reference of the term *kuna* in this system is to all members of ego's own generation to whom any kind of relationship can be traced. Despite the use of Chamba idioms, and the persistence of vague patriclan groupings, inheritance, descent, and succession rules diverge from the central Chamba type. The major contribution of Chamba organization occurs in the conceptualization of the Sama–Ndagana contrast through which political and ritual offices are related—although succession to these offices is on the adopted model. Even the Sama–Ndagana contrast is modified by adopted features, such as palace service for twins, which is foreign to Chamba organization.

The non-Chamba character of Bali kinship and clanship emerges more clearly in Bali Nyonga, where even terminology is unfamiliar. Organization is analogous to that at Bali Gangsin, but on a far larger scale and with greater emphasis upon locality as a principle of administration. The kinship terminology is formally similar to Bali Gangsin, although the special relationship between mother's brother and sister's son is terminologically marked (*nimban*, a term of address for mother's brother; *məndzad*, sister's child); Mubako terms are retained only for the grandparents (*do*, grandfather; *ka*, grandmother). Lineages, called *nggəd*, formed by the descendants of a common FFF, are landowning, exogamous, and constitute ritual

units within which kin terms have their full force. The fact that
ritual offerings are given to the F, FF, and FFF may be instrumental
in defining this unit. A special relationship is traced between an
individual and his or her mother's *nggəd*, to whom he or she is
məndzad. But this relationship does not imply recognition of broad
matrilateral connection, since it concerns two patrilineages.

Overview

The examination of Chamba sociation presented here from the perspective of clanship significantly complements the view from kinship. As we expected on the basis of their kinship terminologies, it
is apparent that central Chamba share a system of double clanship.
The peripheral Taram and Dirrim Daka, as well as many of the
Chamba's neighbors, have a basically similar system but without
patriclans. The evidence points to cultural similarities among matrilineal peoples at the eastern end of the West African middle-belt.
On the basis of this evidence, I have suggested that the emergence
of patriclanship might be connected with changes that accompanied
the extension of Nakɛnyare chiefship among Daka-speaking communities, concurrent with the emergence of an extensive Chamba
identity that subsumes the speakers of the two Chamba languages.
More generally, it seems that current ethnic identities have been
imposed during the last two centuries on more fluid conceptions of
resemblance and difference (Fardon 1987; forthcoming). With greater
confidence, I have speculated that the present clanship systems of
Donga and Bali Chamba developed from a central Chamba system
of double clanship. Donga clanship resembles a mirror image of the
Daka type, a central Chamba clanship system without matriclans.
The emigrant Bali Chamba have been subjected to more pervasive
non-Chamba influences, especially in Bali Nyonga, but Chamba cultural influence persists in the organizational distinctions drawn in
terms of a modified Chamba opposition between Sama and Ndagana. In both cases, Chamba ethnicity has assumed political importance with the foundation of conquest chiefdoms by emigrant
raiders.

All the evidence examined supports a very broad trend of development which, I have argued, is characterized by the displacement of consociating by adsociating idioms of Chamba organization. This suggests to me that the Chamba capacity to respond to the destabilization of their earlier regional system around the end of the eighteenth century may be attributable, at least in part, to the capacity of their organizational resources to manage the shift from consociational to adsociational modalities.

PART IV

CHAMBA POLITICAL DEVELOPMENT

CHAPTER 9

THE POLITICS OF CONSOCIATION:

RITUALIZED CHIEFSHIP

In Part 4 of this book I present an account of broad trends in Chamba political development that can be related to the historical narrative of Part 2, the transformational analysis of Part 3, and the interpretative account of Mapeo politics through which the reader was introduced to Chamba. Chapters 9 and 10 are concerned with centralized chiefdoms, the forms of political organization on which Mapeo Chamba turned their backs before the colonial period. Chapter 11 takes up the narrative account of Chamba political development that I pursued as far as the late nineteenth century in Part 2.

On the basis of the information preserved, I have distinguished two ideal types of Chamba chiefdom: the ritualized chiefdom, of which matriclan chiefship is the most evident feature, and the conquest chiefdom, founded by raiders, that is characterized by patriclan chiefship. A discussion of similarities and differences between these two categories provides the major theme in these chapters, and is presented against a covert chronological framework, since throughout the nineteenth century ritualized chiefdoms tended to be replaced by conquest chiefdoms, and aspects of this trend continued into the colonial period. In detail, matters are complex, but the broad trend is striking, and the movement between types is more far-reaching than a simple contrast between succession rules would suggest. There seem to be thorough-going differences between community-wide organizations headed by patriclan chiefs and those headed by matriclan chiefs. Using the terminology introduced in my discussion of sociability and elaborated in Chapters 7 and 8, the subject of this chapter, the constituent clan units of the matriclan chiefships, is incorporated and interrelated in terms of consociation. In the patriclan chiefships, the subject of Chapter 10, this incorporation and interrelation is achieved through an emphasis on adsociation. I suggested earlier that this distinction implies the co-occurrence of two different styles of reciprocally constituting people, or categories of people, and the differences between them.

The consociational style of chiefdom—with its emphasis upon feminine mediations, consubstantiality, and inclusive idioms of organization—can be grasped most clearly from the way in which the matriclan chief's status is relationally construed. There are a number of elements to this style of organization which, if not wholly mutually consistent, nonetheless consistently load significance of a particular type upon the chiefship. I deal with these from perspectives suggested by several key relationships: between the chief and the living members of his community, between the chief and his officials, between the chief and the ancestral sprites, and between the chief and the natural world.

The Chamba matriclan chief shares characteristics with many other African holders of high office. He is a provider, encharged with rituals that aim to assure the fertility and well-being of his people, their animals, and their crops. Installation rites effect a transformation in his status necessary for his rituals to be effective, but by the same token the chief is estranged, endangered, and may die. The Chamba matriclan chief embodies responsibility for the members of his community, and this embodiment is a crucial element of his relationship with them.

Many writers have interpreted similar concepts of African chiefship. Luc de Heusch has suggested symbolic analyses of a range of central African chiefships (especially 1958, 1962, 1982a, 1982b). Jean Claude Muller has argued that Rukuba chiefship is based on the scapegoating of a chief who transgresses in order to assume his position (1980). Robert Armstrong claims that an Idoma chief is symbolically dead (1980), while Alfred Adler emphasizes the identification Moundang make between chiefs and twins (1982:230–258). In comparison to these and other cases (Feeley-Harnik 1985), Chamba ritual chiefship is not an extreme example: the chief does not transgress through incest or cannibalism; he is not considered a witch, as in some nearby Cameroonian societies; his position is not elaborated in mythology, nor is an identification made between chiefs and twins; he is not considered to be dead, although rites of passage, including chiefmaking and funerary rituals, invoke some of the same conventions.[1] I am reluctant to treat Chamba chiefship as a philosophical statement on the nature of the world, as Vaughan (1980) has suggested for the Marghi, since the chiefless Mapeo Chamba do not hold to a noticeably different philosophy from their chiefly Chamba neighbors.[2] Rather than pursue the idea of a pervasive African philosophy of leadership, I hope to explain why ritual chiefship is *not* a pervasive feature of Chamba organization. This fact cautions against construing ritualized chiefship as an intrinsic or inevitable aspect of Chamba thought or organization.

Ritualized chiefship is a historically specific Chamba institution that is found in chiefdoms themselves interrelated by a skein of resemblances. This network of resemblances is most extensive from the viewpoint of Yeli. It is worth repeating the data that have been established historically: the *gat.kuna* matriclan of Yeli is considered to be the same as the *gang.kuni* matriclan of Sugu, Nya Gangngwu (the royal mother of Sugu), and Da Dukdu (the source of the migration which established the *gang.kuni* chiefships). The royal matriclans of Kiri and Danaba (*gang.kuni*), and Yebbi and Gurum (*gang.tim.nɔ.kuni*), all claim to have reached their present sites from Yeli. To the south, the Yeli *gat.kuna* is related to the clan of the same name that holds the chiefships of Balkossa, Bangla and, historically, Sapeo. The accession to office of these chiefly families predates the Fulani jihad in every case. Later Chamba foundations were established under the auspices of patriclan chiefship, whereas the matriclan chiefdoms survived only in hill refuges, and even there some of them were displaced.

As indicated by these data, ritualized chiefships had their inception in pre-jihadic times and survived defensively installed in the hills. Matriclan chiefship did not persist in the raiding confederacies, nor does it appear to have answered the organizational requirements of conquest chiefdoms. A historical perspective suggests that some capacities and limitations may be inherent in matriclan chiefship, or in the politics of consociation more generally.

Clanship and Chiefship

Chamba represent their local communities as associations of clans. In different contexts, they may choose to emphasize matriclanship, patriclanship, or some combination of both, as providing a basic charter for association. Clanship is always potentially contrastive. Given this choice of idioms, the vesting of chiefship in a matriclan has important consequences for the manner in which the office itself and the relationship between the chief and his people are envisaged. As discussed in Chapter 8, matriclan sociability is grounded in a shared interest in substance—in the correct development of the body, in its health, in witchcraft and slavery, both envisaged as corporeal states, in the physical disciplining of younger members of the clan, and in the moveable wealth acquired by clansmen. Matriclan categories are nominally solidary units, extended to incorporate "children" and "grandchildren." Matriclan internal histories tend to be submerged by public advertisement of their mythological origins.

By virtue of the inclusive character of matriclanship, matriclan chiefship is described as the property of the community as a whole (our chief rather than their chief); by contrast, the patriclan chiefship is envisaged to be the property of a distinct group exercising dominance on behalf of an interest group. Chiefship is bestowed upon matriclan chiefs by chiefmakers or priests (kamɛnbu, in Daka; vom.wana, vom.gara, in Leko) appointed from clans distinct from the chief's, most commonly from patriclans considered to have been settled in the chiefdom territory prior to the installation of the chiefly matriclan (Jangani in Sugu, Nyɛmnɛbba in Yeli, Kpemɛmbu in Gurum). Chiefs are characterized as immigrants in the traditions of both the patriclan and matriclan chiefdoms (Chapters 4 and 5), but the matriclan immigrants are accepted for their ritual potency by local clansmen who grant them chiefship. Patriclan chiefs, however, arrive as conquerors already confirmed in office by their close military allies. The implied social contracts are different. The patriclan chief is representative of power as might; the matriclan chief is the orchestrator of a type of power we distinguish as prepotency, a quality that partly invests and is made to invest his person, and partly inheres in his relationships to others.

The fitness of the chief for office depends on his being without serious physical deformity. Epilepsy, lack of bodily control, which Chamba associate also with the accidental damage to the body by falling into fires, absolutely disqualifies a candidate. Leprosy, the progressive decay of the body, is given as the explanation for the demise of matriclan chiefship in both Gurum and Sapeo.[3] The physical integrity of the chief remains a communal concern even after his death. The grave of the matriclan chief is sealed, and the slightest crack developing in its clay covering entails sacrifice to avert severe misfortune in the community, in the form of wild animals or tornadoes. Unlike the bodies of the patriclan chiefs or priests, which are parted to allow their patrikinsmen to augment their skull shrine, the body of the matriclan chief must for safety remain intact. In Yeli, this bodily integrity is demanded of all members of the royal matriclan. Should they be buried outside Yeli, or should the blood of girls' tooth evulsion fall upon the ground, or should the foreskins of circumcised boys not be returned to Yeli, epidemic disease (most probably smallpox) would break out, and only the intercession of the Yeli priests could avert annihilation. In matriclan chiefships, the welfare of the community is associated with the chief's body; in patriclan chiefdoms, the power of the ruling stratum is associated with the chief's skull.

During his reign, the chief is required to finance the rituals performed by his priests on behalf of the community.[4] He cannot attend many of them and, since he is expressly debarred from entering a graveyard, he sends in his place men to represent him. Yeli dogma has it that no members of the royal matriclan should see corpses. Apart from his regular ritual responsibilities, he has a periodic duty to organize witch-finding in the community by submitting a member of each matriclan to trial either by poison, or by an ordeal which involves lifting a stone from a boiling pot of "medicines" without blistering. Convicted witches, and their matrikin, may be beaten to death with sticks (never shot or stabbed), or sold by the chief into slavery outside the community.[5] The chief physically does little toward the performance of these rites; his task is to enable and to delegate to others who perform with reference to him. The chief is the exemplary center around which matters may be enacted.

The chief is unmoving; he is also vulnerable. His death is likely to occur at the time of circumcision, when the priests of the patriclans separate a part of the bodies of the boys entering adulthood, and the coolness of the chief is menaced by the hot blood from the boys' wounds. The center should be cool, if the chief and the community are not to endanger one another. The chief's anger endangers his people; sexual pollution might render his rites ineffective; but, reciprocally, the heat of the shedding of blood menaces the chief's life. Here, schematically, are some of the ways in which sociability between the chief and his people is modeled upon matriclan sociability. The ritualized chiefship is matriclan sociability writ large.

In detail, the relationships vary in different matriclan chiefdoms but, as I shall show in the next chapter, regardless of nuance, matriclan chiefships contrast with patriclan chiefship defined in terms of patriclan sociability. However, to gauge the full extent of the contrast, it is necessary to augment the analysis of the relation between the chief and his people by an analysis of the relation between the official actors who hold centerstage in the ritual drama of the chiefdom. The center of the chiefdom is occupied by four distinct statuses: of the chief, the chief's assistants, the priests, and the blacksmiths. Ritual regulation depends upon the different contributions that these officials are empowered to make. Their individual efforts are orchestrated around the figure of the chief, with respect to whom their statuses are defined, and who is himself defined in relation to them.

Chiefs, Assistants, Priests, and Smiths

Chiefs and Chiefly Assistants

In the matriclan chiefdoms, descriptions of the ritual regulation of the community's welfare consistently return to the chief. The stages of the life cycle, hunting, farming, the annual cycle of rituals, the rites of both cults and shrines, and the detection of witchcraft all require instigation or endorsement by the chief. Unlike Mapeo, where informants are forced into particularistic accounts of ritual regulation, commentators in the matriclan chiefdoms have recourse to a notion capable of interrelating their various ritual activities. It appears to matter less that the allusions to chiefship are symbolically consistent than that the idea of chiefship may constantly be called upon to synthesize disparate activities by reference to a figure implicated in them all.

Idcally, the chief lived in the capital, usually the largest of the villages within his chiefdom, while the headship of outlying hamlets was vested in "children" of the royal matriclan, known as *mi.sani,* in Daka, or *wa.sama,* in Leko. This ideal was not often realized, and the most heterogenous ties were recognized between the chief and his subchiefs. The organization of the subchieftaincies was supposed to mirror that of the chiefdom on a reduced scale, so that subchiefs had their own chiefly assistants and priests. Again variation tended to be the rule. The complexity of the organization of the center differed from chiefdom to chiefdom. It was normally expected that the chief and his assistants would live in the capital, whereas the priests would live in hamlets outside it. The smiths either lived outside the capital or in a special smiths' quarter. The statuses of the chief, the priest and the smith were not always contrasted in identical terms but, what contrasts were made, pointed to variations on a limited set of themes.

The human actors in the drama of ritual regulation were further related to two other orders of being: animals and ancestral sprites. In Chamba cosmology, the relationship between men and sprites is the dominant axis of ritual exchange. At his installation the chief (*gangi,* Daka; *gara,* Leko) was brought into closer association with the ancestral sprites (*wurumbu,* Daka; *vɛnɛbbira vunɛdbira,* Leko), and with the royal animals: the leopard (*gbe,* Daka; *gɔa,* Leko) and the lion (*nyiki,* Daka; *gba'al nyiga,* Leko).[6]

The chief's association with the sprites is both general, that is to say with the sprites as a category, and particular, by virtue of his relation to earlier chiefs. The association between the chief and the sprites is marked in several ways. The Chamba Daka and Chamba Leko idiom for enthroning a chief is to "sit him on the stone," (*pɔksi gɔn da vani,* Daka); each chiefdom has one unworked stone on which the installation ceremony is performed. Design in stone is interpreted as the handiwork of the sprites, who are said to use stone where men would work in iron. Once the chief has entered his new status, his advice, or particularly the counsel about succession he confides before his death, is known as *wurum.mumi*, the speech of the sprite. The leaf placed on the back of a chosen chiefly candidate in the *gang.kuni* chiefdoms is known as sprite leaf (*wurum.ya*). *Wurum wɔki* is the "water" (i.e. beer) offered on the royal graves, themselves a class of *wurum.bum*, a sprite place or shrine. The brilliant white guinea-corn paste, or beer lees from the first brewing, which is daubed on the royal regalia and graves, is called *wurum.ken*; the small pots that hold the beer offered to the royal ancestors are *wurum.dubu*; *wurum.sɔmi* is the royal spear, and so on. In the matriclan chiefdoms, some of the most important natural products that in Mapeo are the prerogative of the matriclans are due to the chief on account of his relationship to the *wurumbu*—the only possible planters of crops not planted by men.[7] Most important of these resources is the highly valued tamarind crop, used as a bitter additive to soups and porridge.

Men inevitably suffer a relative deficit of power in their dealings with the ancestral sprites. In the Mapeo case, we saw how practitioners of *jubi* had to take precautions not to offend the *wurumbu* during their dealings with them. To the extent that the chief becomes sprite-like he is empowered, but to the extent that his status remains that of a human in close and constant relation with the sprites, he is also endangered.[8] Chamba conceptions play on this ambiguity. The chief is powerful, like the leopard or lion, his animal symbols. These large carnivores are a chiefly perquisite to be delivered to him if they are killed and only he, or another specifically encharged by him, may wear the chiefly leopard skin. But the chief's behavior is hedged around by prohibitions against conduct that would make him unacceptable to the sprites. Many of these are reminiscent of the taboos, *girani*, imposed on those in the vicinity of the cults. He may not commit adultery on pain of death. Even to sit on the sleeping mat of another man might pollute him. The prohibitions are most elaborate for the chief of Yeli, the most potent matriclan chief. He may not wear shoes, eat from metal bowls, or use any other European-introduced appliances (such as lanterns).

Ideally he should not travel at all, but should he do so his food must be carried with him from Yeli. He may not enter the royal graveyard, the place of his kindred royal sprites, nor take part in many of the rites carried out at his behest.

In all the matriclan chiefdoms, stories are told of chiefly candidates who fled their election, or of chiefs who did not long survive their installation. In Gurum, the first chief of a new chiefly clan is supposed to have been caught in a hunting net and elected before he was able to escape (see Chapter 5). In the past, it is asserted, candidates did not promote their chiefly candidacy; the first Sugu chief to canvas the chiefship in colonial times is recalled as the chief who shouted and sought it (*Gang Virɛn kɛte*). Formerly, to become chief was akin to dying, and another chief of Sugu is remembered as *Gang We bari*, "chief death has come."

The anticipated concurrence of the deaths of chiefs and the circumcision of boys tells the same story of the chief's close relationship to the *wurumbu*. Some informants claim that this is because circumcision sets were widely spaced, and few chiefs could hope to see many of them. Other informants are less prosaic. In Gurum, the old form of chiefly investiture was said to involve a reclothing of the chief. His gown and goods were removed, and each of the chiefmakers supplied him with a new item. His knife was broken into two parts from which the smiths forged two new circumcision knives. The first circumcision set of the new reign was operated upon with the knives that belonged to the chief's predecessor, but the next set would be circumcised with the new chief's knives. Before this could happen, he would have to die, either through natural causes, through the *jubi* or cults practiced by the priests, or through strangulation.

Yeli Chamba disclaim this practice but note that circumcision is dangerous to the chief. The hot blood is inimical to his coldness, and although the priests asperge the blood with water, the chief will eventually die—if not during the first circumcision he holds, then during a later one when his strength to withstand heat begins to fail. In this case, the knives of circumcision are forged from the late chief's knife. The relationship between circumcision and the chief's death is not automatic, as Frobenius had supposed (Frobenius 1913), but whatever gloss is placed on the event, the different life cycle

rites everywhere are felt to be interrelated so that chiefly installation is similar to death, and the death of chiefs is associated with
the circumcision of boys.

Priests and Chiefs

In many cases the chief's death provides the occasion for an expression of a latent antagonism between the chief and his priests. Many
informants, if questioned about the past, emphasize that real power
resided not with the chief but with his priests. "What did the chief
do?" informants rhetorically ask themselves. "Nothing," comes the
reply. The priests, and not the chiefs, were masters of the major cults
(*jubi*, Daka, *voma*, Leko) of the land. Whereas succession to chiefship was supposedly restricted to a section of the royal matriclan,
and appears to have been usurped by other sections from time to
time, succession to priestship tended to be either fraternal or filial.
The old priest chose a successor whom he would instruct in the
proper ways of conducting rituals. This training may often have been
incomplete on the death of the previous incumbent, but there was
an ideal image of continuity through knowledge. The chief had only
to embody his office; the training necessary for this is said to have
been imparted to him by the priests in a brief period subsequent to
his installation. Priests were technicians who had served a long apprenticeship. In many places, at least where informants are willing
to discuss the matter, full succession to priestship was dependent
upon the completion of rites to remove the skull of the previous
priest. Whereas the chief was defined largely in terms of what he
was and what he did not do, the priestly role was more active; priests
actually carried out the ritual regulation of the community.

The contrast between priestly and chiefly offices is developed in
all the chiefdoms. In all of them the priests are responsible for the
choice of the chief, for his installation, for carrying out the rites that
he finances, and for burying him secretly during the night when he
dies. In Gurum, a particularly elaborate organization of offices was
based on the opposition between twelve chiefly assistants, who lived
in the capital and were responsible for propitiation of the shrines of
the chiefdom, and twelve priests all drawn from the same patriclan
who were in charge of the cults of the chiefdom and lived outside

the capital. It is recalled that the priests would approach the chief en masse; they would beat the ground with their staves (which symbolize the cults), and threaten to beat the chief himself if he failed to speak well or to supply them with beer, fowl, and animals to repair their cults. This type of distinction between control of cults and shrines does not appear in the other matriclan chiefdoms, in which the priests are responsible for both types of rites.

In the Leko-speaking chiefdoms, and perhaps more generally, a distinction is drawn between the coolness of the chief and his compound and the heat of the priests and their *voma*. A similar theme emerged in the foundation story of Balkossa (Chapter 5). By virtue of his coolness, the chief is associated with the color black (use of black cloth was a chiefly prerogative in Yeli), with the sprites (who favor dark and cold places), and with health (since illness is also heat). The favored sacrificial animal on the chief's grave was the black ram, considered cold on account of its color and the general coldness of sheep. Priests were hot on account of the hot *voma* that they handled. Indeed, heat is generally transferred to those who have seen many *voma*, for which reason it is said that young pregnant women avoid stepping over the outstretched legs of seated older women. Illness is associated with heat, and many healing rites draw upon the notion of cooling by asperging with water. As a precaution, water is sprinkled upon the participants in cult rites, and upon women attending fertility rites. The chief's compound is the cool center of the capital and must be ritually protected against all influences that would tend to heat it. The chief himself refrains from attending the main *voma* rites, although his priests may bring the cult performance to the area outside his compound and will inform him of the results of their rites. The chief's place at the rites is taken by a representative to whom is delegated only those powers the chief himself has; significantly, this man may not be chosen from members of the royal matriclan.

Blacksmiths

The fourth figure in the ritual regulation of the chiefdom is that of the smith. One smith represents all of the members of his group to the chief and is known as the chief of smiths (*kpe.gangi*, Daka;

gat.lama, Leko). To understand the role of the chief of blacksmiths, we need to digress briefly to look at Chamba conceptions of smiths more generally. Chamba blacksmiths are members of an endogamous and hereditary occupational group denied commensality with the rest of the population. In the past, and to some extent nowadays, Chamba did not live with blacksmiths, marry or have sexual relations with them, eat with them, or attend their cults and rites. In some contexts, smiths are not considered Chamba (Sama or Samba) at all. In the Mapeo area, where most smiths are of Vere origin (although Chamba speaking), the denial of Chamba status may seem understandable. However, it should be recalled that a number of Mapeo patriclans are considered to be of non-Chamba origin, which does not prevent them from being considered Chamba once they become more Chamba-like in language and culture. If Mapeo Chamba choose to emphasize the Vere origin of their smiths, they are only conforming to a more general pattern of social organization that contextually withholds Chamba status from smiths, even where no other ethnic origin can be imputed to them.

In general, the non-Chamba status of the smiths is a direct inversion of the status of the chief, who is the Sama or Samba par excellence, and the contrast between the two statuses is evaluative. However, looked at closely, the opposition is more ambiguous; the smiths are both like and unlike the chief. Chamba statements, for instance, associate blacksmiths with dark forces: dirt, death, and witchcraft that in their different ways are antitheses of the associations of chiefship. Dirt (*liga*, Daka, *lira*, Leko), although used to describe mundane filthiness, has connotations of sexual pollution. Chamba cults impose prohibitions against sexual intercourse on cult participants, or sometimes on the entire village, for a period before their performance. Those who do not observe the taboos are said to have dirty hands (*wa liga*, Daka; *nen lira*, Leko) and must take special precautions to avoid the cult apparatus, which would be heated by contact with them. Blacksmiths, by virtue of their occupation, are in a permanent state of filthiness. Traditionally, the products of the forge or pottery were either washed or brushed with burnt feathers to clean them before they could be brought into the compound of the purchaser.[9]

By virtue of the privileged positions that the chief and priests enjoy with respect to the sprites, they have to maintain a constant state of cleanliness, especially manifest in the permanent injunctions upon them to avoid sexual pollution. Chamba rituals and statements on rituals make great play with the notions of dirt and washing, and in these terms the smith and the chief are in contrasted states. As a consequence of these ideas, the dirtiness of the smiths' occupation tends also to attract the sexual connotations of pollution, so smiths are generally considered to be promiscuous.

Blacksmiths are also stigmatized by the belief that they are witches themselves and assist the anti-social behavior of other witches. Unlike other identified witches, the smiths' essential labors on behalf of the community preclude their being beaten to death. Chamba tend to suggest conspiracy in witchcraft of all their neighbors and strangers more generally, so in one sense smiths attract suspicion of witchcraft by virtue of being permanently resident strangers. The iron goods manufactured by blacksmiths include ritual paraphernalia, as well as the mundane hoes, arrow- and spearheads, knives and so forth. Rattles, iron or clay figurines, metal bullroarers, and other cult apparatus are supplied to cult practitioners upon payment. During the manufacture, the blacksmiths' wives are forbidden to enter the smithy. Not only do the smiths know the supposedly secret contents of the cults, but there is also a suspicion that the cults may be ineffective against smiths. This is a matter of interpretation: some practitioners claim that once the items have been installed they become effective even against their makers. Others, including many of the smiths, claim that the smiths cannot be threatened by their own manufactures. The equivocation is part of a more general uncertainty about whether the cult apparatus is effective in itself or by virtue of the relation to the sprites that it mediates.

More directly to the point, Chamba claim that one of the techniques used by witches to kill their victims is the introduction of small iron needles into proffered calabashes of beer. A slight of hand is used to conceal the needle under a thumb nail, from where it is dropped into the beer. Chamba conceptions of witchcraft make no consistent distinction between mechanical means of causing death, poisoning, and the intrinsic capacities of witches. Accusations of witchcraft impugn the morality of the individual and his or her motives for killing, regardless of which technique of killing is applied. Blacksmiths find their morality under suspicion because they connive with witches by supplying them with needles. Some commentators speculate that the blacksmiths are themselves implicated in flesh debts between witches, a belief that not only serves further to sully the smiths' reputation, but also attacks witches with the accusation that they practice commensality in meals of human flesh with blacksmiths. To return to the chief, not only is he contrasted to the blacksmiths through his cleanliness and essential Chambaness, but his freedom from the taint of witchcraft allows him to organize periodic witch-finding ordeals. The welfare of the community is predicated on the assumption that the chief is never what the smith notoriously is—a witch.

A third stigma on the reputation of blacksmiths comes from their association with death, and especially the deaths of chiefs. We saw that the deaths of chiefs are associated with circumcision, and that this association has a material basis as the chief's knife furnishes the metal used in the circumcision knives, forged, of course, by the smiths. But smiths are specifically encharged with chiefly burial. Chiefs are interred during the night at a spot in the royal graveyard chosen by one of the priests. In the matriclan chiefdoms where I was able to elicit an opinion, the task of physically excavating the shaft and niche grave was said to fall to the blacksmiths. They also were encharged with plastering the mouth of the grave, which was closed with a flat rock. Graves other than chiefly graves are normally reused. They are merely closed with a rock or large inverted pot; but the grave of a matriclan chief must be sealed completely, and the chief's skeleton must remain entire.

There is a mundane explanation for these precautions. At installation the chief is given sprite-like characteristics, and his death completes his transformation to a sprite. However, unlike the ordinary dead, the chief remains a named individual through whom requests can be made of the sprite world. His successors, through their priests, will continue to invoke his name among those of the chiefs consigned to the underworld. Thus, it is important that his bodily remains not be confused with that of another, as is sometimes said to occur when graves are reused. Some elders request to be buried in fresh graves for this reason. But this would explain only the need for a new grave and not the specific observances which occur only at the burial of matriclan chiefs. Implicitly, we appear to be dealing with a contrast. Members of most Chamba patriclans remove and preserve the skulls of their dead.[10] These are either stored together in pots near the graves, where their individual identities soon become confused or, as in the case of important officials, kept in separate pots to receive offerings. The same custom is followed for patriclan chiefs.

Another distinctive feature of the treatment accorded to the chief's body also emphasizes the special nature of matriclan chiefship. Matriclan chiefs are buried in a particular section of the graveyard belonging to their matriclan, where the small pots kept to receive offerings of beer to the clan dead are also accumulated. In this respect, the very existence of a matriclan graveyard is unusual because Chamba are normally buried with their patrikin. The existence of a matriclan graveyard, the impartibility of the chief's body, and the withholding of his skull from his patrikin all point toward the dominance of consociating idioms of relationship in these customs. The bodily idiom of matriclanship is asserted against the patriclan's claim on his skull, and the relationship of embodiment, which characterized sociability between the chief and his people during his life, persists after his death as an expression of the dependence of their welfare upon his bodily integrity. The relationship between these notions recalls that leprosy and epilepsy, the conditions of bodily decay and the loss of bodily control, are the two specific diseases that disqualify a candidate from election as chief. It also recalls that the ultimate sanction at the disposal of the Yeli chief was the dread disease of smallpox (*kona*, Daka; *bəgələga*, Leko), considered by Chamba to be the most contagious of epidemic attacks against the body.

If the blacksmiths were indeed only dirty witches associated with the deaths of chiefs, then their standing would be low. But there is another viewpoint from which their status is redeemed. Leo Frobenius recorded a very full text of a legend that retains wide currency among Chamba. The story concerns the introduction of several basic elements of culture by the blacksmiths. According to Frobenius' version (1984:54–56):

> ... long ago Chamba did not know about fire. They left calabashes of water to be heated by the sun and then mixed in flour to make their food; until, that is, a smith appeared to show them how to use a flint and iron to produce fire and pottery in which to cook food. The smith then left. He reappeared again to change sexual customs. Chamba men had sexual relations with their wives by putting their penises under their wive's armpits. They considered the vagina unclean, because blood ran from it periodically, and so they only inserted medicine into it [Frobenius uses the term *gana*, medicine, a common variety of which is a four-cornered succulent, called *gan.vana*, "male medicine"]. The smith demonstrated to the Chamba how to crouch on a mat in order to have sexual relations. One of the women became pregnant, and the Chamba slit her open to remove the child. Both mother and child died. When a further woman became pregnant the smith called two women and showed them how to smooth oil into the woman's stomach, how to stand before and behind the woman to assist her parturition, and how to cut the umbilical cord with a guinea corn stalk and bury the placenta. Then the smith showed how to make doors in the huts, for before they had none. The people asked the smith to stay and live with them. Later, an old man died and the smith showed how to carry him to the tomb, and how to leave a metal object (like a hoe or axe) beside the corpse. Then he showed them how to celebrate after the burial and brew beer. And, after the burial, how to take two pots of beer to the grave, blow the *lera* flutes and remove the metal from the tomb in order to make the rattles and bullroarers for the cults. If the women asked for the source of the noise, the men were to say that the "grandfather" had come out [of the tomb]. All of this Chamba learned from the smiths, who gave them metal weapons for

men, hoes for women, and the knowledge of removing iron from graves.

The versions of this story I have heard are less comprehensive. I was never told that smiths introduced effective copulation among Chamba, and the Chamba custom of opening the stomachs of pregnant women is said only to have killed the women themselves (or, as one practical commentator put it, there would have been no Chamba left). Food is said to have been cooked in the hollows worn by women grinding corn on rocks; while the problem posed by huts without doors is recalled to have been that anyone sitting under the eaves during a rainstorm got wet legs. There is a problem in assessing just how seriously this story is taken. My impression is that, although the tale may be fun in the telling, the notion that some elements of culture are attributable to blacksmiths is seriously entertained, notwithstanding their otherwise scorned status.

Chambas' low regard for the personal morality and cleanliness of blacksmiths does not lead them to deny the contribution that the smiths have made to Chamba culture, and the tale includes contributions not specifically related to the smithing skill. The participation of the blacksmiths is required at a number of the annual rites of the chiefdoms. As well as donating specific manufactured goods, the blacksmiths are the chief's drummers responsible for beating the royal iron gongs and drums. This vigorous activity consciously recalls the rhythmic beating and blowing necessary to the smith's trade. Like the chief himself, and the subchiefs, the chief of blacksmiths is permitted to carry the curved wooden stick over his shoulder (*toma*), and to be addressed as chief. During the annual royal rite at Yeli, when the ancestors of *gat.kuna* are propitiated to assure the fertility of women, animals, and crops, the chief and the chief of blacksmiths sit together, on a new mat which the blacksmith chief has made for the occasion, outside the royal graveyard to await the return of the people from the ritual of blessing. This seems a curious conjunction of the pure and the impure, but informants say it is possible because the chief smith, unlike the priests and like the chief, is cool, because if blacksmiths were hot they would be unable to work with fire and hot metal as they do—I also have been struck by the way in which Chamba smiths seem able to handle burning charcoal and heated metal without suffering injury. The idea that smiths have to be cool to withstand their occupation is better founded empirically than the notion that they are heated by it.

In Gurum, the relationship between the chief and his smiths has been differently institutionalized. Gurum smiths, I was told, do not fear or respect the chief, or show him the courtesy that others would. Talking of the past, it is claimed that if the chief, on emerging from his compound early in the morning, caught sight of a smith, he would disappear inside and not be seen again for the remainder of the day. To the question of what the chief feared, the response seems to be ridicule. However fine a gown the chief bought, it is said that the blacksmith would buy one just as ornate and attire himself disrespectfully in the finery of a chief. Why should the chief's only riposte to the blacksmith's ridicule be to disappear? The answer can only be speculative, but we know that the chief is endangered by his relationship to the sprites, and that at his death the blacksmiths will come to bury his corpse. The blacksmith, on the other hand, uses special powers routinely without ever being endangered by them. He, and not the chief, was responsible for the introduction of important elements of culture, and while the chief is forced to remain secluded and relatively passive by the taboos imposed on his conduct, the blacksmiths' activities are described by resonant verbs of beating and blowing. He pursues his labors actively, which makes him dangerous to others who have to protect their coolness. Whereas the chief has to be kept cool, the blacksmith is resistant to heat in his nature. In these respects, the chief and the blacksmith represent opposed faces of potency, a situation that is consonant with the smith's immunity from punishment and, at the risk of overinterpretation, betokens a certain hollowness in chiefly power.

The ritual regulation of well-being in matriclan chiefdoms, predicated on a particular type of relationship between chief and community, also rests upon the sorts of potency attached to the statuses of the four types of office discussed here. The chief embodies the welfare of the community, he directs and provisions the necessary rites, but cannot carry them out himself. The chief's assistants personate the chief, by acting in his stead in places and at times when

Figure 13 Celebrations during the Annual Royal Death Rites at Yeli

he cannot be present without being endangered. The priests control the heat of the cults, and maintain the knowledge of techniques that control the most important cults of the land that ward off disease. They choose the chief, install and instruct him, and finally assimilate him at death to the remembrance of past chiefs with whom he will intercede on behalf of his successor. For their part, the smiths are both defiled and powerful. Without them, farming, war, and, it is claimed, the regeneration of life itself, would be impossible. The relationships involved can only be approximated oppositionally; beyond bold contrast is ambiguity and uncertainty.

In different ways, all of these figures are estranged from the community in terms of their special powers; together they orchestrate potency at the center of the chiefdom. As the embodied exemplar of his people, the chief is conductor of this orchestra. But as the example of Mapeo reminds us, this orchestration is not inevitable. Certain Chamba societies are sustained in the absence of an exemplary center by means of an allocation of precise responsibilities to competing groups; not all ritual efficacy is monopolized at the center, even in the ritualized chiefdoms. Although the more potent cults are controlled by the chief and his priests, lesser cults dealing with different common ailments remain in the ownership of the community's constituent clans. Beneath the appearance of ritual hierarchy flows an undercurrent of clan-based competitiveness that is intensified because of the incorporation of the clan-owned offices and some of their cults into the central organization of the chiefdom.

Delegated Chiefly Functions and Annual Rites

In Chapter 2, I demonstrated the competition between patriclans in Mapeo by describing how each found a time in the annual cycle to command the attention of the community, during which they performed the rites particular to their clan culture. At Yeli, in contrast, delegated chiefly functions dominate the yearly rites. Since Yeli and Mapeo are separated by a few miles, the natural order of events is identical. The new year (ze pua) begins, as in Mapeo, when the first of the new harvest is eaten around December or January (these first two months are called guinea-corn harvest month, yɛt kɛdn soa, and chief's guinea-corn harvest month, gat yɛt kɛdn soa, when everyone cooperates to harvest for the chief). Once the harvest is brought in, funerary rites (val.batna, death beer) may be held for those who died during the wet season. These rites are completed during March (yɛb yɛl soa, the red earth, or "building" month), and April (gɔnga la soa, the month of burning guinea-corn heads). If the rains arrive on time, May is the month of sowing guinea corn (yɛt lum soa, corn-seed month).

During the remaining months, the Yeli calendar begins to diverge from that of Mapeo. Every other year, the Gbannɛbba of Yeli, custodians of the chief's lera flutes, organize a festival of lera singing and dancing, which is partly held in honor of the chief and known simply as lera beer (lɛd.batna).[11] In the following month of the shea tree (kɔl soa), when the harvest of shea butter kernels takes place, the chief's head priest, Dura, organizes the rite of val.batna, death beer, by means of which the dead of the royal matriclan are assimilated to the gat.kuna memorial site. This rite is designed to make offerings to the gat.kuna dead and to secure fertility for the chiefdom. July is the month of the guinea-corn skull or death (*so yɛt vara*), since seed planted after this time will not germinate. Dura is responsible for breaking the seed gourd (*yɛt lum pɔba*) to signal the end of the planting season. In *so kɛla*, the pot month, which has no agreed etymology, Dura is sent by the chief to the hills to make an offering to the royal ancestors in the hope of achieving a good harvest. This rite begins the period of taboos, *giri nyama*, during which a man should not have sexual relations before going to farm, and loud noises may not be made.

Around August, in the month of *so dinga*, the "black month" when the previous year's corn harvest is exhausted, Dura and his Sama clansmen undertake the important task of clearing the area around the small hut in the bush where the smallpox spirits are called to receive offerings. The localization of these spirits is the basis of Yeli's claim to ritual preeminence, and the rite that assembles them is considered the most dangerous of the year. Immediately afterwards the Nyɛmnɛbba, who are the chiefmakers of Yeli, begin the *voma* rites of *vom.ninga*. They are also, by virtue of their prior occupation, nominal owners of all the land excepting the grave sites they are said to have given to other clans. This is the uncircumcised month (*so za*), because the true character of the harvest is unknown. Harvest is the test of the crop, just as the true character of a boy can only be assessed from seeing his reaction to the pain of circumcision. Both are known after cutting. The rites of the Nyɛmnɛbba are succeeded by those of Jɛngnɛbba, the chief's bodyguards. The stalks of the guinea corn swell, (*so nyia*, "trunk month"), and the heads of corn fill out and begin to hang down—in fear of *voma*, Yeli Chamba say. The final month of the year, *so la*, "fire month", marks the time for the burning of the bush and for the offering of *vom za'an batna*, "beer for getting up the cults," to the cults owned by members of the community.

Although brief, this discussion serves to illustrate that, unlike Mapeo, the Yeli calendar revolves around delegated duties performed on behalf of the chief by his different officials. Whereas Mapeo rituals are almost solely concerned with cult observances, Yeli Chamba operate on a more varied set of rites involving the *lera* flutes, sacrifices to the past chiefs, offerings to the collective dead of the royal matriclan, and direct propitiation of the spirits of smallpox. These differences arise from the different ways in which time is appropriated for the ritual events in Yeli and Mapeo, and imply a number of political differences between the two communities.

Variation and Change in Matriclan Chiefdoms

I have formalized Chamba expectations of matriclan chiefship into a pattern of associations that I term consociation. The pattern derives from my attempt to translate and interrelate statements I have heard, and to relate them to Chamba standards that normally prevail in given conditions. This type of analysis does not account either for variations that exist between different chiefdoms, or for the changes undergone by chiefdoms individually. It deals in what they share, rather than what separates them. But it can contribute to the historical perspective by providing a summarizing set of expectations that possibly informed and inflected Chamba agency. In concluding this chapter, I return briefly to the historical narrative of Chamba political development.

We know that the establishment of the matriclan chiefdoms of the central Chamba area predated the Fulani conquests (Chapter 6). Traditions maintain that the earliest chiefdom established by Daka speakers was among the Jangani peoples in the hills around Da Dukdu. This chiefdom, which hardly exists today, was the source of both the twin chiefdom of Sugu and Nya Gangngwu, and the ritual paramount of Yeli (Chapter 5). Various contemporary features of organization are considered by informants to be explicable in the light of this history. The close relations of Sugu and Yeli are particularly evident in the necessity for them to confirm one another's chiefs in office. It is believed that the apparatuses involved in the control of rain and smallpox were transferred from Sugu to Yeli, because of which the chief of Sugu continues to send delegates to Yeli when rainfall is insufficient.[12] By a rule, to my knowledge, unique among Chamba, the chief of Yeli changes his patriclan affiliation upon accession to become a member of a section of the Jangani patriclan (the Lum.nɛbba section of Jangan.nɛbba, in Leko).[13] Children born subsequent to his installation will belong to this clan rather than their father's natal patriclan. The custom is considered to be a recognition of the original claim of the Jangani to ownership of the land. The chief of Yeli encompasses in his own status a relation more normally expressed between a matriclan chief and a patriclan priest. Chiefly families that invoked an origin from Yeli to support their legitimacy established themselves throughout the central and southern Shebshi Mountains. All claim to have sent periodic offerings to Yeli in the time before the Fulani jihad, although the establishment of an independent smallpox shrine within the chiefdom of Gurum, again justified by a foundation story associating it with Yeli, suggests that some attempt at ritual self-sufficiency may have been made there. Members of these chiefdoms also subscribe to the dogma that all Chamba come from Dayela.

By examining kinship, clanship, and the organization of ritualized chiefdoms, we have been able to flesh out these historical recollections with more precise notions of the kinds of organizational devices that sustained these interrelations. In doing this, we have also noted anticipations that Chamba informants voice about the values associated with matriclanship and matriclan-based chiefships. The contemporary culture of matriclanship and the way that informants recollect the period in which matriclanship thrived are intimately related. In terms of this relationship, present organization may be depicted as a decline from a previous ideal, which remains visible only in traces and vestiges. Yeli informants find in their present chiefdom a shadow of the importance that it once occupied. Apart from retaining links with Sugu and Mapeo, Yeli is virtually cut off from its old hegemony by the modern Nigeria–Cameroon border. But when the Chamba chief of Ganye, the modern administrative capital of the central Chamba, was created a second-class chief in 1983, the aged Yeli chief was brought to Nigeria to be present at the ceremony. And, although the Ganye chiefship is a modern creation, its incumbent was validated by the presence of a member of the *gang.kuni* royal family. Obviously, the older ideals still lend themselves to annexation to the confusing standards of modernity.

Chamba informants note other emendations of the ideal matriclan chiefdom pattern. The chiefships of Gurum, Yebbi, Sapeo, and the Danaba subchiefdom of Dim Kusumi have all been taken over by patriclan owners. In Sugu, the male chief is said to have increased his authority at the expense of the female chief, claimed by many informants once to have been preeminent. In Yeli, the traditional division of powers between an immigrant chiefly family and indigenous priests has been complicated by the creation of a priestly role vested in the Sama patriclan, the occupant of which is encharged to carry out rituals on behalf of the chief. More generally, informants, especially older individuals, claim that the behavior of chiefs changed during the late nineteenth century and colonial period. The ideals of matriclan chiefship became subverted as chiefs began to act more like their counterparts among the Chamba of the patriclan chiefdoms, the Fulani, and latterly, in terms of the responsibilities devolved upon them by indirect rule.

Matriclan chiefship implied an ideal. It was presumably honored in the breach in its own day; it certainly subserves some present interests that are occasionally politically transparent, but its present importance is often attributable to the desire to see beyond a morally confused present. Like matriclanship itself, matriclan chiefship is not simply a romantic vision of the effects of extreme closeness. Togetherness carried costs of contagion and danger. If we cannot recover the events of the pre-jihadic period with certainty, we can at least know the period through its forms and ideals. In the next chapter, we will examine how those forms and ideals changed.

CHAPTER 10

THE POLITICS OF ADSOCIATION:

DOMINANT CHIEFSHIP

So closely do the presuppositions of Chamba politics of adsociation converge with our own that, without the contrasting frameworks of ritual involution (in Mapeo) and consociational incorporation (in the ritualized chiefdoms), we might overlook the fact that dominant chiefship is a political style. At its inception, this variant of Chamba political organization, modeled on patriclan sociability, must have been unprecedented. We have seen how the ascendancy of consociational forms was increasingly challenged by adsociational idioms of relationship during the nineteenth century. The later the foundation of a chiefdom, and the more numerous and diversified the non-Chamba elements incorporated within it, the greater the predominance of patriclan sociability it displays. Contrast with the ritualized type of organization is most marked in the Chamba conquest chiefdoms outside Chambaland (the Benue and Bali Chamba). To a diminishing degree, the contrast is also evident in the northern Shebshi conquest chiefdoms, in the chiefdoms of the northern residual Leko, in the erstwhile matriclan chiefdoms that changed to patriclan type during the nineteenth century, and in the matriclan chiefdoms that retained their forms but tended to change their functions in the course of the later nineteenth and twentieth centuries. The extent to which these chiefdoms reflect features of a dominant chiefship corresponds to the general degree of displacement of matrilateral by patrilateral idioms of organization.

I begin this chapter by itemizing a number of related indices of the movement toward patrilateral idioms or adsociation, and account for them in general terms. I subsequently survey the regional variability of this style of Chamba politics. Because adsociational incorporation developed in the context of the Chamba Leko diaspora, we find a variety of local detail adopted from new neighbors. Nonetheless, by reference to the contrastive frame of consociational organization, we can see that, whatever the local variants, common developments occurred in the course of transition between types.

In comparison to the ritualized notion of chiefship discussed in Chapter 9, the type of chiefship discussed here illustrates changes in its forms, functions and very conceptualization. Chiefships tend to become vested in patriclans rather than matriclans. This tendency co-occurs with the shedding of a number of their earlier matriclan characteristics, such as danger to an individual chief, and the ritual protection of the community. Furthermore, concomitant with the increase in patriclan forms, the chiefship is redefined in terms of dominance by force, specifically the force of the patriclan owners. The treatment of the chief's body is instructive: the bodily impartibility of the dead chief, so strongly marked in the matriclan chiefdoms, is replaced by chiefly skull shrines, modeled on patriclan custom and expressive of the exclusive relationship between the patriclan, and its past and future members.

However, the changing position of the chief is only an index of a more general decline in importance of the older notions of mutuality. Consociation, as I have termed it, is variously attenuated. A more general index is the restriction in the organizational importance of many aspects of matriclanship. Matriclanship within Chambaland continued everywhere to be important throughout the colonial period and up to the time of my fieldwork. However, even in this, attenuation was noticeable. Partible inheritance is tending to be replaced by a filial norm throughout Chambaland. With the demise of the Chamba cults, matriclanship is no longer an important criterion of membership in these institutions for the majority of younger people. The illegality of slave status and child pawning has further lessened the importance of the relation between mother's brother and sister's son. Greater mobility means that many children are born or brought up in places where their close matrikin do not reside. As a consequence, individuals live in places beyond the range of the cults, and many Muslims and Christians would anyway refuse to make the payment for "repair" of cults, which is a collective responsibility of matrikin. Most younger Chamba informants now claim they have abandoned exogamic restrictions upon marriage or remarriage within a matriclan (discussed in Chapter 8). Before the colonial period, patriclanship developed in importance in many places, to the detriment of matriclanship. Preferential marriage between immigrant patriclans was practiced in the chiefdoms of the northern Shebshi Mountains. Outside Chambaland, in the Benue and Balı chiefdoms, matriclanship had died out perhaps as early as the time of the foundation of the conquest chiefdoms. Although the degree to which matriclanship has been attenuated is variable, and depends upon the political history of the political unit in question, the trend toward attenuation has been pervasive.

The changes in chiefship, kinship, and clanship correlate with a modification in the basis of incorporation into the polity. Whereas consociation, particularly in the idiom of mutual ritual responsibility, had underpinned the incorporation of differentiated elements within the matriclan chiefdoms, in the patriclan chiefdoms incorporation is envisaged to result from military alliance or conquest. The significance of this change is not only in the historical circumstances under which the chiefdom came into being, although these seem to be reflected fairly faithfully, but also in the persistence of domination as the most explicit rationale for the contemporary organization of the chiefdom. The organization of the conquest chiefdom is explicitly derived from military superiority rather than from any other criterion, even where this capacity is expressed in terms of the ability to provide order or protection from outsiders.[1] Narrative differences consistent with this occur in the foundation stories of the ritualized and conquest chiefdoms: the former appeal to the ritual abilities of the incomers, the latter to their military capabilities.

In this context, it is easy to appreciate the importance attached to annual martial ceremonies in all the conquest chiefdoms. These celebrations tend to displace the earlier importance given to cult rites of harvest. Rites of destruction outweigh rites of reproduction. In part, this change is also indicative of the different status accorded peoples considered indigenous to the chiefdoms. In the matriclan chiefdoms, such people tend to be the priests, chiefmakers, custodians of the preeminent cults, and the directors of the annual harvest celebrations. By contrast, in the neighboring northern Shebshi chiefdoms of Chambaland little recognition is given to indigenous ritual efficacy; where it is recognized, compliance with the wishes of the chiefly clan tends to be coerced. In the northern residual Leko chiefdoms, chiefly and priestly clans are settled in different areas and their rites are considered antithetic. The differences between the cases will become apparent in the survey of adsociational political forms to which I shortly turn.

In the midst of these changes, a terminology of subjection was introduced into Chamba language from a Hausa/Fulani model. Chamba Daka has no terms by which to distinguish freemen or rulers from commoners. There is a term for slave, *kəsani*, and two common terms for outsiders, which can be applied to other groups of Chamba as well as their neighbors: *sɛnɛni*, stranger, and *dɔ*, a derogatory term denoting language difference that connotes primitiveness. Nowadays, this term is used of adherents of traditional religion by converts to world faiths. Otherwise, a number of useful composites are available (such as *gang.tu.bu*, people of the chief, *kamɛn.tu.bu*, people of the priest) which may be used to designate members of a clan that owns an office; and they might apply *nɛ.dɔkɛn* (a compound of the pejorative *dɔ*) to nonmembers. But there is no specific terminology to distinguish those who rule from those who are ruled, except to speak of a chief and his people; this omission is simply explained by the absence of any such relation in the acephalous and consociated types of chiefdoms in which Chamba lived before the Fulani jihad.[2]

With the advent of overt politics of domination, terms were adopted from the Fulani and Hausa to express this new relation, which was not one of slavery, but of subjection to the authority of others through physical force. *Dimu* was adopted from the Fulani to describe a freeman and *talaka* from Hausa to describe, pejoratively, the status of a commoner. During the course of my research in Mapeo, I rarely heard these terms used, except in relation to outsiders considered to have been conquered by the Fulani. They were not used frequently by elders in the southern Shebshi mountains, except in relation to the controversies surrounding the transference of chiefship to patriclan owners in Gurum. But in the chiefdoms of the northern Shebshi Mountains, they were used so frequently as to figure in any description of political organization. Although the terms are borrowed, it could be argued that they answer a potentiality of Chamba adsociational organization that had not been actualized previously.

In concert with these formal changes in organization, there was also a change in the mode of exploitation within the community and between communities. Whereas gifts, labor parties, certain natural products, and, to some extent, trade were the main sources of revenue for matriclan chiefs, the patriclan chiefs exploited tolls on traders and pastoralists crossing their territories, practiced forced appropriation, and both raided as well as manipulated legal procedures to secure slaves for sale. The chief's ability to provision his officeholders and their clanspeople, particularly with horses and gowns, was enhanced at the same time his responsibilities for the ritual regulation of his chiefdom were eroded. The result was the emergence of differences in wealth between classes within the chiefdom, a situation that had scarcely existed previously. Even in the case of Yeli, which had received gifts or seized goods from those communities of Chamba that recognized its capacity for ritual violence, the goods received were consumed through the ritual cycles of the chiefdom and the cult rites of the priests. The necessity for chiefs to provision their supporters generously was built into the techniques used by Chamba bands to raid their neighbors.

In the early stages of expansion, only a small raiding band would have been needed to successfully attack small communities of ill-defended people. However, as illustrated in Chapter 4, the tendency to split was a dominant feature in the histories of all the Chamba-led alliances that left the Chamba area, as well as in the chiefdoms of the northern Shebshi Mountains. Because the resources were there for the taking, and the most recently raided or threatened were themselves available to augment the fighting strength of the alliances, the pressures that promoted fissioning must have been difficult to resist.

Many of the patriclan chiefdoms settled in the plains. Those, like Donga and Bali Nyonga, that managed to defend or expand an exposed settlement through the turbulent times of the late nineteenth century were generally forced to find organizational means to control fissioning, most frequently through the delegation of limited powers to subchiefs and ward heads, and the proliferation of offices and privileges for non-succeeding royals. In all cases, effective administration demanded that ethnic and territorial differences become entrenched in offices and their associated privileges. The movement of matriclan chiefly capitals out of the hills during the late nineteenth and early twentieth centuries also tended to introduce adsociational mechanisms into government. This movement coincided with the separation of a chief from the bulk of his people and with a need to deal with the external agencies of the Fulani and colonial administrations.

In short, the provisioning of the consociated polity's rituals centrally was first overturned in the Chamba raiding bands, and later routinized into expropriations from neighbors, in the case of the conquest chiefdoms, and internal expropriations, in the case of those refuge chiefdoms in which the chief was able to manipulate alliances with either Fulani or Europeans.

In general, ethnic difference is handled differently in consociated and adsociated chiefdoms. In the ritualized chiefdoms ethnic difference usually calls forth recognition in terms of a ritual division of responsibility; this tendency is especially visible in the manner in which duties are distributed between immigrant chiefs and indigenous priests, but it also occurs in the ritual cycles of communities like Mapeo. Thanks to the scattering of marriages, and the absence of ethnic difference between most matriclans, ethnic difference cannot furnish the basis for unequal incorporation into the political community. In conquest chiefdoms, the attenuated regard for matrilateral connection, the direction of marriages (in some cases) toward political allies, and the demise of the notion of shared ritual responsibility for communal welfare correlate with the emergence of an ethnic principle of differential incorporation. Ethnic difference comes to be seen as an argument supporting differential rights rather than differential capacities and responsibilities.

The five factors just enumerated: the change from ritual to dominant conceptions of chiefship, the control and attenuation of matrilateral relationships, the incorporation of subjects on the basis of domination, changing modes of exploitation, and the increasing political salience of ethnic difference, are aspects of the process by which ritualized Chamba chiefdoms were replaced by ethnically divided chiefdoms and city-states. In a wider context, we can see the political process as an indication of a cultural transformation. In most cases, the development of these chiefdoms was impeded by their own small size, by the strength of their neighbors (especially the Fulani), and by the advent of proto-colonialism. However, the examples of Bali Nyonga, Bali Kumbad, Donga and Binyeri, at the height of their powers, show that this mode of organization was potentially able to support political communities as large as the largest of the matriclan chiefdoms (between five to ten thousand inhabitants, to judge by early colonial censuses; see Appendix 3).

The transformation in Chamba political style may in part be seen in terms of a reaction to the Fulani jihad of the nineteenth century. But it would be a mistake to see Chamba reactions solely as emulative. At least since the eighteenth century, central Chamba had two idioms of sociability at their disposal. Earlier events, culminating in the process of Chamba ethnogenesis through the expansion of matriclan chiefdoms, were predominantly acted out in terms of the consociating idioms of sociability, whereby perceptions of difference between sociates were consistently interpreted in terms of their mutual responsibilities. Difference was accommodated as special aptitude in the pursuit of shared goals, or abrogated more radically in an appeal to shared characteristics.

To the extent that chiefship appealed to force, techniques of violence were effected through ritual. The events of the early nineteenth century were not amenable to response in these terms. The organization of physical violence had always concerned Chamba patriclansmen, and the idioms of patriclanship stressed historical difference and cultural variety. Regardless of Fulani influence, if patriclanship was to be emphasized as a basis of collective action, then consociational idioms were bound to recede in importance. During the later nineteenth and twentieth centuries, the divisive force of adsociational idioms came to invest the politics of matriclan chiefdoms, and the Chamba identity itself, both of which had been established consociationally.

Some matriclan chiefs acquired the support to act in the same manner as their patriclan counterparts, although they retained some aura of their earlier position as embodiments of their communities; Chamba ethnic identity became one more of the exclusive and exhaustive identifications which made up the colonies of Nigeria and Cameroon, and later those independent states. Chamba idioms of sociability underwent, in their own terms, something akin to the processes of rationalization that Weber analyzed in western and ancient civilizations. The pertinence of consociational idioms of organization was gradually restricted from areal, to community, to clan, and finally to domestic relations involving the family home and immediate kin, as political relations were increasingly taken over by patriclan chiefdoms, colonial administrations and, finally, the governmental frameworks of regions and the state. The later stages of this development belong in the next chapter; in the remainder of the present chapter, I shall review the forms of patriclan chiefdom that arose among Chamba before the colonial period.

Types of Chamba Patriclan Chiefships

The Northern Residual Leko

Historically, these remnant Chamba chiefdoms were displaced from the northernmost pre-jihadic area of Chamba settlement, where they had bordered the Bata. Following the foundation of Tchamba by the Fulani, the chiefdoms were forced into the mountains and paid tribute to the Fulani to avoid being raided. Not all of the northern residual Leko lived within the chiefdoms. Instead there was, and still is, a mixture of communities living along the hillsides, some of which are directed by priests, and others by chiefs. Linguistically, there are resemblances between the Chamba Leko dialect spoken here and that spoken by the Bali Chamba; certain organizational themes also recur. The chiefly communities (such as Saptou and Kollu) draw their chiefs from members of the Sama patriclan. The chiefly clan possesses no *voma* cults, its rites concern the *lera* (here pronounced *lela*) flutes, and the skulls of the Sama clansmen, especially those of the chief (*vara*, skull).[3] Rites concerned with *lela* and *vara* occupy the places that would be taken by cult rites in the matriclan chiefdoms at the times of planting and harvest. Not only does the smith have no role in these rites, but it is said that any blacksmith witnessing the royal skull rites would die. However, disease-causing cults are still the prerogative of matriclans, as in Mapeo or the ritualized chiefdoms.

Those communities of the northern Alantika Mountains that are without chiefs are headed by their priests, *wana*, who are also custodians of the major *voma* of the harvest. At places like Lowol (Dzap.kolu in Chamba), the priestly patriclan is Nyɛmnɛbba, identical to that of the "owners of the land" in Yeli. Like the chiefdoms, these communities were forced to pay tithes to the Fulani of Tchamba, although they claim to have recognized no relationship with the Chamba chiefdoms of the area. An injunction against marrying girls of *gat.kuna* appears in these chiefless communities, justified by the supernatural dangers of mixing the cold (chiefs) with the hot (priests), that is also the theme of the foundation story of Balkossa (Chapter 5). Both chiefly and chiefless communities recognized Yeli as the controller of smallpox, and offerings are claimed to have been sent via the chiefdom of Kollu in case of an epidemic outbreak.

Northern residual Leko organization articulates contrasts we have encountered before. Cold chiefs associated with rites of *lera* are contrasted with hot priests, controllers of *voma*. But, in contrast to the southerly Leko, the two types of official are not incorporated into the same political community. Since this is the single most important difference between the two areas, it would appear that this development is associated with the vesting of chiefship in the exclusive idiom of patriclanship. Chiefly skull shrines assume prominence in chiefdoms not vested in a matriclan, thus preempting consociating ritual, which is governed by the impartibility of the chief's body. Although the point can be no more than speculation, it seems likely that northern residual Leko organization represents an early Chamba transformation towards adsociational forms of organization, either by reaction to Fulani inroads or, perhaps, in response to other northern influences mediated by the Bata. The same themes are submitted to a different resolution in the Bali Chamba chief-doms, suggesting that the basic matrix of organization predates the diaspora.

The Northern Shebshi Chiefdoms

The northern Shebshi chiefdoms were established within Chamba-land by immigrants of varied Chamba and non-Chamba origins dur-ing the nineteenth century. The non-Chamba, mostly Vere and Bata/Bachama, have become Chamba to the extent that their origin is recalled only by their patriclan name, *Ka* or *Kambu* (Bata) and *Mɔmbu* (Vere), and in a few ritual practices considered not to be Chamba. The founders of these chiefdoms seem to have arrived rela-tively well-mounted and armed, and they were initially able to es-tablish their settlements in the plains. However, the later expansion of Fulani into the Nassarawo Plain during the second half of the nineteenth century forced them into the hills. No matriclan chief-ships are reported from this area, and I was able to find only two exceptions to the rule that officeholders are all appointed on the ba-sis of patriclanship. Unlike chiefdoms farther south, elaborate ritual cycles are not characteristic of the area, nor is there evidence of at-tempts to incorporate indigenous groups fully into the processes of appointing the chiefs of the territories, as occurs to the south. Sub-tribal differentiation forms the basis for access to offices, and con-quest is emphasized as the foundation of the relation between rulers and ruled. This is further reflected in the prominence of martial rites in the chiefdoms. Much the same titles and categories of office are recognized throughout the area and, by comparison with the matri-clan chiefdoms, the sets of officials include a relatively large number of warrior titles, but relatively few priests.

The most numerous and powerful of the northern Shebshi patri-clans, or patriclan clusters, was the Yambu, one section of which rules the Polla chiefdoms, while another rules the chiefdoms of Tola and Binyeri. A third section supplies chiefmakers to the Yambu chiefdoms. Like the southern matriclan chiefdoms, those of the north have chiefmakers called *kamɛnbu* but, unlike the southern chiefdoms, the chiefmakers are drawn not from the indigenous population but from closely allied or related patriclans. The Chamba axiom that "you cannot give yourself chiefship" is barely honored. The chiefs of Tola, Binyeri, and the smaller places also ruled by Yam.tub.bu, are appointed by priests of the related Yam.dəgum.bu patriclan. In Polla, chiefship is given to a member of the Yam.də.bu patriclan by a head chiefmaker drawn from Mombu, a small incorporated clan of Vere. Since the relation of alliance and co-residence between Yambu and Mombu is considered to be of such long standing, they may lay claim to a closer relation of common parentation, or "one father." At Polla Djalo, a second and less important chiefmaker is appointed from the *gang.tim.nɔ.kuni* matriclan. This office is said to have been instituted when a section of Jangani was incorporated during the passage across the Nassarawo Plain. Initially, it was given to the son of a marriage between a chief's daughter and a Jangani man.

The roles of the priests of the Yambu chiefdoms are more restricted than those of their southern counterparts, since the most important "cults of the land" are considered to be ones that belong to the Yambu patriclan, *ya.bum.ani* and *jɛrubi*, which remain under the control of the chiefly clan. Propitiation of shrines, considered to be local haunts of the sprites, as in Gurum and Sugu, is virtually unknown. The only one at Polla is said to have been bought from the local Mangla and given into the custody of the Vere priest. In the past, for most members of the chiefly clans are now members of world faiths, the most important observances were centered on the skull shrine at Vanku, the earliest Yambu settlement on the northern Shebshi Mountain fringes, where chiefs were taken to be installed and where the previous chiefs were solicited for assistance.

Other titles are similarly monopolized by members of the royal clan or their allies. In the southern Shebshi chiefdoms, the warrior offices, *nya.gang.bu*, are said to be later introductions filled largely on an appointive principle. Once patriclan chiefship was instituted in Gurum, the offices were given to children of daughters of the royal patriclan. In Polla Djalo, Mbulo, Dalami, and Mbangan, war leaders were members of the royal clan. The sole exception to this generalization is to be found in Tola and Binyeri, where a number of warrior titles were given to the indigenous peoples who threw in their lot with Damashi, the leader, to raid west of the Shebshi Mountains.

Apart from the offices of chiefs, chiefmakers, and war leaders,

there were few specialized positions within the northern Shebshi
chiefdoms, and the sets of offices show little of the variation that
characterizes the southern chiefdoms. Polla Djalo is claimed to have
had two special officials, drawn from the royal clan, who were encharged with funerals of royal clansmen. *Dako* took charge of funeral arrangements, whereas *kuni* was responsible for the digging of
graves. Both of these offices are now defunct. Additionally, an official
known as *kpanate* was found throughout the northern Shebshi
chieftaincies. He provisioned the chief's household; he brewed beer,
received portions of animals caught in the hunt, and organized work
parties. This office may be of Bachama origin, since he is reported as
an official among them, and *kpana* seems to be a common Bachama
title (Meek 1931b:5–6). Throughout the northern Shebshi area, the
duties attached to the office appear to have been sufficiently onerous or servile to discourage chiefly clansmen from attempting its
monopoly.

In Binyeri and Tola, many offices other than the priestships and
chiefship were occupied by indigenous allies of the Yambu. However, these allies occupied their own hills and therefore remained
residentially discrete. The chief's assistant, *gban*, the divider and
provisioner, *kpanate*, and various titled war leaders were drawn
from local peoples called Dangsabu, Tolabu, Kokumbu, and Nyi-
sabu. Small incorporated patriclans of Jangani and Vere had no special offices but claim to have acted as the enforcers of the chief's
decisions; they captured thieves who would then be bought back by
their kin to avoid sale into slavery, and they urged the exchange of
members between matriclans to avoid revenge killings between patriclans in case of murder. The local peoples within Binyeri and Tola
either retained or developed chiefly organization on the arrival of
the immigrant Yambu. Although their chieflists begin at the time of
the arrival of Damashi, they claim to have had chiefships before
then. These local peoples have their own cults, shrines and graves,
which they manage independently. Only the indigenous chief of
Gang Pana has been co-opted into the ritual organization of the
chiefdom in the role of head diviner to the Binyeri chief.

The Bachama-founded chiefdom of Mbulo is virtually identical
in organization to the Yambu chiefdoms. The chief is appointed
from a section of Kambu called Kam.vowe.bu, and his assistant from

a different section called Kam.jibawe.bu. The *kamɛn*, alternatively known as *kpane*, is drawn from a matriclan simply known as *kamɛn.kuni*, although earlier occupants of the office are recalled to have been Yambu. The war leader, *nya.gang*, is drawn from the chiefly clan section and is said to have been the heir apparent to the throne; he appoints an assistant, *trigali*. The leader of the cavalry is known by the Bachama title *kpanduwe*; and a provisioner, *kpanate*, was chosen from the Yam.dɔ.bu. The indigenous Mangla, most of whom live within Mbulo, are granted no particular offices, but their leader, Gban Mangla, was given a small offering to bring rain in the event of drought. It is indicative of the position of the Mangla that informants, including the incumbent Gban Mangla in 1978, note that his failure to summon up rain led to Gban Mangla receiving a beating and being told to try again. Like the Yambu of Polla, and the Jumamɛmbu of Mbangan, the Kambu took the skulls of their chiefs and elders to be installed in a shrine in the vicinity of Vanku, the site where the immigrants had first congregated.

The Farang chiefdoms conform to the general northern Shebshi type. The chief was appointed from a section of Farnɛpbu by chief-makers belonging to Yam.dɔ.bu. Warrior offices of *nya.gang*, *turi-gari*, and *kpanduwe* were given to members of the royal clan, as was the office of chief's assistant, *gbani*, and that of the royal gravedigger, *kuni*. The role of *kpanate* was filled by an appointee.

The Leko-founded chiefdom of Mbangan was ruled by Juma-mɛmbu, who were appointed by Vere chiefmakers. Additionally, there were the usual offices of war leader, a "brother" of the chief, a counselor, a provisioner, and an official responsible for gravedigging and transporting skulls to Vanku, here called *gbanso*.

The repetitive terms of organization of the northern Shebshi chiefdoms recur in the central plains chiefdom of Dalami. The chief, his war leader *nya.gang*, and the leader of the women's cults, *mala*, his paternal aunt, are all drawn from the royal patriclan now called Lamnɛpbu, after the Da Lami River on which the chiefdom stands. Informants of the clan say their ancestors formed a section of the Sama patriclan of Kollu among the northern Leko. However, the relationship between chief and priests conforms to the northern Shebshi rather than northern Leko pattern. The priestly and chief-appointing office of *kamɛn* is owned by a section of Yambu, known

here as Yam.kamɛn.bu, whereas a clan of immigrant Lamja that intermarried with the chiefly clan provide the chief's counselor, *da
gban*, and assume chiefship during an interregnum. Additionally,
there are clans of Jangani and Vere, and the allied clan of Tiranɛpbu
holds the neighboring subchieftaincy of Tim Dəng. Dalami, it may
be recalled, maintained its plains settlement by virtue of clientship
to Yola.

The terms of northern Shebshi chiefdom organization are highly
repetitive; important offices are distributed between a few patriclans
that are interrelated through common parentation, prolonged co-
residence, and alliance. The officeholding clans are virtually all immigrants to their territories, whereas local clans are rarely given important positions within the chiefdoms. Clearly, the chiefdoms have
exerted influence upon one another and have adopted similar office
sets; a great part of their similarity is probably attributable to their
co-residence and alliance during the period of the Vanku settlement.
Although not particularly remarkable in themselves, these organizations acquire greater significance when they are compared with
those of the matriclan chiefdoms. The results of such a comparison
indicate the extent to which the divisive idiom of patriclanship has
been elevated to virtually the sole basis of incorporation within the
political community of the conquest chiefdoms.

The Benue Chamba

Although our sources on the emigrant Benue Chamba are limited to
investigations in Donga, which give us a partial account, they are
sufficient to demonstrate the preeminence of patriclanship in general, and of the royal patriclan in particular. The chiefly patriclan,
Sama, provides the majority of the most important officeholders of
the chieftaincy. Meek and Garbosa both give lists of Donga officials
(Meek 1931bI:334–38; Garbosa n.d.:35–37); neither suggests internal classifications of the offices, but Donga elders were of the opinion that the fourteen officeholders were in two groups of seven, only
one of which was responsible for chiefmaking.[4]

Foremost in the chiefmaking group is *gbana*, the chief's assistant, who is appointed from the patriclan of the same name. Meek,
using a Jukun title, refers to him as *abo*. *Kpəngate*, the next most

senior official, is appointed from the "brother" kindred of Janga, and called *kpwati* in Jukun. Garbosa claims him to be responsible for war, and Meek states that he may take charge of any troubles arising in outlying villages.

According to Meek, the officeholder who is third in seniority is *kuni*, drawn from the Denkuna clan. This official places the hippo-hide whip on the shoulder of a new chief to signify his election. Garbosa says that this office was traditionally reserved for a woman whose mother had been a member of the royal clan. Because of her constant companionship to the chief, she was called "the wife of the gara." Donga elders I consulted agreed both with the view that *kuni* was a woman and that she was drawn from the Denkuna patriclan. It seems possible that title and clan name are related, since the suffix -*kuna* would normally denote a matriclan in Chamba Leko.

Nya is the senior official responsible for the organization of war. Both Meek and Garbosa distinguish the duties of *nya* and *kpangate*, the war counselors, from those of *gangum* and *galim*, the leaders of the warriors. Contemporary elders state that suitable candidates were appointed to this office regardless of clan.

Tigye is the custodian of the royal drums. This title is reputed to have been given to Garkiye, founder of Donga, by his father's successor at the Gankwe camp. The office was also given to a Jibu at Donga, who was later said to have betrayed the trust placed in him.

Mala, the paternal aunt of the chief, is a member of the Sama clan. She may appeal on behalf of those estranged from the chief or who wish to influence his judgment. For Meek, she is "queen over women," and Garbosa claims that she would be able to succeed in the absence of a male heir to the chief (an unlikely circumstance given the scale of polygyny). She is also the custodian of the women's cults of *vomkima* (equivalent to *vom.kena*, women's *voma* among Chamba Leko). The seventh official, or *vompobiya*, also a member of the royal clan, is the chief of the men's *voma* cult.

Six of the seven titles are similar to central Chamba terms. Three, *gbana*, *kuni*, and *mala* are identical; *nya* may be related to *nya.gang*; *kpangate* could be a variant of *kpanate*, and *vompobiya* is a variant of the central Chamba *vomba*, *vomwana*, or *gatvoma*; only *tigye* is unique.[5]

The *voma* cult seems to have been attenuated into a single institution particularly associated with rainmaking. It retains its associations with the calabash horns and basket rattles, which are also used in similar rites in Chambaland (Meek 1931bI:348–349). In Donga, *voma* is under royal control. The women's cults, also associated with rainmaking, were owned by the various Donga patriclans but were under the direction of *mala*, also a member of the royal patriclan. These cults probably retained associations with disease, since Meek remarks that they might effect a cure for male impotence (1931bI:347). Otherwise, the most important rites appear to have revolved around skull shrines owned by each clan. The skull rites of the royal clan are reported to have been carried out in secret so that the people would not realize that these rites did not differ from their own (Meek 1931bI:365–366). Of the seven titles, two (in addition to the chiefship itself) are vested in the royal clan and another may have been reserved for a royal relative. An additional title is given to a closely related clan, whereas another two are appointees. Therefore Donga, in restricting access to crucial positions, conforms to the conquest model of Chamba political organization.

The development of martial ceremony suggests further convergence between Donga and the other conquest chiefdoms. Two martial rites were held. The first, after the harvest, was called *ding sukbia*, "washing the spears," and involved spears belonging to Donga clans, termed *ding sa kuna*, literally "the spear that looks out for the family." The occasion of sacrificing chickens in front of these spears was also an opportunity to treat the warriors with "medicines" (Meek 1931b:340–341). A larger ceremony and military display, designed to instruct younger warriors, was held around October and called *purma*; it closely resembles the *lela* ceremony of the Bali Chamba (for descriptions of *purma* see Meek 1931b:349–355; Garbosa n.d.:91–93).

We know little of the relations between the Donga Chamba and their non-Chamba neighbors. Garbosa tells of how the population of Donga increased as people flocked there in search of security. Subchiefs were recognized as leaders of some of these elements. Garbosa also records that the administration of allied tribes was achieved through the appointment of mediators. The mediators dealt with representatives of the tribe who, in turn, had responsibility for internal administration (n.d.:96—98). This model may have been adapted from the Fulani category of official known as a *jekada*. Bali Chamba organization diverges from this model in respects that are reminiscent of northern Leko organization.

The Bali Chamba

Considered together, the five Bali chiefdoms have made a particular and distinct adaptation to their Grassfields environment. We noted in Chapter 8 that these changes included substantial alterations in their systems of kinship and clanship along Grassfields lines. In addition to the attenuation of matriclanship, which also occurred in Donga, the Bali Chamba instituted title lines and positional succession. However, not unexpectedly, these chiefdoms, regardless of scale and incorporation of non-Chamba, share significant features that can be related to their Chamba cultural patrimony.

Linguistic evidence points to a historical relationship between the core of the Bali emigrants and the contemporary Chamba Leko of the northern residual area. For the latter, the term Sama refers to the royal patriclan; Dagalbira is the term used for the Daka and Nakenyare, as well as for the Leko of Yeli, when a speaker has the origins of the Yeli chiefly family in mind. In the Bali chiefdoms, the term Sama includes the meaning of princes or royals more generally, and the term Ndagana covers the sense of non-royal among its meanings. It seems reasonable to suppose that the contrasted Bali terms, Sama and Ndagana, derive from the paired terms used by northern Chamba Leko. Although there are differences in the way that the distinction is actualized, Bali Chamba subscribe to a set of associations in which the Ndagana are the custodians of *voma* and the Sama the custodians of *lela* (*lera* in its southern Leko pronunciation).[6]

The same contrast is found among the northern residual Leko, where *voma* is the prerogative of priests and *lela* of chiefs; and where chiefly and priestly communities are residentially discrete. But in Bali, the antithesis between chiefly and priestly rites has been contained through recognition of the chief himself as titular head of both sets of rites. The rites are clearly derivative of their central Chamba forms. *Voma* retains its associations with the guinea corn harvest, although maize is now the Bali staple. The calabash horns and rattle sacks continue to furnish the musical acccompaniment for the public dances, and are hidden from women (except in the case of Bali Kumbad, which is recognized as exceptional by Bali Chamba).

Although local political considerations have by now led to an extremely heterogenous collection of appointees to *voma* titles, the rites are associated historically with Chamba clans, and particularly that of Djab.nɛbba. The generic term for priestly officials, *nwan.voma*, is also derived from a central Chamba term, *wana*. In common with the Donga *voma* institution, the Bali *voma* rites appear to have undergone attenuation. Informants suggest that the Bali *voma* is a composite institution, since the priestly officials bring the cult objects associated with different named *voma* in their bags. The names of these *voma* are the same as those of some named and separate institutions among the central Chamba. Like central Chamba priests, the Bali *nwan.voma* are said to be responsible for the installation of the chief, and for carrying his corpse to the grave and burying him. According to Bali Gham informants, the chief (*gala* in Bali dialect), but not the chiefs' children, may attend sacrifices at *voma*. This suggests that some of the antagonism between priestly and royal status has been retained in the contrast between Ndagana and Sama categories, which the chief, but not his children, transcends.

The rites of *lela* are organized by the royal office holders. The term *lela* refers not only to the bamboo flutes (here, as among the northern Leko, in a set of four), but also to the annual martial rites of the same name, which are very similar to the Donga rites of *purma*, in which sacred spears and flags also figure. In both senses, *lela* is strongly associated with the chief himself, as the owner of the flutes and the central figure of the martial rites. In Bali Gham, and most probably elsewhere, although the knowledge is not public, some of the Sambila and the senior Ndaganbila are responsible for the ceremony of "begging" the *lela* flutes in the royal grave hut.[7] Those of the Sambila who take part in this rite are called *vatyɛbba*, "the children of the skull" (*vara*). Even in the absence of the esoteric details of these rites, we are able to recognize another pervasive feature of the idioms of patriclan chiefship in the importance ascribed to chiefly skull rites. A further indication of the significance of these rites is clear from the prestige that accrued to Bali Nyonga when the skull of the hero leader of the united alliance, Gawolbe, was retrieved from the Bamileke who had taken possession of it after their victory against the Chamba at Nkɔm (Hunt 1925).

Whereas the general division between the two types of office-holder and the two types of rite is admitted in all the Bali settlements, the lists of officeholders that I and previous researchers have collected show great variation, both between chiefdoms, and in different accounts of the same chiefdom. Suffice it to note here that, in the dynamic political organizations that the larger Bali states constituted until after the onset of the colonial period, the perquisites of office were considerable, and competition for them was not deflected by the countervailing attractions of local government frameworks to the extent that occurred among central Chamba. In part this was because of the prominence enjoyed by Bali Chamba as mediators of German colonial administration, and in part because Bali Chamba were not competitors with Fulani, as the central Chamba found themselves.

A point of note concerns the continuity of titles between Bali Chamba, Benue Chamba and the central Chamba in a number of cases. The titles of *do kun* (comparable to *kuni*) and *do nyagang* (elsewhere *nya.gang*) recur as war leaders in the Bali chiefdoms (compare Chilver and Kaberry 1968:64) and seem to have been the prerogative of daughters' children of the royal clan. A second, more general, point concerns the non-Chamba features of Bali organization. As in Donga, circumcision sets, also recognized by central Chamba, attained greater significance thanks to the organization of age-graded regiments in terms of them, and to the establishment of warrior lodges. The greater scale of the larger Bali chiefdoms demanded administrative refinement in the recognition of quarter organization under ward heads. Adoption of positional succession tended to undermine the conceptually corporate status of Chamba patriclans in favor of title lines, and saw the institution of title lines for queen mothers. Palace organization achieved greater prominence with the adoption of large-scale polygyny for the chief and a system of palace service for some young men.

The claim to northern Chamba origin and, bizarrely, to kinship with Fulani,[8] subserved particular interests that Bali Chamba had in distancing themselves from their Grassfields neighbors. Self-conscious anachronisms, such as the building of a single round hut in the palace, the necessity for the chief to plant a small guinea corn field in order to offer guinea corn seeds to royal dead, the weaving of grass mats of northern pattern to be sat upon by chiefs, and the importance attributed to a "traditional" Chamba dress which, apart from using a two-part kilt as the lower garment, bears no resemblance to any garment worn by central Chamba, are part and parcel of political claims made in cultural terms within the Grassfields context.

Given the large numbers of Grassfields peoples incorporated within the Bali chiefdoms, it is no surprise to find that most aspects of Bali Chamba culture are very similar to that of other peoples in the same milieu. But, all the differences between Bali Chamba and central Chamba admitted, it is remarkable that a presumably small, emigrant force, cut off from its homeland since the early nineteenth century, and in an environment different in many ways from that which it had left, was able to maintain not only its language (in four of the five chiefdoms), but also so many features of distinctively Chamba political organization. This signals the extent to which elements of Chamba descent were successful in retaining control of the alliances they recruited and, additionally, the historical tenacity of the individuality of Chamba patriclan culture. This trait inheres in the way that Chamba conceive of their patrimony, and which, through their regard for it, their patrimony comes to be stamped upon all Chamba organizations that draw heavily upon idioms of patriclanship.

Summary

Despite the fact that the four geographic areas of Chamba patriclan chiefship examined in this chapter (the northern Leko, northern Shebshi Mountains, Benue Chamba, and Bali Chamba) developed in virtual independence throughout the nineteenth century, the organizational solutions they brought to bear on problems of incorporation were strikingly similar. In each case, patriclan chiefs developed strategies to incorporate, or distance themselves from, the powers of clan-owned cults that were seen to be antithetical to chiefship.

Maximum chiefly control over these cults emerged in the emigrant chiefships, where Chamba elements drew together to protect their interest against that of their numerous non-Chamba allies. In the northern residual Leko chiefdoms, an opposing strategy was evinced in the residential separation of chiefly and priestly communities. The northern Shebshi chiefdoms, founded among ethnically diverse members of the extensive Chamba people, represent, as we might anticipate, an intermediary strategy, in which the cults were neither wholly subject to chiefly direction nor wholly separated from the chiefship.

In terms of their common features, patriclan chiefdoms may be contrasted with their matriclan counterparts. The divisive idiom of patriclanship, which gained ascendancy as the basis of power shifted from ritual potency toward military supremacy, was reflected in the new pertinence of ethnic difference, the preeminence of patriclan rites, especially concerned with the chiefly skull line, and the new prominence accorded martial rites.

Concurrent with this development, the older communal concern for fertility (of women, animals, and crops), embodied by the chief, was replaced by an emphasis upon the destructive force at the command of the community, of which the chief was the epitome. This display of force, most cacophonously developed with the introduction of muskets in the Bali chiefdoms, was designed both for internal and external consumption. Where the matriclan chiefs' powers depended to a great extent upon their abilities to withhold fertility from their people or, in the case of the Yeli chief, to visit smallpox on them, the patriclan chiefs relied upon more direct means to affect the bodies of their subjects. Decline in the ritual vulnerability of the body of the chief and in the bodies of his subjects proceeded concurrently. In Chamba terms, both adsociation and consociation are finally underwritten by violence, but the presuppositions on which violence rested differ. Ritualized chiefship presupposes a mutual vulnerability that derives from close relation; dominant chiefship rests upon the disciplines that can be inflicted on unrelated bodies.

My argument has been that these developments are most easily comprehended by accepting that Chamba sociability had always been susceptible to two different constructions, which were cued contextually. Given the contexts in which conquest chiefdoms were founded, Chamba agents were liable to cue in, that is, interpret and act in terms of, an appropriate set of expectations about sociability and its effects. Put another way, from their understanding of what they would take to be the material conditions of enactment, Chamba would be predisposed ("choose" may be too purposeful a word) to construe and act upon and through others in different ways. Nineteenth century conditions consistently favored an approach to construing and acting in terms of adsociating idioms, and the successful adaptation of the Chamba to a changing political context suggests that the ability to make contextual adjustments had survival value. Twentieth-century contexts gradually evolved circumstances in which congruent images of family, clanship, community, and government were insufficient guides to judicious action. The range of circumstances which they might appropriately inform was restricted finally to the local and familial.

CHAPTER 11

COLONIAL DISJUNCTION:

THE POLITICS OF MODERNITY

This descriptive chapter picks up the narrative threads I left at the end of Part 1 and examines political developments among Chamba after the imposition of colonial rule. It leads toward the socio-cultural context in which I carried out my local researches with Chamba between 1976 and 1987 and to the limits of the model through which I have tried to interpret and explain some aspects of precolonial Chamba political development.

Colonization, evangelization, Islamicization, western education, colonial and later national administration, and all their minion "-ations," beginning with exploration, were to alter the political context of Chamba agency and, finally, the forms that agency took. The pertinence of previous notions of sociability became restricted to local, domestic, and kinship affairs, and to the vestiges of earlier political organizations that had been co-opted into more modern schemes of administration. It is from these sources that I have tried to reconstruct the range of their previous importance. These changes ushered in what I term modernity, a word that covers a confusing and contradictory set of tendencies. The colonial disjunction was, in its effect, a separation between the forms of agency relevant to local and domestic matters and those required for judicious action in larger forums. If the relationship between the two is in fact less clearcut than this definition may make it seem, the polarity is nonetheless genuine. Earlier Chamba idioms moved easily between the referents of immediate parentation and the largest traditional units of organization. Modern political affairs are not amenable to conceptual as-

similation or movement on the same scale. Modern Chamba ethnicity, along with the related notions of Chamba culture, tradition,
or custom derive most immediately from the colonial experience
and its aftermath. For the Chamba of Chambaland, these developments have taken barely a century.

The emigrant Chamba of the Benue and Bali conquest chiefdoms came into contact with Europeans earlier than the Chamba
speakers who had remained in Chambaland. Chamba of the middle
reaches of the Benue met the MacGregor–Laird expedition in 1854,
when the future chief of Donga was encamped at Ganako, near Ibi,
on the Benue River (see Chapter 4; Baikie 1956; Crowther 1855).
When in 1900, control of the Royal Niger Company's "Upper Benue"
Province was assumed by the British government, most of the Benue
Chamba found themselves in Muri Province of Northern Nigeria
(Fremantle 1922:2–3). The Bali Chamba were also contacted and
brought into the European colonial project at what is in Chamba
terms a relatively early date. After 1889, when the German explorer
Eugen Zintgraff arrived in Bali Nyonga, that chiefdom became an
important post in the heart of the German colony. In the absence of
Fulani rulers to act as administrators, Zintgraff proposed that the
Bali Chamba might act as mediators of German interests in the Bamenda Grassfields. For a short time, Bali Nyonga, then known as
Baliburg, was supported by the Germans in its attempts to dominate
its neighbors.[1]

Farther inland, and removed from the major waterways, Chambaland was not directly affected by either of these series of events.
Heinrich Barth recorded some information on the tribes and languages south of Yola, but was prevented from confirming his reports
in person (Barth 1857 II chapters 35–36). The German explorer
E. R. Flegel passed through Chambaland in 1882 and left us his itin-
erary (Flegel 1883). Another German expedition under von Uechtritz
and a French expedition under Maistre crossed Chambaland in the
1890s and left brief accounts of this part of their journeys (Passarge
1895; Maistre 1895). When Chambaland was eventually colonized,
its partition was a purely accidental result of the competition to control Yola, the Fulani capital of Adamawa, and thereby the trade of
the Emirate as a whole. The 1880s coincided with consolidation of
British trading interests and a belated foray into Africa by Germany.

By the middle of the decade, British traders reached Yola and established a trading post on a hulk moored in the Benue River. Then, in 1886, Britain and Germany extended the boundary they already recognized northward to a point on the Benue east of Yola (Rudin 1938:67–68). Thus, Britain gained control of Yola, whereas Germany acquired the Fulani subchiefdoms to the south, which were nominally subject to the Emirate capital.

Further clarification of the boundary was agreed with the demarcation of the "Yola arc" in 1893. The authority of the Emir of Adamawa was to be restricted to the western (British) side of a boundary that passed through the Shebshi Mountains before making a thirty-mile detour to the east of Yola (Weladji 1974:164, 169). The chiefdoms of Chambaland apart from the few most northerly and westerly outposts of the Nakenyare (notably Binyeri), were ceded to Germany. A working party set out to demarcate the boundary in 1907. From Yola they worked their way through the Shebshi Mountains, and in 1909 signed the protocol confirming the boundary (Whitlock 1910).[2] The Germans appear to have begun touring the central Chamba area in 1907 (C.778 Crane 1958), and in 1913 they built a customs post at Mayo Kalai (near present Jada), the earliest European station among the central Chamba.[3] Only two years later, action by combined Anglo-French forces ended German colonial interests. Cameroon was occupied and German administration was terminated before it could become established. This sequence of colonial endeavor followed by truncation was to be repeated for almost another half century. Nonetheless, the short period of German colonialism demarcated boundaries and spheres of interest that confronted later administrations as entrenched positions. To see how this occurred, we must look at the terms within which Germany established the colonial status of the central Chamba.

The northern part of the German "Kamerun" colony held out little prospect of easily exploitable resources, especially as communications to the coast were severely stretched. Initially, the Germans left the transportation of resources from the interior to the coast in the hands of native carriers. Administration of the interior was effected indirectly through Fulani princes, part of an organization which has been discussed by Rudin (1938). Rudin (p.299) summarized the rationale of this administration as follows:

Greatest leniency toward native ways was evident in Adamawa, at any rate towards the Fulbe [Fulani] people through
whom the Germans administered that part of Adamawa.
Care was taken not to disturb Islam by the admittance of
Christian Missionaries into the region; at the same time
thought was given to the welfare of the aboriginals whom
the incoming Fulbe had conquered in the early part of the
nineteenth century or had driven into the mountains. The
resident commissioners appointed to advise the native [i.e.
Fulani] princes were instructed to keep a protecting arm on
the enslaved people, since, it was reasoned, from the latter
must come part of the colony's future labour supply, the
Fulbe themselves being far too proud to work.

According to the same author, the control which the Fulani
exercised over "aboriginals," who were "enslaved" or "driven into
the mountains," was "well organised" and "quasi-feudal" (Rudin
1938:136). The stark contrasts we found earlier in travelers' reports
are reiterated by this sympathetic commentator; the misunderstanding of Fulani–Chamba relations, so convenient to a colonial power
with slender resources, was virtually complete.[4] Fulani political organization was not "feudal" but based upon different types of exploitation within a framework of ethnic pluralism locally adapted
by contingent alliances, often expressed through nominal conversion to Islam. The central Chamba experienced colonization as a
period of intensified Fulani dominance during which the various ac-
commodations reached between Chamba and Fulani were often superseded by the Fulani mandate to rule on behalf of the Germans.

The Fulani chiefs recognized by the Germans dealt with their
subjects not directly but through *jekada*, appointed officials who
acted as intermediaries between the Fulani and the Chamba and
were often resident in the Chamba communities given over to their
control. The Chamba chiefdoms were simply carved into a set of
administrative spheres under the leadership of the old Adamawa
subchiefdoms. Most of the communities of the Alantika Mountains
and the immediately neighboring plain (Mapeo, Sapeo, Lapeo, Balkossa, Garamba, Jaggu, and Duna) were under the administration of

the Fulani of Laro; a smaller number of communities to the north was attached to Tchamba (Saptou, Kollu, Yeli). The chiefdoms of the southern Shebshi Mountains (Sugu, Nya Gangngwu, Kiri, Da Dukdu, Danaba, Gurum, and Yebbi[5]) were administered by the Fulani of Koncha. Nassarawo controlled the remainder of the plain and those chiefdoms of the northern Shebshi Mountains that lay within the German territory. Laro, Tchamba, and Nassarawo were supervised by the German resident at Garoua, whereas Koncha, which had become the most powerful among them, was under a resident farther south in its sister community of Banyo (K4 Mair Letter to Resident June 1918). The great freedom of maneuver allowed the Fulani is remarked in later British reports and instanced by the ability of Fulani chiefs to exchange parts of their territories (G2.2 Nassarawo District History). Their main responsibility appears to have been tax collection: on the establishment of the customs post at Mayo Kalai in 1913, a poll tax of six marks and a cattle tax of one mark were introduced. Fulani rulers were officially permitted to retain a proportion, apparently a quarter, of tax collected.

Fulani chiefs enjoyed variable degrees of success in their dealings with the Chamba communities entrusted to them. Greatest success was achieved in cases where a preexisting relationship had existed. Koncha, for instance, appears to have managed its relations with Sugu peacefully thanks to the recognition of alliance relations prior to the colonial period.[6] Sugu informants stress the cordial relationship between them and the Koncha Fulani. But relations between the Koncha Fulani and the Chamba of Gurum and Yebbi were marked by sporadic violence and the absolute refusal of the Chamba to acknowledge their appointed Fulani rulers.

Raids by Fulani against Gurum probably occurred frequently, although it is now difficult to disentangle specific attacks from the general recollection of hostilities. One large-scale attack appears to have been launched from Laro in the 1870s (Relly 1954, quoting a 1935 report by Savani, which I have not seen). The hinterland of Gurum also suffered during the passage of the von Uechtritz expedition through the Shebshi Mountains (Passarge 1895). When Strümpell toured Gurum in 1907, he seems to have received a cautious, but eventually friendly, reception from the chief, who refused to have anything to do with Koncha but was willing to pay tax via Nassarawo so long as Gurum remained independent. The German official apparently saw no reason to end Gurum's independence (Strümpell 1907). Perhaps Gurum officials saw in the Germans a useful counter to the ambitions of the Fulani. If British reports and Gurum recollections are to be believed, the policy was not wholly successful.

While "on tour" in 1921, the Yola Resident, C. Migeod, met Gang Maken, the Gurum chief with whom Strümpell had dealt in 1907, and who may have acceded around 1897. He learned that in 1907 Gurum "threw off the yoke of Kwancha," which seems a rather florid description of the matter described by Strümpell. A period of independence seems to have ensued until 1912 when Mai Gari, the Fulani chief of Nassarawo throughout the German period, summoned the chief of Gurum to meet him at Danaba where he informed him that the Germans ordered Gurum to pay taxes. The date of this event corresponds approximately to that of the establishment of the first German customs post in Chambaland. Gang Maken was persuaded to comply with the request by gifts of gowns to his headmen, perhaps an old counter in dealings between Chamba and Fulani, and "by soft words and promises," the substance of which is unspecified. During World War I, demands for labor and corn became excessive, so the chief of Gurum went to the nearest British officer at Mayo Farang and "told him all he knew about the Germans." Following this (presumably in late 1914 or early 1915), the chief of Nassarawo, accompanied by German soldiers, attacked Dabora within the Gurum chiefdom, killing ten people and carrying away ten more (B3.X Migeod 1921).

This confrontation with Nassarawo does not appear to have been the sum of Gurum's tribulations, although further interpretation of rather garbled records becomes difficult. In 1920, in the course of an exchange of letters between the Yola Resident and W. D. K. Mair, the officer in charge of the "Chamba patrol," the Resident claims that Koncha and Nassarawo raided Gurum with the assistance of German troops and carried off a hundred people. Mair's reply is intended to clarify the issues involved so that a decision about the future administrative status of Gurum could be reached; his information is drawn from the Fulani chiefs of Koncha and Nassarawo. From the chief of Koncha, he learns that the Sugu Chamba are "friendly," but the Gurum Chamba "dangerous." (We might also note that the sale of slaves to Fulani continued in Sugu at this time.) Gurum was nominally part of Nassarawo, but the Nassarawo chief refused to go there and claimed that a German had once tried to collect taxes from Gurum, with an escort of eight soldiers, but had soon given up. Mai Gari, the Nassarawo chief, had himself raided for slaves near Gurum, but not to Gurum itself; the Yola Fulani had also attempted raids but abandoned them when they lost too many men (G2.2C Correspondence 1920).

In the collective Gurum memory, one raid stands out. Known simply as the "Koncha war," this attack is said to have caused the death of many Gurum men, and the capture of many others. Gurum Chamba claim that the raid was supported by Germans, some of whom were killed during the action. Perhaps P. S. Crane refers to the same events in his report of "running battles" between Gurum Chamba and forces from Koncha and Nassarawo, during which two German soldiers were killed (C778 Crane 1958). Since Strümpell makes no reference to these hostilities, they must have occurred after 1907. Whether they formed part of the campaigns of World War I, or whether they occurred as part of a German attempt to assert administrative control and impose taxation just prior to the war, cannot be ascertained on the basis of the records to hand. In either case, it is obvious that German administrative policy was particularly unsuccessful with respect to Gurum, and that the overall beneficiaries of German colonization were the local Fulani chiefs, who were supported in their attempts to exert authority over previously recalcitrant Chamba communities, at the same time that the international boundary permitted their independence from their nominal overlord at Yola.

Thirty years after Flegel crossed the Nassarawo Plain, Germany lost its Kamerun colony to the British and French. British reports were later to speak of German atrocities, and the Chamba would remember the German period as one of hardships and sufferings. Given the slight colonial presence, it is legitimate to wonder how far these recollections were offered in the knowledge of British antipathy to Germany, and to what extent they referred to the short period of the war itself. The visible legacy of the German period to the new administration lay in the administrative framework that had been put in place. The campaign of 1915 left Britain and France in control of the old German colony. Letters from the British officials expressed the hope that Yola would be reunited with its old subchiefdoms in Adamawa, thus reestablishing a viable traditional unit of administration. In fact, Adamawa had never been successfully centralized, and the British view probably reflected palace propaganda; in any case, Adamawa was never reconstituted since the majority of its territory was ceded to France (K2 two volumes). Administration by the sole British officer in charge of what had become known as the Southern Mandated Territories continued to be based at Koncha until the formal transfer of that chiefdom to France in 1920. Two years later, Britain was granted a League of Nations' mandate to administer most of central Chambaland, but only had gained Nassarawo, of the Fulani chiefdoms that had administered the area on behalf of the Germans.

At this point the British found themselves faced by seemingly irreconcilable demands. While the Cameroon was occupied territory, they were bound to continue administration along German lines;[7] but the territory under their control was not identical to that which the Germans had administered and there was, in any case, considerable uncertainty about the way in which German administration had functioned in practice. Since the resources that could be devoted to the administration of a mandated territory were slight, indirect rule, to which by this time the British had an ideological commitment, was also expedient. This meant using traditional political organizations as instruments of administration; but a difficulty emerged immediately in relation to the term "traditional." In areas where there had existed well-organized, stable political structures, the idea of "traditional organization" could be given substance without undue complication; indirect rule could be justified in terms of this understanding of the "traditional" and practically implemented through the modification of preexisting political arrangements.

In the case of Adamawa (and most of the Nigerian middle-belt), tradition was a slippery concept. The preceding century and a half had been tumultuous. Chamba communities had reacted to the Adamawa jihad in a range of ways; the Fulani had grown in authority, but the problem of organizing stable relations between the center of the Adamawa Emirate and its chiefdoms had proved insoluble. This problem had been exacerbated by the Anglo-German and Anglo-French boundary settlements, which enhanced the powers of the subchiefdoms, now independent of outside Fulani powers, at the expense of the Emir. If to this scenario is added the dramatically fluctuating and local nature of arrangements between Chamba and Fulani, it readily becomes apparent that "tradition" offered a flexible, and not necessarily practical, guiding standard. It was even debatable whether "traditional" arrangements between Chamba and Fulani were still pertinent so long after the first attempt to impose colonial rule. Nonetheless, efforts at administrative reform, when they occurred, were almost invariably justified by appeal to some "traditional" state of affairs.

It is difficult to know whether the key to present administrative success was seriously sought in the past, but the surviving colonial records make it clear that change was certainly justified by reference to the past. The self-conscious sense of tradition, so much part of Chamba modernity, must derive in part from accommodation to the types of retrospective arguments endlessly elicited by colonial officers. The fieldworker eliciting oral records in the present is reminded by the colonial records how many times other British visitors had asked similar questions in different political times. Its appeals to tradition notwithstanding, British administration brought into being a system of indirect rule which bore little resemblance to any earlier political arrangement in the region. The histories of the Fulani subchiefdoms clearly illustrate this point.

Laro, Koncha, and Tchamba belonged to the eastern cordon of Fulani chiefdoms established along the Faro–Deo river system in the earliest years of the jihad. Although transfigured by their colonial roles, there is at least a genetic link between the colonial and nineteenth-century organizations of these chiefdoms. Nassarawo is, to all intents and purposes, a colonial creation. In the first half of the nineteenth century, Fulani had not settled the northern half of the Nassarawo Plain in large numbers. The few Fulani there appear not to have fought the Chamba. Sources are not completely clear on the point, but for reasons that may have been connected with the control of trade crossing the plains, the first Emir of Yola, Modibbo Adama, decided to send a son, Hamidu, to take over the "Chamba fief" (G2.2 Nassarawo District History; Vicars-Boyle 1910). Hamidu founded the village of Nyibango at some time around the middle of the century, although the dating is disputed. Again, there are no reports of fighting between Chamba and Fulani. On the demarcation of the Anglo-German boundary, Mai Gari, grandson of Adama, left Nyibango and crossed to the German side of the border to settle at Ubawo, which became known as Nassarawo. Under the Germans, Mai Gari was put in charge of much of central Chambaland as well as sections of neighboring Koma, Vere and Vomni. The new Anglo-French boundary placed Nassarawo and virtually all its territory in British hands and, after a short period of captivity to atone for connivance with the German war effort, Mai Gari returned to Nassarawo with a salary of three hundred pounds a year to carry on business as usual.

The boundary makers had been kind to Nassarawo and to Tchamba, which fell into the British and French sectors respectively, but the chiefs of Laro and Koncha found themselves in difficulty, since the new boundary bisected territories that they had administered under the German regime.[8] In 1920, the chiefs of both Koncha and Laro elected to move to the British side of the international boundary and established themselves at Namberu and Toungo respectively. Koncha, Laro, and Tchamba continued to administer the small rump of Chamba Leko, sandwiched between the Alantika Mountains and the Faro–Deo Rivers, on behalf of the French. As a result of these maneuvers, both the British and French considered that they were maintaining legitimate "families" or "lines" in office, which accorded with one understanding of the way in which "tradition" should inform administration.

In the longer term, British administrators saw the reconstitution of the Adamawa Emirate as the most economical way to integrate the territories that had to be administered under mandate. Yola, the Emirate capital, had become part of Nigeria under the Anglo-German boundary settlement, and so it seemed that making Yola overlord of the southern mandated territories was not more than restoring some part of a preeminence violated by the earlier boundary. But Mai Gari of Nassarawo flatly refused to have his chiefdom incorporated into Adamawa and wrote a strongly worded letter to the Resident at Yola expressing his distaste for the scheme (K4).[9] However, by the chance death of the Lamido of Yola in 1924 and the appointment of Mai Gari (Muhammad Bello) as his successor, the problem was neatly circumvented. In the same year, Nassarawo, Toungo, and Namberu were incorporated within the Yola Emirate and thus, according to an assessment report of 1930, reverted " . . . to their status prior to the delimitation of the former Anglo-German boundary" (G2.2A Logan 1930). Certainly, Yola was once again able to lay claim to hegemony over a large tract of territory, but in any sense other than this the statement could hardly be more self-deluding. Nassarawo, Toungo, and Namberu scarcely existed before the colonial period, and the territories they administered had, more often than not, either remained entirely outside pre-colonial Fulani authority or else had contracted fluid alliances with the Fulani as and when it suited them. In effect, the central Chamba found themselves administratively reshuffled into the Yola Emirate,[10] a situation many of them had been doing their utmost to resist throughout the nineteenth century. Worse yet, Chamba subordination appears to have been achieved by the European colonial powers quite unwittingly. Much of the remainder of the British colonial period was spent extricating the Chamba from the Fulani domination created by these realignments; this exercise, necessarily, was carried out under the guise of new understandings of the increasingly distant "traditional" relations between the two peoples.

British administration was short of staff during the entire period of the mandate. In the 1920s, administration was carried on first from Koncha, before the boundary settlement with France, and then from Toungo, when Chambaland formed part of a South Cameroons Division. Later it was conducted from Yola, after Nassarawo, Toungo, Namberu, Binyeri, Gurum, and Yebbi had been incorporated into the Emirate. All these administrative centers were Fulani settlements. The District Officers (Mair, Glasson, and Logan bearing the brunt of the work for more than a decade) were able to do little more than tour their areas, accompanied by predominantly Hausa and Fulani retinues.

However, by the end of the decade attempts were made to introduce reform at the village level. Although Fulani dominance was encouraged at Emirate and, to some extent, district level, steps were taken to allow Chamba a degree of autonomy in village administration. The *jekada* system, through which the Fulani had administered the Chamba villages under their control, was dismantled after 1924, and Fulani district heads were encouraged to deal directly with their village heads. Village units were redefined as territorial rather than "tribal" entities in 1930, in an attempt to make the heads more than "tax collecting agencies" (G2.2 Walker 1931). But still the Chamba, who were numerically preponderant in Nassarawo District, were recognized as chiefs in only ten of the twenty-four village areas. A British officer's claim that Fulani were henceforth to be ruled by Fulani and "pagan" by "pagan" was not strictly accurate (G2.2 Walker 1931).

From the early 1930s, the search began for means of making a major reform of Chamba administration. Since change had to be grounded in better understanding of the past, a spate of reports ensued.[11] The past, however, was not an altogether helpful guide. Chamba communities nurtured their own grievances and rivalries. Administrative practicalities had previously necessitated giving Binyeri, Gurum, and Yebbi district status. The three districts were reluctant to forego their status, but federation would not be feasible if every traditional unit of similar size had to be recognized as a district (Logan 1932 Letter R.H.). Not all Chamba lived in the mandated territories, and historical arguments were going to be needed to support the establishment of any administration which crossed the boundary between Nigeria and the Cameroon mandate (G3 N. J. Brooke 1933 Note). In addition to these practical problems, an undercurrent of the older simplistic analysis persisted, wherein regional politics were viewed in terms of a cleavage between Fulani and "pagans." J. H. Shaw declared that Fulani had "superior political ability" and were recognized as "natural leaders" by the Chamba, who were riven by internal dissent (G3 Shaw 1936 *The Chamba Tribe*).

Nonetheless, proposals for reform were made. A report by Welch in 1933 appears not to have been acted upon, but a detailed report by Shaw in 1936 (*op. cit.*) did form the basis of a reorganization implemented two years later. A new Chamba district was to be recognized by reconstituting a Sugu chiefdom and placing the chief of Sugu on a par with the Chamba chiefs of Gurum, Yebbi, and Binyeri. These Chamba chiefs were to be formed into a new council with the Fulani District Head of Nassarawo, still the largest district, as its head. The judicial system was to be based upon the administrative districts, but with the district court of Nassarawo, sitting in the emerging Fulani township of Jada, acting as court of appeal for the implementation of Islamic law throughout the area. The new organization was officially inaugurated by the Lamido of Yola in May 1938.

Although optimistic reports were made during its first year (G3A, Vol. II Report by Shaw), in the longer term, reorganization was not considered a success. A letter from the District Officer at Jada to the Adamawa Resident summed up the problems (C 778 Paul 1951):

> The war and the lack of organised touring for some twelve years largely spoilt the 1938 organisation, and in plain fact there is now less administration of the Chamba by the Chamba then there was before 1938. Wakilin Chamba, Hamman Tukur (District Head of Nassarawo R.F.) who was intended to be a sort of guide, and helper and chairman, has become a District-Head-in-Chief of the five districts, and is officially responsible for the administration of all of them. No attempt has been made to make all the subordinate staff in the four districts of Binyeri, Yebbi, Gurumpawo, and Sugu Chambas, although this was the intention, and it could have been completed long ago.

What occurred was another chapter in the remarkable colonial career of the Fulani of Nassarawo. Under successive British and German regimes, and through a couple of border adjustments and two wars, Nassarawo had been transformed from a petty village into a District Headship controlling all of Chambaland under the British mandate. Moreover, all this had happened under the aegis of tradition. In part, success has to be attributed to the political acumen of the Fulani chiefs of Nassarawo; in part, they were also the beneficiaries of highly stereotyped European impressions of the regional organization. But above all, they thrived because of the slight economic potential of this part of Adamawa in European eyes, relatively inattentive to the slaves and ivory and kola routes, which had made the area a Fulani *El Dorado*. The point is explicitly made in the Yola Gazetteer for 1937 (91–92):

> In comparison with the rest of the Northern Provinces, the administrative development of Adamawa has been retarded and there are three specific reasons for this—first, the direct set-back caused by the war; second, the diversity of the primitive pagan tribes and of their languages and cultures and third, its inaccessibility. The only route by which bulk produce can be economically exported is the River Benue during its brief high water season of mid-July to mid-September. The produce trade is monopolised by the two shipowning firms, and their mutually agreed price for the ground-nuts has been very much lower than that paid at the buying stations on the railway. Consequently, although the emirate is rich in produce, particularly ground-nuts, its revenue is small and the margin between this and ordinary expenditure allows little scope for development schemes.

However frank this account intended for a British readership, the Chamba gained the impression that the preeminence accorded the Fulani derived from a British misunderstanding about the past. After all, investigations were always phrased in "traditional" terms. This charitable interpretation of the form British rule took is still maintained by many Chamba who grew up in the colonial period, and it influenced the way in which Chamba demands for greater autonomy were phrased when they began to be made at the beginning of the 1950s. To understand this development an account must be made of influences not directly connected to the colonial offices.

Although there is no record of economic agents in Chambaland, missionary activity got under way at the end of the 1920s. The Protestant Sudan United Mission was the first to be established in

Gurum, and later the Roman Catholics began missionary work in Sugu and Mapeo.[12] At the same period, more Chamba began to convert to Islam. There is a unanimous denial that Chamba seriously converted to Islam before the colonial period (compare Blench 1984). Certainly, some chiefs adopted nominal signs of Islam if they entered alliance with the Fulani, but their conduct was unaffected by this. A story told of Damashi, the most famous Chamba ally of the Yola Fulani, recounts how he accepted part of the Koran from Modibbo Adama and pledged to convert to Islam. When he returned home Damashi summoned his wives (fourteen or twenty-four according to different accounts), with the intention of sending all but four away, but he found that they pleased him so much that he abandoned the idea of converting to Islam and kept his wives instead. The chief of Sugu is said to have adopted the trappings of a Fulani-style investiture when he had to be installed at Koncha, during the German colonial period. This, however, did not prevent his holding Chamba rites and festivals.

By the 1920s, and perhaps earlier, Eid celebrations at the end of the period of fasting had been introduced into the Sugu cycle of rituals (Migeod F. W. H. 1925:196), just as Christmas has been adopted into the Mapeo cycle as a community festival. In Mapeo, conversion to Islam seems to have begun in earnest during the 1940s; Fr. Malachy Cullen, one of the earliest Catholic missionaries in Mapeo, refers to the conversion of youths to Islam in a manuscript of 1944 (Cullen 1944 Yola Mission). Elsewhere, conversion began a little earlier, but Chamba Muslims are adamant that the Fulani jihad is misnamed, since no attempt to convert Chamba was made, and the objective of the war was booty and slaves.

In many cases, there is evidence that aspiring Chamba Muslims have attempted to attract Koranic teachers from outside the immediate Fulani community in order to avoid the association between conversion and fealty. Nonetheless, the politically dominant position of the Fulani under colonial administrations created pressures on Chamba Village and District Heads, or those with pretensions to occupying such offices, to convert to Islam. The more important the office, the greater the likelihood that the occupant would be a Muslim; a rule that is supported by the fact that all informants who attempt to argue against it have to resort to the same two cases of District Heads who were Christians, both of whom were removed from office.

Conversion of local administrative cadres to Islam proceeded concurrently with conversions to Christianity effected through the mission schools. Thanks to its association with schooling, and with the professions followed by the schooled (many of whom left Chambaland), Christianity was seen as a young man's religion, necessitating a considerable apprenticeship. For a variety of reasons, therefore, different categories of people tended to supply the material for the first generation of converts to world religions, and conversion tended further to differentiate their life chances. Uncertainty about social roles was often accompanied by a series of conversions back and forth between "paganism," Islam, and Christianity.[13]

Along with a proto-national context beginning to make itself felt in Chambaland, these several factors affected the way in which Chamba agitation for a reversal of their subordinate position began to be expressed. What became known as the "Chamba Separatist Movement" started among the mission-educated Chamba of Numvani, the Sudan United Mission station which had been established in Gurum, where Chamba opposition to Fulani domination was historically strongest. The protesters were young, Christian, and literate, and their fears had been compounded by the prospect of indirect elections to be held in the north of Nigeria in 1951–1952 on the basis of a revised constitution.[14] Unless change occurred, they felt the Fulani would manage to dominate the new electoral system just as they had dominated the old administrative organization. Knowing the British penchant for traditional legitimations, the document expressing their demands began by asserting that they had never been conquered by the Fulani, but had been put under them by Europeans. In the preceding years, they had received none of the benefits enjoyed by other districts. They wanted a Chamba chief and wakili (first minister) to govern them, and they wanted roads, schools, wells, and dispensaries built. But they would forego all of these advantages rather than live any longer under the Fulani.

Their demands were put to the Touring Officer, H. J. A. Cassidy, who reported back to the Senior District Officer, W. H. Paul, while the latter was himself approached by Chamba who journeyed to Yola to express similar grievances (C778 Separatist Movements). The Gurum Chamba seem to have enlisted the support of some of the Chamba at the Sugu Catholic mission, for another group approached the Touring Officer there with a familiar list of grievances: the Chamba were the largest tribe in Adamawa without their own division, they received no benefits in return for their taxes, and the Native Authority employed only Fulani even in Chamba territories.

The reactions of the various British officers differed. Some seem to have favored suppression; noting the activity of middle-belt politicians in the area, they suspected a conspiracy and took steps to forestall it.[15] The District Head of Gurum was ordered to issue a warning to the "ring leaders" of the Separatist Movement, as one British officer called them, to cease their propaganda. But the reaction of the Senior District Officer was sympathetic. In a letter written to the Resident in September 1951, W. H. Paul endorsed many of the Chamba demands and suggested various reforms to "Chambaize" the Native Authority. These included: the abolition of the office of Wakilin Chamba (occupied by a Fulani), a reorganization of the large Fulani-led district of Nassarawo, and the recruitment of Chamba to positions in the Native Authority. But little seems to have been achieved by 1955, other than a request to Wakilin Chamba to restrict his activities to the Nassarawo District. A suggestion was put forward for the formation of a District Council before the visit of the United Nations Trusteeship Committee, but it is not clear whether it was acted upon (C778 letter from Resident 30.9.55). The idea of a Chamba Federation was discussed again in a 1955 report by the Assistant District Officer, D. S. Sorrell, who proposed the inclusion of Toungo District in any future federation, but noted that the Mumuye already outnumbered Chamba in Binyeri, which might therefore be excluded (C778 Sorrell). Again, nothing happened. But in the same year, the District Head of Nassarawo retired, and a British Officer was stationed at Jada to preside over monthly meetings of the District Heads who would take care of their internal affairs free from the influence of the Fulani chief who had "overshadowed the lesser chiefs and in his later years tended to become overbearing and to interfere in district affairs, with consequent discontent" (C778 Crane 1958).

London in 1957 was the scene of another conference held to revise the 1954 constitution. Chamba demands were part of a pattern of similar agitations which had to be addressed (Crowder 1973:294):

> By far the most complex problem confronting the delegates was that of Nigeria's minority groups, and the demand for the creation of new states that had grown up amongst them. One of the main results of the accentuation of tribal politics in the years of the Macpherson constitution was the increase in the minority reaction against the major tribal groups dominating the political life of the Regions. This minority movement, always potentially existent because of historical and ethnic factors, took the form of political associations seeking the separation of so-called minority areas and the creation of new states.

The 1957 conference referred this "knotty matter" to a minorities commission headed by Sir Henry Willink. Crowder notes that the tour of the commission led to a "vocal outcry" on the part of minority groups throughout the country (1973:295). A detailed report, largely sympathetic to the Chamba grievances against both the Fulani and the British as their supporters, was submitted to the Commission by the Assistant District Officer, Peter Crane.[16] He demonstrated the way in which British administration had worked to the detriment of Chamba interests and outlined the specific problems. The Chamba resented being called "slaves," they objected to the pressure exerted by the Native Authority to make Islam the official religion of the area, they complained that little development of essential services had taken place, and that few Chamba were employed by the Native Authority. In sum, the report stated (C778 Crane 1958):

> They resent the fact that their chiefs become willy-nilly tools of the Fulani, encouraging the Moslem faith and exerting their influence to secure the election of district councils that will do as they are told and of electoral colleges that will elect the Yola nominees to the Federal and Regional legislatures. This the chiefs do through fear or be-

cause they are themselves corrupt and depend upon the favour of Yola for their continuance in office.

Crane argued that the only solution would be the separation of a Chamba Native Authority from Yola and the curtailment of Fulani influence within such a unit.[17]

The British Trusteeship of Cameroon was running out. A referendum was held to determine whether the people of the territories wished to join Nigeria, or Cameroon, or remain under British Trusteeship. The initial vote, in 1959, was for delaying independence (by votes of 70 percent in Gwoza and Adamawa), and Chamba petitioned the United Nations and Britain to be allowed a further five to ten years in preparation for independence. The remainder of Nigeria became independent in 1960. The Plebiscite Commission interpreted the 1959 vote as a protest against the Native Authority; therefore, in 1960, a Commission of Inquiry under the chairmanship of Mohammed Tukur was convened "to ascertain the wishes of the people of the Trust Territory regarding their grouping into Divisions and Native Authorities." The litany of Chamba grievances, elicited at a number of mass meetings, is familiar. The Chamba Native Authority constituted in 1937 had never been "more than an exercise on paper." Development programs were implemented slowly, and local (i.e., non-Fulani) men held few posts other than the most junior (Tukur 1960:2–3). When reform was attempted it tended to be "bypassed by informal Fulani organization." Above all, the Chamba wanted local autonomy and an administrative headquarters built in a Chamba, rather than Fulani, town. Mohammed Tukur's synopsis of the state of affairs was uncompromising (1960:6):

> . . . what emerges from this sequence [of recent events] is that all the efforts to liberalise and broaden the bases of Native Authorities have, in the case of Adamawa, been met by passive resistance by the Yola Fulani who have been so concerned with trying to maintain their dominant position that they cannot, or will not, take account of local discontent, and what concessions have been made to local feelings have held an academic interest only. There has, throughout,

been a complete lack of real contact between rulers and the ruled and as the education and political awareness of the latter have increased so have their demands for greater and more effective participation in local government affairs . . . What the Adamawa Native Authority . . . [was] eventually persuaded to do has been too little and too late; now they have been overtaken by events.

Finally, on the eve of decolonization, real change would occur. The large Fulani-dominated district of Nassarawo was split into the districts of Jada, Koma, Leko, and Mbulo, the last three of which were given Chamba heads. Along with Toungo, Sugu and Yelwa (an amalgam of Yebbi and Gurum, formed in 1957), the districts were amalgamated into a new Ganye Division. Before they left, the British had new local government offices built to the south of the Fulani-dominated town of Jada in a little market settlement called Ganye. Today, Ganye is the largest town of the Division. A second plebiscite was held in 1961, this time without the option of referral. The Northern Cameroon Trusteeship voted to merge with Nigeria but, within this vote, the Chamba came out strongly for merger with Cameroon. This was not an anti-Nigerian vote, and certainly not pro-Cameroonian, but once again a reflection of Chamba fears of rejoining the Fulani of Yola who had so effectively retained the political whip hand over them through successive administrative regimes.[18]

Chamba complaints to the United Nations, and a petition to be allowed to join Cameroon, were unavailing. The Northern Cameroon Trust Territory merged with Nigeria in June 1961, and the southern areas, including Ganye Division, insisted on the formation of a state independent of Adamawa. This was granted with the formation of Sardauna Province. Attention now centered on the internal administration of Ganye Division. Experiments were made with various types of presidencies and rotating chairmanships during the 1960s; eventually it was decided that Ganye should have a paramount chief, and the first Sarkin Ganye was elected in 1971 by the Village Heads, after the District Heads had been unable to agree to one of their members taking the office. Since then, there has been tacit agreement to treat some offices and headships as Chamba and others as Fulani. Matters have come to a head only when this agreement seems to have been breached. When a Fulani was appointed in succession to the retiring Chamba head of Leko District, the ensuing disturbances precipitated the imposition of martial law, and some Chamba lost official posts while others were taken into detention.

Despite goodwill, the ethnic legacy of the jihad and colonialism demand sensitive handling. The ten years since I first began fieldwork have seen the election of a Local Government Authority and its subsequent dissolution, the creation of districts that were later abolished, and the elevation of the Chief of Ganye to a second-class chief. The implication of these political shifts and changes is simply that Ganye Division of Gongola State has shared in the different experiments in governmental style that were attempted during the first twenty-five years of Nigerian independence.

Overview

Between the 1890s and 1960, we are clearly dealing with a historical disjunction in Chamba affairs that corresponds fairly closely to events unfolding as a result of encapsulation throughout colonial Africa. During this period the pertinence of the way I have explained Chamba precolonial politics becomes increasingly attenuated with the declining autonomy of Chamba communities. Looked at closely, the pace of change is slow and its mechanisms quite subtle. Because the Chamba lived in a region that was in turn the hinterland of a German colony, a mandated territory, a trust territory, and then a belated addition to an independent country, almost every development in Nigeria occurred here late and half-heartedly.

Colonial administration on a scale almost comparable to that in other parts of the Nigerian middle-belt was established in the 1930s, but was virtually non-existent in the 1940s. Missionary activities started late, and therefore educational change also came late. In consequence, the emergence of a modern elite conversant in nationalist politics occurred only in the 1950s. Islam for long buttressed the local Fulani ascendancy that was maintained in the face of colonial negligence. Economic development came slowly, although the number of local markets increased steadily. Chamba were virtually excluded from cash employment with the Native Authority, produce prices were lower than elsewhere and communications were so poor that production of surpluses on a large scale would have served little purpose.

On the face of it, very little seemed to be happening before the 1950s; but appearances may deceive. From a patchwork of cultural, historical, dialectal, language, and other differences, there was emerging the idea of a Chamba people faced by common problems that called for collective solutions. Such practical interests were not the sum of factors interacting to give rise to modern Chamba ethnicity, with its associated notions of a Chamba tradition, culture, and past, but they furnished a considerable motivation to the complex. For alongside the internal squabbles over precedence, there emerged the idea of Chamba as a minority in a system that tended to favor larger groupings. In practice, this battle came to be fought out in what later was organized as Ganye Division. So, although Chamba ethnicity is not restricted to Ganye Division, it is there that the internal divisions were most clearly subordinated to the idea of a Chamba entity and, in contrast to peoples in other regions dominated by Fulani, there is no evidence of Chamba attempting to pass as members of other ethnic groups (Burnham 1972; Schultz 1984 on Cameroon). In local terms, Chamba is itself a high-status ethnic identity. Within Ganye Division, the demands of the early Chamba separatists have been answered.

Outside Ganye Division various of the Chamba-language groupings have remained much less closely involved with a notion of Chamba identity than they might have become in the arena where political questions eventually resolved themselves into Chamba or Fulani terms. For this, like the dualism of "pagan slaves"–"Muslim rulers" that it replaces, remains a substantial simplification of the ethnic distinctions pertinent to other local issues.[19] Nonetheless, the ethnic momentum is inexorable. The remaining Chamba Leko in North Cameroon, at least those who have not resettled across the border in Ganye Division, still live under Fulani lamidos. But they maintain close contact with their relatives among the Leko speakers of Ganye Division and some have traveled to Bamenda and then return to spread the news of powerful Leko-speaking Chamba there. In 1954, the Donga chief and Chamba historian Garbosa traveled to see for himself the Bali chiefdoms of Bamenda in Cameroon, and some Bali Chamba told me of correspondance with Benue Chamba and mutual visits since then. The yearly calendar of the Nigerian Chamba Progressive Cultural Association carries photographs of prominent individuals from the Benue Chamba and Ganye communities. The ethnographer does not stand apart from all this. Given the convergence between these ethnic developments and the conventions of the monograph form we must surely question the authorship of an ethnographic account, for the ethnographer also is not autonomous of the historical process.

PART V

CONCLUSION: THE TRANSFORMERS

AND THE TRANSFORMED

CHAPTER 12

AGENCY AND TRANSFORMATION

IN CHAMBA HISTORY

Résumé

I began the argument of this book with a problem that seemed a mirror image of E. R. Leach's concern in *Political Systems of Highland Burma*: how did people who differ from one another as much as Chamba ever come to consider themselves members of a single ethnic category? The answer has led us far afield. But my concern to retrieve a Chamba history over the last two hundred and fifty years has remained self-consciously oriented to the present: the extensive curiosity of the study has been bounded by the current notion of a Chamba people.[1] Even in the guise of historian, as I argued at the end of the last chapter, the ethnographer as writer is constrained by the outcomes of history. In this case, the way I am able to write about Chamba is possible only because there was a Chamba ethnogenesis. The authorship of a monograph such as this is a complex historical product as much as the result of individual cerebration.

My approach to Chamba ethnicity has stressed two perspectives between which there is tension. Chamba ethnogenesis depended upon antecedent conditions that can be approached historically by asking about the practical salience of ethnic-like distinctions that Chamba recognized before the present century. Pursuing this line of inquiry we can outline a genealogy of the idea of Chambaness and ask why one ethnic idea came to assume greater prominence than others that were potentially able to define competing boundaries. Among the specific problems that can be addressed from this point of view, the fact that speakers of two different languages came to recognize common ethnicity is only the most obvious. Just as remarkable is the way in which the most extensive ethnic connections have been mobilized to draw not only the Chamba of Chambaland but also those of the emigrant conquest chiefdoms into the notion of a single people. Despite the fact that the Chamba-led raiding alliances were multi-ethnic in composition, and large numbers of the participants did not consider themselves members of any of the categories from which Chamba has developed, their descendants have, nonetheless, become Chamba today. In historical terms, being Chamba has not meant the same thing to different people at various times and places.

But against this developmental approach to history, we can contrast an appreciation of history that emphasizes disjunction rather than continuity. From this perspective, we would want to note that Chamba ethnicity shares a form with other ethnic identities in modern African states. However different the processes by which ethnic identities emerged in particular cases, these processes shared a common end-result in the phenomenon of contemporary ethnic separatism. This, in turn, suggests the complexity of the historical processes to which we must appeal in order to explain the contemporary phenomenon.

The three substantive parts of this work have developed interrelated perspectives on these historical events that, respectively, emphasize variations, common themes and developmental processes. Initially, I sketched in different aspects of Chamba variation that were so substantial as to suggest a microcosm of West African social and cultural forms. We discovered that in looking at a single people we had to admit differences of language and dialect, mode of livelihood, strategic location, systems of kinship and clanship, as well as political organization. To order this variety I proposed typologies: Chamba Leko and Chamba Daka as distinct languages with original eastern and western provenances; raiders and refugees as two reactions to the political instabilities of the nineteenth century; double clanship, matriclanship and patriclanship as organizational mechanisms; ritualized and conquest chiefships as two ways of envisaging the importance of the chiefdom in Chamba political organizations.

Having proposed means for arranging the differences of concern to the analysis, I suggested interrelations between the forms. The first step was to see how far the form and content of historical traditions could help in reconstructing a sequence of events during the last two and a half centuries. The fragmented nature of the evidence required detailed investigation if reconstruction was to carry any conviction for an audience of regional specialists. I proposed a distinction between two idioms of oral tradition which by and large corresponded to the way in which history was evoked in patriclan and matriclan chiefdoms. The former class of narratives detailed epic journeys of war and conquest that involved alliances of Chamba and non-Chamba patriclans. The latter class detailed the way in which indigenous populations had been encompassed by the ritual efficacy of immigrant matriclans. The two types of narrative corresponded to the manner in which matters falling respectively within the domains of patriclanship and matriclanship tended generally to be treated in oral accounts.

But beyond this sociological glossing of the difference, I suggested that the difference between forms and contents of narratives was amenable to historical analysis. A variety of types of evidence pointed to the conclusion that the accounts from matriclan chiefdoms referred to circumstances that predated the nineteenth century, although by how much is a matter for speculation. These traditions, though highly variable in their detail, envisaged the expansion of a form of ritualized chiefship that became established among the Leko-speaking Chamba of Yeli and was later to be accepted by Chamba-Daka speakers to their west who, by identifying themselves as Nakɛnyare, became distinguished from uncentralized Daka speakers. The Nakɛnyare identity was the historical product that logically mediated the differences between the speakers of the two Chamba languages. Without that identity, there could not have been a later extensive Chamba ethnogenesis.

The oral traditions of the conquest chiefdoms and their patriclan chiefships refer us to a later set of events, roughly contemporary with the Fulani jihad in Adamawa. From the detail of numerous accounts, we can derive an overall impression of the way in which displaced raiders, with an initial composition predominantly from the eastern Chamba-Leko chiefdoms, incorporated the peoples through whom they passed and eventually settled to establish numerous Chamba conquest chiefdoms hundreds of miles from their homelands. The record is not as complete as we might wish. We lack materials from many of the Chamba emigrant chiefdoms and from the peoples whom they raided and incorporated. Nonetheless, the records we do have are sufficient to establish the broad features of the events that concern us.

The middle chapters of my account, in Part 3, shift attention from variations to common themes. On the basis of a detailed account of kinship and clanship in Mapeo I investigated the contrastive idioms of Chamba matriclanship and patriclanship. Relations between members of these two clan categories, what I termed sociability, are differently construed. Matriclanship is evoked in references to common bodily concerns, which beg an assumption I termed consubstantiation; matrikin share a common substance and this underlying similarity between them is the presupposition that justifies their common interests in one another's bodily states. Patrikin envisage the differences between them to arise from more irrevocable differences of spirit and incarnation. This distinction, between forms of sociability that have elective affinities with forms of clanship, invests not only the relations between co-members of a clan category, but also the relations between the clans and the form of government that is associated with royal matriclanship or patriclanship. Developmentally, as I argued in Chapter 8, we can arrange the Chamba political organizations about which we know in terms of the dominance of one or other form of sociability: ritualized chiefdoms are conceived, predominantly, in the idiom of matriclanship. In the uncentralized community of Mapeo, the two idioms are roughly counterposed with equal importance, whereas in the conquest chiefdoms within Chambaland, and to an increasing extent in the conquest chiefdoms founded among non-Chamba, patriclanship became dominant. In order to dispel an elision between ethnicity and culture which such analyses tend to introduce by default, I also demonstrated that the information we have shows that the neighbors of the people who were to become Chamba shared forms of organization very similar to the early, matriclan, Chamba types.

The third substantive section of the book, Part 4, contrasts two polar types of Chamba chiefdom in terms of their predominant forms of sociability. I argue that matriclan chiefdoms rested on presuppositions about power different from those of the patriclan chiefdoms, founded later by raiders who saw themselves as conquerors. Ritualized chiefship can be understood as matriclanship writ large,

in which the chief embodies the welfare of his people. Ritual concerns cluster around the impartibility of royal bodies and the vulnerability of the chief. Ritual regulation of communal welfare is a
cooperative exercise to which different sections of the community
make complementary contributions. By contrast, the conquest chiefdom is envisaged in terms of the military power of a dominant stratum of allied patriclans whose separation from the people over
whom they rule is emphasized in their monopoly over office and
martial ritual. There has been a consistent trend for the older conception of chiefship to be eroded by the newer.

In the preceding chapter, I began to examine the historical limits to the model I propose. I have appealed to historically specific
ideas of agency and sociability (see below) that I argue have undergone transformation. There is a point at which transformation becomes a less helpful way of approaching change than disjunction. In
the terms of my opening paragraph, a genealogical approach becomes less appropriate than one which stresses radical change. This
is not to claim that my model loses all applicability, rather that the
practices currently informed by the suppositions I try to summarize
are of such local and domestic importance that they are of only marginal significance in explaining contemporary political affairs. In
theoretical terms, our abstract concepts like agency and sociability
reciprocally define epochs to which they are appropriate. When political conditions change radically, and our terms no longer seem to
assist us, we may decide to construe the exhaustion of their salience
in terms of a historical disjunction.

Agency and Sociability

With the completed analysis before us it is appropriate to return to
the issues that I broached in the introductory chapter. The analysis
itself clarifies what I hoped to propose in abstract terms. My use of
concepts is eclectic, and both the concepts to which I appeal and the
ethnography I present have accumulated in a piecemeal fashion over
a long period (Fardon 1980, 1983, 1986a, 1986b, 1987, forthcoming).
The process has been one of trial and frequent error, and like all
ethnographic and theoretical formulations this one also is for the

time being. Tracing intellectual respectability for ideas after the event is an overridden anthropological hobbyhorse, so I shall try to restrict my comments to sources that have borne directly on my reasoning.

I have written of typological change in terms of transformation— an approach normally considered antipathetic to interpretative understanding, which I also claim to have espoused (albeit Weber is the classic source of both). I have also introduced concepts like sociability and agency, which I have claimed to mediate these antitheses. I had best be more explicit about the assumptions I am making.

Although the literature on African history has grown enormously in recent years, I can find only partial parallels to the problems posed by this study and the solutions attempted. Doubtless, any ethnographer describing a relatively undocumented people would say the same. Anthropologists who have historical leanings have tended to be attracted to states rather than acephalous societies or small chiefdoms (e.g. Smith 1960, 1978; Nadel 1942; Peel 1983). Comparing these accounts to the classic accounts of uncentralized societies written at the same period could give the impression that the inhabitants of the latter conceive the present with less historical insight; the more likely case is that historical reasoning is differently expressed. Even in settings where the continuities between kinship and government are more vital to the political process, anthropologists have usually been confronted with greater political coherence than in the myriad Chamba communities (e.g., Henderson 1972; Muller 1980; Willis 1981; Packard 1981). To an extent then, a transformational account that relies on typology is methodologically appropriate for discussing an unusually heterogenous people, no section of whom can be argued to be typical of anything other than the pervasiveness of differences.

But transformational analysis is also associated with structuralism, and particularly with the mentalistic ontology of Lévi-Strauss, to which I would not subscribe. The great power of the related notions of structure and transformation, like their generative counterparts in psychoanalytic theory, means that their crude deployment is liable simply to echo back the preconceptions on which they are based (see Douglas 1967; Willis 1967; Sperber 1975, among many dissenting voices). Luc de Heusch's description of structuralism as "an innocent method" is too disarming (1981:10). The transformational analysis of institutions needs to be founded in interpretative sociology, if we wish to argue that the transformations we detail reflect any agency other than our own.

Structural method is a specific application of our general appeal to formal logical properties in an effort to realize coherence and patterning. But anthropology exists by virtue of the encounter of (at least) two complex agencies: the agency of the people we study, presented to us through their practices, among which we are especially reliant on what they say to us and to each other, and our own agency, finally expressed through our writing about them. Especially in the case study of Mapeo, but more generally throughout this book, I have tried to explain the meaning of institutional configurations both as they seem to Chamba informants and, by drawing on Chamba accounts, in terms of the meaning they have for the analyst by virtue of the presuppositions on which they draw. My account of meaning is collaborative in the sense that it is neither my account, since it is informed by what Chamba told me, nor is it the Chamba account, since what they told me was not told in the form I present it. Moreover, I have put their statements to the service of super-local affairs which are less situationally specific than issues they would address. My typologies present complexes of institutions in the context of the general meanings that I attribute to them by virtue of specific statements I have heard and practices I have seen. These are not the "actors' models," since the actors do not formulate models to address the problems I have posed. But neither are they akin to structuralist models, since they are cued by the way in which actors do explain their own practices rather than by the idea of an underlying generative structure. Like all ethnographer's models, they issue from the complex exigencies of an encounter between a historically constructed writer–researcher–regional specialist and the people among whom he lived and to whom he talked. The formulations proposed in a written account attempt to mediate the interests of these agencies; as such they are resistant to simplifying accounts of their status that might explain them simply as analysts' models or as folk models. The writer may appear to have the whip hand by

virtue of control over the means of dissemination, but the informants have played the major role in determining the terms of access
to what he wishes to explain.

In *Political Systems of Highland Burma*, Leach also presented
polar types of political organization along with the meanings that
his informants derived from their reflections on their institutions.
Thus, his typology was interpretative as well as institutional. However, when he turned to consider why transformation occurred he
appealed to a transcultural actor by introducing the assumption of
individual maximization of political advantage, what I referred to
in Chapter 1 as Leach's espousal of machinating man. This crude
appeal to transactionalism begs numerous problems. If individual
maximization applies by definition to every individual in whatever
circumstance, then Leach's concept is tautologous and, worse still
from an ethnographic viewpoint, completely uninformative. Moreover, it is inconsistent simultaneously to propose that political
types are culturally construed and that political agency is universal
and, therefore, unproblematic.

To avoid such assumptions, I have stressed the cultural nature
of the agent, an idea that I consider a dynamic counterpart to many
anthropologists' current preoccupations with personhood. Discussions of the person, dormant for a period at least in British anthropology, have come to renewed prominence with the rediscovery of
the pertinence of important works by Mauss and Leenhardt, especially to the comparative study of gender relations (Mauss 1938;
Leenhardt 1947; M. Strathern 1985a; 1985b). Taking my starting
point from these writers, I understand by agency a theoretical account of a horizon of assumptions and anticipations about the self
and the self's relations to others and the wider environment that we
can assume to inflect social practice. As the concept is ambitious,
any particular analysis can deal only with some aspects of agency
that fall under this definition. Here, for instance, I have not dealt
except in passing with gender relations. Agency is therefore a theoretical construct, both in the sense that we are directed to certain
facets of the concept in terms of the problems we address at any
time, and also because agency is not something we can know directly. The idea of agency appeals to the view of the human subject
proposed by the philosopher Charles Taylor that, "social theory has

to take subjects as agents of self-definition, whose practice is shaped by their understanding" (1983:29), while simultaneously recognizing that in knowing these self-definitions we confront a problem of principle, succinctly expressed by a sociologist, Anthony Giddens, in that "rationalization is the causal expression of the grounding of the purposiveness of the agent in self-knowledge and in the knowledge of the social and material worlds which are the environment of the acting self" (1976:85, emphasis removed).

To summarize, practice is shaped by understanding, but that understanding is not necessarily expressed in verbal rationalizations of conduct. Put another way, practical consciousness need not be exhausted by the accounts of actions we are offered, for these accounts are pointed activities in their own right. Taking the actor's point of view, whatever that may mean, is not a simple expedient, if we accept that a viewpoint is not of necessity discursively available to those who inform us. An actor's account is a situated explanation of something that we may interpret as evidence for a theoretical conception of agency, but not as a window on it. The individual agent's situated self-description is not in itself the explanation we are in search of but part of the human behavior that we wish our account of agency to encompass (Bourdieu 1977). Following Taylor once more, to argue other than this would imply acceptance of an "incorrigibility thesis," recognizing incomparable reasons in every culture and even every individual (1983:36); to endorse such a view would compromise the possibility of translation, at the same time as creating an unnecessary boundary problem between supposed "culture gardens" (Fabian 1983). These problems are not resolvable in any final sense. In asking about agency we beg the question of what enables people to act as they do under circumstances as they construe them. In short, we want to know why certain conduct is appropriate for a self in a particular self-construed environment (Hallowell 1955). Any account we may offer is subject to the corrigibility thesis we apply to other situated understandings.

The resolution I have proposed for the purpose of this account involved counterposing to the notion of agency the idea that Chamba recognize competing idioms of sociability. I do not suggest that these idioms are distinctively Chamba features but, in the absence of a fuller regional account, it is not possible to specify the precise historical and geographical pertinence that might be attributed to them. By sociability I have meant a set of expectations about the way in which persons may be anticipated to relate to one another. I have suggested that the contrasts between idioms of sociability can be drawn pervasively between levels of analysis that we normally separate, such as the normative, the emotional, the practical, and so forth. The idioms define person and relationship in terms that are themselves relational. It is not possible to write about person other than in terms of relationships between people, nor does relationship make sense outside the terms of personhood it supposes.

The terms I have used to contrast idioms of sociability have been designed to differentiate between two senses of "oneness" or "togetherness" that are expressed by the same Chamba terms. I have argued that this single term conceals a covert category that we could express as the difference between types of difference. The first term, borrowed with modified sense from Schutz (see Chapter 1), is consociation. I use the term to stress the sense of "with" (con-). The second term, adsociation, is coined. By adsociation I refer to the togetherness of people who are brought under a single referent but between whom difference is not subverted. The general form of the distinction is not original and corresponds in some respects to Victor Turner's distinction, drawing upon Martin Buber and others, between structure and communitas (V. Turner 1969).

The use to which I put the terms is quite unlike the purpose to which Turner employed his distinction. Like Turner, I claim that one of the idioms, consociation, radically subverts difference as it is construed in terms of the alternative idiom, adsociation, in my terms. But I argue that the idioms are equally organized, so that while one may offer an alternative to the other, neither is anti-structure except when looked at in relation to the alternative vantage. The idioms are associated with different forms of social experience, but both are stable. Hierarchy is conceivable in either of the idioms but is differently construed in the two cases. Table 9 summarizes the distinctions that I have drawn in terms of sociation at different points in the text.

The distinction between types of sociability is most clearly discerned where it closely converges with conventional anthropological distinctions between matriclanship and patriclanship, and

between matrilateral and patrilateral kinship. Because of the significance of clan organization in central Chamba communities, other
means of organization, such as affinity, tend consistently to be interpreted in terms of their ramifications in the domain of clanship. A
similar situation is operant in matters of laterality, specifically those
that concern the closest and most distant matrilateral kin (all of
whom Chamba could claim in some context to have "one mother").
Thus we are able to note consistency between the idea of substantial
connection between mother, child, and mother's brother and other
facets of their relation, for example, that they are supposed to share
close and affectionate ties. In addition, the sister's child may joke
with his maternal uncle, steal small items from his compound, and
jokingly abuse his wife, whom he may also marry on his uncle's
death. Such relations are permissible with no other senior-generation
kinsman nor the wife of any such. Traditional partible inheritance
meant that moveable properties were passed from maternal uncle to
nephew. Close matrikin share bodily concerns. Reparation to cults
is paid by matrikin to achieve a cure for one of their members.

But there is a shadow side to extreme closeness between matrikin. The development of his nephews and nieces is monitored by
their maternal uncle who arranges for the expulsion from the community of children who cut upper before lower teeth. The conviction of a witch also implicates his or her close matrikin. Physical
punishment is supposed traditionally to have been meted out by
mother's brother to his nephews or nieces, and never by their father.
The transference of children to cancel blood debts took place only
between matriclans, and formally the mother's brother had the right
to sell his nephews and nieces into slavery. Taken together, these
features, affectionate or otherwise, constitute the close mutuality of
immediate matrikin to which I apply the term consociation.

Attitudes to close patrilateral relatives, who share "one father,"
contrast with these point by point. Patrikin share reincarnation,
spirit and name. The father and his sister are normatively figures to
whom respect should be shown. Patrikin are responsible for the individual's social maturation. Hence, they carry out rites at birth,
circumcision, tooth evulsion for girls, and finally at death. The
skull, or some other durable relic of the individual, eventually finds
its way to the patriclan shrine, taken there by a son or brother's son.

TABLE 9

The Axes of Sociability in Chambaland

	Consociating	Adsociating
Idiom of Relation	The relationship, traced matrilaterally, through a feminine mediation, presupposes shared substance, possibly also witchcraft substance. In this respect, the relationship is based upon a denial of difference between those related. Consociation invests the body.	The relationship, traced patrilaterally, through a masculine mediation, presupposes reincarnation and the inheritance of name. Those related share responsibilities associated with their cyclical incarnations into the same patriclan. These responsibilities may be expressed through preservation of skulls or personal relics.
Normative Definition of Inter-Generational Relations	*Mother/child*: parentation relation expressed in affection. Mother and child share common substance.	*Father/child*: parentation relation based upon respect. Father and child share incarnation in the patriclan, and, therefore, common descent from patriclan forebears.
	Mother's brother/sister's child: terminologically a collateral relationship. The MB is the only senior kinsman with whom there is a joking relationship. The relationship is defined in terms of the authority of MB over the bodies of his sister's children (Zch), with	*Father's sister/brother's child*: terminologically, a collateral relationship based on respect and a degree of avoidance.

	whom he shares substance, and in terms of the substantial claim of the ZS on his MB's moveable property, on his death, and against his property through petty theft and privileged treatment during his life. i. The MB may sell his Zch into slavery ii. He alone may legitimately administer corporal punishment iii. He disposes of his Zch whose bodily development is considered anomalous (breech births, upper teeth cutters) iv. He organizes payments to cults which "catch" his Zch *Mother's brother's wife/husband's sister's child: the only joking relation with a spouse of senior generation kin.*	*Father's sister's husband/wife's brother's son: no kin term used; virtually unrelated.*
Inheritance	Moveable/substantial property is inherited between MB/ZS and M/D.	Compound, land and tools (hoe, spear, axe, bow and arrows, associated with the male as farmer, hunter and warrior) inherited from father.
Clanship	*Time referent:* matriclans, other than chiefly clans, claim mythological origins through	Patriclan narratives are sequential accounts of development, with legendary elements.

TABLE 9—*Continued*

The Axes of Sociability in Chambaland

Consociating	Adsociating
relations to shapechanging animals, or other metaphoric relations. Their names are those of: animals, birds, insects, fish, and phenomena like mist or stones.	Their names refer to localities, to non-Chamba peoples or sub-Chamba ethnic distinctions, to offices vested in the clan, or to the name of the clan founder.
Distribution: matriclans are dispersed categories a similar number of which (approximately a dozen) is found in every local community.	Parts of patriclans form co-residential units. The number of patriclans varies widely in different local communities.
Interrelation: local variation in matriclanship is reduced through the recognition of nominal and conventional equivalences. Further relationship is created through numerous relations of common parentation between clan categories.	Patriclans, whether resident in the same community or not, share parentation only if relationship is generally accepted on the basis of their historical narratives. An exception to this generalization would be Mapeo where ritual involution has led to co-ownership of patriclan cults being expressed as common clanship.

matriclans are internally differentiated into named sections, the identities of which should be concealed from outsiders. These section distinctions emerge in relation to witchcraft accusations, disputes over office, and, in the past, the slave origins of some sections.

Patriclans do not invariably have sections. If they do, the identities of the sections are generally known. Slave status is not recognized in the patriclan.

Extension: matriclans are extended categories. Children of matriclan men are collectively "children borne by the matriclan," their children are collectively "grandchildren of the matriclan." These are relations of parentation and may form the basis for claims to siblingship.

Patriclans are slightly extended. The sons of patriclan women are individually related to the clan and perform specific obligations and enjoy limited rights. They would not normally claim classificatory siblingship on this basis.

Co-operative action: the proper performance of matriclan affairs rests on the division of responsibilities between full members, "children" and "grandchildren." The term for matriclan (*kuni*, Daka, or *kuna*, Leko) may refer to the simple or extended membership. Although, from the point of view of kinship relations, the groups acting in the name of the matriclan consist of cognates, in Chamba terms they all belong to the extended matriclan.

Groups formed to act in the name of the patriclan are predominantly agnates. Children of patriclan women discharge specific functions, but the main division of labor is between classificatory fathers and sons.

TABLE 9—*Continued*

The Axes of Sociability in Chambaland

	Consociating	Adsociating
	Common affairs: groups appealing to matriclan identity are responsible for the maintenance and performance of matriclan cults, and for the payment to other cults which have "caught" one of their members. Matrikin are collectively vulnerable to contagion of some cults. They do not usually take part in physical violence; the sanctions at the disposal of the matriclan rely on ritual means. If a clan member is killed, the matrikin may accept a transferred member as compensation.	Groups acting under patriclan auspices maintain patriclan cults and shrines, including graves and skull shrines. They organize the individual passage through life in rituals of name giving, circumcision or tooth evulsion, burial wakes, and rites of remembrance. In the past, they resorted to self-help to avenge murder and to protect rights in property and women. But patrikin could not accept compensation by transfer of personnel for a murdered member.
Rights in Land and Natural Products	Matriclans collectively owned rights in the natural products of areas of bush (Mapeo). In matriclan chiefships, these rights were subject to the overriding right of the chief to certain products.	Localized patrikin are considered to own the land on which their hamlets are built and the area where their dead are buried. In the matriclan chiefdoms, ritual responsibility for fertility devolves on indigenous patriclan owners of the land. Tracts of farmland were owned by the individuals who had last culti-

vated them. Since the patrikin were guarantors of these rights, the land also belonged to the patriclan.

Organization of Chiefships	In matriclan chiefships, a chief with predominantly ritual duties was chosen by priests from a section of the community other than his own. With his priests, chief's assistants and smiths, the matriclan chief was considered to regulate the fertility and health of the community. The potency of the chief was justified in terms of his membership of the royal matriclan, in the Nakenyare case by reference to Yeli. The chief embodied the welfare of his people, and his protection, even after death, depended upon his bodily coolness, freedom from pollution, and impartibility.	In patriclan chiefships, a chief with predominantly martial functions was chosen by members of allied or related clans. With his military officials and assistants, he maintained the dominance of an alliance of patriclansmen. The preeminence of the chief and his supporters was justified by conquest. The chief presided over rituals to ensure success in war. His priests monopolized the most important cults, and after his death added his skull to the royal skull line.
Ethnic Differentiation	Immigrant/indigene distinctions in the matriclan chiefdoms supported the distribution of complementary offices and ritual functions amongst sections of the community. Ethnic difference was the basis for ritual co-operation.	In patriclan chiefdoms, stratification is based upon ethnic and Chamba subtribal distinctions. A dominant alliance, defined ethnically or sub-tribally, attempts the monopoly of offices and ritual functions. Ethnicity is the basis for exclusion from office and ritual responsibility.

Similar presuppositions are evident in the organization of clans.
Patriclans are numerous and their names evoke their historical particularity via their ancestral places, ethnic origins, or important offices. Matriclans appeal to mythological origins, in the restricted
sense of my contrast between myth and legend (Chapter 7). They are
less numerous than patriclans and the same matriclans are considered to exist throughout Chambaland and beyond. Access to patriclan affairs is restricted to daughter's children, but matriclans are
extended into the broad categories of parents, children and grandchildren, between whom classificatory kinship relations are recognized. Patrikin own farming land, while matrikin own rights in
natural products. Patrikin may react violently to the theft of their
daughters and, especially, wives. They are responsible for seeking
redress for the death of one of their members. But matrikin are the
patient of revenge; they will receive the bodily equivalent for the
member they have lost.

The two polar types of chiefship can be interpreted as clanship
writ large. Patriclan chiefship derives from conquest and is explained in these terms. The chief is a martial figure who dominates
the community with the assistance of closely allied patriclans who
share the offices of the chiefdom. Matriclan chiefship is the embodiment of the community. The matriclan chief orchestrates the ritual
activity of his chiefdom's specialists who are drawn from different
sections of the community, both indigenous peoples and immigrant.
The ritualized chief is endangered by his office; for him chiefship is
also a death sentence.

Chamba discourse and practice appear to presuppose two vari-
eties of difference. One type of difference lends itself to consociating
relation. Here, difference is apparent. Relationship is underwritten
by the supposition of shared substance, which radically negates difference in terms of underlying similarity. The sharing of substance
implies a particular vision of the possibility of mutuality within distinctive temporal and spatial frameworks. The past is a mythological
realm and spatial variation is denied. In contrast to these, adsociating idioms bridge different forms of difference in which similarity is
constituted as resemblance rather than continuity. The temporal
framework of this type of difference is historical; its spatial understanding is correspondingly specific and particular. Relationships

between units defined by adsociation, such as patriclans, are frequently antagonistic.

Nevertheless, adsociating and consociating idioms do not altogether coincide with conventionally discerned distinctions between matrikin and patrikin. If they coincided exactly, coined terms would be superfluous. However, we saw how, under duress, the mythological facades of the matriclans tended to crumble as people proposed historical differences to support political claims or to distance themselves from accusations of witchcraft or imputations of slave status. Conversely, patriclans belonging to a single cluster could choose to trivialize the differences between them, like the founders of the Yambu sections, who were considered to have adopted the names of trees under which they camped as names for their patriclans. Between matriclans and patriclans and larger ethnic units, relations of privileged abuse are glossed by informants in terms of the "oneness" or "togetherness" of those united in this way. Age mates, considered to have been born so closely "together" that seniority is disputed, are lifelong consociates who both joke and evince a tender concern for their mutual welfare while enjoying physically close relations witnessed in mutual embraces and playful struggles. Proverbially, Chamba tell us that the friend, that closest of others, is greater than matrikin.

To distinguish what I am proposing here from a structuralist account, I have used the terms contrast and difference rather than opposition to refer to divergences between the two idioms of sociability. In this, I have been influenced by Foucault's conception of *epistemei* underlying the possible forms in which difference may be recognized (Foucault 1970). This position radically differentiates Foucault's early writings from those of the structuralists, in whose mentalistic ontology all difference is, essentially, the same kind of binary opposition.[2] I would follow him in claiming that agents are enabled to act by virtue of their recognition, in the world they act upon, of types of difference that exist there. In societies like those of the Chamba, where the world to be acted upon consists predominantly of others rather than things (Goody 1971; 1976), there is ample justification for dwelling upon the way in which others are construed to be like or unlike oneself. For if this understanding is acted upon it provides us in our turn with insight into why activities took the course that they did. Before making the final connections between this essentially static view of differences and the developmental account I have proposed, I have to digress briefly to discuss the ethnographic basis from which my account is inferred.

Ethnographic Interpretation

However a reader chooses to evaluate my argument, I would suggest that it is potentially detachable, at least to an extent, from the ethnographic information I have presented. It is certainly my aim that this should be the case, although it is a difficult aim to achieve. The author of a clutch of distinguished monographs has expressed the opinion that success in monograph writing lies in simplification (Cohen 1974:47). But clarity for the reader is achieved by strong authorial guidance, and another school of thought takes exception to the tendency of anthropological writing to become monologue.[3]

My own view is that since authorial direction is inevitable, it may as well be explicit. The sandwich construction of the traditional monograph, with a statement of intent and parting homily framing the ethnographic meat, has always seemed a reasonable recognition by the author that there is a distinction between what his or her readers are likely to accept, or reinterpret, and what is liable to end on the historical scrap heap of ideas. Dan Sperber has put the case for a separation between anthropology and ethnography more strongly than I would be able to defend, even proposing that data and interpretation should be published separately (1985). I prefer to imagine a distinction between the two in relation to our techniques for reading a text. In these terms, a theoretical interpretation is relatively more disposable than, say, a fragment of reported speech or a situated observation. But we, nevertheless, need the anthropological framework of the writing in order to encompass the older account, by which I mean to treat that account as the product of an earlier relationship between agencies that has to be interpreted from our present viewpoint. We shall certainly want to recognize presuppositions in earlier writers, which are only apparent from a contemporary viewpoint, but the anthropological context of writing provides important material from which these suppositions may be inferred.

My appeal to contrasting idioms of sociability was not induced from the quantity of secondary data that I have used in this book, but from participation for a year in Mapeo social life, when appeals to such idioms were part and parcel of practical pursuits. The idea was generalized as an account of Chamba political development later and more reflectively; only retrospectively does there appear to have been much plan to the procedure. Knowing this is also important to evaluation of the thesis. My interpretative perspective derives from the accident of doing fieldwork in a particular place. I have no way of knowing whether my comparison would work in the same way if my Chamba center had been elsewhere. Calls for reflexivity in our practice have recently been interpreted as appeals for revelations about the ethnographic context of work. There is clearly a case to be made for greater awareness of the way in which the subjects of ethnographic investigation preempt the terms under which they consent to become an object of study. But calls for reflection on our practice are equally justifiable in relation to the more conventional area of anthropological theory. There is an important difference in grounding between structuralist methodology and that interpretative practice which is dependent upon the "loitering with intent" that goes into fieldwork. However, the fieldwork experience, which is local, short-term, and attended by so many accidental features, is rarely the sufficient basis for an ethnographic account that aspires to encompass a greater temporal and areal extent.

The generalization of my interpretation of Mapeo fieldwork into a developmental account of Chamba politics has to appeal to justifications different from those I can use to support my views about Mapeo itself. Although I have spent periods of a few months in other Chamba places, my involvement with those communities has been less intense than it was in Mapeo, and my interpretations less tried by that most practical necessity of attempting to behave appropriately in terms of them. The evidence, therefore, becomes more formal, in the literal sense that it depends upon the comparison of forms (of clan and chiefdom organization, of the terms of oral accounts, and so forth). Within the limitations of time and acquaintanceship, interpretative familiarity is open to testing.

But as my analysis deals with places and times more remote from the place in which I carried out fieldwork, so it becomes increasingly dependent upon types of information and reasoning other than those that derive directly from the field situation. Such reasoning may be referred to as the ethnographer's interpretative understanding. Although this understanding does not by itself legitimize the fieldworker's efforts other than rhetorically, it provides him or her with insights that can be extended to a range of materials that accrue in numerous ways. Analysts may look for formal similarities in areas to which anthropological theory guides them, such as kinship and clanship, and ask of the information available whether there is good reason to infer something very different from what is more adequately documented elsewhere. In the absence of evidence to the contrary, we generally extend our insights as long as they seem to be making sense of the materials we have. Insofar as this is true, then the temporal and spatial extent of the subject to which our analysis applies is determined not by an ethnic boundary but by the informativeness of the analysis itself. I shall consider the limits of my own analysis below.

From Interpretation to Transformation

My supposition that Chamba agency has inflected the outcomes of Chamba history makes sense of information that would otherwise appear random. It does appear to be the case that the idioms of organization I have identified as consociational have consistently receded in importance before adsociational idioms of relationship. Given a Chamba agency informed, that is both enabled and restricted, by suppositions of aptness in relations between people, it seems retrodictable that Chamba organizations would have changed in the way that they have. It also became retrodictable that people whose agency was informed by other notions would not have created the same historical changes as the Chamba. These considerations lead us to demonstrate the ways in which Chamba historical development can be construed to have rested importantly upon the ways that Chamba agency was inflected by understandings about sociability. This "construing" was itself made possible through fieldwork, which is the method crucial to the study, despite my account being historical and comparative. The reader can independently assess the inferences and connections to which I appeal to generalize the Mapeo account, but he or she cannot independently reassess the practical experience of fieldwork on which that account is based.

To look upon Chamba history as an outcome of Chamba agency is not to claim that individual Chamba were somehow masters of their own destinies. An analysis in terms of agency is just as far removed from transactionalism as it is, for different reasons, from the idea that agency is just the representation of the actor's point of view. Weberian sociology, to repeat terms I borrowed earlier, is a "sociology of fate" (B. Turner 1981). This implies that a distinction has to be drawn between the terms within which we represent purpose and those that represent the results of activity. Neither the resources of reflection at the disposal of acting agents, nor their resources of enactment, could be assumed to determine the results of social action without jettisoning an entire sociological literature devoted to the exploration of unintended consequences of activity, and to the practical effects that accrue to accepted standards of reflection through action.

There are principled objections, therefore, to eliding agency with result or effect. I have previously suggested that western analysts tend to treat agency as a term competitive with power. In emphasizing the power relations of enactment, we correspondingly diminish the role of agency in explanation, sometimes to the extent of encompassing agency as an effect of power, as in Foucault's later conflation of "power/knowledge" (Fardon 1985b). Conversely, constructions of universal agency that are culturally nonspecific, such as transactionalism, have difficulty in distinguishing intention from result. Both viewpoints are able to ignore the complex play of agency and power that suffuses Weberian sociology, notwithstanding the widely recognized bias towards fatalism in the writings of its founder. Both are able, also, to misconstrue the analytic creation of power and agency. The allocation of responsibility for outcomes between agency and power is modeled after the event in analytic terms. Within these terms, agency is imputed to actors from the evidence of their speech and practice. Reattribution of these imputed qualities is tantamount to redescription of the activities themselves, in that it supplies purpose to them. In terms of anthropological practice, this implies a research methodology curious about indigenous agency, and a method of presentation that attempts to justify to a readership the attribution to agents of foresight in defined terms and of specified extent.[4]

Any analytic focus renders some factors exogenous to its interests. Because they are not the major focus of this study, I have dealt in only general terms with external factors that canalized Chamba agency. Thus, we have seen that the rise of the Fulani Emirates of Adamawa and Muri, as a context, was a source of opportunities and constraints for Chamba activities. Much the same has been claimed of the advent of proto-colonialism and of the process of colonization and subsequent political decolonization that brought into being the two independent states in which Chamba now live. Broader regional or world-system analyses would suppose a context in which Chamba agency appeared negligible. A context derives from a focused curiosity. The redeeming feature of an academic division of labor is that someone is left to perform the task of interrogating the degree to which people's destinies were shaped by their own agency. Often, this has been the job of anthropologists.

However, external relations are only a part of the matrix of power relations within which Chamba history can be envisaged. If my analysis of agency has any validity, it seems necessary to argue that Chamba agents were ensnared also in the presuppositions of their own practices. Their capacity for acting was constrained or enabled by the resources of reflection and enactment at their disposal. The evidence for a proposition of this sort can be found in the very similar developments that spatially separated Chamba polities underwent. The logic of these similar institutional developments was not inherent in the institutions themselves, but had to be realized by agencies that created, recreated, modified or changed them. The strong correlation we have established between raiders and the politics of adsociation, and refugees and the politics of consociation, seems to be a property of the agency we have attributed to Chamba actors.

The argument involves the appropriateness of images under different circumstances of enactment. The consociated matriclan chiefdom responds to the purposes for which Chamba of these communities oriented their communal organization: to assure well-being, to expel witches, to control cyclical developments in the farming year and the human lifespan. The adsociated chiefdom organized the use of violence to guard the interests of its minority leadership. The two forms are appropriate to different aspirations.

Because these aspirations are achieved through institutional-ized means, which are interrelated themselves through common presuppositions about sociability, seeking to achieve a purpose in terms of one institution entails elevating the relative importance of other institutions to which it is related. Thus, the emergence of pa-triclan military organization implies the downgrading of matriclan-ship and its consociational idioms. The greater the scale of military adventures, and the more non-Chamba who are incorporated, the greater the degree of reliance upon patriclanship to achieve future purposes. This is the progression we witness in comparing the con-quest chiefdoms of Chambaland with those founded outside Cham-baland. Conversely, incorporation into the matriclan chiefdom tends to emphasize the importance of the chief's embodiment of the com-munity's welfare. Thus, in Yeli, which attempted the most wide-ranging ritual paramountcy, we find also the greatest elaboration of chiefly embodiment and chiefly vulnerability. The implied logic of these developments is not a static property; instead it is one that is revealed only as agents act under given circumstances in terms of their understanding of the idioms that relate them to those others whom they wish to affect. The test of our analysis is the extent to which it can encompass temporal and spatial change, in other words, the extent to which agency and transformation shed light upon one another.

Ethnicity, Tradition, and Modernity: The Limits of the Analysis

The limits to my analysis, which I began to explore in Chapter 11, coincide with the limits to credibility of the agency hypothesis that I have formulated. The incorporation of Chamba into national and world societies has changed the way that Chamba agency may be construed. Education, conversion to world religions, and participa-tion in Nigerian and Cameroonian politics and economics are fac-tors with which I can deal only negatively here: by showing that they mark the end of a relatively unreflective and coherent agency through the introduction of a disjunction between the techniques for assessing activity in local and domestic groupings and those appropriate to the wider society.

Nowadays, the complexities of public life can no longer be grasped by assimilation to relations of parentation and the idioms of sociability they connote. Or, to more exactly describe the circumstances of my own fieldwork, Chamba idioms of sociability remain adequate only for a diminishing minority of older people and, to a lesser degree, the untraveled among the youngsters. Something of this change had perhaps already occurred in the indigenous rationalization that accompanied the foundations of the Chamba conquest chiefdoms, which better equipped them to deal with both Fulani and European forms of imperialism. The change has been most marked in the diminishing pertinence of the consociating idioms of relationship, whose significance has already been restricted to locality, kin and the family, and which will be further eroded by the gradual decline in the practice of matrilateral inheritance of property. The other associations of this idiom with indigenous ideas of disease, with slavery, with witchcraft, and with the disposal of infants who had anomalous physical characteristics, make it peculiarly susceptible to threat from modern legal statutes, as well as the influences of Islam and Christianity, neither of which have yet shown syncretist tendencies, at least that I know of in central village Chambaland.

The emergence of the modern concept of Chamba ethnicity is one of the starkest examples of this change. Precolonially, the relativistic terms such as Leko, Daka, Nakɛnyare, and Sama only permitted the situational emergence of a notionally extensive Chamba ethnicity. Historically, we have seen that the possibility of this extensive identity was tied, among other things, to the consociating relations envisaged between Leko and Daka speakers because of the importance of the "same" chiefly matriclan among them both. We could say that the possibility of a Chamba identity was established consociationally. The totality of Chamba ethnicities, including those of the Benue and Bali Chamba, was uncoordinated. Particular ethnic designations traded upon locally recognized authenticity defined from the pivotal position of the community. The magisterial survey was simply unavailable to Chamba of the precolonial period. The center of gravity has shifted now. In discussions of ethnicity in a national context, the educated Chamba speaker no longer places himself within a local community from which he regards the similarities and differences of his neighbors. Instead, he seems to talk from an aerial vantage, surveying the distribution of ethnic groups within the nation and mapping an exclusive and exhaustive set of ownerships upon the national territory. This is a simple enough way of thinking, one that is integral to our own territorial conceptions of nationhood, but one impossible in a community that lacked maps and viewed its neighbors across the ground at eye-level—impossible also, it might be added, before the assumptions made about the position of states in a world order of states had been extended by analogy to the position of ethnic groups in a national order of such groupings.

A similar change is occurring in Chambas' reflections on the concept of tradition. The category of "tradition" is flattening what is understood as Chamba custom to a single dimension, a process that is analogous to changes in the understanding of ethnicity. The ways in which attention is engaged by evidences of what is taken to belong to the past in present affairs is altering in more and less subtle ways.

In 1977, during major public celebrations held at Ganye to welcome the introduction of universal primary education, I witnessed festivities held in the public space in front of the divisional chief's palace. (He, incidentally, is called by the Hausa term, Sarkin Ganye, in part, local commentators suggest, to finesse the implications of a Chamba or Fulfulde title. He is from Sugu and became a Muslim before election as the first paramount chief, and earlier worked in the veterinary service.)

Seated under an awning constructed from a framework of poles was the chief, attired in Fulani-style robes and turban, his traditional councilors, who also have Hausa titles and are appointed from both Fulani and different Chamba communities, and an assortment of officials representing local government, state administration, police, schools, army and prisons. The chief's retainers sang praise songs and announced his movements by setting up a vigorous refrain on the drums and horns they have adopted from the Fulani. Chamba from the villages and Koma from the hills entered the central space to perform publicly the flute dances that accompanied chiefmaking, circumcision, and death. The more picturesque elements of tradition were well represented: the Chamba masked dancers, with their raffia bodies and gaping-mouthed wooden heads, the exponents of traditional circumcision dances, a splendidly drilled semi-professional troupe wearing well-laundered narrow-loomed cloth skirts, the Koma jesters or buffoons clad in baboon skins, blowing their shrill whistles and discomforting the wealthy with demands for money, to the amusement of onlookers. Bank notes were affixed to the sweating brows of the dancers and musicians to attest the approval and demonstrate the wealth of the patrons of the festival.

The local populace formed a dense arc around the three sides of the palace forecourt. Had they come to see the dances, the officials, the chief, the dramatization of wealth they cannot hope to possess? Was it just as well to be seen there, or were public gatherings simply irresistible? It was difficult to tell. When I asked, the responses often invoked the idea of tradition. But the form of the answer was revealing. Whereas Chamba elders would preface their remarks with the inevitable "We Chamba . . . ," the younger men tended to slip into "they." Which "they?" Well, the people who live in the villages, or the elders, or the people in the past, and so forth. This notion of tradition is the reflex of a conception of modernity. Traditions are what you *have* by virtue of belonging to a particular people, but they come from the past across a divide between "us" and "them." All Nigerians have traditions in the same way (and for the same reasons) that they have ethnic identities. The important thing about traditions is that they are as aesthetically pleasing, rhythmic, and exciting as the next man's. For the educated national, traditions are the visible manifestation of ethnic origin, and subject to the judgments made of appearances in general, at least in this context.

A term like tradition has to be understood in terms of its reflective use. In the new national context, its use signals a new form. The articulate sense given to the concept of tradition by contemporary Chamba of Ganye brings the past to bear upon the materiality of the present under a particular guise, which can only be understood against the background of the contemporary administrative setting and multi-ethnic make-up of the Ganye town, and the relations between this administrative center, the state, and the Nigerian nation.

Bali Nyonga in Cameroon is the locale of a different festival, which I witnessed in 1984. Resplendently attired in "traditional" Chamba gowns (which have no counterpart in Chambaland), the men of Bali Nyonga enact the martial *lela* ceremony, as they claim to have done every year since they started their trek south. Standards similar to those supposed to have led the Chamba raiders on their migration are taken by armed warriors to be washed ceremonially in a nearby river. Then they are paraded through the town before the throng join the Chamba flute band in the forecourt of a substantial palace. Members of the warrior lodges dance forward to salute the chief with cacophonous volleys from their muskets. The festival re-enacts the drama of Bali conquest in the Grassfields. More press-ingly, it reminds the Bali Nyonga's neighbors of their might in the context of contemporary land disputes that derive from the events of Chamba conquest and the subsequent role that the Bali played in support of German administration. In contrast to the symbols of "traditional" northern Nigerian chiefship, which the Ganye celebra-tion shares with many similar events in that country, the Bali stress a distinctive "Chamba" patrimony (albeit that patrimony now con-sists of elements from diverse sources) which differentiates them-selves from their neighbors.

Such observations concerning tradition are not unique to Ganye or Bali Nyonga, and in relation to the contemporary situation, my remarks about them are only programmatic. However, I offer these remarks to indicate that this book finishes when it does not because I have doubts about the contemporary pertinence of anthropological research, but because appeal to agency as an analytically salient con-ception implies an acceptance that when the analysis is no longer attributable to actors it is, correspondingly, no longer illuminating about their activities. The analysis I have proposed is reconstructed from the restricted pertinence Chamba idioms of sociability have in village, and more generally, domestic affairs. I know that these idi-oms remain an important factor in negotiating the relations between the villages of origin of town officials and the people who have re-mained behind, but to pursue the analysis further would go beyond the boundaries of my research and import suppositions from village culture into a national context where their pertinence may be different.

Agency, like most words that address social phenomena, is an ambitious term. More cautiously, I could have referred to aspects of agency, admitting that no amount of attribution by analysts can fill the contexts that the term begs. However, the term is far less ambitious than many others that anthropologists use routinely, such as culture, worldview, actor's point of view, and so forth, and it has the virtue of asking us to ground interpretation in action and event. Throughout this book I have drawn attention to, what I called in Chapter 1, the problematic relation between ethnic- and culture-bearing subjects. Chamba ethnicity is a modern phenomenon; so, by implication, is any notion of Chamba culture. The attribution of cultures to "tribes" once served the rhetorical purpose of drawing attention to the respect which should be shown towards those who disagreed with western ideas, when our capacity directly to impose our own notions was greater than it is now. But the elision of ethnic and cultural subjects has had unanticipated effects in the contemporary world. While these effects are not academic reasons for reexamining the relationship between the two, the realization that the relationship between ethnicity and culture emerged under historically specific conditions, of whatever complexity, does constitute such a reason.

In the Chamba case, I have argued that clans and localities were, at one time, more clearly represented as culture-bearing units than the extensive Chamba people. Although my information is not completely adequate, I have also suggested that cultural similarities do not end with the extensive people. None of this will surprise anyone with interests in the same matters; these are things that have always been said. But the realization has not been as central as it should. In part, we are led astray by our words. In order not to be incomprehensible, or unreadably longwinded, there has to be recourse to Chamba, Chamba culture, or Chamba agency (and for Chamba read any other people) as a shorthand way of identifying a subject. But, inevitably, the identification is an anachronism, and it begs the similarity between ethnic and cultural subjects that can only be explored when ethnicity and culture are distinguished and dismantled.

In subnational ethnic groupings, as in nations themselves, the building of ethnic and cultural subjects, and of an identity between them is a contemporary project to which anthropological writings may contribute. But this is a different issue from the tendency anthropological writings have to contribute definitionally towards the creation and elision of ethnicity and culture. Whatever the tendency to backslide into ways of writing we have absorbed professionally, I suggest that terms like culture, worldview, and their virtual synonyms require sustained criticism if they are not to connive in current political debates by positing ahistorical difference between peoples in the way that notions of evolution once posited historically unsubstantiated development.

MAPEO CLANSHIP:

A NUMERICAL ANALYSIS

The following table (Table 10) is based upon a survey of the patriclan affiliation of 260 compound heads in twelve hamlets of Mapeo and provides data that support my interpretive argument in the main text. The survey included most of the compounds of Mapeo village, but excluded the Chamba who had left the Mapeo refuge to settle in neighboring Tisayeli or in any of the numerous plains villages founded, or augmented, by Mapeo elements.

Major patriclan *jubi* are those that Mapeo Chamba describe as establishing "one father" relations between co-owning clans. The table includes twenty-five patriclan names. Because the materials relate only to Mapeo village, this understates the number of patriclans that would have occupied the Mapeo hills during the refuge period. The most important omission is probably that of the Sanbu of Tisayeli, who are members of the *jub.Jangi* alliance under their own priest, *wani*. The table also ignores conversion to world religions. Not all the respondents are members of the *jubi* associated with their patriclan; previously, compound heads would have been members.

Given these reservations, the table can be interpreted as follows: *bən.təng* groups six named clans of predominantly northern origin (Yangur are sometimes supposed to derive from a more northern ethnic grouping of that name; Liranɛpbu, Libbu, and Jabbu are said to be of Bata/Bachama origin). *Ya.gum.ani* groups the Yambu clans. The first two clans are considered identical to the two major clans of the northern Shebshi chiefdoms (Yam.tub.bu, and

TABLE 10

Mapeo Patriclanship

Major patri-clan *jubi*	Patriclans al-lied by *jubi*	Number of Re-spondents as percentage of total	Alliance as percentage of total
bən.təng	Yanguru.bu	16.0	
	Liranɛp.bu	5.4	
	Lib.bu	1.9	
	Jab.bu	1.2	
	Wɔsan.bu	3.5	
	Gbəng.bu	0.4	28.4
Ya.gum.ani	Yam.tub.bu	2.3	
	Yam.dəgi.bu	7.7	
	Yam.kəm.bu	1.2	
	Yam.kpub.bu	1.2	
	Yam.san.bu	1.9	
	Yam.iran.bu	0.8	15.1
Jarɔ	Tiranɛp.bu	11.2	
	Daka.bu/Dɔ.bu	7.3	
	Kpem.bu	3.1	
	Lamnɛp.bu	1.5	23.1
Jub.Jangi	Jang.bu	7.3	
	Jang.bu	7.3	
	Dəng.bu	3.1	
	Dang.bu	0.8	18.5
Kɔna	Jangan.bu	4.6	
	Sankirtan.bu	0.8	
	Gban.ḅu	6.5	11.9
Others	Danu.bu (*tɛgi*)	1.2	
	Wum.bu	1.9	3.1
Total		100.1	100.1

Yam.də.bu); the other four are peculiar to Mapeo. The cult of *jarɔ* groups four clans of western origin (Tiranɛpbu are chiefs of Tim Dəng near Dalami, and originally from farther west; Dakabu are also from the west; Kpembu are the clan of the chiefmakers of Gurum; Lamnɛpbu are the chiefly clan of Dalami). *Jub.Jangi*, the harvest cult, is associated with the Leko (*Jangi* means Chamba Leko in this context). The two Jangbu clans are distinguished by reference to their distinct priestly offices, *wani*. *Kɔna* groups clans that trace some kind of connection to Yeli (Gbanbu, the Mapeo representatives to Yeli; Janganbu, the clan of the Yeli chief; Sankirtanbu, the clan of the python chief who claims to have exercised influence on behalf of Yeli among the Koma). The cults are concerned with the following ailments: *bən.təng*, broken bones and deformed births; *ya.gum.ani*, swellings and ulcers; *jarɔ*, madness; and *kɔna*, smallpox. *Jub.Jangi* is the cult of the harvest rather than an ailment, and

TABLE I I

Mapeo Matriclanship

Matriclan	Derivation	Members as percentage of sample	Alliance
kɔm.kuni	Koma Hill	18.0	People from
nɛ.kusum.be.kuni	people	4.0	the hills
dəng.kuni	(disputed)	17.0	Chiefly
gang.van.ji.kuni	Chief of the red rock	2.0	clans
kongla.kuni	elephant	18.0	People of
yɛt.kuni	bushcow	13.0	the bush
wana.kuni	dog	11.0	
su.kuni	sun	3.0	
jam.kuni	mist	11.0	
kpe.kuni	blacksmith	3.0	
Total		100.0	

the *wanbu* have the ability to cleanse compounds of the pollution of breech births. The numerous clans are thus grouped, approximately in terms of origin, into larger alliances through the *jubi*, which place them in the communal etiology and calendar. The cults also perform at funerals of their members.

Table 11 presents data on matriclanship derived from 256 adult men and women who comprise the population of four Mapeo hamlets. One matriclan *wɔ.yit.kuni*, loves guinea-corn clan, has only minor representation in Mapeo and is absent from the sample. There are also no members of *gang.kuni* in the table. The table shows the ten matriclans that are long established in Mapeo. Alliances group eight of the ten. The other two unrepresented clans also have allies through the joking relations between matriclans.

Table 12 presents the matriclans and patriclans in Mapeo in terms of their overall memberships and of their proportional representation in the whole community. For the purposes of constructing the table, I have assumed that compounds have an average membership of six (excluding members absent for schooling or employment), which yields a population of 1,560 for twelve Mapeo hamlets (which I suspect is rather lower than the real figure). Assuming constant proportions of clan membership among this population, nominal figures can be attributed to the clans. The calculations are somewhat arbitrary, but the results in the patriclan and matriclan domains are so divergent that less crude calculations would not affect the points I want to make.

Given the range of clan sizes, the average membership (a) is not particularly informative. Looking at range (b), we find that six of the ten matriclans have more than a hundred members, but only seven of twenty-five patriclans attain this size. All but 12 percent of the population (c) belong to large matriclans, taking a hundred members as large, but more than a quarter of the population belong to small patriclans. Almost 90 percent of the population belong to matriclans with memberships in excess of one hundred and fifty members. If the sample could be expanded to include other villages of the Mapeo area, the results would be reinforced, since we would have to include a number of extra patriclans but virtually no extra matriclans.

The figures support my point that Mapeo Chamba experience

TABLE 12

Numerical comparison of Mapeo matriclanship and patriclanship

a. Average size of membership: matriclan $1560 \div 10 = 156$
patriclan $1560 \div 25 = 62$

b. Range of membership:	*patriclans*	*matriclans*
0–50 members	15	3
50–100 members	3	1
100–150 members	5	0
150–200 members	1	2
200–250 members	1	1
250–300 members	0	3

c. Proportion of population belonging to clans in each size range (in percent):

clan size	*patriclans*	*matriclans*
0–50	23.1 percent	08.0 percent
50–100	13.5	04.0
100–150	36.2	00.0
150–200	11.2	22.0
200–250	16.0	13.0
250–300	00.0	53.0

patriclanship particularistically and matriclanship as a more general idiom. Since the number of matriclans is roughly the same throughout Chambaland, and since the differently named matriclans of separate communities are considered "the same," the point would be further reinforced for Chambaland as a whole. See also Chapter 8 for the comparative implications of these points.

CHAMBA LANGUAGE

Linguistic researches into the Chamba languages are not advanced, and I am not a linguist, so these notes are offered only in the absence of a better informed summary.

Chamba Leko Dialects of Chambaland

Most of the dialects appear to belong to two clusters, but a third residual category of dialects reminds us that the diaspora may have obliterated the evidence of a more complex pattern of variation.

Northern Chamba Leko

This cluster includes Kollu, Saptou, Vogba, Nyemdelou, and Kachalla Voma; Noss (1976) calls the grouping Wangai dialect.

Speakers of the southern dialects of Leko refer to these northern Leko speakers collectively as Janga. The term is pejorative, and is also used by central Daka speakers for the Leko as a whole. *Jang* carries connotations of hill-dwelling backwardness, though there seems to be no etymological reason why it should do so. Chamba Daka speakers sometimes gloss *Jang* in terms of their identical verb "to throw away," i.e., people who should have been thrown away. However, this sheds no light on the Leko usage and is best seen as another example of the Chamba penchant for derogatory etymological glosses of ethnic terms. The root appears as a patriclan name in Mapeo (see Appendix 1). Although I have no data to indicate whether there are variants of the northern Leko dialect, informants claim that there are.

Prominent phonological variants between northern and southern Leko dialects include replacement of [r] by [l] in some contexts, e.g. *gala* for *gara*, chief; *lela* for *lera*, flute; *wala* for *wara*, groundnut, and so forth (but not *vara*, skull; or *yera*, guinea corn), and other variants *bana* for *batna*, beer; *afinbea* for *abinbea*, our. There are two historical justifications for dwelling on this point: (1) the same variants occur in the Daganyonga Chamba Leko dialect of Bali Chamba, a relation also confirmed by the researches of Pastor Hamidou Jean of the Samba Literacy Centre, Balkossa, and (2) the extension of the northern Chamba Leko dialect seems to correlate with historical traditions of the dominance of the Sama patriclan.

Southern Chamba Leko

Informants' accounts suggest that there is minor dialectal variation among almost all the communities of the southern Chamba Leko, and the situation is probably rather similar in the north. Three dialect groups were most commonly suggested:

BALKOSSA

This group includes Alani and Wapeo and forms the Samba-Leko group of Noss (1976). The dialect is spoken in and around the chiefdom of Balkossa, and probably also in Sapeo, Nigeria. It has been transcribed by Noss, and is to be the medium for Bible translation into Chamba Leko. Noss also includes the hill community of Sim Kola in this group. Informants with whom I have discussed Meek's schedule of terms from the Benue Chamba of Donga (1931b), claim that Balkossa speech is the most closely related to Donga speech among the dialects in Chambaland.

YELI

The group includes Kubi and forms Meek's Lekon schedule (1931b). The distinctive Yeli dialect is spoken only in Yeli and its surrounding villages. The dialect is sometimes called *mɔ.ba.yɛli.kɔ*, after the common phrase from which Leko also derives ("I say that . . . ").

BANGLA

This dialect group includes Malkoga, Audi, and Duna. It is the southernmost of the Chamba Leko dialects and is spoken by members of the communities established after dispersal from the Bangla Hills during the colonial period.

These three dialects account for the majority of the southern Leko population; distribution of the southern dialect correlates with the area over which the chiefly matriclan *gat.kuna* once ruled. The minor variants correspond to three distinct chiefly territories. Two further Chamba Leko dialects are noted by Noss, whose comments I am unable to amplify: Sampara, with about five hundred speakers living to the north and west of Balkossa, and Denu, spoken around the place of that name (in which some informants would include Jampeu and Simkola). The dialects are readily mutually intelligible although, if Yeli and Balkossa speech forms are a guide, there are lexical differences between them.

Outlying Chamba Leko Dialects

At least three distinct dialects of Chamba Leko are spoken in small communities separated from the main body of the contemporary Chamba Leko people. Each of the three appears to diverge from the main Leko dialects (both southern and northern) more markedly than any of these dialects does from the others.

WOM

According to Meek, this dialect is spoken by a group of 500 people living in an area known by that name. They call themselves Pereba and they are neighbors to the Vere in Nigeria (1931b I:384).

MUMBAKE

The dialect is used by some villages of Leko speakers on the northern edge of Chambaland in Nigeria (Meek 1931b I:388). Meek's information on both of these groups is very meager.

KOLBILA

A dialect "spoken by about 2,500 people in the environs of Bantadje south of Mount Vokre by Poli" (Noss 1976:8). Podlewski gives a population of about 1,000 (1971:73). My schedule from Kolbila shows numerous differences from the major Chamba Leko dialects.

All three of these groups appear not to consider themselves ethnically Chamba, despite similarities of language. I have not visited either Wom or Mumbake. At least in the cases of Wom and Kolbila, it is evident that cultural similarities can as easily be traced with their neighbors as with Chamba. In the absence of more specialized linguistic and ethnographic work, it is difficult to know what inferences should be drawn.

Chamba Daka Dialects of Chambaland

The research efforts on Chamba Daka language have been even more modest than those expended on Chamba Leko, and I have little data on which to base my comments. However, it seems that Chamba Daka dialects differ in grammar, phonology, and vocabulary. The two major central dialects are Nakɛnyare and Mapeo. Raymond Boyd is currently engaged on research that will clarify the relationship between them.

Nakɛnyare Dialect

Despite the local importance attached to very slight speech differences, this is a single dialect spoken throughout the chiefdoms of the Shebshi Mountains and the western Nassarawo Plain. Meek's Gandole schedule from the west of the Shebshi Mountains clearly demonstrates that the foundation of chiefdoms in that area was accompanied by the spread of the Nakɛnyare dialect (Meek 1931b).

Mapeo Dialect

The distinctive speech of the Chamba around Mapeo seems to pose more problems of comprehension to Nakɛnyare speakers than Nakenyare speech does to Mapeo Chamba. This is understandable since the Mapeo form is cut down and glottalized compared to its more western counterpart; initial [y] or [w] are typically substituted by glottal stops, whereas medial stops become voiced. The result is considered more abrasive than the mellifluous and flowing Nakenyare by speakers of both dialects.

Divergent Daka Dialects

I have to deal with the remaining Daka dialects under two headings to separate those that have persisted within the area of the Chamba chiefdoms from those found on the peripheries of the centralized Chamba lands.

PERIPHERAL DAKA DIALECTS

Early reports of the existence of these dialects have never been seriously investigated. Our sources at best indicate that there are such dialects and that they are diverse. Meek collected wordlists from two peripheral Daka groups: the Taram to the south of central Chambaland and the Dirrim to the southwest. Dirrim may also be spoken to the north of the Kam River, around Garba Chede, although Taram is probably restricted to an area around Gumti (personal communications from A. Edwards and R. Blench). Meek's wordlists reveal two divergent schedules of what are, nonetheless, recognizably Chamba Daka terms. In a colonial report, R. Logan suggests further categories, but without lexical foundation: Dakka (around Dawo on the southern peripheries of Chambaland), Sonkol (originally from south of the Taraba River, they are said to have lost a language of their own and to speak "Dakka"), Kokon (another southern peripheral group), and Taram Dakka (presumably Meek's Taram) (1932 Rhodes House). However superficially, these data do suggest a patchwork of Daka dialects to the south and southwest of the present-day Chamba chiefdoms. Other information leads us to suppose that this pattern may once have extended throughout Chambaland.

CENTRAL DAKA DIALECTS

In the absence of linguistic investigations, we are again dependent on informants' statements. These propose that dialects of Chamba Daka are spoken among such peoples as the Jangani (largely within Sugu), the Mangla (Mbulo and neighboring chiefdoms), the Kolen, Dangsa, Tola and Gang Pana (all of the northern Shebshi Mountains), as well as the Lamja (north of the central Chamba chiefdoms).

Taking all the linguistic information on Chambaland together, and ignoring its variable quality, an intriguing picture emerges. Large speech communities seem to correlate closely with the existence of chiefdoms. Closely related chiefdoms appear to speak related dialects. In the absence of centralized political organization, we encounter linguistic fragmentation; whereas in the presence of centralization we find indications that linguistic diversity was previously greater. It is evident that there is a large area of chiefdoms among Chamba Daka in which Nakɛnyare is the normal means of communication, and two major Chamba Leko dialects that are associated with two different chiefly dynasties. There are indications that cultural uniformity may be more generally related to political centralization.

CHAMBA POPULATION

With population, as with language, we are handicapped by reliance on unreliable sources, where we have any sources at all. It is difficult to fit traditional units and modern administrative units, although the two are fairly close in the southern and central Shebshi chiefdoms. The chiefdoms of Gurum and Yebbi were combined in the census figures of 1976 as the district of Yelwa. In 1936, the Chamba populations of Gurum and Yebbi were respectively 8,000 and 3,300. By 1976 their combined Chamba population had risen to 29,500. If they had maintained their respective sizes then the Gurum Chamba population would have been about 20,000 and the Yebbi population about 9,000–10,000.

If we look at another chiefdom, Sugu, a roughly parallel set of figures emerges. There were 7,000 Chamba in Sugu in 1936, which had risen to 23,500 forty years later. However, Sugu District, which was reconstituted by the British, did include some of the Leko settlements of the eastern Alantika Mountains that had not traditionally formed part of the Sugu chiefdom. This suggests that a population of 7,000 may have been slightly in excess of the population of traditional Sugu around the mid-1930s, but colonial underestimates of population might compensate for this factor. If the figures are far from reliable, they at least provide an order of magnitude; in the precolonial period the best guess is that the largest chiefdoms had populations of about 7,000–8,000, while the smaller chiefdoms were in the range of 1,000–2,000 (for more detailed discussion see Fardon 1980 II, Appendix; I have drawn on estimates in files: B3.Z;

G3 Vol.1; C778 Paul; Sorrell 1955; Crane 1958; and Tax Returns for
Ganye Division 1977–78).

Populations in the northern Shebshi Mountains were either on
the same scale or perhaps slightly smaller than the settlements to
the south. The largest chiefdom of Binyeri had a population of about
9,000 in 1936, consisting of about 4,000 Chamba who ruled over
about 5,000 Tola, Mumuye and Tiba. During the colonial period, the
Chamba population of Binyeri dropped sharply as a result of migrations into the Nassarawo Plain and fell below 1,500 in the 1950s.
Dalami, in the middle of the Nassarawo Plain, was estimated to have
a population of about 2,000 in the 1890s, roughly similar to its 1930
population of 1,700 (Passarge 1895:252). The other intrusive chiefdoms of the northern Shebshi Mountains had smaller populations.

The hill refuges around Mapeo contained some thousands of
Chamba who dispersed rapidly once farming in the plains became
possible. Some estimates have put the number of Chamba in the
Mapeo refuges at 6,000 (C778 Crane 1958), although a figure of
3,000–4,000 seems more credible.

The residual chiefdoms of the Chamba Leko in the Alantika
Mountains were smaller than those of the central Nakɛnyare, and
presumably only a fraction of their size prior to the diaspora. Nowadays, none of them has a population of more than a few hundred
(Paris 1983; ORSTOM 1971; Lembezat 1961). Their present-day
small size has been accentuated by migration into Nigeria, especially during the early colonial period, and into less remote areas of
Cameroon after independence.

If the population was roughly 2.5 times greater in 1976 than in
1936, and if the 1936 figure is fairly close to the nineteenth century
population, we can guess that there might have been about 60,000
Chamba in central Chambaland, the majority of whom would have
lived in the chiefdoms of the Shebshi Mountains. Prior to the Leko
diaspora, the population of Chambaland might have been consider-
ably larger, although by just how much would depend on the number of Chamba chiefdoms that previously existed between the Faro
and Deo Rivers. We are unable to achieve precision, but the picture
of relatively small populations, with relatively numerous dialect variants is pretty clear.

Appendix 4

ETHNOGRAPHIC ABSTRACTS

The organization of the main text of the monograph reflects a sequential argument concerned with Chamba variation, chronology, thematic resemblance, and historical development. Appendix 4 adds materials that are not specified in the text. As so much of the main text is concerned with Mapeo, I have not thought it worthwhile to include data from Mapeo in the abstracts.

Bali Chiefdoms

Language, dialect, location: five chiefdoms of Northwestern Cameroon founded by immigrants under Chamba Leko leadership. Four chiefdoms remain Leko speaking (locally termed Mubako or Daganyonga); the largest, Bali Nyonga, is Munngaka speaking.

Population: in 1913, Bali Nyonga 29,240; Bali Kumbad 3,200; Bali Gham 1,521; Bali Gashu 1,200; and Bali Gangsin 105. In 1953, Bali Nyonga 18,277; Bali Kumbad 6,350; Bali Gham 4,954; Bali Gashu 674; and Bali Gangsin 278 (E. M. Chilver 1964 TS).

Chieflists: for earlier versions see Chilver 1964, 1970; Hunt 1925; Jeffreys 1962. Chief Gawolbe (Ga.wəl.be: chief of water) died at Nkəm around 1835–1840. Other chiefs include the following:

Bali Nyonga
Nyonpasi, d. 1860?
Ga Lɛga, d. 1901
Fon Nyonga II, 1901–1940

Bali Kumbad
Ga Labi, n.d.
Ga Gbanyi, killed at Bali
Nyonga, n.d.

V. S. Ga Lega II, 1940–1984

Ga Nyamnyi, n.d.
Ga Labi II, 1920–1980
Ga Nyamnyi, 1980–

Bali Gham
Ga Langa, reigned 60 years,
n.d.
Ga Wəlbe, n.d.
Ga Labi, fl. 1889–1923
Ga Nyam, 1923–1958
M. S. T. Ga Labi, 1958–

Bali Gashu
Ga Nyam, n.d.
Ga Su, n.d.
Ga Wəlbe, fl. 1926–1949
Do Gashu, 1949–

Bali Gangsin
Gavabe, n.d.
(hiatus)
Gangsin, fl. 1926–1943
Do Gavabe, 1943–

Jeffreys includes three additional chiefs of Bali Kumbad who do not occur on other lists. Relationships between the leader of the united alliance and the founders of the Bali chiefdoms are disputed locally.

Sources and observations: basic materials to be found in the researches of E. M. Chilver and P. M. Kaberry, especially for Bali Nyonga. My research was based in Bali Gangsin for ten weeks in 1984, supplemented by visits to other Bali chiefdoms, particularly Bali Gham and Bali Gashu.

Balkossa (Val.kɔsa, slave of death; also Tadnu)

Language, dialect and location: Southern residual Chamba Leko refuge chiefdom located in Alantika Mountains. Speakers of mə.ba.lekɔ.

Population: 378 in 1982.

Chieflists: Valkosa; Buba (Ding ke mu ga); Gaji (reigned 1 year); Tema; Jima; Lanawa; Misa 1968–1986.
Descended to the plain under Tema (about 1900?).

Sources and other observations: archival and published sources are slight; I carried out one interview in 1976–78 and a number of interviews in 1984 with representatives of both chiefly and priestly clans.

Binyeri–Tola

Language, dialect and location: speakers of Chamba Nakɛnyare dialect, living in the northern Shebshi Mountains.

Population: in 1936, 4,000 Chamba and 5,000 Tola; by 1950s only 1,500 Chamba.

Chieflists: Virtually identical lists in Logan 1926; 1932 and Fardon 1980. Logan 1926: 1. Damashi, 2. Nyeri (son of 1), 3. Gang Jeni or Gidaudu (son of 2), 4. Sule (son of 2), 5. Jaune (son of 3), 6. Mabanso (son of 4) 1924–25, 7. Bello (son of 4) 1925, 8. Umaru (son of 5) 1926.

Sources and other observations: Published references are largely concerned with putative exploits of Damashi. My information is from interviews held with officials of Yambu, Tola, Gang Pana, etc. in 1977.

Dalami

Language, dialect and location: Chamba Nakɛnyare-speaking chiefdom in the center of the Nassarawo Plain.

Population: about 2,000 in the 1890s; 1,700 in 1930s; 600 in 1977.

Chieflists: 1. Gang Jeren (founder), 2. Gang Lawe, 3. Gang Bakassi, 4. Gang Yetchen, 5. Gang Wukeni, 6. Gang Tangen, 7. Gang Gini, 8. Gang Ganen (alive in about 1903 when oldest informant born, and chief in German times).

Politico-ritual organization: similar to northern Shebshi type. Lamnɛpbu appointed to *gang, nyagang,* and *mala;* Yambu are *kameni,* Dɔbu are *gbani.*

Sources and observations: few published/archival sources; although Passarge (1895) is an early reference; my data are from interviews in 1977.

Donga

Language, dialect and location: Chamba Leko-speaking immigrants to the Benue Plains.

Population: estimated at 8,000 in late nineteenth century.

Chieflists: See Fardon (1980; 1983) for interpretation of Garbosa's data to produce this list:
1. Loya Garbosa fl.1810–c.1825; 2. Pyemishena (Ga Kola) c.1825–c.1850; 3. Shimbura (Garkiye) c.1830–c.1865; 4. Nubumga Donzomga (Garbasa) c.1860–c.1885; 5. Gargbanyi 1885–1892; 6. Garbosa I 1892–1911; 7. Garkiye II 1911–1921; 8. Garbasa II 1921–1931; 9. Garbosa II 1931–1982 (author of history of Donga).

Sources and observations: see especially Garbosa and Meek; I made a short visit in 1977.

Gurum

Language, dialect and location: Chamba Nakɛnyare of the central Shebshi Mountains.

Population: 8,000 Chamba in 1936; perhaps 20,000 in 1976.

Ethnic and clan composition: early chiefs of *gang.tim.nɔ.kuni* claiming Yeli connection; later chiefs of Gangwɔknibu with Bata or northern associations, and Taksabu. Priests from Kpemɛmbu are considered indigenous to area. A number of other patriclans are known, including Danubu, Nupabu, Lambabu, and Sangamɛmbu.

Chieflists: The listings are highly variable and contentious because of chiefship disputes (see Fardon 1980 II:252–53 for six lists). Between four and six matriclan chiefs may have reigned before the middle of the nineteenth century; thereafter, succession for the next five reigns rotated between Gangwɔknibu and Taksabu; from about 1900, with the installation of Gang Makɛn, Gangwɔknibu retained control of the chiefship.

Politico-ritual organization: southern Shebshi type. Ideally, twenty-four officials divided into twelve chief's assistants (*gbanbu*) and twelve priests (*kamenbu*). Priests are drawn from Kpemɛmbu and considered indigenous, in charge of *jubi,* and conceptually opposed to chief. All but one of the chief's assistants are drawn from matriclans (the exception being *gang.ta*). Other officials are in charge of four great shrines of chiefdom: the grave of last matriclan chief; the smallpox shrine of Dim Timi; the royal graveyard; and the shrine in the custody of *masa* the head diviner (see Fardon 1980 I:258–68; II:110–14 for details).

Sources and observations: three months' fieldwork in 1977–78. Copious references to chiefship in British colonial records, see especially G2.2C.

Mbulo (also Gang Bakɛni)

Language, dialect and location: Chamba Nakɛnyare of the northern Shebshi Mountains.

Population: 2,060 Chamba in 1930.

Chieflists: Ninth chief in list met the Germans.

Sources and observations: Noted by Passarge: my interviews in 1978.

Northern Residual Leko

Language, dialect and location: Speakers of the northern dialect of Chamba Leko, and live in the northern Alantika Mountains.

Population: very small, e.g. Kollu 68, Kachalla Voma 150, Lowol 197 (1982).

Chieflists: Germans arrived in reign of third Kollu chief in present site; war with Fulani of Tchamba in reign of third chief of Saptou (in both cases informants claim that full chieflists are forgotten).

Sources and other observations: interviews 1984.

Sapeo

Language, dialect and location: Chamba Leko speakers of the southern Alantika Mountains.

Population: 400 in 1930; 1,320 in 1977.

Chieflists: Eighth chief appointed at the end of World War I.

Sources and other observations: Frobenius worked there, but it is difficult to tell which of his information is from Sapeo; interviews in 1976–77.

Sugu (Ga.Su.bi)

Language, dialect and location: Chamba Nakɛnyare of the southern Shebshi Mountains.

Population: 9,800 in 1936; 14,700 in 1954; 23,600 in 1976.

Chieflists: Chieflists consistently show eight to nine chiefs before Gang Kusum (reigning in 1923) (Fardon 1980 II:248).

Sources and observations: colonial reports, Frobenius, interviews 1976–78.

Yeli or Dayela

Language, dialect and location: Chamba Leko speakers of mɔ.ba.yɛli dialect living in the central Alantika Mountains.

Population: 46 and 96 in two hamlets (1982); 186 and 90 (1936) for Yeli Manga and Yeli Petel. A part of Yeli Manga has been moved to the Nigerian side of the border.

Ethnic and clan composition: chiefs of *gat.kuna,* priests of Nyɛm-nɛbba, chief's priest of Sama, also Jɛngnɛbba, Gbannɛbba, Kun-nɛbba, Lɛnnɛbba and Jangannɛbba (or Lumnɛbba, the clan of the acceding chief).

Chieflist: The Yeli chieflist is thought to contain about thirteen names, but informants could not recall them all or agree about the order of any but the most recent.

Sources and observations: fieldwork for six months in 1984; interviews 1976–77. Some references in Frobenius.

NOTES

Chapter 1. Ethnicity, Agency, and History

1. Emphasis upon theoretical discontinuities in anthropology was most marked during the 1970s, a trend foreshadowed by E. Ardener in his identification of the "New Anthropology" (1971), but also shared by Marxist and feminist anthropologies as well as semantic anthropology (Fardon 1985a). The reemphasis upon continuity as a perspective has paralleled changing political awareness. Just as colonialism has come to mean more than a particular set of governmental institutions, anthropological texts have been discovered to be textured by presuppositions more deeply imbedded than our explicit theories. E. Said's *Orientalism* (1978) was, of course, a crucial mediator of Foucault's ideas in this respect. Perspectives emphasizing discontinuities have become paradigmatic in discussions of anthropology, while continuity has tended to be stressed in relation to ethnographic reporting. I am not aware of an attempt to defend explicitly the emergence of these viewpoints.

2. The literature is copious, but a representative sample would include: on *The Nuer* (Karp and Maynard 1983; Geertz 1983); on ethnographies as texts (Marcus and Cushman 1982; Marcus and Clifford 1985); on ethnographic writing styles (Clifford 1981; 1983; Nash and Wintrob 1972); on anthropology and colonialism (Asad 1973).

3. The most comprehensive critique in British circles is implied in the "Manchester manual" for fieldwork (Epstein 1967).

4. See note 3. The studies of Evans-Pritchard's writing style do not make much of, what seems to me, the very characteristic device of sheer repetition, e.g. the famous passage on the pervasive nature of Zande witchcraft (Evans-Pritchard 1937:63–64).

5. See van Binsbergen 1985; for regional approaches, see contributions by Lancaster 1974, discussions in Tardits ed. 1981.

6. But to say this is not to forget that, as A. Giddens has noted, social reproduction is not an "explanatory concept" but a "contingent phenomenon which requires explanation" (Giddens 1981: 64).

7. The quickest route through would be to read the next chapter on Mapeo, then go on to the concluding chapter of Part 2. The book is difficult to understand without reading Chapter 7, but the introduction and conclusion to Chapter 8 summarize results for those willing to take evidence on trust. Chapter 9, the first half of Chapter 10 and the conclusion, Chapter 12, together contain the main points of my argument. These would have been the major parts of a book written with no ambition to contribute to regional understanding.

8. Adsociating and consociating can be construed as relational counterparts of the current anthropological preoccupation with personhood in its different constructions, especially those represented by M. Strathern's explorations of the metaphors attaching attributes to actors (1981; 1985). For the purposes of this book, I restrict my curiosity to the expressions of attachment between agents that inform political action, particularly such action in societies whose material reproduction rests upon women, agricultural labor, and elementary means of destruction (see Goody 1971; 1976).

9. In Chapter 12 I note an important distinction between Turnerian *communitas* and the notion of consociation that I am suggesting.

Chapter 2. Mapeo: The Politics of a Ritual Involution

1. Within Chambaland the non-chiefly refugees of the northern Alantika Mountains may be similar to Mapeo in some respects. But the populations of their communities may be numbered in hundreds rather than thousands and are ethnically less heterogenous than the Mapeo population. Mapeo might also be similar in some ways to the non-centralized Daka on the peripheries of Chambaland. Our information on these people is too slight to pursue the point, but the particular circumstances of the nineteenth century foundation of Mapeo would argue against pursuing the analogy with these older polities too far.

2. The name of the festival that I transcribe as *jub.kupsa* is pronounced *ju'kupsa*. Similarly, *jub.nyɛm* is pronounced as *ju'nyɛm*. In both cases I have retained the prefix *jub-* to indicate that these are members of the general class of ceremonies of *jubi*. Many of the plains villages that take part

in the cycle initiated at Mapeo dispersed from the hill refuges once the plain was opened to secure cultivation. Some others appear to have remained in the plain during the nineteenth century under the umbrella of Dalami. In other cases, preexisting villages were augmented by clan sections leaving Mapeo during the colonial period.

3. As is frequently the case when places in Chambaland have both Leko and Daka names, the locative suffixes make sense from different vantages. Thus, Ma.peu, the Leko form, used at Yeli, makes sense from an easterly perspective; Dim.Ma, makes sense from a westerly perspective. Yeli sources support a version of Mapeo history in which incoming Daka speakers swamped a previous Leko-speaking population. The same variant is suggested by the members of the chief of the red rock matriclan (*gang.van.ji.kuni*) and the people of the hill matriclan (*ne.kusum.be.kuni*), who represent themselves as the original inhabitants of the Mapeo hills. Interestingly, there is a version of Yeli history that also suggests that the incoming matriclan of the chief (*gat.kuna*) took over chiefship from the chiefs of the red rock clan (*gat.bəng.yel.kuna*).

4. Pronounced '*urumbu* in Mapeo dialect; transcribing Mapeo and Na-kɛnyare variants in the main text would not serve the interests of clarity.

5. See Appendices 1 and 2, and note 7 for population estimates.

6. Between 1978, when I left Chambaland, and 1984, when I returned briefly to Mapeo, a tarred road had been laid between Ganye and Kojoli.

7. If we are to believe the earlier population estimates the refuge population may have been double that of the present population of the Mapeo hamlets.

8. Since named cults are usually owned by more than one clan, the number of cult groups is much higher. It is difficult to produce an exhaustive figure for Mapeo cult groupings, since the owners and holders of many cults are resident in the plains villages. I roughly estimate that the number of cults should be multiplied by a factor of between four and five to arrive at the number of cult groups, that is approximately two hundred.

9. I shall not attempt to deal now with the organization of esoteric rites, but I intend to discuss these features as part of a subsequent volume.

10. Ownership is simply stated by an individual in the claim that it is his. But the context in which the statement is made is crucial, since the same words might be used by another person to state membership only (I explain this point later in the text).

11. The verb used here is *gut* which means catch or clutch. The same verb would be used of a cult which catches someone with illness, or of someone catching a chicken or fish; the verb appears to imply vigorous seizing activity. In these terms the activity of the cult holder is distinct from the more passive ownership of the cult's father(s).

12. In Yeli, the terms *gidna* and *girba* correspond to the Mapeo terms *girani* and *gira*, meaning forbidden and menstruation. This is another of the numerous convergences in Daka and Leko ritual lexicons.

13. *Wani*, the Mapeo Chamba term for priest is the same as *wana*, the Leko term. Elsewhere, Chamba Daka speakers use the term *kameni*. Mapeo Chamba cannot gloss their term, nor can the Chamba Leko of the Bamenda Grassfields, but the Chamba of Yeli derive it from *wana*, a cooking hut, and claim that the priest "cooks" the cult rite. This etymology relates to their general association between cults, *voma*, and heat.

Jem gang is a chief of women's cults (*jem* is the women's equivalent of *jubi*). I shall discuss women's rites in a volume on Chamba religion.

14. This even applies to the dancing cults of the harvest celebrations, which in some contexts Chamba would say are not *girani*, (*git.so*). Although no illness is associated with the cults, the new crop cannot be eaten before the cults have performed, so guinea corn is *girani*, and the women who dance to the cult music should not see the calabash horn instruments, which are *girani* to them. In fact, each cult defines a complex set of *girani*. The members of *karbangi*, considered one of the most contagious of cults and restricted to mature men, may offer beer to non members, under certain restrictions, when they meet to drink during a funeral celebration for one of their members. The beer is not *girani*. Adequate attention to the complexity of Mapeo Chamba idioms and uses of prohibition belongs in a detailed account of religion and ritual.

15. The apparently obvious association of broken chicken bones and broken penis (members mimic the effect of their cult with a crooked index finger) was never offered to me. I suspect that Mapeo Chamba elders find arbitrariness intrinsically meaningful, and that this differentiates their approach to ritual from that of, for instance, Yeli elders. This is another of the issues which must await a second volume.

16. This suggests an important clarification of the idea that matrikin are collectively vulnerable to the contagion of some cults. Chamba explicitly dissociate this idea from that of collective guilt. Individuals are persuaded to act correctly by the effects their actions may have on their matrikin; cult practitioners are dissuaded from activating the more indiscriminate cults to

catch offenders retrospectively by the argument that they may catch someone who is innocent, perhaps even an innocent close relative.

17. This cult is called *ya.bum.ani* by the Yambu of the northern Shebshi Mountains. It appears that Mapeo Chamba are correct to see the cult as one owned by Yambu in all areas of Chambaland, almost as a sub-ethnic preserve.

18. Although I have been offered this gloss on several occasions, I have also heard it refuted. *Nyɛmi* "home," and *nyɛmi*, the name of the harvest *jubi*, differ in tone. Leko-speaking informants in Yeli claim the name of the Mapeo rite derives from the patriclan name of the custodians of the Yeli harvest rite, Nyɛm.nɛbba. Prompted by an investigator, Mapeo Chamba often seem to offer etymologies of their ritual lexicon that strike them as close in sound, and credible in sense. However, as they admit, much of this lexicon derives from Leko loanwords.

19. The Gbanbu or Gbanmɛmbu (children of Gbana, the common title for a chief's assistant) claim to have originated from Yeli, and this claim is accepted at Yeli. The right and responsibility of taking Mapeo offerings to Yeli to avert smallpox and locust infestation, and the preeminence of Gbanmɛmbu at *jub.nyɛmi*, with the implication that they were the earliest settlers and therefore owners of the land, constitute the Gbanmɛmbu case for asserting chiefship over Mapeo.

20. For specific patriclan alliances see Appendix 1.

Chapter 3. Contemporary Variations: An Overview

1. The border at this point follows the watershed of the major river systems along the peaks of the mountains. This decision of the European powers effectively cut off the strip of land on the left bank of the Faro River (home of the residual Leko) from "mainland" Cameroon, with serious results for its economic development. Currently, plans are underway to bridge the river.

2. This variant, apparently cognate with the central Chamba term Daka, has to be interpreted in terms of other uses of the terms Ndagana and Ndaganbila by Bali Chamba; for these, see Chapters 8 and 10.

3. The French spelling is Tchamba and the most common German spelling Tschamba. Other ethnic terms found in variant spellings include Nakɛnyare (Nagayare), Daka (Daga), Leko (Laego) (e.g. Frobenius 1913; Strümpell 1910).

4. The convergence of lexical items is instructive since it occurs in contexts where mutual influence might be anticipated: kin and clan terms, some specialized ritual terms, and a number of terms for animals, plants and trees. There is also evidence for parallel innovation; the different terms for sprite in Leko and Daka are similarly related to different terms for death, skull, spider, relic, etc. Similar idioms occur in such interests as chiefmaking. I hope to clarify these relations in a subsequent publication.

5. Chamba Leko (Mubako) survives in four of the five Bali chiefdoms, the exception being Bali Nyonga where Munngaka is spoken. The Donga Chamba claim to speak, as they told me, "bad Jukun." However, Meek did collect a Leko wordlist there in the 1920s. The situation in the remainder of the Benue Plains is unclear. Chamba Leko is said to persist in Suntai, Nyakola, Nukpo, Tissa, and Kungana (Roger Blench, personal communication 1986).

6. Koma is not an emic term. Our knowledge of these peoples will be immeasurably enhanced with the publication of the results of research led by Michel Dieu and Louis Perrois. Dieu's personal communication to Boyd (in press) suggests the existence of three linguistic communities. Some Chamba attempt to gloss Koma as "my slave," kɔ.ma. In general, Chamba terms for their neighbors: Koma, Moma, Pere, Kaga, Mumuye, etc. tend to simplify complex dialect chains and cultural differences of degree.

7. Koutine or Kutin is an abusive term, said to be derived from the Fulfulde kutiiru, dog (Boutrais 1978:113, 113fn.). Boyd records three linguistic groups, from secondary sources: Koutine (Kutin), Potopo, and Patapori (Boyd in press). Mohammadou has recorded oral traditions which suggest that Potopo are immigrants claiming a western origin (perhaps in the same terms as the gang.kuni of Yeli and Sugu) (Mohammadou 1978). Koutine call themselves Pere, variants of which are also employed by Chamba Leko (Pere, Peli, Pyeri, Pednebba). The Linguistic Atlas of Cameroon records three main dialects of Pere: per-mure, zongbi, and dan-murɛ (Potopo). It is becoming clear that the languages of the Pere, Koma, Vere (Kobo), as well as Dowayo and Duru (Di) are very closely related.

8. I have never worked among Chamba who happily accept the term Daka applied to themselves (excepting the occurrence of the term as a patriclan name in Mapeo). Adrian Edwards, who has worked to the west of the Shebshi Mountains, found that Daka was an emic term, and recorded the disappointed remark of one chief that some Daka were too ignorant to have realized that they were Chamba (personal communication).

9. Literally, "you/do/presently/what/interrogative." For simplicity I render the ethnic term Nakɛnyare, which is closer to its pronunciation when used as an ethnic/dialect marker.

10. It is indicative of the way Chamba do not consistently separate language, dialect, culture, and ethnicity that Nakɛnyare speakers often include the Mapeo dialect of Chamba Daka in the class of Jang or Leko languages. The criteria for this are largely cultural and geographic.

Chapter 4. Historical Variations: The Chamba Raiders

1. *Labarun Chambawa da Al'Amurransa* and *Salsalar Sarakunen Donga*. Garbosa writes that he began his researches in 1923 and wrote an early version of his book then. A second version was begun in 1932–3. The published version contains information on his trip to Bamenda (1954) and seems to have appeared about 1960, although it is undated. According to E. M. Chilver, this is the date at which the texts were microfilmed by University College Ibadan and the Historical Society of Nigeria. I follow Garbosa's spelling of most titles and place names. I am indebted to the late Hamman Erasmus Diori for a translation and paraphrase dictated from the original Hausa in 1976.

2. Chamba are sometimes called Dingyi in reports emanating from the Benue area, e.g. Fremantle 1922, Temple 1922.

3. According to Meek, the Ndoro chief of Galea carries the title *gara* (Chamba Leko for chief) and traces descent from Gakirra, who received his title from a Chamba leader called Garboshi (Loya Garbosa?) to whom the Ndoro had become "subservient" (Meek 1931b II:590). Roger Blench, in a personal communication (1986), reports that Chamba Leko speakers have descended into the plain from the Fali Plateau, home of the Ndoro. All but the oldest Chamba Leko descendants in the hills now speak Ndoro. It is unclear from Garbosa's text whether Gildu and Giendu are variants of a single place name or two different places.

4. Also called Gangkwe and later Garkola (Ga kola, chief of Kola) after the chief installed there.

5. Chamba raids in the Benue Plains were mostly directed against speakers of Jukun languages, which may be important given the accounts of Chamba involvement in the downfall of the Jukun. Garbosa refers to these people as

Kutep or Ichie, and Zomper. Meek derives the latter term from the Jukun "cannibal" and claims them to be hill dwellers of the Takum area. Garbosa lists Jenuwa, Akente, Akyuma, Bika, Likam, and Markam as conquered places in Kutep country. I retain Garbosa's ethnic names in the text; most can be related to languages listed in the Jukun cluster of Jukunoid languages listed by Williamson (1971:272–3).

1. Jukun
2. Ashaku, Nama, Mbembe
3. Kentu, Ichen, Nyidu
4. Kpanzo, Hwaye and Kpwate, Eregba, Appa, Boritsu
5. Kutep (also known as Mbarike and Zumper, and perhaps including Garbosa's Lissam, Likam and Markam).

Secession from Garkiye's group heading towards Arufu was led by the chiefmaker Gahwan. His group is said to have left the main body at Utu and to have continued behind Garkiye's as far as Fyayi. From there, the group moved to Lumtu before dispersing to found Rafin Kada, Akati, Gaya, Garvyon, and Bason (Garbosa n.d.:60–63; Meek 1931a:57).

6. Garbosa calls the leader of this group Gamie, and also credits the group with the foundation of Bakundi, Gamie, and Gauma. Another group under Galim Kama fought the Ndahawa section of the Kentu, who were hill dwelling subjects of Jukunised Kpwate (Meek 1931b II:605–10, for the incorporation of Kentu in Chamba alliances). Gankwe is said to have been established among the Hwaye.

7. The settlement neighbored Gandiko under a chief called Ama, founded after the failure of a raid against Wukari (Baikie 1856:125). Gandiko and Gankera are both said to have been subject to Jibu (Crowther 1855:84). Neither of these statements can be related to Garbosa's narrative, although he does note hostility between the Chamba group and Jibu.

8. Nukpo takes its name from the Kentu section incorporated there. Garbosa names Garnyama of the Samdinga section of the Sama patriclan as leader of this seceding group.

Gban Tinyisa of the Kola clan led a group to the base of Mount Nyibwuen, near Kumbo, where he ruled over the Kpanzo. This group was later resettled at Tissa on the orders of Nubumga Donzomga. Other groups may have left to Kunabe and Aka (Meek 1931b I:332; Garbosa n.d.:21–2,43–4, 63–4).

9. Garbosa claims that a sister of Garkiye, called Ka Nadera, refused to allow the chiefship to be inherited by the brothers of her late husband. She did this on the authority of her husband, titled Galim Kpanga (21–2).

Meek's version of events states that an older sister of the late chief refused the chiefship to the sons of Garkola and gave the insignia to her husband (Meek 1931b I:332). The account is confused and certainly cannot stand the interpretation Meek tries to place upon it—that it is a token of matrilincality.

10. Shimbura (Garkiye), who was born in Dindin (i.e. Chambaland), and Nubumga Donzomga (Garbasa), born at Gildu or Giendu, are both claimed by Garbosa II to have had mothers of Chamba Pyeri origin (n.d.32). This supports the suppositions that Chamba Leko and Pere (Koutine) were neighbors prior to the diaspora and that the Den Bakwa were largely drawn from the more southerly Chamba Leko, who would have bordered the Koutine plain.

11. The influence is probably exaggerated. Akiga lists white seeded guinea corn (the Chamba staple), guinea corn beer, ordinary and bambara groundnuts, goats, hunting nets, various cults, marriage by purchase (rather than by exchange) and the title *kur* for warrior leaders, which was bought from Donga and Takum, as Chamba introductions (Akiga 1939:70,88,94,125, 184,382). To this list East, Akiga's translator, tentatively adds the introduction of iron working, which is highly unlikely (East 1939:16). Adrian Edwards tells me that the Tiv term Ugenyi is applied to early raiders, some of whom may be of Jukun origin, and that the Chamba claim to the foundation of Kashimbila would be contested by Tiv (personal communication). Nonetheless, Tiv retain vivid recollections of Chamba raids (see also Akiga Sai and P. Bohannan 1954:296–99).

12. Descriptions of the available sources of Bali history can be found in Chilver and Kaberry 1970:251–2, and E. M. Chilver's reports to the Bali Historical Society compiled in 1964 and revised 1970. These valuable documents have unfortunately not been published. I have worked from a typescript of Part Two, filed at the Institute of Human Sciences, Garoua, and a manuscript of Part One, kindly loaned by the author. Chilver's reports synthesize data available up to 1970. My bibliographic notes refer to the most important of these and add a few more recent references.

For the two streams of Chamba migration, see Mohammadou 1978:38.

Koncha: vague references to an origin from the Koncha area, convergent with Garbosa's account of the Tipchen camp, appear in most Grassfields traditions (Kaberry and Chilver 1968:16). These traditions also accord with traditions of the residual Leko (see also Moisel 1908:117; Keller 1909, who claims a migration from Garoua; Hurault 1975:7; Hunt 1925). For incorporation of the Potopo, apparently a chiefly stratum of the Pere, see Boutrais 1978:116.

Tignere: Chilver, discussing present Bali Nyonga composition, suggests that groups of Buti may have been incorporated in this area (Buti Koncha, Nabuli, Babele, and Buti Suga or Sugnebba). They may already have been raiders in touch with Tikari (Chilver 1970[1964]:11). For the histories of other Buti raiders, see Siran 1980, 1981.

Galim: for attacks on the Nyam Nyam by Chamba and Pere either at or near Galim, see Mohammadou 1978:102–5; Boutrais 1978:116.

Tibati: this appears to be the area in which Chamba recruited Mbum elements (called Kufad), see Kaberry and Chilver 1961:358–9; Mohammadou 1978:102–5. Chilver (personal communication) suggests that some Kufad may have been previously incorporated by Buti and joined the Chamba together with them. The Mana Mbum may have been located on the southward trajectory of the Ba'ni, see Faraut 1981.

Banyo: more Buti were incorporated here (Kaberry and Chilver 1961: 358–9). Mohammadou records an attack on Buti around Mount Djoumbal (1978:102–5). Hurault writes of Fulani activity displacing Chamba from Mba (1975:7). The fullest account of the Chamba involvement in local politics is in Mohammadou 1967:89–90.

Tikari: Chilver records Tikali in the Chamba chiefdoms: they must have been recruited during a move below the Mbam River (see Price 1979 for the distribution of Tikari chiefdoms).

Bamum: Chilver notes the presence of Bati within the Ba'ni, that is the group of Gawolbe's adherents. They are distinct from the large Bati contingent recruited by Nyongpasi after Gawolbe's death, and must have been picked up on raids south of Bamum before entry to the Grassfields (Kaberry and Chilver 1961:358–9; Chilver and Kaberry 1968:17; Chilver 1964 Part I).

13. Evidence for Koma involvement is admittedly slight. But the Bali "scouts," *gwe*, closely resemble in dress the Koma jesters.

14. Early raids on the northeastern Grassfields, perhaps around the turn of the eighteenth century, are recorded from Nkambe, Wiya, War, and Nso (Nkwi and Warnier 1982:81; see also Chilver and Kaberry 1968:15–18). Tardits claims that Chamba were present on the Bamum plateau from the late eighteenth century (1980:120–2). Some reports, supported by present oral traditions, suggest successive waves of Chamba immigration (Hawkesworth 1926; Ga Muti and Chief of Bali Gham; Newton 1934:para 7). These raids are difficult to attribute to particular Chamba groups. They may represent early Daka or Peli inroads, or even distant raids from Loya Garbosa's early camp among the Ndoro. But, given the generic terms by which early raiders

are identified in Grassfields traditions, it is equally possible that the raids may be attributable to some other source, perhaps Buti or Tikari. A second wave of attacks from around 1820 is clearly associated with the traversing of the Grassfields by Gawolbe and his Ba'ni (Nkwi and Warnier 1982:116–119, 127,134; Hunt 1925:para 17; Chilver and Kaberry 1968:17; Jeffreys 1962).

15. It is unclear whether the Bali Muti group separated from the main body of Chamba (in Meta, according to Moisel 1908; or near Bafut, according to Keller 1909), or continued with them up to Nkəm. Chamba unity prior to Nkəm, where Gawolbe was killed, has become local dogma and has clear implications for contemporary Bali relations. However, elders of the smaller Bali chiefdoms (Gham, Gashu, and Gangsin), stressed that the Peli had preceded the main migration and borne the brunt of the fighting. Whatever the case, the Peli sections are said to have been repulsed from Bafut and continued into the Benue regions, supporting Garbosa's account (Nkwi and Warnier 1982:120). Nkəm was a large settlement on a hill near present Bafu Fondong; once established there, the Chamba sent out raiding parties into Bamileke country (Jeffreys 1962a:170,188). This hill is still know as Pa'ali (Bali) Hill. Dschang traditions, collected by the chief of Bali Gham and myself in 1984, suggest that the Bali were driven from the hill by the combined forces of Bafu and Dschang, apparently in the course of a night attack. The later histories of the Bali chiefdoms are easily accessible in English language sources (see Chilver, Kaberry, Jeffreys, Nkwi and Warnier, etc., for the incorporation of pa Tie (Bati) by Nyongpasi, see Tardits 1980).

16. The descent of the founders of the two larger Bali chiefdoms, Bali Nyonga and Bali Kumbad, from the hero leader Gawolbe (Ga wəl be, chief of water) is questioned by the members of the three smaller Bali chiefdoms who represent themselves as the true sons of Gawolbe.

17. In different areas the constituent Yambu clans are differently named. In the northern Shebshi Mountains the three clans are named after trees, *tubi*, the shea butter tree, *də*, the palm tree, and *dəkum*, another tree which I cannot identify. I was told that the ancestors of the clans camped under the different trees. To further questioning, an informant offered that the names were arbitrary, if a Yambu had sat under a mango tree there would be a Yam.mango clan.

18. Another version, recorded by Logan (Rhodes House 1932), claims that the Mangla were persuaded to descend because of an earthquake, which shook their hill as they fled the Chamba. Like many other Chamba traditions, this has evidently been highly durable during the colonial period.

19. For a fuller account of Mbangan traditions see Fardon 1980.

20. Logan 1932 (Rhodes House) makes "Bonsokso" father of "Kiningwai" who was father of Damashi. Acccording to this account, Damashi was born at Gang Pana and later moved to the east of the Alantika Mountains to live at Doroba (presumably Dorba near the Faro–Deo confluence). Polla Djalo elders argue that Damashi was delegated from Vanku to visit the Emir by their own leader.

Chapter 5. Historical Variations: Chamba Refugees

1. Sugu (*Su.gu, su* + locative) is a Leko name; in Chamba Daka the place is called Ga.su.bi.

2. Sugu elders of my acquaintance were not aware either of the godlike status or the joking relationship.

3. *Vom.gara, vom.wana,* and *vom.ba* are Leko terms synonymous with the Daka *kamɛni,* priest, cult master and installer of the chief.

4. Other versions make San.nyɛng.jimi the principal Gurum actor in these events; my version is from Amza of *gang.tim.nɔ.kuni.* The story was known to colonial officials and appears in historical summaries by P. S. Crane (1958 Ganye).

5. This story was also known to colonial officers, (G2.2C Percival 1937).

6. An alternative gloss, offered by the incumbent in 1977, is that the role was given to the chief's estranged father, *gang.da.*

Chapter 6. Regional Variations: An Areal Perspective

1. Yeli sources claim that exchanges of cattle against produce were made with the Fulani, and that the chief of Yeli retains the right to receive Fulani cattle that die since he is "owner of the land."

2. It appears on maps as the Réserve Forestière et de Chasse du Faro. Frobenius, largely basing his account on fieldwork among the southern residual Leko, refers to a settlement between Yelba and Uro Mali, located on the left bank of the Deo River just below the Faro–Deo confluence, called "Dengi-diu" (Frobenius 1913 III:270). This would appear to be Dɔngadiu, the place of the Dɔnga, a current patriclan.

A number of traditions refer to place names constructed from chief, *ga*, and a locative suffix (which changes according to the relative position of the speaker to the site); thus *Gat.gu* seen from Balkossa, or *Ga.diu* seen from Duna.

From Duna informants I was also given a location that seems to refer to Pere (Koutine), *Peri.gu*.

Garbosa, from the Donga perspective, at first calls the area originally occupied by the Chamba Leko, Denga or Dengha, which is also the name he gives to the Chamba, and later Dindin or Dindi (Garbosa:7–11). Meek, presumably from the same sources, refers to the general area of Chamba settlement as Dindi and claims Sapeo, Mapeo and Zolba (Dollba), the latter also named by Garbosa, as its major towns (Meek 1931b:329). Although they may have been inhabited prior to the nineteenth century, both Mapeo and Sapeo are represented as refuge settlements in their own traditions. If Meek's Zolba is Dorba, just east of the Faro–Deo confluence, this tradition may be better founded, since residual Leko traditions claim Dorba to have been an early meeting place of Chamba and Fulani. Other names recorded by Mohammadou (Sunbunga, Kolongti, Gadjikaro, Galtu, Sangani) and myself (Sanbura, Papayo) appear to refer to settlements on both sides of the Deo River.

Terms similar to Garbosa's Dengha, for Donga Chamba, occur frequently in reports from the Benue: Dinga (Meek 1931bI:329), Dingyi (Meek 1931a:45), Denye (Temple 1922:80).

3. Adrian Edwards found evidence of Jukun connections among the western Dirrim section of Chamba. The Koutine or Pere are said to be composed of a ruling people, Potopo, (from Jukun territories in the west according to Tignere sources, or Kundi according to Koncha sources) who imposed themselves on the indigenous peoples (Mohammadou 1978: 102,164; Lacroix 1952:28).

4. Conflict with the Bata is reported by Garbosa to have occurred prior to the arrival of the Fulani, whom he calls Mallawa da Ba'awa (10–11). B. Glasson suggests that a Chamba town had been established around Lamorde Jongum, but that the Chamba were driven out and forced to flee across the Deo River where they founded Tchamba at the foot of the Alantika Mountains (J8 Glasson 1922). Later, the Chamba were again driven out by the Bata. This report would appear to be the source of Meek's note to the same effect (Meek 1931b:329 fn.). Mohammadou has recorded that the Fulani took Tchamba from the Bata who had settled there after expelling earlier Chamba occupants (Mohammadou 1978:29–42). In an earlier published version of these events, the Bata are said to have expelled the Chamba from

Dorba and to have been in their turn expelled by Fulani who built Chamba alongside the Chamba town of Diddo (Mohammadou 1964:25–27). (One version of Yambu history claims they began their westward movement from Dorba, Logan 1932 Rhodes House). Stevens' account of Chamba/Bachama relations refers to sporadic trade in iron, salt, horses, and slaves in the area (Stevens 1973:366). One of the stereotyped Bata jokes at the Chamba's expense rests on their reputation as slave raiders (op.cit.366). Unlike the Bata to the north of the Benue, the Bachama, Malabu and Gudu employ a term similar to the Chamba for slave (see the wordlists in Meek 1931). Barth recorded that the Chamba had driven the "Kotoffo" (Koutine, Pere or Potopo) to the south in the process of establishing Tchamba (quoted in Meek 1931b:329). The general picture of a southward movement of population prior to the jihad seems well attested, but the vocabulary of driving and conquering has not occurred in versions of similar traditions which I have heard.

5. The ancestors of the chief's head priest, titled Dura, are said to have been Bata or from an area bordering the Bata. Initially, they held no position in the royal cycle of rituals, which were performed by the chief's assistants and by *wanbira*, priests, of the indigenous Nyɛmnebba patriclan, the "owners of the land." But by turning meat rotten and beer sour, the new arrivals forced the chief to give them an important directing role in royal rituals, so they could "get something to eat." Dura is drawn from the Sama patriclan and attends both the rites of the chief and those of the priests; as he puts it he works for both of them.

6. E. Terray has recently supported a distinction between clan and locality as bases of organization (1985). Chamba organization suggests that there is a missing temporal dimension to the argument. Relations of co-residence seem to have been reinterpreted as common descent after a migration has taken place. Retrospectively co-residence becomes patriclanship. See Chapter 8 for the trans-ethnic importance of matriclanship.

7. According to traditions at Bali Gham, also recorded by E. M. Chilver in her report to the Bali Historical Society.

8. Garbosa records a list of Chamba clans, presumably collected from his informants in the 1920s, but he seems to jumble them. The earliest names in the list are Donga patriclans corresponding to those collected by Meek and by myself.

Sama: the ruling clan of Donga. In the text, Garbosa refers to sections within the clan. Presumably, this is nominally the same clan as that found in the northern residual Leko chiefdoms, and more widely among the Leko of Chambaland (for instance at Yeli). It is also the name that the ruling clan of Dalami claims to have borne before changing to Lamnepbu.

Janga: this clan name might be related to the Leko Janga.

Poba: a patriclan of this name is found in Duna, a modern settlement established after dispersal from the Bangla Mountains.

Gbana: a clan found in different areas of Chambaland (Yeli, Mapeo, Sapeo), and named after the official drawn from its ranks, *gbani, gbana,* chief's assistant.

Nupabi: perhaps the same as the Nupabu of Gurum, a member of which clan is the priest of the Danubi shrine.

Pyeri: a variant form of the Chamba term for Koutine, Pere or Potopo.

Laga, Kpenga and Sobaa look like more patriclan names.

Additionally, Garbosa appears to have recorded some matriclan names: shikunkuna, salkuna (grass clan), denkuna, dungbalkuna (hippo clan), zabilkuna, zamkuna (mist clan), nyamkuna (sun clan), zagbonkuna and sarkuna. I have translated only the least speculative of the names. It is difficult to know where Garbosa found these names. He does not appear to have derived them from Meek, whose lists from Kubi and Daka sources are different (Meek 1931b I:378,398). Matriclan organization does not appear to persist in Donga at present. The only conclusions to be drawn would be that matriclan organization persisted in some of the Chamba settlements outside Donga, or that elders in Donga were able to recall the previous terms of matriclan organization.

A final group of names in Garbosa's list seems to be drawn from outside Donga: Zangani or Zanghani Gurum, Balla, Darim, Yama, Dakka and Girim. Zangani Gurum is evidently Jangani Gurum, Yama may be Yambu, Dakka is Daka, Darim and Girim might be Taram and Dirrim, but I cannot account for Balla.

9. According to contemporary recollections and colonial records, such as Crane 1958, one of the exchanges was of hoes and honey against cattle.

10. Tribute is recollected to have been paid at a rate of twenty measures of corn per household per year. Assessment reports suggest that Chamba guinea corn farms averaged 1.5 to 2 acres yielding about 450 measures of corn per acre (Logan 1925; Hopkins 1930: both G2.2E Toungo District Assessment; Logan 1930:G2.2A Nassarawo District Assessment).

11. Raids, in the past, on traders passing Mapeo are noted by early British officials (K2 Vol.II). Passarge had first hand experience of Chamba exactions on crossing the Shebshi Mountains, while Strümpell notes that Chamba of the plains could also menace traders (Passarge 1895; Strümpell 1907). Slave trading appears to have continued in the area into the 1920s, when it is reported from Sugu (B3.Z Glasson 1923). See also Maistre 1895; Detzner 1923; and discussion in Chapter 11.

12. H. Relly (1954 ISH Garoua, quoting a report by Savani 1935 that I have not seen) clarifies a general memory at Balkossa of a significant victory against the Fulani. Garga, a brother of Haman Tukur the late chief of Laro, refused to recognize the succession of the latter's brother. Despite help from Emir Sanda of Yola, the forces from Laro could not manage to dislodge Garga from Balkossa where he was assisted by his Chamba allies. Balkossa sources vividly recall the battle, for which staves were planted to impede the Fulani horses and the smiths heated arrow heads in order to pierce the mail armor of the cavalrymen. The account recalls other instances when Chamba and Fulani interests coincided.

Chapter 7. Kin as Sociates, and Sociates as Kin

1. For instance Chamba do not seem to have developed notions of destiny or fate, such as reported by Fortes and Horton from West Africa, ([1959]1983), or elaborated notions of personal constituents such as described by Héritier 1977.

2. The Chamba Daka phrase gɔn bit, he became, refers to transformations of state or condition: humans become wurumbu and vice versa; in the matriclan origin stories animals become humans and vice versa.

3. Although it is not my purpose to develop a model having comparative applications in this publication, there is a striking convergence between my formulation of Chamba clanship and Fernandez' account of Fang clanship that I read subsequently. "The principal connotation of paternal origin was divisiveness, even conflict. The principal connotation of maternal origin was unity and common purpose" (Fernandez 1982:95). Similar connotations are to be found in publications on many middle-belt peoples of Nigeria and Cameroon (e.g. Fardon 1984/5 for a review).

4. This reciprocal might suggest kaka as the term for grandmother (as among Nakɛnyare). If so, ka could be a Leko loanword.

5. The idiom of transformation used in this story is the same as that used for the man/*wurum* relation (see note 2).

6. There is general agreement that *dəng.kuni* is the Mapeo branch of the matriclan elsewhere known as *təmsi.kuni*, the sheep clan. Most informants deny knowledge of the etymology of the term *dəng*. One other school of opinion derives the term from a similar term said to mean entrance hut (but not the common term for this hut). This school reasons from the fact that those with a plaint wait in the chief's hut or that the chief is the entrance to the village for strangers. More hostile opinion claims that the clan members cannot reply to questions about their origins or rights to the land (*dəngi sɔ*, did not reply). The latter etymology is also seized upon by the clan's joking partners, the *kɔm.kuni*, whom the *dəng.kuni*, equally conventionally, claim to be Koma slaves.

7. The following description by a Chamba Leko writer became available to me after I had written this passage:

> We speak of integration into Chamba society when the stranger is Chamba himself. Chamba society is divided into clans [matriclans]—lam-kuna, saal-kuna, deng-kuna—that are found everywhere. A stranger who is Chamba belongs to one of these clans, and in the new village he finds aunts, uncles, nephews, brothers and sisters, and brothers-in-law and sisters-in-law with whom he can attend clan reunions. (Bernard 1982:6)

The writer of this passage is a Chamba Leko from Balkossa (although the name is the same, this is not the Bouba Bernard who was my helper and host in Yeli). He goes on to contrast the happy situation of the Chamba stranger with that of the non-Chamba stranger who has no kin and ceases to be a stranger only after many years of residence. The article makes no reference to patriclanship as a basis for incorporation into the local community.

8. In Mapeo, informants insist that a patriclan member should be able to recite the names of seven forebears in order to demonstrate non-slave status. These forebears are not necessarily lineally related members of the clan, simply previous members who have died. The regulation is in keeping with the Chamba notion of shared descent rather than lineal descent, which would be difficult to sustain given that reincarnation is considered to take place in any section of the clan.

9. But this does not imply collective guilt for actions of a clan member; Chamba cult practitioners are often persuaded to refrain from activating

their cults because the contagion may seize an innocent matrikinsman of the guilty party.

10. Not all clans retain skulls, but all maintain some kind of collection of relics that are terminologically the same as skulls.

Chapter 8. Transformations in Sociation

1. Dr. Paul Nkwi of the University of Yaoundé kindly sent me a Bali Kumbad kinship schedule in 1981; my subsequent inquiries in Bali Gangsin revealed the schedules to be virtually identical. Meek's incomplete Chamba Leko terms are from Kubi, where the dialect spoken is the same as that spoken at Yeli (Meek 1931b).

2. Yeli Chamba discriminate one among the maternal uncles as the senior, *mun.doa*, literally mother's brother-grandfather. I occasionally heard Mapeo Chamba refer to *pɔb.wari*, big MB, to denote a senior member of the matriclan. Strictly this is a position of preeminence within the clan rather than a kinship status. Whereas the Mapeo usage was always subject to argument, the Yeli use seems to correspond, virtually, to a corporate office.

3. I was given such a term, *wanu*, literally equivalent to *minɔ*, in response to earlier inquiries in Sapeo, made during my fieldwork among Chamba Daka. But I have not been able to check this subsequently.

4. I noted earlier that locality relations seem to be susceptible to reinterpretation as relationships of common descent following migrations and dispersion. Hypothetically, an expansion of polygyny would undermine matrilocality and subsequent dispersion could produce the pattern of patriclan affiliations found in Chambaland today.

5. Garbosa's chieflists are suggestive here. In localities where Chamba formed a small element of the population of a chiefdom, they appear to have used matrilateral relations to retain control of the chiefship. For instance, the Chamba who left the Den Bakwa at Jenuwa are credited with the foundation of a number of small chiefdoms; the chieflists from these places show numerous instances of candidates being appointed from a patriclan different from that of their predecessor. The chieflist of Gardanpua shows two instances of matrilateral succession which transferred the chiefship from Ngwuma to Janga and then to Pyeri (Garbosa:48). Instances of matrilateral succession also seem to occur in the chieflists of Akate, Rafin Kada, Bason, Garvyon, and Gaya, where patriclans of Nupabi, Pyeri, Kwasa, and Zangani held chiefships at different periods. The chiefship of Chanchanji

may also have changed hands matrilaterally, since chiefship was held by Kwasa, Saka, and Jahun (Fulani) (Garbosa:60).

The founders of Kungana and Gamie, who according to Garbosa left the original alliance before Jenuwa was reached, also established chiefships that were to circulate between different patriclans: Sama, Kwasa, Ngwuma, and Za (Garbosa:40–43). The type and extent of Chamba Leko dominance of the southern Benue Plains during the nineteenth century is in urgent need of investigation in the field.

6. I have not collected a term other than *man.zala* or *man.jala* for joking relationship among Chamba Leko. However, some Pere informants seem to consider the term to be of Fulani origin.

7. See Chapter 5, note 8.

Chapter 9. The Politics of Consociation: Ritualized Chiefship

1. John Middleton (1982) has counseled caution in the use of our term chief to translate African concepts of preeminence. With this in mind, it could be argued that the Chamba terms for preeminent position (*gangi*, Daka and *gara*, Leko) mask covert distinctions between two types of leadership.

2. I would go further and express dissatisfaction with the more than rhetorical (Bloch 1983) uses of terms like worldview or culture which we totalize on the basis of quite disparate inferences (see Chapter 12).

3. Epilepsy and leprosy are the causes of "bad deaths" for which normal funeral rites are not held. In Mapeo, leprosy and epilepsy are the prerogatives of two cults viewed as morally ambiguous by many informants who would claim that the disease, which sanctions the cult, is out of proportion to the rights that the cult may be deployed to protect (for instance unharvested crops). Bodily deformities would probably also debar a candidate for patriclan chiefship. But the condition is not stressed or averred to in stories, as in the case of ritualized chiefship. See also Note 5.

4. The ability of the chief to do this derived especially from rights in natural products (such as tamarind) and from the organization of large work parties. Both of these rights have been substantially eroded in importance and at present hardly exist outside recollection of them.

5. The transmission of witchraft matrilaterally, and the insistence that witches were beaten to death with staves (never shot or stabbed), seem to draw upon related features of substantial or consociating idioms. More tenu-

ously, there might be echoes of the substantial idiom in the favored ordeal by blistering. As I wrote in Note 3, the association between chiefship and witch-detecting may also have been drawn in patriclan chiefships, but I never heard it stressed.

6. I would again draw attention to the clustering of lexical similarities about these terms in Leko and Daka, see also Chapter 3, Note 4.

7. This is an informant's gloss rather than mine. In Nakɛnyare Chamba, guinea-corn seeds, prior to harvesting, may be referred to metaphorically as *wurum* eyes.

8. The relation is more complex than the "betwixtness" normally implied in the notion of mediation. Rather than being between, the chief partakes of both terms, as well as animality. In this he is not unique, but his status is more marked than that of ordinary men of whom this is also the case (see Chapter 7).

9. The reader will have detected what structuralists would call a "thermo-dynamic" theme to Chamba thought about ritual (compare de Heusch 1985). I shall give a more comprehensive account of this in a volume on Chamba religion. The theme is apparent in brushing with feathers which, some say, mimics the smiths' habit of brushing the anvil stones in the forge so that impurities do not enter the iron.

10. Where skulls are not taken, other relics can substitute for them or be used additionally to them. These relics are known by the same terms as skull.

11. The association between chiefship and the *lera* or *lela* bamboo flutes is made most directly in the northern residual Leko chiefdoms and the, per-haps historically related, chiefdoms of the Bali Chamba. There are some suggestions in informants' accounts that one of the grounds for this asso-ciation may be that the flutes are an item of culture not given by the smiths and, by virtue of this, are quintessentially Chamba in terms of some con-texts of ethnicity.

12. Despite the international border that separates the two places, and the Muslim faith of the current Sugu chief, this custom persists, and a visit was made in 1984. Just as I revise these notes, a letter has arrived to tell me of the death of the Yeli chief in early 1986, but since it would be inappropriate to speak of death before the funeral wake, he is said to have journeyed to Sugu.

13. French colonial reports claim that the Jangani were the original inhabi-

tants of Yeli as well as Sugu (Floch 1938; Relly 1954). I was told that the earliest inhabitants were Nyɛmnɛbba.

Chapter 10. The Politics of Adsociation: Dominant Chiefship

1. This difference could also be understood as a different metaphorical construction of power used to argue a different collective destiny relation (see Fardon 1985a b).

2. Recall here that central Chamba of Mapeo and the refuge chiefdoms deny slave status in the patriclan; it is recognized in the matriclan as a corporal status. The early colonial belief that Chamba were Fulani slaves caused an affront that has not been forgotten (see Chapter 11).

3. This does not affect matriclans that remain cult-owning categories.

4. The seven other title holders are: *gangum* and *galim*, warriors who additionally appoint their own officials; *zegna*, an interpreter and announcer; *fawe*, claimed to be an aide to *nya* or supervisor of palace repairs; *kpanduwe*, who had responsibilities in relation to royal deaths and funerals (oddly this appears to be the Bachama title for a cavalry leader, and is found in that sense in the northern Shebshi chiefdoms); *kungana*, said to have been in charge of divination and of an oath cult; and *kpandilgshi*, responsible for royal attire.

5. The root form of the verb to supplicate is the same in Leko or Daka, *pɔb.nbia* or *pɔb.ani* (see also Chapter 3, note 4, and Chapter 9, note 6).

6. For descriptions of *lela* and *voma* see Chilver and Kaberry 1968; the earlier German accounts on which they draw; Soh 1975; and Bali Historical Society 1978. I shall examine these in detail in a subsequent ethnography.

7. Here translating *pɔb-*, see note 5. The idiom is identical in Chambaland.

8. The first *Chamba National Almanac* (1961) describes Chamba and Fulani as of the "same stock." A stranger claim to ethnic separatism was made to me by a Bali man who claimed his ancestors were Europeans from Bali.

Chapter 11. Colonial Disjunction: The Politics of Modernity

1. See Zintgraff 1895 and Hutter 1902 for accounts of the disturbances in the wake of this policy, and Chilver 1967 for an overall assessment of German rule.

2. The passage of the different border demarcation expeditions is recorded in a number of reports (Whitlock 1910; short notices by von Stephani in Globus and DKB 1907-10); for the later expedition see especially Nugent 1914 (also summarized in Calvert 1916), and Detzner 1923, for a German viewpoint. Nugent's report was given to the Royal Geographical Society, and in the ensuing discussion Sir Claude MacDonald clarified the arbitrary nature of the original boundary:

> In those days we just took a blue pencil and a rule, and we put it down at Old Calabar, and we drew that blue line up to Yola, and that is the boundary which Captain Nugent has described to you so charmingly and in such detail this evening . . . I recollect thinking when I was sitting having an audience with the Emir, surrounded by his tribe, that it was a very good thing that he did not know that I, with a blue pencil, had drawn a line through his territory.

3. Strümpell's reports of 1907 clearly refer to explorations into relatively uncharted territory. Detzner, recalling the border expedition of 1912, refers to recent pacification of Chambaland (1923:38,48). Moisel's maps (D2 and D3 for Chamba and E3 for Pere) show German and French expeditions up to 1911; most of them were part of the explorations of the 1890s or the later border demarcations. I have not been able to trace reports from the remaining half dozen or so (of a total of about sixteen itineraries shown).

4. For instance, Detzner's expedition of 1912 appears to have been thoroughly under the control of Fulani guides and interpreters. He reports a highly stereotyped view of Chambaland, apparently generalizing from the existence of slave villages to the general subjection of all non-Fulani *Heidensklaven* (Detzner 1923).

5. Gurum and Yebbi seem to have been transferred from Koncha to Laro late in the German colonial period. Earlier, they had been unwilling to have anything to do with either. Relly records a large-scale raid from Koncha on Gurum, which may have occurred prior to German colonization (Relly 1954).

6. Three Sugu chiefs are recalled to have been installed by the chief of Koncha during the German colonial period. In two cases, the chiefs reigned for a short period only.

7. Although the mandate was granted in 1922, this continued to be the case until 1924, after which the mandated territory was administered as an integral part of Nigeria. In 1947 the League of Nations' Mandate was ratified as a United Nations' Trusteeship (Burns 1955: 237).

8. The Anglo-French boundary at this point followed the watershed of the major river systems along the ridge of the Alantika Mountains. The logic of the arrangement is difficult to discern, if there was one. The Faro-Deo river system cut off a thin strip of land from access to Cameroon. This land, the homeland of the Chamba Leko among others, has become in some ways an adjunct of Nigeria. The Alantika Mountains, which perhaps looked like a natural boundary feature on a map, are in fact less of an obstacle than the rivers in flood. In 1924, Nassarawo had a population, underestimated one suspects, of about sixteen thousand, compared with about thirteen thousand in Namberu and Toungo together. In 1930, Namberu was absorbed into Nassarawo.

9. This antipathy concerned succession to the office of Emir, which his father, Hamidu, although a son of Adama, had never occupied.

10. Temporary exceptions should be noted in the cases of Gurum and Yebbi, whose hostility to any form of Fulani administration led to their spending the years 1921–26 in Numan Division before joining Yola, and of Binyeri which was incorporated into the Emirate in the same year.

11. See in particular: J8 Percival 1938, G3 Shaw 1936, Logan 1932 Rhodes House, G2.2C Percival 1937, 3058 Welch 1936.

12. The Gurum S.U.M. mission was set up by Mr. and Mrs. Fleming in 1929. After 1947 it was run by Danish Lutherans. See Nissen 1968, especially Chapter 32, for an account. The Roman Catholic mission was established at Sugu and Mapeo in 1940–41.

13. See Bruce 1982 for a similar account from elsewhere in the middle-belt.

14. The Richards constitution introduced in 1947 was to be replaced, and consultations "at every level" were encouraged so that accusations of foisting a new constitution on Nigerians, regardless of their will, might be avoided. Consultation took place over a couple of years and against the background of increasing "retribalization" (see Crowder 1973, chapter VXI Three Constitutions, for a concise account).

15. At the time, there was support among minority peoples for the creation of a "middle-belt" state that would be independent of the northern Emirates dominated by the Muslim Hausa, Fulani, and Kanuri.

16. Peter Crane has kindly discussed this important document with me. Apparently, it was considered to fall outside the Commission's terms of reference and was only glanced at by Sir Henry Willink. There are copies of the report in both the Nigerian Archives, Kaduna and Rhodes House, Oxford.

17. However patchy the record of movement to self-regulation among the majority Chamba of Nigeria, it is salutary to compare their experience with that of the minority Northern Cameroon Chamba. At approximately the same time as the more sympathetic British officials were endorsing some aspects of Chamba separatism, H. Relly on the other side of the border was suggesting that the declining authority of the Lamido of Tchamba could be restored by recognizing his traditional rights to gather tithes from non-Fulani. Augmenting his wealth, in this way, was supposed to restore his credibility as an administrator. Exactions by their Fulani rulers is the major reason offered by Cameroon Chamba Leko for resituating many of their villages (or offshoots of them) just inside the Nigerian side of the border.

18. For the very similar Marghi case, see Vaughan 1964.

19. An outstanding example of the tendency to envisage the nation as an assemblage of discrete ethnic groups which exhaustively classify population may be found in a recent account of Nigerian ethnic groups (Gandonu 1978); I have explored the convergence of ethnic and national presuppositions in an article (Fardon 1987).

Chapter 12. Agency and Transformation in Chamba History

1. I noted earlier that my definition of Chamba may be slightly more inclusive than that of most contemporary Chamba. Some peripheral groupings, like the westerly Daka and perhaps Lamja, appear to equivocate about their Chamba identity. Other linguistic Chamba, like the Kolbila, Wom, and possibly Mumbake, have shown no predilection for notional incorporation into the extensive ethnicity. But by and large, resemblances that can be interpreted to underwrite the common ethnicity of the major Chamba groupings (of Bamenda, the Benue Plains, and Chambaland) have been co-opted into this scheme, despite the very substantial differences between these groups. Conversations with some of the younger and more mobile Chamba suggest that ethnic associations in towns and colleges may be playing a role in continuing this process. Colonial policy was certainly a crucial catalyst prior to independence. The western border of Daka and Chamba may still be a relic of the old Anglo-German boundary.

2. The category of opposition has been negligently defined. Without endorsing other parts of his analysis, I think that Hallpike clearly demonstrates the highly variable relations between paired terms (1979:224–234).

3. See also Chapter 1, note 2. The mirror image of the absent author, which

some commentators now find dishonest, might be the spurious first person, and that could be worse. I am dubious about the extent to which readings can successfully be coerced by writing styles, rather than, for instance, preconceptions about the status of things written.

4. Through our analysis, indigenous statements about agency tend to become redescribed as conditions of enactment. For instance the statement that ancestors have effects is translated in terms of a world in which the effectiveness of ancestors has to be taken account of when deciding what to do next (thereby differentiating this from another world in which this is not the case).

GLOSSARY

Adamawa.　　The Fulani Emirate named after Modibbo Adama, its founder. It is also known as Fombina.

Bali Chamba.　　The conventional term for the inhabitants of the five Chamba-founded chiefdoms of North-West Province, Cameroon: Bali Nyonga, Bali Kumbad, Bali Gangsin, Bali Gham, and Bali Gashu. The term derives from Ba'ni in Munngaka. They call themselves Ndaganbila in Mubako (see Leko).

Bata/Bachama.　　Northern neighbors of the Chamba. Chambaized clans of this origin are found throughout Chambaland and formed part of the Chamba-led migrations. Chamba call them Ka, Kagbira, Kambu, Kagnεbba etc.

Benue Chamba.　　My shorthand for the chiefdoms founded by Chamba emigrants west of the Shebshi Mountains and south of the Benue. The term excludes Bali Chamba, but includes Donga, Takum, Suntai, and so forth.

Bangla.　　An indigenous term for the Chamba Leko of the southernmost range of the Alantika Mountains (called Bangla Hills). On descending from their hills the Bangla colonized areas on both sides of the international border.

Chambaland.　　The term I use to refer to the homeland occupied by people who consider themselves to be Chamba. The boundaries are not constant. The Leko diaspora evacuated its eastern area, whereas the foundation of Nakεnyare chiefdoms extended it to the west. I contrast Chambaland to the peripheral Daka and emigrant Chamba chiefdoms.

Daka.　　An indigenous term with different senses. As a language, it is distinct from Chamba Leko. As a culture, it is contrasted with Leko, Nakεnyare, and Sama in different contexts. As an ethnic identity, it may refer to the speakers of a Daka language, or carriers of a Daka culture, depending on context.

Daka, peripheral.　　My term for Daka speakers not assimilated into the Chamba chiefdoms.

Daka, central subtribes.　　My term for more or less incorporated Daka-speaking groups within Chambaland, e.g., Jangani in Sugu, Mangla in Mbulo. I suppose that central subtribes were previously peripheral.

Fulani.   Also referred to as Fulbe, Peul, etc. in the literature. In Chamba experience, initially pastoralists whose numbers were swelled by immigration from the north prior to and during the jihad (q.v.) in Adamawa(q.v.). Their language, Fulfulde, is a northern Cameroonian lingua franca.

gat.kuna (Leko) and *gang.kuni* (Daka). Synonymous terms in the two Chamba languages for the "matriclan of the chief," which held the chiefships in the major southern chiefdoms of Chambaland among both Leko- and Nakɛnyare-speaking (q.v.) Chamba.

gbana (Leko) and *gbani* (Daka).   Synonymous terms for a chief's assistant, or for the class of chief's assistants (for other individual titles see text, Part 4, and Appendix 3). The title frequently occurs in a patriclan name (e.g. Gbanbu in Mapeo; Gbantinɛbba in Yeli).

girani.   Chamba Daka idiom of prohibition, contagion, and danger.

gang.tim.nɔ.kuni.   Erstwhile royal matriclan of Gurum and Yebbi: "the matriclan of the chiefs of the east."

Jangani.   Apparently, the indigenous peoples of the southern Shebshi Mountains, especially numerous in Sugu and other southern Nakɛnyare chiefdoms. See also central Daka subtribes.

Jihad.   Islamic holy war. From the Chamba perspective, especially that launched in Adamawa (q.v.) in 1809 by the Fulani. Hostilities joined before the official declaration are not distinguished from the jihad. Chamba Daka just call this Puli-gagi, Fulani war.

jubi.   Chamba Daka for cults, singly or collectively. The term encompasses women's cults which may be distinguished as *jem*. See also *voma*.

kamɛn.   Chamba Daka term for priest, installer of chiefs, and cult master. See also *wana*.

Koutine.   Southern neighbors of the Chamba. Clans of this origin are found in the residual Leko chiefdoms and in the Chamba raiding alliances. Chamba call them by variants of Pere, the name they call themselves: Pyeri, Peli, Pednebba, etc.

kuna (Leko) and *kuni* (Daka).   Almost synonymous terms for matriclan categories, either simple or extended. The Leko sense also includes bilateral relatives, especially "brothers."

Lamidate.   In Chamba experience, a Fulani chiefdom.

Lamido.   The head of a Fulani chiefdom; also used by Chamba for Muslim Chamba Divisional and District Heads.

lera, or, *lela*.   The sets of bamboo flutes (numbering between four and six) found throughout Chambaland. In some Chamba chiefdoms they are associated with the chief. In the Bali chiefdoms, *lela* also refers to an annual, preeminently martial, ceremony.

Leko.   As a language, it is contrasted to Daka; the term derives from "I say that," *mə.ba.leko*. As a culture, it is contrasted with Daka and has eastern connotations.

mala.   Paternal aunt in either Leko or Daka.

Mapeo.   Large refuge community previously on the north face of the Alantika Mountains, where a distinct dialect of Chamba Daka is spoken.

muna.   Maternal uncle in Chamba Leko.

Mangla.   An apparently indigenous Daka subtribe (q.v.) in the Shebshi Mountains; now mostly in Mbulo.

Nakɛnyare.   Local term for dialect and culture derived from "how are you doing?," *n.nak.ɛn.nyare*. Linguistically and culturally contrasted with both Leko and Daka. I distinguish southern *(gang.kuni* chiefdoms), central (Gurum and Yebbi) and northern (Binyeri, Mbulo, etc.) Nakɛnyare chiefdoms in terms of the area of the Shebshi Mountains they occupy, their form of chiefship (matriclan; matriclan superseded by patriclan; patriclan), and the dates of their foundation.

pɔbi.   Chamba Daka for maternal uncle.

Residual Leko.   My term for the remnant Chamba Leko-speaking populations that took no part in the Leko diaspora and sought refuge in the Alantika Mountains during the nineteenth century.

Sama.   Chamba Daka for Chamba. Chamba Leko term for a patriclan cluster found throughout the residual Leko area, especially in the north, where it is the chiefly clan. Also the chiefly patriclan of Donga. In the Bali chiefdoms, the term has many nuanced associations with royalty.

Samba.   Chamba Leko for Chamba.

Vere.   Northern neighbors of the Chamba. Patriclans of Vere origin are found throughout Chambaland, especially as allies of the Yambu (q.v.) and as smiths in Mapeo. Known to Chamba as Mɔma (Leko), or Mɔmi (Daka).

voma.   The Chamba Leko term for cult, synonymous with *jubi* (q.v.). Women's cults may be discriminated as *vomkena*.

wana (Leko), *wani* (Mapeo), *nwana* (Bali).   Virtually synonymous with the Daka *kamen* (q.v.). Also known as *vom.wana*, or *vom.gara*, or *vom.ba* in different areas.

Yambu (Daka), Jengnebba (Leko).   A widely distributed patriclan cluster with internal sections. It is especially associated with chiefdom foundation in the northern Shebshi Mountains, the exploits of the hero leader Damashi and, thus, martial aptitudes.

Yeli (Yɛli in Leko) or Dayela (Da'Yɛla in Daka).　　Chiefdom of central Alantika Mountains, where a distinct dialect of Chamba Leko is spoken, mə.ba.yɛli. It is considered to have been founded by Daka from the west and to retain Daka cultural features. It is supposedly the source of the Nakɛnyare chiefly families. Previously, it controlled smallpox, locust infestation and rainfall in the Nakɛnyare chiefdoms, in Mapeo, and in some of the residual Leko chiefdoms.

Yola.　　The third and permanent capital of the Adamawa Emirate (q.v.).

REFERENCES

The references are divided into three sections: general references to ethnographic studies and standard anthropological concepts and theory; references specifically to Chamba and their neighbors; and unpublished references chiefly drawn from governmental and other institutional archives.

General References

Adler, Alfred
  1982   La mort est la masque du roi. Paris: Payot.

Anderson, Benedict
  1983   Imagined Communities: Reflections on the Origin and Spread of Nationalism. London: Verso.

Ardener, Edwin
  1971   The New Anthropology and its Critics. Man NS 6:449–67.

Armstrong, Robert G.
  1960   The Development of Kingdoms in Negro Africa. Journal of the Historical Society of Nigeria 2:27–39.
  1980   The Dynamics and Symbolism of Idoma Kingship. *In* West African Culture Dynamics. D. K. Swartz and Raymond E. Dumett, eds. The Hague: Mouton, World Anthropology.

Asad, Talal ed.
  1973   Anthropology and the Colonial Encounter. London: Ithaca Press.

Barth, Frederick ed.
  1969   Ethnic Groups and Boundaries: The Social Organisation of
          Culture Difference. London: Allen and Unwin.

Beattie, John
  1960   On the Nyoro Concept of *Mahano*. African Studies 9:145–50.

Binsbergen, Wim van
  1985   From Tribe to Ethnicity: the Unit of Study as an Ideological
          Problem. *In* Old Modes of Production and Capitalist Encroach-
          ment. Wim van Binsbergen and Peter Geschiere, eds. London:
          Routledge and Kegan Paul, and Leiden: African Studies Center.

Bloch, Maurice
  1983   Marxism and Anthropology. The History of a Relationship.
          Oxford: Oxford University Press.

Bourdieu, Pierre
  1977   Outline of a Theory of Practice. R. Nice, transl. Cambridge:
          Cambridge University Press.

Burnham, Philip
  1972   Racial Classification and Ideology in the Meiganga Region,
          North Cameroon. *In* Race and Social Difference. P. Baxter and
          B. Sansom, eds. Harmondsworth: Penguin.
  1979   Raiders and Traders in Adamawa: Slavery as a Regional Sys-
          tem. *In* Asian and African Systems of Slavery. J. Watson, ed.
          Oxford: Blackwell.

Bruce, Richard
  1982   The Growth of Islam and Christianity: The Pyem Experience.

In Studies in the History of Plateau State Nigeria. Elizabeth Isichei, ed. London: Macmillan.

Clarke, Peter B.
    1982   West Africa and Islam. London: Edward Arnold.

Clifford, James
    1981   On Ethnographic Surrealism. Comparative Studies in Society and History 23:539–64.
    1983   On Ethnographic Authority. Representations 1:118–46.

Cohen, Abner
    1974   Two Dimensional Man: An Essay on the Anthropology of Power and Symbolism in Complex Society. London: Routledge and Kegan Paul.
    1981   The Politics of Elite Culture. Explorations in the Dramaturgy of Power in a Modern African Society. Berkeley: Campus.

Cohen, Ronald
    1978   Ethnicity: Problem and Focus in Anthropology. Annual Review of Anthropology 7:379–403.

Crowder, Michael
    1973   The Story of Nigeria. 3rd ed. London: Faber and Faber.

Douglas, Mary
    1967   The Meaning of Myth with Special Reference to *La Geste d'Asdiwal*. *In* The Structural Study of Myth and Totemism. E. R. Leach, ed. London: Tavistock, ASA 5.

Dumont, Louis
    1970   Appendix: Caste, Racism and "Stratification": Reflections of a Social Anthropologist. *In* Homo Hierarchicus. Louis Dumont. St. Albans: Paladin. (1st publ. 1960)

Epstein, A. L. ed.
    1967   The Craft of Social Anthropology. London: Tavistock.

Evans-Pritchard, E. E.
    1937   Witchcraft, Oracles and Magic among the Azande. Oxford: Clarendon Press.

Fabian, Johannes
    1983   Time and the Other: How Anthropology Makes its Object. New York: Columbia University Press.

Fardon, Richard
    1985a   A Sense of Relevance. *In* Power and Knowledge. Richard Fardon, ed. Edinburgh: Scottish Academic Press.

Feeley-Harnik, Gillian
    1985   Issues in Divine Kingship. Annual Reviews in Anthropology 14:273–313.

Ferguson, Adam
    1966   An Essay on the History of Civil Society. Edinburgh: Edinburgh University Press. (First publ. 1767)

Fernandez, James
    1982   *Bwiti:* An Ethnography of the Religious Imagination in Africa. Princeton: Princeton University Press.

Fortes, Meyer
    1983   Oedipus and Job in West African Religion. Cambridge: Cambridge University Press. (1st ed. 1959)

Foucault, Michel
    1970   The Order of Things. An Archaeology of the Human Sciences. London: Tavistock. (1st ed. 1966)

1980   Two Lectures. *In* Power/Knowledge: Selected Interviews and Other Writings 1972–1977. Colin Gordon, ed. Brighton: Harvester Press.

Gandonu, Ajato
    1978   Nigeria's 250 Ethnic Groups: Realities and Assumptions. *In* Perspectives on Ethnicity. Regina E. Holloman and Serghei A. Arutiunov, eds. The Hague: Mouton.

Geertz, Clifford
    1983   Slide Show—Evans-Pritchard's African Transparencies. Raritan 2:62–80.

Giddens, Anthony
    1976   New Rules of Sociological Method. London: Hutchinson.
    1981   A Contemporary Critique of Historical Materialism. London: MacMillan.

Goody, Jack
    1971   Technology, Tradition and the State in Africa. London: Hutchinson.
    1976   Production and Reproduction: A Comparative Study of the Domestic Domain. Cambridge: Cambridge University Press.

Hallowell, A. Irving
    1955   Culture and Experience. Philadelphia: University of Philadelphia Press.

Hallpike, C. R.
    1979   The Foundations of Primitive Thought. Oxford: Clarendon Press.

Henderson, Richard N.
    1972   The King in Everyman. Evolutionary Trends in Onitsha Ibo Society. New Haven: Yale University Press.

Héritier, Françoise
    1977   L'Identité Samo. *In* L'Identité: Séminaire. Dirigé par Claude
            Lévi-Strauss. Paris: Grasset.

Heusch, Luc de
    1958   Essais sur le symbolisme de l'inceste royal en Afrique.
            Brussels.
    1962   Pour une dialectique de la sacralité du pouvoir. Annales du
            Centre d'Etude des Religions 1:15–47.
    1981   Travel Memories. *In* Why Marry Her? Luc de Heusch. Cam-
            bridge: Cambridge University Press.
    1982a   The Drunken King or, The Origin of the State. Roy Willis,
            transl. and annotator. Bloomington: Indiana University Press
            African Systems of Thought Series. (Original: Le roi ivre ou
            l'origine de l'Etat. Paris: Gallimard. 1972).
    1982b   Rois nés d'un coeur de vache. Paris: Gallimard.
    1985   Sacrifice in Africa: A Structuralist Approach. Manchester: Man-
            chester University Press.

Horton, Robin
    1983   Social Psychologies: African and Western. *In* Oedipus and Job
            in West African Religion. M. Fortes and R. Horton. Cambridge:
            Cambridge University Press.

Isajiw, Wsevolod W.
    1974   Definitions of Ethnicity. Ethnicity 1:111–24.

Karp, Ivan and Maynard Kent
    1983   Reading *The Nuer*. Current Anthropology 24:481–503.

Lancaster, C. S.
    1974   Ethnic Identity, History, and "Tribe" in the Middle Zambezi
            Valley. American Ethnologist 1(4):707–30.

Leach, E. R.
 1954 Political Systems of Highland Burma. London: Bell; Cambridge, Massachusetts: Harvard University Press.
 1982 Social Anthropology. Glasgow: Fontana.

Leenhardt, Maurice
 1979 Do Kamo. Person and Myth in the Melanesian World. Chicago: University of Chicago Press. (First publ. 1947)

Lévi-Strauss, Claude
 1976 Tristes tropiques. Harmondsworth: Penguin. (Original publ. 1955)

Marcus, George E. and James Clifford
 1985 The Making of Ethnographic Texts. Current Anthropology 26: 267–71.

Marcus, George and Dick Cushman
 1982 Ethnographies as Texts. Annual Review of Anthropology 11: 25–69.

Mauss, Marcel
 1979 A Category of the Human Mind: the Notion of Person, the Notion of "Self." In Sociology and Psychology. Marcel Mauss. London: Routledge and Kegan Paul. (Original publ. 1938)

Middleton, John
 1982 *Review of* Explorations in African Systems of Thought. Ivan Karp and C. S. Bird, eds. Africa 52:101–03.

Muller, Jean-Claude
 1980 Le roi bouc émissaire: Pouvoir et rituel chez les Rukuba du Nigeria Central. Quebec: Serge Fleury.

Nadel, S.F.
  1942   A Black Byzantium: The Kingdom of Nupe in Nigeria. London: Oxford University Press for the International African Institute.

Naroll, Raoul
  1964   Ethnic Unit Classification. Current Anthropology 5:283–91.

Nash, Dennison and Ronald Wintrob
  1972   The Emergence of Self-Consciousness in Ethnography. Current Anthropology 13:527–42.

Packard, Randall M.
  1981   Chiefship and Cosmology: An Historical Study of Political Competition. Bloomington: Indiana University Press.

Parkin, David
  1983   Introduction. In Semantic Anthropology. David Parkin, ed. London: Academic Press ASA 22.

Peel, J. D. Y.
  1984   Making History: the Past in the Ijesha Present. Man NS 19: 111–32.

Riches, David
  1985   Power as a Representational Model. In Power and Knowledge. Richard Fardon, ed. Edinburgh: Scottish Academic Press.

Said, Edward
  1978   Orientalism. London: Routledge and Kegan Paul.

Schultz, Emily
  1984   From Pagan to Pullo: Ethnic Identity Change in Northern Cameroon. Africa 54(1):46–63.

Schutz, Alfred and Thomas Luckmann
  1973   The Structures of the Life-World. London: Heinemann.

Simmel, Georg
  1950   The Sociology of Georg Simmel. Kurt H. Wolff, transl. New
          York: Free Press.

Smith, Abdullahi
  1971   The Early States of the Central Sudan. *In* History of West Af-
          rica. Vol. 1. J. F. Ade Ajayi and Michael Crowder, eds. London:
          Longman.

Smith, M. G.
  1960   Government in Zazzau: A Study of Government in the Hausa
          Chiefdom of Zaria in Northern Nigeria from 1800 to 1950.
          London: Oxford University Press for the International African
          Institute.
  1978   The Affairs of Daura: History and Change in a Hausa State
          1800–1958. Berkeley: University of California Press.

Sperber, Dan
  1975   Rethinking Symbolism. Cambridge: Cambridge University
          Press.
  1985   Interpretive Ethnography and Theoretical Anthropology. *In* On
          Anthropological Knowledge. Dan Sperber. Cambridge: Cam-
          bridge University Press.

Strathern, Marilyn
  1981   Culture in a Netbag. Man NS 16:665–88.
  1985a   Kinship and Economy: Constitutive Orders of a Provisional
          Kind. American Ethnologist 12:191–209.
  1985b   Knowing Power and Being Equivocal: Three Melanesian Con-
          texts. *In* Power and Knowledge. Richard Fardon, ed. Edinburgh:
          Scottish Academic Press.

Taylor, Charles
1983   Social Theory as Practice. Delhi: Oxford University Press.

Terray, Emmanuel
1985   Sociétés segmentaires, chefferies, états: Acquis et problèmes. Canadian Journal of African Studies 19:106–15.

Turner, Bryan S.
1981   For Weber: Essays on the Sociology of Fate. London: Routledge and Kegan Paul.

Van Den Berghe, Pierre
1981   The Ethnic Phenomenon. North Holland: Elsevier.

Vaughan, James H.
1964   Culture, History and Grass-roots Politics in a Northern Cameroons Kingdom. American Anthropologist 66:1078–95.
1980   A Reconsideration of Divine Kingship. In Explorations in African Systems of Thought. Ivan Karp and C. S. Bird, eds. Bloomington: Indiana University Press.

Willis, Roy
1967   The Head and the Loins: Lévi-Strauss and Beyond. Man NS 2: 519–34.
1981   A State in the Making: Myth, History and Social Transformation in Pre-colonial Ufipa. Bloomington: Indiana University Press.

Wright, Patrick
1985   On Living in an Old Country. London: Verso

Published References concerning Chamba, Their Neighbors, or the Adamawa Emirate

Abubakar, Sa'ad
    1977   The Lamibe of Fombina: A Political History of Adamawa 1809
           1901. Zaria and Ibadan: Ahmadu Bello University Press and
           Oxford University Press.

Adamu, Mahdi
    1978   The Hausa Factor in West African History. Zaria and Ibadan:
           Ahmadu Bello University Press and Oxford University Press.

Akiga Sai, B.
    1939   Akiga's Story, Translated and Annotated by Rupert East. Lon-
           don: Oxford University Press for the International African
           Institute.
    1954   The "Descent" of Tiv from the Ibenda Hill, Translated and An-
           notated by Paul Bohannan. Africa 24: 295–309.

Baikie, William Balfour
    1856   Narrative of an Exploring Voyage up the Rivers Kwora and
           Binue—Commonly Known as the Niger and Tsadda—in 1854.
           London: John Murray.

Barth, Heinrich
    1857   Travels and Discoveries in North and Central Africa. London:
           Longman, Brown, Green, Longmans and Roberts.

Bennett, Patrick R.
    1983   Adamawa-Eastern: Problems and Prospects. In Current Ap-
           proaches to African Linguistics. I. R. Dihoff, ed. 1:23–48.

Bernard, Bouba
    1982   The Stranger among the Chamba. In Grafting Old Rootstock.
           Philip A. Noss, ed. Dallas: Museum of Cultures.

Blench, Roger
    1984   Conflict and Co-operation: Fulbe Relations with the Mambila and Samba People of Southern Adamawa. Cambridge Anthropology 9:42–57.

Bohannan, Laura and Paul Bohannan
    1969   The Tiv of Central Nigeria. Ethnographic Survey of Africa: Part 7, West Africa. Darryl Ford, ed. London: International African Institute.

Boutrais, Jean
    1978   Peuplement et milieu naturel en zone soudanienne: Le Cas de la Plaine Koutine (Cameroun). Cahiers O.R.S.T.O.M., Sér. Sci. Hum. 15(2):103–43.

Boyd, Raymond
    forthc.   Adamawa-Ubangi. In Current Trends in Linguistics: State of the Art Reports: The Niger–Kordofanian–Congo Language Family. J. Bendor-Samuel, ed. The Hague: Mouton.

Burns, Sir Alan
    1955   History of Nigeria, 5th ed. London: George Allen and Unwin.

Calvert, Albert F.
    1916   The German African Empire. London: T. Werner Albert F. Laurie.

Chilver, E. M.
    1961   Nineteenth Century Trade in the Bamenda Grassfields, Southern Cameroons. Afrika und Übersee 45:233–58.
    1967   Paramountcy and Protection in the Cameroons: the Bali and the Germans 1889–1913. In Britain and Germany in Africa: Imperial Rivalry and Colonial Rule. Prosser Gifford and Wm. Roger Louis eds., New Haven: Yale University Press.
    1981   Chronological Synthesis: the Western Region, Comprising the

Western Grassfields, Bamum, the Bamileke Chiefdoms and the Central Mbam. *In* The Contribution of Ethnological Research to the History of Cameroon Cultures (In two volumes). Claude Tardits, ed. Paris: Editions du C.N.R.S.

Chilver, E. M. and P. M. Kaberry
1965   Sources of the Nineteenth Century Slave Trade: Two Comments. Journal of African History 6:117–20.
1968   Traditional Bamenda: The Pre-colonial History and Ethnography of the Bamenda Grassfields. Buea, Cameroon: Ministry of Primary Education and West Cameroon Antiquities Commission.
1970   Chronology of the Bamenda Grassfields. Journal of African History 11:249–57.

Chukwudi Unomah, A.
1982   The Lowlands Salt Industry. *In* Studies in the History of Plateau State, Nigeria. Elizabeth Isichei, ed. London: MacMillan.

Crowther, Samuel
1855   Journal of an Expedition up the Niger and Tshadda Rivers, Undertaken by MacGregor Laird, in Connection with the British Government in 1854. London: Church Missionary Society.

Detzner, Hermann
1923   Im Lande des Dju Dju. Berlin: August Scherl.

Dieu, Michel and Patrick Renard
1985   Atlas linguistique de l'Afrique Centrale: Atlas linguistique du Cameroun. Yaoundé: CERDOTOLA/DGRST.

East, Rupert
1935   Stories of Old Adamawa. Lagos: West Africa Publicity Limited.
1939   Akiga's Story. London: Oxford University Press for the International African Institute.

Faraut, F.
    1981   Les Mboum. *In* The Contribution of Ethnological Research to
              the History of Cameroon Cultures (In two volumes). Claude
              Tardits, ed. Paris: Editions du C.N.R.S.

Fardon, Richard
    1983   A Chronology of Pre-Colonial Chamba History. Paideuma 29:
              67–92.
    1984   Sisters, Wives, Wards and Daughters. Africa 54:2–21 (Also
              1985, Africa 55:77–91).
    1985b   Secrecy and Sociability: Two Problems of Chamba Knowledge.
              In Power and Knowledge. Richard Fardon, ed. Edinburgh: Scot-
              tish Academic Press.
    1987   African Ethnogenesis: Limits to the Comparability of Ethnic
              Phenomena. *In* Comparison in Social Anthropology. L. Holy,
              ed. Oxford: Basil Blackwell.
    forthc.   L'Alliance et l'ethnicité: Aspects d'un système regional de l'Ada-
              maoua. *In* Les Complexités de l'Alliance, Volume 4. F. Héritier-
              Augé, ed. Paris: Editions des Archives Contemporaines.

Flegel, Robert
    1883   Rob. Ed. Flegel's Reise nach Adamaua, März 1882 bis März
              1883. Petermann's Mittheilungen aus Justus Perthes Geogra-
              phischer Anstalt 7:241–49.

Fremantle, J. M.
    1922   Gazetteer of Muri Province. London: Waterlow and Sons.

Frobenius, Leo
    1913   Und Afrika Sprach, Vol. 3, Rev. ed. Berlin: Vita Deutsches
              Verlagshaus.
    1984   Ethiopiens du Nord Cameroun. Garoua: Centre de Recherches
              et d'Etudes Anthropologiques. (Manuscript translated from:
              Dichten und Denken im Sudan, Bd. 5. Eldridge Mohammadou,
              transl.)

Garbosa, Bitemya Sambo, Gara of Donga
   n.d.   Labarun Chambawa da Al' Amurransu
   n.d.   Salsalar Sarakunen Donga

These works were privately published in a single undated volume. Apparently written by 1956 (see Chilver 1967:479fn), the texts were microfilmed in 1960 by the Historical Society of Nigeria and University College Ibadan respectively.

Greenberg, Joseph H.
   1966   The Languages of Africa, 2nd ed. The Hague: Mouton.

Hurault, Jean
   1975   L'Histoire du lamidat Peul de Banyo (Cameroun).
           Extraits des Comptes des Séances d'Outre-Mer.

Hutter, Franz
   1902   Wanderungen und Forschungen im Nord Hinterland von Kamerun. Berlin: Braunschweig.

Jeffreys, M. D. W.
   1957   The Bali of Bamenda. African Studies 16:108–13.
   1962a   Some Notes on the Customs of the Grassfield Bali of Northwestern Cameroon. Afrika und Übersee 46 (3):161–67.
   1962b   Traditional Sources Prior to 1890 for the Grassfield Bali of Northwestern Cameroons. Afrika und Übersee 46 (3–4):168–99; 296–313.

Kaberry, P. M.
   1952   Women of the Grassfields. London: H.M.S.O.

Kaberry, P. M. and E. M. Chilver
   1961   An Outline of the Traditional Political System of Bali Nyonga. Africa 31:355–71.

Keller, Jakob
   1909   Die Bedeutung des Bali-Volkes für die Evangelisierung des
           Hinterlands von Kamerun. Evangelisches Missionsmagazin:
           157–63.

Kirk-Greene, A. H. M.
   1958   Adamawa Past and Present. London: Oxford University Press
           for the International African Institute.

Lacroix, Pierre-François
   1952   Matériaux pour servir à l'histoire des Peuls de l'Adamawa.
           Etudes Camerounaises 37–38:3–61.

Last, Murray
   1974   Reform in West Africa: the Jihad Movements of the Nine-
           teenth Century. In History of West Africa, Volume 2. J. F.
           Ade Ajayi and Michael Crowder, eds. London: Longman.

Lembezat, Bertrand
   1961   Les Populations païennes du Nord Cameroun et de l'Adamaoua.
           Ethnographic Survey of Africa: Part 9, French West Africa.
           Darryl Forde, ed. London: International African Institute.

Maistre, C.
   1895   A travers l'Afrique Central du Congo au Niger 1892–93. Paris:
           Hachette.

Meek, C. K.
   1931a   A Sudanese Kingdom: an Ethnographical Account of the Ju-
           kun-speaking Peoples of Nigeria. London: Kegan Paul, Trench
           and Trubner.
   1931b   Tribal Studies in Northern Nigeria (In two volumes). London:
           Kegan Paul, Trench and Trubner.

Migeod, F. H. W.
1925   Through British Cameroons. London: Heath Cranton.

Mohammadou, Eldridge
1964   L'Histoire des lamidats Foulbe de Tchamba et Tibati. Abbia
        6:15–158.
1967   Pour une histoire du Cameroun Central: Les Traditions histo-
        riques des Vouté ou *Baboute*. Abbia 16: 15–127.
1978   Les Royaumes Foulbe du plateau de l'Adamaoua au XIX siècle.
        Japan: Institute for the Study of Languages and Cultures of Af-
        rica and Asia.
1983   Le Peuplement de la Haute-Benoue: 1. Les Habitants de la zone
        centrale. Garoua, Cameroon:ONAREST/C.N.R.S.

Moisel, M.
1908   Zur Geschichte von Bali und Bamum. Globus 93:117–20.
1912   Mapsheets: D2 Schebschi Gebirge; D3 Garoua; E3 Ngaundere.
        Berlin: Dietrich Reimer.

Nissen, M.
1968   An African Church is Born. Denmark: Purups Grafiske Hus.

Njeuma, Martin Z.
1978   Fulani Hegemony in Yola (Old Adamawa) 1809–1902. Came-
        roon: privately published.

Nkwi, P. N. and J. P. Warnier
1982   Elements for a History of the Western Grassfields. Yaoundé:
        University of Yaoundé.

Noss, Philip A.
1976   Samba-Leeko: Outline of Phonology. Bulletin de l'Atlas Lin-
        guistique du Cameroun 2:5–38.

Nugent, Capt. W. V.
    1914   The Geographical Results of the Nigeria-Kamerun Boundary
            Demarcation Commission of 1912–13 (with discussion). Geo-
            graphical Journal 43:630–51.

O.R.S.T.O.M.
    1971   Tableau de la population du Cameroun. 3ème ed. Paris.

Palmer, H. R.
    1911   Notes on the Kwororofawa and Jukon. Journal of the African
            Society 11:401–15.
    1930   A Muslim Divine of the Sudan in the Fifteenth Century. Africa
            3:203–16.

Paris, Frederic
    1983   Géographie de l'Onchocercose au Nord Cameroun. Garoua,
            Cameroon: Institut des Sciences Humaines.

Passarge, Siegfried
    1895   Adamaua: Bericht über die Expedition des Deutschen Kamerun
            Komitees in den Jahren 1893–94. Berlin: Höfer und Vohsen.

Podlewski, A. N.
    1971   La Dynamique des principales populations du Nord-Cameroun,
            2ème Livraison, Piémont et Plateau de l'Adamaoua. Paris: Ca-
            hiers ORSTOM, Sér. Sci. Hum. VIII.

Price, David
    1979   Who are the Tikar now? Paideuma 25:89–98.

Rudin, Harry
    1938   Germans in the Cameroons 1884–1914. London: Jonathan
            Cape.

Ruxton, F. H.
1907   Notes on the Tribes of the Muri Province. Journal of the African Society 7:374–84.

Samarin, William J.
1971   Adamawa-Eastern. *In* Current Trends in Linguistics, Volume 7: Linguistics in Sub-Saharan Africa. Thomas Sebock, ed. Paris: Mouton.

Siran, Jean-Louis
1980   Emergence et dissolution des principautés guerrières Vouté. Journal des Africanistes 50:25–57.
1981a   Eléments d'ethnographie Vouté pour servir à l'histoire du Cameroun central. *In* The Contribution of Ethnological Research to the History of Cameroon Cultures (In two volumes). Claude Tardits, ed. Paris: Editions du C.N.R.S.
1981b   Appellations et attitudes: Le Système de parenté Vouté. L'Homme 21: 39–69.

Stevens, Phillips K. Jnr.
1976   The Danubi Ancestral Shrine. African Arts 10:30–37.

Strümpell, K.
1907a   Dans l'Ouest de l'Adamawa. (Original: Deutsches Kolonialblatt 23:1139–42)
1907b   L'Exploration du Faro. (Original: Deutsches Kolonialblatt 22: 1088–92)
1912   L'Histoire de l'Adamawa d'après les traditions orales. (Original: Mitteilungen des Geographischen Gesellschaft in Hamburg 26:46–107).

All three works by Strümpell above were translated by Eldridge Mohammadou, and appeared *In* Peuples et états du Foumbina et de l'Adamawa (Nord-Cameroun). Yaoundé: Travaux et Documents de l'Institut des Sciences Humaines. Collection Archives Allemandes du Cameroun No. 1.

Strümpell, K.
1910   Vergleichendes Wortzeichnis der Heidensprache Adamauas.
        Zeitschift für Ethnographie 42:444—88.

Tardits, Claude
1980   Le Royaume Bamoum. Paris: Armand Colin.

Temple, O. and C. L. Temple
1922   Notes on the Tribes, Provinces, Emirates and States of the
        Northern Provinces of Nigeria. 2nd ed. Lagos: CMS Bookshop.

Vicars-Boyle, C.
1910   Notes on the Yola Fulanis. Journal of the African Society
        10:73—92.

Weladji, C.
1974   The Cameroon-Nigeria Border (Part One). Abbia 27—28: 157—75.

Whitlock, C. F. A.
1910   The Yola-Cross River Boundary Commission, Southern Nige-
        ria. Geographical Journal 36:426—38.

Williamson, Kay
1971   The Benue Languages and Ijo. In Current Trends in Linguis-
        tics, Volume 7: Linguistics in Sub-Saharan Africa. Thomas Se-
        beok, ed. Paris: Mouton.

Zintgraff, E.
1895   Nord Kamerun. Berlin: Pätel.

Unpublished References

British Colonial Records at the Nigerian National Archives, Kaduna.

All the references are from the *Yola Profile;* the letter–number citations are those under which they are catalogued.

K2   The Cameroons: Assumption of Mandate, Volume I: Yola Sector 1915; Volume II: Yola Sector 1916–17.

K4   The Cameroons British Occupied Territory: Incorporation in the British Empire and in the Yola Emirate 1917–24.

B3.X   Recurrent Reports on the Southern Mandate with Associated Papers 1919–22: Quarterly Reports by W. D. K. Mair and C. Migeod.

B3.Z   Recurrent Reports on the Southern Mandated Districts with Associated Papers 1923–31:
       Glasson 1923. Report on Sugu.
       Glasson 1924. Ethnological Appendix to Toungo District Report.

G2.2   Nassarawo District Miscellaneous Papers 1925–37:
       Memorandum of 31.1.25. Confirming installation of D. H., Nassarawo.
       Hopkins 1929. Report on Mapeo and Lendo Village Groups.
       Logan 1930. Reorganisation of Village Units.
       Walker 1931. Nassarawo District Assessment.
       Percival 1935. Note on Tax Collection in Kubi and Mapeo.
       Anon. n.d. Nassarawo District History.

G2.2A Logan, R. 1930. Nassarawo District Assessment Report.

G2.2B Chamba, later Binyeri, District Miscellaneous Papers 1918–37:
       Logan 1926. Genealogical Tree of Binyeri.
       Percival 1935. Note on the Administrative History of Binyeri District.

G2.2C   Gurumpawo and Yebbi District Miscellaneous Papers 1920–39:
Resident, Yola 1920. Letter to W. D. K. Mair.
Mair 1920. Letter to Resident, Yola.
Logan 1926. History of Gurumpawo.
Shaw 1936. Letter to D. O., Yola.
Percival 1937. Gurumpawo District.
Percival 1937. Yebbi District.

G2.2D   Toungo District Miscellaneous Papers 1923–40.

G2.2E   Toungo District Assessment Papers 1925 and 1930:
Logan 1925. Toungo Assessment Report.
Hopkins 1930. Toungo Assessment Report.

G3   Chamba Area Re-organisation 1933–40 (In two volumes: Volume I
1933–37).
Welch 1933. Report on Proposals and Further Report.
Shaw 1936. The Chamba Tribe.
Brooke 1933. Handing-over Note.

G3A   (Volume II 1937–40) Reports on Re-organisation.

3058   Chamba Marriage—Wife Stealing:
Welch 1936. Report on Chamba Marriage and Wife Stealing.

C778   Chamba Federation: (1) Separatist Movements:
Paul 1951. Letter to Resident, Yola.
Cassidy 1951. Reports on Separatist Movements.
Paul 1951. Chamba District Affairs.
Sorrell 1955. Report on Chamba Federation.
Crane 1958. The Chamba Subordinate Native Authority: A State-
ment Prepared for the Visit of the Minorities Commission to
Adamawa Province in Feb. 1958 by P.S. Crane A.D.O.

J8   The Chamba: Collected History and Anthropological Papers:
1921–38:
Lilley 1921. Historical and Ethnographical Notes on the Chamba
People of Dakka.
Glasson 1922. The Chamba.
Glasson 1923. Additional Chamba Notes.

Logan 1929. Historical Notes on the Chamba.
Percival 1938. The Chamba, etc. Notes on Origin and Organization.

K5   Strümpell, K. 1912 History of Adamawa. English translation, apparently of a previous French translation of the original, see Strümpell under ethnographic references.

Sources at the Local Government Headquarters, Ganye, Nigeria

Crane, P.S. 1958. Histories of Gurum and Yebbi Districts.
Local Government 1976–78. Population Figures by District and Village for Assessment of Taxation.

Cameroonian Archives consulted at Local Stations of the Institute of Human Sciences

FRENCH REPORTS AT GAROUA (NORTHERN STATION)

Floch, Jean 1938. Eléments d'une notice sur la subdivision de Poli.
Relly, Henri 1954. Rapport de tournée éffectuée dans le lamidat de Tchamba du 9 Juin 1954 au 22 Juin 1954.

Both of these reports draw heavily upon earlier documents that I have not seen. Relly's historical sections quote passages verbatim from a report of 1935 by Lt. Savani.

BRITISH REPORTS AT BAMENDA (NORTHWESTERN STATION)

Hawkesworth, E. G. 1926. An Assessment Report on the Bafut Area of Bamenda Division, Cameroons Province.
Hunt, W. E. 1925. An Assessment Report on the Bali Clan in the Bamenda Division of the Cameroons Province.
Newton, R. 1934. An Assessment Report on the Ngemba.

Archival Sources in Rhodes House, Oxford

Crane, P. S. 1958. The Chamba Subordinate Native Authority. Also in British Colonial Records at the Nigerian National Archives, Kaduna: C778. q.v.

Logan, R. 1932. The Chamba Tribe in Adamawa (and accompanying letter).

Tukur, Mohammed 1960. Report on the Cameroons Commission of Enquiry. Submitted to Alhaji Ahmadu Bello, Premier of Northern Region, 1 February 1960

Other Sources

Chilver, E.M.
   1964   Historical Notes on the Bali Chiefdoms of the Cameroons Grassfields. Report Number 1 to the Bali History Committee: Origins, Migration and Composition. MS revised 1970, courtesy of the author. Report Number 2: Settlement and Composition. TS 1964. Institute of Human Sciences, Garoua

Cullen, Fr. Malachy
   1944   Notes on the Mapeo Chamba: Origin, Custom, Juju. MS Yola Catholic Mission

Fardon, Richard
   1980   The Chamba: a Comparative History of Tribal Politics. Ph.D. thesis, University of London.
   1986   Report on Ethnographic and Historical Researches amongst the Pere of North Cameroon. Garoua (Cameroon): Institute of Human Sciences.

Mohamadou, Aliou
   1975   Le Lamidat de Koncha au XIX siècle. Memoire de DES d'Histoire, University of Yaoundé

Rubin, A. G.
    1969   The Arts of the Jukun-speaking Peoples of Northern Nigeria.
            Ph.D. dissertation, Indiana University.

Soh, Pius Bejeng
    1975   A Study of Lela, a Bali Chamba State Cult of the North-West
            Grassfields of Cameroon. Memoire de DES de Sociologie, Uni-
            versity of Yaoundé.

Stevens, P. K.
    1973   The Bachama and their Neighbors: Non-kin Joking Relations
            in Adamawa, North-East Nigeria. Ph.D. dissertation, North-
            western University.

I am also indebted to numerous letters especially from E. M. Chilver and
Adrian Edwards, as well as Roger Blench, Raymond Boyd, Peter Crane and
Arnold Rubin. Dr. Elias Nwana kindly made publications of the Bali His-
torical Society (Volumes 1 and 3) available to me.

INDEX

SUBJECT AND PLACE INDEX

AUTHORS CITED

Archival sources are abbreviated as follows: Br. British, Fr. French.

Abubakar, S., 141, 142
Adamu, M., 138
Adler, A., 216
Akiga, Sai, 80, 347
Anderson, B., 109
Ardener, E., 339
Armstrong, R., 138, 216
Asad, T., 339

Baikie, W., 81, 262, 346
Barth, F., 18
Barth, H., 66, 262, 352
Bateson, G., 19, 156
Bennett, P., 64
Bernard, B., 355
Blench, R., 64, 82, 275, 344, 345
Bloch, M., 357
Bohannan, L., and P., 86, 347
Bourdieu, P., 295
Boutrais, J., 344, 347, 348
Boyd, R., 64, 344
Brooke, N. (Br.), 272
Bruce, R., 361
Burnham, P., iv, 11, 282
Burns, A., 361

Calvert, A., 360
Cassidy, H. (Br.), 270
Chilver, E., v, 78, 85, 86, 87, 88, 205, 207, 347, 348, 349, 352, 359
Chilver, E., and Kaberry, P., 257, 347, 348, 349, 359
Chukwudi, Unomah A., 138
Clarke, P., 141
Clifford, J., 339
Cohen, A., 23, 306
Cohen, R., 18
Crane, P. (Br.), iv, 263, 267, 277, 278–79, 350, 353, 361
Crowder, M., 278, 361
Crowther, S., 81, 262, 346
Cullen, M. (R. C. missionary), 275

de Heusch, L., 293, 358
Derrida, J., 17
Detzner, H., 148, 354, 360
Douglas, M., iv, 24, 292
Dumont, L., 19
Durkheim, E., 24

East, R., 86, 141, 347
Edwards, A., iv–v, 344, 347, 351
Epstein, A., 339
Evans-Pritchard, E., 339

Fabian, J., 295
Faraut, F., 348
Feeley-Harnik, G., 216
Ferguson, A., 22
Fernandez, J., 354
Flegel, E., 262, 267
Floch, J. (Fr.), 359
Fortes, M., 354
Foucault, M., 23, 305, 309, 339
Fremantle, J., 84, 262, 345
Frobenius, L., 121, 124, 197, 223, 230–31, 343, 350

Gandonu, A., 362
Garbosa II, Bitemya Sambo, Chief of Donga, 78–85, 99, 144, 206, 282–83, 345–47, 351
    history by: dramatic intention of, 80–81;
        writing of, 345
    on Chamba Kinship, 181–94
    on Donga organization, 252–54, 352–53
    chieflists given by, 336, 356–57
Geertz, C., 339
Giddens, A., 295, 340
Glasson, B. (Br.), 116–18, 271, 351, 354
Goody, J., 77, 88, 305, 340

Hallowell, A., 295
Hallpike, C., 362
Hawkesworth, E. (Br.), 348
Henderson, R., 292
Héritier, F., 354
Hopkins (Br.), 353
Horton, R., 354
Hunt, W. (Br.), 205, 257, 347, 349
Hurault, J., 347, 348
Hutter, F., 359

Isajiw, W., 18

Jeffreys, M., 349

Karp, I., v
Karp, I., and Maynard, K., 339
Keller, J., 347, 349
Kirk-Greene, A., 98

Lacroix, P-F, 141, 351
Lancaster, C., 339
Last, M., 141
Leach, E. R., 5, 15–16, 30, 287, 294
Leenhardt, M., 294
Lévi-Strauss, C., 23, 292